IMAGES FROM
VEDIC HYMNS AND RITUALS

IMAGES FROM VEDIC HYMNS AND RITUALS

Sadashiv Ambadas Dange
R.G. Bhandarkar Professor and Head, Deptt. of Sanskrit, Mumbai University (Retd.)

ARYAN BOOKS INTERNATIONAL
NEW DELHI

IMAGES FROM VEDIC HYMNS AND RITUALS

ISBN-81-7305-190-9

First Published in 2000 by
ARYAN BOOKS INTERNATIONAL
Pooja Apartments, 4B, Ansari Road, Darya Ganj
New Delhi-110002 (INDIA)
Tel.: 3287589, 3255799 Fax: 91-11-3270385

Computer Typeset at ABI Prints & Publishing Co., New Delhi
Printed in India at B.B.N. Printers, New Delhi

TO

(Late) Fr. (Dr.) ADOLF ESTELLER, S.J.

Whose love and scholarship
regarding the Ṛgveda
could never be doubted
In spite of the fact, that
his writings about Ṛgveda being

A PALIMPSEST

aroused controversies
which he boldly faced
till his death
with a sincere zeal
to find out
the original un-mutilated words
in the *mantra-s*
of
Ṛṣi-kavi-s.

PREFACE

In this volume some concepts, images and symbols from the Ṛgveda are presented. They have been thoroughly discussed and checked, over the years, at various meetings of scholars in the field. Studies on some of them have also been published in reputed research-journals.

In the recent years my effort has been twofold, through publications. On the one hand, it followed the norm of providing details in line with the usual research methodology; and, on the other, essential thought from the Vedic tradition was sought to be placed before the interested general reader, avoiding too much of intricacy but with necessary references and comparisons. This latter phase of my effort has necessitated the selection of parts to give an idea—and a fairly good idea—of the whole. This is clear from the two recent volumes published under the title *Divine Hymns and Ancient Thought.* (Vol. I: *Ṛgveda and the Ancient Thought*; Vol. II: *Ritual and the Quest for Truth).* In this volume also quotations from the texts are given in the italics transliteration, in addition to references to the texts where necessary. However, while giving quotations, as noted above, accent marks are not indicated as not being absolutely necessary for the treatment here.

This volume has been published as separate from the earlier title, as the former volumes were of the nature of selection of text, while this volume does not have 'selections' as such. However, as some important concepts and items are included in this volume, it could be lined up with the earlier two to have an idea of the variety of concepts, images and beliefs in the Vedic tradition.

Jacket design with the picture and the line-drawings have been done by Mrs. Vidya Joshi, Lecturer in Art, at the J.J. School of Arts, Mumbai. My thanks to her for the same.

I thank the Publishers, Vikas Arya of Aryan Books International, for bringing out this volume also neatly, and within a reasonably short time.

Mumbai **Sadashiv A. Dange**

CONTENTS

INTRODUCTION

Sacrifice formed an integral part of ancient societies. The Vedic records are quite numerous to attest this point; and the Ṛgveda reflects the ideas of the ancient Vedic seer-sacrificers regarding the interaction of social needs on the one hand, and a variety of sacrificial rituals, on the other. The Ṛgveda is the source from which many later ritual practices developed. Though it is not quite possible to present details from the Ṛgveda of the types of sacrifices that developed in the later period, it seems quite probable that major sacrificial types are suggested in the Ṛgveda. Sacrifice was believed to be a medium through which the priest-seers could be assured of divine help for prosperity on the earth. One of the major sources of divine help for prosperity on the earth was assured timely rain, in spite of the fact that rivers also were seen as 'Mothers' to help the productivity of land. However, rivers were praised and deified more for providing areas for sacrifice, especially the Soma-sacrifice; for there was already established a close relationship between the river-waters and the pressed out shoots of Soma. Also rivers came to be deified more as resorts for a sacrificial bath, rather than for ease in agriculture. It is hard to find a one-to-one correspondence between the river-waters and agricultural activities, though the word *sīrāḥ* (I.179.9, IV.19.8) might be taken to indicate canals or water courses; and also we have the word *kulyā* (III. 45.3; V.83.8; X.43.7), indicative of artificial rivulets. In any case, rain was the major source for the growth of the pastures; and there are a number of instances to that effect. Rain was the virtual 'Father' and the 'seeder' of,the mother earth. As such various images sprang round the formation of rain in the clouds, and its release on the earth. Chapter 1 takes a survey of the various images, concepts and symbols that were invented by the such Vedic seers. The cloud was seen variously as the serpent, the frog, the leather-bag that pours out rain, the measure that sprinkles the 'corn' of rain, and so on. It has been pointed out in this chapter (and also in the subsequent ones, where occasion arose) that the images and symbols of the Vedic seers have been influenced by folk-beliefs, at that period, and which are current even today. In certain cases, there appears to have developed a pattern of visions among the seers. According to this pattern, which was based upon beliefs current in the ancient Ṛgvedic past, the seer projected himself as being on par with the lord of the cosmic activities, calling himself the 'First born of the Ṛta — the Universal order'. In this he went into (or placed himself in) a state of trance and proclaimed that he knew the working of the universe. This secret knowledge of the working of the universe was not associated in this context, with the activity of creation so much as it was with the wonder of the release of rain. The hymns of Dīrghatamas (I.164) and that of Vasukra (X.27) stand testimony to this fact. These two hymns, studied here, have parallel ideas, and reflect ritual details for the gain of rain. According to the vision of these seers, especially that of Dīrghatamas, the thunder, prior to rain, is the prototype of speech — it is the cosmic speech; and, in a complex imagery, the thunder is the bellowing of the cosmic cow, which is another symbol for speech. In a step further, we are presented the symbol of the Akṣara — the "non-oozing" supreme principle on the one hand, and the mystic 'syllable' on the other. The *Akṣara* oozes (*kṣarati*) with the loud expression of the thunder from the rain-cow (cloud); and the splutter of the thunder (=speech) is heard in various sounds in the cosmos in the rain-drama. As its another aspect, it gives rise to the various syllables in ordinary speech. The seemingly complex image works with a simple conviction that gradually unfolds its meaning. The cosmic cow thunders and causes the Akṣara to ooze. On the one hand, the oozed out *Akṣara* is the 'milk' in the form of rain. On the other, the *Akṣara*—'syllable'—develops into alphabets. This is a unique presentation; and Dīrghatamas has to be credited squarely for it. This is where the rain-symbolism, developed out of necessity from the needs of pastoro-agricultural life, gets a base of proto-philosophy. It is necessary to point out, that the later Vedic philosophical concept of *akṣara brahma* (as reflected in the Upaniṣads) has its roots in the symbolism reflected in the imagery of the gain of rain. Gain of rain was also seen as the fluid of germination from the cosmic foetus in the form of the rainful cloud. This was only an extension of the belief that rain was not a lifeless liquid; it was the life-procreating fluid of germination, its another symbolic, and more popular, name being *retas*. Another striking image that the seers of Ṛgveda had developed is, that of the 'Son-husband' in one. In other words, the husband who is the 'seeder', and procreator, is also the son. This image is different from that of the later popular one, first presented by the Aitareya Brāhmaṇa (VII.33), according to which the son is the husband himself born afresh from his wife, now his mother, in his form of the son—a thought that obtains even among the so-called rustic people who sing, "The wife has delivered; and the husband is the new-born babe". The concept of the son-husband, referred to above, is not from the social actuality. It got formed in the context of the fertility of waters. This son, that is also the 'seeder' husband, is the fire that is believed to be in the midst of the water-females, that get fattened up and are expected to provide water continuously for agriculture. The concept is seen in the deity Apāmnapāt, which is Indo-Iranian and is praised in the Ṛgveda and in the *Avesta*. The fire-male among the water-females is seen in three strata — heavenly (sun and solar water in the orb), mid-region (lightning fire and the waters, both posited in the cloud) and the fire that is believed to stay in terrestrial water-courses (*payasvān agniḥ*). On the same analogy, Soma is seen as the son-seeder of the waters called Vasatīvarī at the ritual of the Soma-sacrifice. Actually, as stated above, this concept is not restricted to the Ṛgveda and the later ritual literature. It is the gift of the wider agricultural stage of life — a fact supported also by myths.

The concept of the "crying worlds" works on a belief, also not restricted to the Vedic literature, and found widely. It was believed, that, in the ancient times, Sky and Earth were together in a mass, clasping each other in a close embrace. This is an un-sophisticated proto-philosophical version of the highly philosophical idea of the complete whole (*pūrṇam*) of the cosmos, the primeval egg (*brahmāṇḍa*) being yet another version of the same concept. The 'crying worlds' are referred to in the Ṛgveda by the term *krandasī* (dual). The mythical version, is, that they were separated — a stage necessary for healthy reproduction and creation. As they were separated, they groaned and roared (*krand*). By extension, the word *krandasī* came to denote the unit of the thundering sky and the resounding earth in the context of the release of rain. But, it has to be marked, that the word *krandasī* does not legitimately belong to rain-symbolism, for which the 'bellowing of the cow' (*gaurī*, the sky-cow, or the cloud-cow) is the right image. The concept of the sky and the earth together forming one whole, though now separated, is related to creation and has been utilised, later, in the context of consecration for sacrifice.

And, the sacrificer to be consecrated was believed to be so consecrated in the midst of this whole. Thus, he became the foetus of Heaven and Earth. In the same way Soma, the juice of whose shoots came to be an important aspect of the Soma-sacrifice, was also thought to be the foetus of Heaven and Earth. Parjanya (the god of rain) is said to be the father of Soma. As a ritual-drink, various images centred round Soma. Like the fire-god, Agni, he is the god that could not only be seen but also touched. The pressing of the shoots of Soma for being offered into the fire, and also to the various gods, brought him on par with the sacrificial victim. In one aspect he symbolised the lord of water, as noted above; and, in another, he came to be the divine victim, being also the 'king' of vegetation. He was believed to have arrived on the earth from heaven, where he was believed to be staying in the midst of the stars. This is one aspect of the imagery about him. Another one, and allied to it, was that he was in the highest heaven of Indra. He was seen as the 'shining drop' (*indu*). Hence, through rain, he was believed to arrive on the earth, on the mountain, in the form of the Soma-creeper. Thence, he was brought to the sacrificial plane in the form of shoots of the Soma-creeper, for being pressed. It was, mythically, believed that he was brought to the earth by the 'daughter of the sun' (*sūryasya duhitā*). The advent of Soma to the earth from his heavenly abode has interesting details in the Ṛgveda which developed, in later times, into interesting myths. As the advent of Soma and his pressing was accompanied by the chanting of various *mantra-s*, he was called *brahmā-sava*; and the imagery took a stride further, when poetry was believed to be aided by the influence of the intake of Soma-juice. There is a probability, that the later concept of Kāvya-rasa was suggested from the imagery centring round the sacrificial pressing of Soma.

In the 'Eye' of Prajāpati we have the germs of a later popular myth of the eye of Śukra, the preceptor of the Asuras. The eye had come to assume the symbolic status of the generative organ, the fluid from which (=tear) was believed to be procreative. This belief, like many others, is not restricted to the Vedic tradition. In line with the belief of the 'eye' falls the one that the orb of the sun is the receptacle of fertile waters. The 'eye' of various gods, and the fertile fluid therefrom, is suggested from the orb of the sun and the waters stored therein. Another aspect of this belief, but somewhat changed, is that of 'Tryambaka', which has been taken to mean 'a god with three eyes'; but, the concept is not indicative so much of the three eyes, as of the 'fire in water' at three strata.

"Sasarparī" had been a problematic word in the Ṛgveda. It never occurs in the later literature. It is proposed, through this volume, that Sasarparī was another name for the Gāyatrī-Sāvitrī *mantra* itself. Also, through the examination of this word new light on the relationship between the Viśvāmitra family and Jamadagnī is shed, as 'Sasarparī' is said to have been presented to the Viśvāmitras by Jamadagnī. In Sasarparī a unique use of a *mantra* and formulae at the time of war is indicated. In "Aspects of War" beliefs regarding divinity of the banners is brought to the fore, along with such things as the dress of the warrior and the preparation for war. Closely associated with war is the word Vāṇa, through the attire of the gods Maruts; but, the concept of Vāṇa changed from that of a war-trumpet, in the Ṛgvedic period, to that of a musical instrument later necessary at rituals. The chapter on "The Birth of Vasiṣṭha" points to the method of deification of humans, and marks a well-known practice seen in later mythical accounts of supernatural births of important humans. It also presents Urvaśī in a new setting, quite different from that of her relationship with Purūravas. Urvaśī, here, is presented as the 'weaver of the web' of life, and the knower of all secrets relating to life and birth. Here we have also the very first ever reference to the jar as the *symbol of the womb*, whence are born Vasiṣṭha and Agastya. Jar, as a symbol of the womb, occurs at various places in later literature, in ritual and folk-beliefs. It also came to symbolise the goddess in post-Vedic literature.

The study of the words *"dvi-barhas"*, *"śiprin"* and *"śipiviṣṭa"* has been included here to give an idea of their socio-mystic background. *Dvibarhas*, like *śiprin*, went out of use in the post-Ṛgvedic period. (We do not count the Atharvaveda as indicative of a separate period). Both these words are indicative of power and status. *Dvibarhas* is mostly an individual who came to be so called as he controlled the happenings in both the worlds — heaven and earth. Śiprin was an epithet of a very few important gods;

but the word also indicated a 'wearer of the *śiprā* (singular) or the '*śipre* (dual) on his helmet'. The *śipre* could be taken out for drinking liquids from and replaced on the helmet. In other words, they were horn-shaped attachments on the helmet, and were a privilege of a very few persons. *Śipiviṣṭa* had become obscure after the early post-Ṛgvedic period itself; and fanciful explanations are noticed. A close look at the word indicates, that, under the avowedly sexual slant of the word, there is a base of fertility. In the same way, the word *śiśnadeva* was explained variously. A fresh look at this word shows that it refers to the followers of the cult of the nude. It is probable that the *śiśnadeva*-s were wonder-mongers not following the Vedic religion, though they might have formed part of the Aryan society. Another interesting word that has been examined in the present study is "Admasad". This word, also, is not found in later literature. The flat meaning 'sitting at food' does not convey any sense, nor does it catch even a glimpse of its inherent meaning. Close examination shows, that it came to stay as an epithet of priests. It is well-known that the Ṛgveda does not mention many of the priests who are frequently mentioned by later ritual texts and *vice versa*. 'Admasad' seems to be a special priest who supervised the material of offerings at the sacrifice, as he is also associated with the epithet '*jāgṛvi*' ("awakener"). However, this office went out of use later.

"Ajāmitā and speech-coupling" explains the source of the concept of *jāmi* and *ajāmi*. This concept is seen worked out to its varieties in the ritual literature. The Ṛgveda had already introduced the concept. A *jāmi* couple (in any context, social or ritual) was to be non-procreative, as both the partners of this couple (or pair) were believed to be of similar nature, or of similar sex. A *jāmi* couple, or pair. was that of two males, or of two females, or of a brother and sister, i.e., of those whose sexual union was either non-productive or was socially forbidden. In the ritual context productivity and procreation were the desired goal. Hence it was seen that pairs of *mantra*-s, or pairs of objects, used were such as were slightly different. This interesting concept pervaded the whole of the Vedic ritual tradition. Hence jāmi (similar) was always sought to be made a-*jāmi* (dissimilar). In the examination of the '*garta*' and '*gartāruk*' a social custom is hinted at.

Vedic people believed in rebirth; and the Ṛgveda stands testimony to this belief. Chapters on "Metempsychosis" and the "vision of Dīrghatamas" deal with this topic. At the period of the Ṛgveda, *ātman* did not indicate 'soul', as was the case with the later period. A difference between *jīva* and *ātman* was maintained in the Ṛgveda.

One prominent trait of the Vedic religion was theriomorphism, according to which prominent deities were symbolised by beasts — mostly domesticated. This is seen with other religions also; and a variant phase of the same concept is that the beasts become the vehicles of these deities and also their special victims. Now, the black deer presents a riddle. This beast had gained a unique importance in the Vedic ritual tradition. It became a symbol for sacrifice, and for Prajāpati. Its skin was used in ritual. Yet, there is no reference to its being sacrificially killed. The riddle is sought to be solved in one chapter. An important aspect of Vedic religion was fresh birth of the sacrificer at the sacrifice. Often the sacrificer was led to the heavenly region and brought back to the earth through symbolic rituals and *mantra*-s. His new birth was sought to be accomplished through the chanting of special *mantra*-s, which were mixed and rearranged. The *Kuntāpa*-hymns are a skilful device for this. The whole plan of this symbolic rebirth is presented in one chapter. The post-Vedic period is familiar with the Mother-goddess, and Tantrism came to be pretty well rooted in the Indian tradition after the eighth century A.D. Scholars have tried, somehow, to connect these concepts with the Veda. A more detailed examination on this point indicates the Vedic concepts and practices that could have been the source of these later traditions. The Dance of Indra and Chāyā from the Atharvaveda gives a glimpse of war-dance in that ancient period and tallies with the war-dance of Mātaṅgī in the Pallava-Pāṇḍya period. Interesting beliefs mingled with imagination in the formation of the concept of the Goddess of speech being also a *puṁścalī* (courtesan). It is shown how this Vedic tradition continued in the later times, through Puranic records. Ritual for any ancient people was a continuous action throughout the year — throughout life. This is seen from the zeal of the Vedic ritualists to connect earlier ritual with the later ones and to maintain this continuity by various ways. The altar served as the symbol, connecting the holy and divine world of rituals to the world beyond it, which is the world of common existence. The vedic ritualists joined the two at the boundaries of the altar. This is seen in the concept of *antarvedi-bahirvedi*. The structure at the joint of the two worlds indicated control of both. This is also why the sacrificial pole was fixed at the centre of the eastern boundary of the altar *(ardham antarvedi ardham bahirvedi)*. This is the source of the special importance that is attached to the threshold of a house, or a temple, and of the various beliefs attached to it.

Chapter 1

FOLK-BELIEFS AND RAIN-IMAGERY OF THE VEDIC SEERS

Rain-gain is a mixed motif in the Vedic seers' imagination. Viewing closely we see that there are two predominant aspects of the seers' vision of the advent of rain from the skies. In one aspect the sky, the cloud or the sun are the male, the male that releases the manly fluid (rain); and, this, in itself is the result of some unseen act of coitus in the cosmos. In another aspect, rain is the result of a fight that goes on in the cosmos. The first aspect we are going to study fully in the pages to follow. The aspect developed further and gave rise to many sexual rituals. In addition to these two main aspects, there are a number of symbols used by the Ṛgvedic seers, and followed by the later ritualists, to indicate rain. The various expressions found in the Ṛgveda (RV) as regards rain, could be divided into two: (i) Originated from the pastoral experiences; and (ii) Originated from the Pre-pastoral experiences. However, this division cannot be stressed too much; and pre-pastoral images could be presented by the seer in later times. Broadly speaking, the motif of the fight between the hero and the wild beast may be taken as a gift of the hunting or the pre-pastoral period. In the pastoral setting the common motif used is that of the oozing of the fat of the domesticated animal as it is being roasted on the fire (cf. RV III. 21.5; also I.145.5ab).

The most dominant motif for the release of rain is that of fight. On the Ṛgvedic plane, Indra is said to have smashed the demons Vṛtra, Śuṣṇa, Namuci and others who are said to control water. The motif of fight, in connection with the gain of rain, is to be found in other mythologies also; and we shall have occasion to refer to such instances in our discussion, here and later. This, probably, was the most original concept of the advent of rain, the basis of it being the actual experience of the rain-shower, from the clouds. The flash of lightning and the thunder suggested the fight, yet unmixed by the motif of sex, gave to the ancient people the first glimpse of the probable reason of the release of rain, wherein they visualized the fight of the flash and the cloud, both taken to be animated with life. A further extension of the same motif is to be seen in the fight between the "Bird" and the "Serpent", the former representing the cloud-fire (the lightning) and the latter the dark elongated or changing cloud.[1]

The bird–serpent fight is seen among many people, as we have remarked above; but, it is to be noted that even this motif has two phases. In one phase it is symbolic of the fight between the solar bird and the serpent of darkness, while in the other it touches the sphere of the gain of rain. As far as RV is concerned, the solar bird motif is found in it; but, it is not connected with the killing of the serpent. The solar bird, on the other hand, is said to stay in the solar waters. This point will be clear in the course of discussion later. The solar orb is believed to be full of waters sucked up from the earth; and in it stays the solar fire like a bird. Analogous with it is the lightning fire-bird that stays in the waters of the cloud. The fight between the bird and the serpent does not form a rain motif in RV Vṛtra is the serpent, no doubt; and he is also called "First-born among the serpents" (RV I.32.3 *ahann enam prathamajām ahīnām*; and, 4—*yad indra ahan prathamajām ahīnām*), when he is said to be killed by Indra in the intoxication of Soma (Soma is also closely associated with the gain of rain, in oral charms and rituals); but, in this exploit Indra is not depicted or described as a bird. In later texts, when Indra is depicted as a bird,[2] he is not involved in the dragon-fight. In the post-Vedic texts the motif of the bird-dragon-fight occurs; but the bird is Garuḍa (the hawk) called Suparṇa; and Indra does not come in the direct fight, but helps this bird and becomes a third party in the gain of rain. Suparṇa, as a bird, is mentioned in RV and other Vedic texts many times; but, it has to be noted, there he is not associated with the dragon-fight, though associated with the gain of rain (RV I.164.46-52, the famous hymn known as "Asya vāmīya"; see chap. "The Thunder-Cow"). The bird-serpent-fight comes first at the Suparṇādhyāya[3] which is a semi-Vedic text, and, later, in the Mahābhārata (Mb).[4] However, the belief in the cloud (or Vṛtra who symbolized it) being the great serpent is well set in the RV. Thus, *ahi-hatya* (meaning "the killing of the serpent") indicates at all places in the RV the fight against the dark waterful cloud-dragon (RV I.61.8; 165.6; III.32.12). The epithet of Indra based on this belief is *ahi-śuṣmaṇ* (RV V.33.5), his other epithet of similar nature being *ahi-han* (*ibid.*, II. 19.3; 13.5). The rain (or the rain-waters, or atmospheric waters) are, before their release, called *ahi-gopāḥ* (I.32.11); and Vṛtra, and other water-controlling fiends are called *ahi* (I.52.10; 64.8,9; 172.1 etc.). The cloud-dragon motif, in the context of rain, is found also among other people, and has been a very popular one;[5] and it must be taken as pre-pastoral. It is very old. It should also be taken as based on the common experience of the association of the serpent and the water, the former staying in it in many places. The lightning being taken as the serpent is only an application of this motif in the sphere of the mid-region. Another phase of the same motif is in the clouds being called *ajagara* (the python). RV does not record it; but AV does record it (AV IV. 15.7, 9 *utsā ajagarāḥ*, "the pythons, the water-springs"; and Sāyaṇa's comment, *ajagara-samānākārāḥ utsāḥ marudbhiḥ pracyutā meghāḥ*, ... "the clouds moved by the winds"). The motif, obviously, is a gift from the folk-belief that the cloud-water is controlled by the lightning serpent that resides in it, on the analogy of the serpents that are believed to control the water-places on the earth. This belief gave rise to the concept of the yellow dragon in China. It is noteworthy, however, that the serpent does not figure in the Vedic rituals as such for rain.[6]

There are instances in the context of rain, where Vedic concepts and deities have been used by folks in later times. On the other hand like the serpent, the frog are closely associated with rain; and, in the Vedic theatre, it finds a place in the RV already (RV VII.103, the famous Frog-hymn). Like the serpent, the frog has been, without doubt, taken by the Vedic seer (Vasiṣṭha) from folk-belief. The frog played a very prominent part in rituals for rain in the folk-tradition. Thus, among the Behirs in Assam, when the rains are delayed, the following is the practice: Women from the low stratum of the society go about catching frogs. The frogs, when gathered, are placed in an earthen jar and are taken in a procession round the locality in a ceremonious manner. The procession goes to every house where women pour water in the jar. Ultimately, it reaches the house of a woman known to be of a quarrelsome nature, and the frogs are thrown there in the courtyard, along with the water in the jar.[7] In a variant of this ritual, all women in the locality gather near a well. There a small girl is asked to hold a small jug containing a frog in her hand; and on her head is placed a lamp; she is made to sit on a mortar turned upside down. In a short time she pretends to be (or is actually) possessed by Indra,[8] and, in that condition, is asked questions about the advent of rain. And she foretells.[9] The point to be noted is, that in these rituals women figure. The frog, like Indra of the Vedic people, is the rainer. Here we have a mixture of the Indra and the frog motifs, on the folk-plane; and there is no reason to doubt that these two got mixed even in the Vedic period, when Vasiṣṭha used the motif of the frog for the gain of rain. In addition, in the Behir tradition we have the women; and this is for the sex-charm. We have the sex-pairing as follows: (i) Frog-girl; and (ii) Frogs-women. The throwing of the frog-jar in the courtyard of the quarrelsome woman suggests the rumbling (quarrelling) of the clouds, which is also the fight-motif. The sex-motif in the employment of the frog(s) is to be noted also in such cases where frog-marriages are performed for the gain of rain.[10] Apart from their part in rain-rituals, the frogs played a very important part in fertility rites, which indicates the belief about their being the male counterpart of the ritual-women. Thus, according to a custom in Orissa, after the period of uncleanliness after delivery, the woman goes to a well or a water-place outside the village. There she prepares a frog with her own hands, out of clay, worships it and comes back home.[11] Even shorn of the idea of sex, the belief in the frog as the terrible controller of all nourishing fluid obtains. Among the Australian tribes near the lake Tyers obtains a myth that all water was inside the belly of a huge frog, in very ancient times. Hence, there was no water anywhere on the earth. It was, hence, decided that the huge frog should be made to laugh, somehow. An eel was entrusted with this task; and when he danced on the tip of his tail, the frog laughed. Immediately there was water everywhere; for it came out of the body of the frog, as it moved when he laughed.[12] The belief in, and the worship of, the frog goes far back. Thus, the terrible Hathor of ancient Egypt, having the face of a cow in one of her aspects, that of the Sky, was also depicted in the form of a female frog in her aspect of the rain-goddess. Human sacrifice was offered to her so that she may release rain.[13] Likewise, among the Zuni Indians the female frog represented the mother-earth.

When the Vedic seer praised the frogs, he was drawing upon a part of this general store of folk-beliefs. The female frog does not appear in the RV; but the AV mentions her (IV.15.14), where she is addressed as *tādurī*, a rather curious epithet which occurs nowhere else, and is indicative of pregnancy, if we follow the scholiast Sāyaṇa (*yāvac charīram tāvad udaram yasyāḥ sā*). However, the RV records the invocation to the frogs for coolness (X.16.14), and the AV refers to the custom of tying a frog to the foot of the bed of a person suffering from fever (AV VII.116.42; and Kauśika sūtra 32.17). This makes clear the belief about the frog being the controller of waters and of coolness. The creature came in the rain-hymn on the basis of this belief. The RV and the AV do not indicate the belief that the creature was sacrificed for the gain of rain, or that it was sacrificed to. In the later texts, however, there is indication that frogs were sacrificed for rain (Mait. Saṁ. III. 14.2-*samudrāya śiśumārān ālabhate parjanyāya maṇḍūkān adbhyo matsyān*). But, for want of an actual ritual, it is difficult to assert that this sacrifice was actual. In all probability, this *mantra* was only an oral charm; but, the fact of the belief remains. Though frogs are not seen as deities in the Vedic texts, there is a clear effort on the part of Vasiṣṭha to see them as wonder-workers that bring rain. The seer Vasiṣṭha says, that the frogs "perform the *brahma* (ritual wonder) that is yearly" (RV VII. 103.8-*brahma kṛṇvantaḥ parivatsarīṇam*); and as they perform this *brahma*, they are the Brāhmaṇas (v.7-*brāhmaṇāso atirātre na some*; and v.8-*brāhmaṇāso somino vācam akrata*). Earlier, in the very opening of the hymn, they are said to be "Brāhmaṇas that abide by the periodic law" (v.1-*brāhmaṇā vratacāriṇaḥ*). The identification of the frogs with the Brāhmaṇas is only one phase of the belief about the frogs, recorded by Vasiṣṭha.

The other is their identification with the clouds, a fact that has to be very carefully noted. The suggestion comes in the very first verse of the hymn, where the creatures are said to utter the speech of the rain-god (Parjanya) himself (*vācam parjanya-jinvitām pra maṇḍūkā a-vādiṣuḥ*). This means, that the frogs are the earthly representatives of the god of rain. This is balanced by the thought that they are the "divines" on the earth, lying idle for the whole year and harbingering the refreshingly benevolent speech of Parjanya. They are said to protect (hold) the yearly deposit of water (v.9-*devahitim jugupuı dvādaśasya*). Now, the frogs that hold the yearly deposit of water cannot be the frogs on the earth. They are their doubles in the mid-region; the clouds. Hence, the expression in the same verse: "The heated vessels get their release" (*taptā gharmā aśnuvate visargam*) cannot be taken to indicate the actual frogs jumping out of the crevices in which they had hidden, due to heat.[14] The heated vessels (*gharmāḥ*) cannot be the frogs; for the latter are already said to be *gharmiṇaḥ* ("those who prepare the *gharma*"); and, naturally, there has to be a difference between the *gharma* and the *gharmin*. The frogs on the earth are the *gharmiṇaḥ*, and they release the *gharma*-s, the clouds. Thus, the expression 'heated *gharma* is symbolic for the cloud here; and, being in association with the thought of the frogs, there could be little doubt that the seer, metaphorically, visualises the clouds as vessels (*gharma*-s); and at the same time he throws the suggestion that they are the mid-region 'frogs'. Thus, the frog has a twofold aspect in the vision of Vasiṣṭha: (i) the earthly water-controller; and (ii) the dark waterful cloud. The thought works on the same line as that which makes the serpent the controller of rain on the one hand; and, on the other, the cloud itself is seen as the serpent. The latter image is common in the RV in the form of Vṛtra. The frog appears to be a later incorporation; for, the serpent motif is common in RV, while the frog-motif comes only once in it, and is scanty in the later texts.[15] Continued use of this sort, gradually, gives the frog and the serpent the status of a symbol for rain control.

The serpent and the frog symbols for the cloud are far less employed in the RV than that of the cow. While these two creatures symbolise the cloud, or the water-reservoir, the cow symbolizes both the cloud and also the streams of rain.[16] Sometimes there is a fusion of the cow and the serpent; and once (VII. 103.10) the frogs are invoked to bestow the "cows" (rains). Indra kills Vṛtra, the serpent; and the latter's mother, Danu, lies shattered as a cow with the calf (RV I.32.1-4,9).

Another important symbol for the cloud is the *varāha*, the boar. This symbol, which is very complex, has its rise, probably, in the pre-pastoral stage of life. Indra is said to have struck the *varāha* that stood concealed in the mountain (RV I. 61.7). The belief became a myth in later times; and it is said that a certain *varāha* bears the wealth of the Asuras, and stands hidden beyond the seven mountains (Taitt. Saṁ. VI. 2.4.2,3). The *varāha* is Viṣṇu in this context due to the obvious influence of the identification of the sacrifice with Viṣṇu. In the original concept, however, the *varāha* appears to be the cloud. This gets support in the fact that *varāha* comes as the cloud in the RV, where he is said to have been struck by Indra; he is called Emuṣa, and is said to be full of boiling milk (RV VIII. 77.10). Elsewhere, Indra is said to have struck the *varāha* with the tip of his finger that was as hard as the tip of metal, *ayas* (RV X.99.6-*vipā varāha*m *ayoagrayā han*; *ayas* is not iron in RV, but copper or bronze). Here the image is of fight, or of hunting, as is the case with Vṛtra. Another image of a similar nature is where the cloud is believed to be a forest or a tree to be cut (RV X.27.22,23; also cf.28.8). In this case the shaft that shoots is the lightning, which is the thunderbolt in the Indra-Vṛtra motif. Now, this motif of shooting enters a new phase of symbolism and gets tinged with sex in the famous hymn of Nābhānediṣṭha (X.61.6-9) and forms the central theme of the notorious myth of the incestuous Father that runs after his own Daughter. Here the incestuous father is seen as Parjanya; the daughter is earth (*Kṣmā*), he is shot at by the archer (called Rudra in the tradition); and the shaft is the lightning (RV I. 71.5). In the origin, however, there is no shaft, and the myth is confined to the ritual of fire-kindling (RV III.31.1). In yet another phase of symbolism, we do not have the point of sex or the shot; we have the bow, or the thunderbolt, moving in the midst of the mid-region waters (RV VIII.100.9; 72.4; X.27.17), which is clearly suggestive of the lightning and the thunder in the waterful cloud, or the mid-region.

That rain was believed to be the body-fluid of the cloud-beast is clear from the image of the *varāha*. In the same category falls the belief that rain is the fluid from the testicles of Śuṣṇa (RV VIII.40.10, 11), which Indra is said to have broken in the act of releasing rain. This supports the general belief in folklore that rain is the fertilizing body moisture;[17] it is the *retas* (semen) in RV. Then we have the perspiration of the Maruts (RV V.58.7-*varṣam svedam cakrire yajniyāsaḥ*; X.67.7-*varahair gharma-svedebhiḥ*), or later, the tears of Prajāpati (Mait. Sam. IV.6.3). The imagery of the frog releasing the waters from his body-joints and other parts has to be taken in the same category of pre-pastoral beliefs.

Other images for the cloud are "the stone-mouthed reservoir" (RV II.24.4 — *aśmāsyam avatam*) and the "water-filled fountain" (*ibid.-utsam udriṇam*; cf. VIII.7.10 *utsam kavandham udriṇam*), or simply "fountain" at various places. Yet other symbols are "divine reservoir" (*divyam kośam*), or "the rivers that ooze from the boiling vessel in the sky" (RV IV.55.6 *gharma-svaraso nadyaḥ*), or even "the great reservoir" (*mahatkośa*, V.63.8), or the *caru* (I.7.6, "small boiling pot"), or "the floating citadel of Śuṣṇa" (VIII.1.28). These images are mostly from the pastoral stage and indicate a seemingly settled life. But there are clear agricultural images, in such cases where the clouds are suggested by the word *sthivi* (cf. X.27.15 where the Maruts are called *sthivimantaḥ*; *sthivi* is corn-measure). Of similar nature is the symbol in the word *dṛti* (leather-bag), which obtains at various places (cf. IV.45.3 where the Aśvins are said to carry the honeyed *dṛti*, *dṛtim vahethe madhumantam*; also V.83.7 etc.) and the "wheelless nourishment" (*acakrā svadhā*; cf. IV.26.4; X.27.19). The most interesting and notable pastoral images for clouds releasing rain can be seen in the allusions to the roasting of domesticated beasts, their fat being caused to ooze on the fire as a sympathetic charm for the gain of rain (X.27.17 *pīvānam meṣam apacanta vīrāḥ*; I.164.43 *ukṣāṇam pṛśnim apacanta vīrāḥ*), which entered the rituals for rain-gain as a sympathetic spell.[18] In the bull-sacrifice the bull was praised as "the source (or foetus) of waters, sprinkled on the plants" (Tait. Sam. III.3.9.1 *apām garbha oṣadhīṣu ny āktaḥ*), which is rendered by Sāyaṇa as "*hutaḥ san megheṣu apām sambandhī garbhaḥ, punar oṣadhīṣu ny aktaḥ*" (cf. also Mait. Sam. II.5.10; Kāṭh.Sam. XIII.9). The ritual of the offering of the drop of fat of the sacrificed bull is thus described by the Śat. Br. (III.8.2.21): "Indeed, these drops being offered into the fire...; from here does the fire seek the shower of rain; with these drops does he gain these drops (of rain); those drops, thus, get showered (herewards)" (*ibid* 22). Rains come through the sieve, as juice is sieved (X.27.17, *pavitravantā carataḥ punantā*), which probably, is a suggestion of sympathetic magic.[19] The same symbol comes elsewhere when Vāyu is said to make a leather-sieve (X.31.8-*tvacam pavitram kṛṇuta svadhāvān*). With the bull-symbolism the motif of sex is deftly employed. The mid-region is conceived as the pasture wherein the bull roars (the thunder-cloud), planting his seed in the cows (clouds) that get fructified (and rain) for prosperity (III. 55. 16,17). The cloud is the black bull in one image; and his thundering roar is believed to be due to the shaft of the lightning (I.79.2 *kṛṣṇo nonāva vṛṣabho yadi-idam*; and the cause given in the earlier half, *ā te suparṇā aminanta evaiḥ*). Just here the image takes a turn and glides swiftly into sexual imagery. The result of the shooting, and the roaring of the "Bull" is the streams of rain-waters. But these are presented in the pet symbol of women; for waters are believed to be females to be fructified by the fire. Here Parjanya is said to advance along with the smiling auspicious women (*ibid-śivābhir na smayamānābhir āgāt*). The concept of the water-females compares with the "streams of clarified butter"... the females.. that are said to go round the mid-region fire (IV.58.8 of *samaneva yoṣāḥ smayamānāsaḥ...ghṛtasya dhārāḥ*), who adores them (*ibid. tā juṣāṇo haryati jātavedāḥ*). It will be interesting to mark how this vision of the seer is enacted in ritual-context, for which we have to recollect a rite in the Mahāvrata according to which young girls went round the fire dancing and calling the "cows" to bathe.[20] At the same ritual a cow-hide (bull-hide?) was pierced with an arrow, which reminds us of the black bull struck with the shafts as noted above. The girls going round the fire in the ritual for rain in the Mahāvrata serve as a sex-charm, and there could be no doubt that they represent the females that arouse the mid-region fire to release the rains. At this juncture we may note, and compare, a few customs that obtain outside the Vedic sphere.

According to a custom that obtains in a region of Africa, in a rite for the gain of rains, a black bull is killed; the partly digested grass in his stomach is taken out; it is placed in a pot which is buried, with mouth open. Into this mouth of the pot little girls pour water till it overflows, indicating the rains from all quarters. Now, the women strip off their clothes and dance a rain-dance.[21] The Vedic rite noted above does not have nudity as a motif at this particular place; but the sex-motif is clear. We shall have occasions to refer to clear examples of nudity and copulation in the Vedic rituals also. Such rituals indicate the pastoro-agricultural stage when rain was the utmost necessity. The Mahāvrata of the Vedic Aryans was a pastoro-agricultural festival-sacrifice, for the gain of rain and prosperity through sex-rituals. Among other Aryan people also the same motif is seen. Thus, among the Germans there obtains a ritual, according to which the rain-charmer causes a naked girl to be led to the river, where water is sprinkled over her.[22] We may compare the Behir girl who foretells the day of rain. Nudity and rain is closely associated in rituals; and nudity is only one aspect of a clear-cut sexual symbol; the other is copulation on the ritual plane, the sanctified plane on the earth. Where nudity or copulation is not present, there are suggestive dialogues or actions. But, in the original rites nudity played a very important part, sometimes gliding into sex; for rain was believed to be the result of sex on the cosmic or the superhuman strata. Among the Tsul tribe of Morocco when rain is wanted, the women of the locality go to a secluded place, where nobody is expected to see them. There they get completely naked and play a sort of a game with a ball.[23] Here, the ball, probably, represents the male member. Now let us note an unusual rite among the Trojas of Central Celebes. These people simulate the incest of beasts when there are conditions of drought. A cock and sow are killed, and laid side by side. This is interpreted as for showing unnatural copulation to cause the heavens to show displeasure by pouring rain.[24] Incest is only one of the motifs employed; but the general principle is copulative pairing (or sex-coupling), which the Vedic people called *mithuna*; and they employed it at various levels with a view not only to cause rain but also the resultant prosperity in corn and cattle. The Brāhmaṇas have a complicated system of these *mithuna*-s. The point to remember is that *mithuna*-formation (or *mithunīkaraṇa*, if we may use a new term) is sex-pairing on the ritual-plane; and the parties that form the *mithuna* are believed to be divine for the duration of the ritual. As a variant of this motif, elsewhere (in Palestine for example), obtains the custom of the marriage of gods. This is accomplished in the following way: Women, including maidens, clothe a fork in the garment of a woman, and call it "the Bride of the gods".[25]

If we carefully examine the material about the beliefs and customs regarding rain-making, the fight-motif appears to be the oldest. The fight is against the power that confines rain or the fertilizing fluids. Now, this power may be the fiend, or the deity of the locality or the tribe in its baser aspect. In the latter case those who fight against this deity are women; and they fight a mimic fight. Thus, among the Bhils of the central part of India, when rains are delayed, women go with bows and arrows to the shrine of the goddess of the village dancing and abusing her in vulgar terms.[26] Here the fight is mixed with sex; and the vulgar abuse is nothing but a rain-charm. On the other hand, among the Celts it was customary to whip the water in a sacred stream and sprinkle the drops on stones.[27] The idea here, as in the fight-motif, appears to be to strike the cosmic waters (symbolically the reservoir-waters), or the water-god, so that he might send rain. Where the rain-controller was believed to be a demon, as in the case of

Vṛtra (or his other representatives in the zoomorphs),[28] the motif takes the form of a regular fight. The ancient Egyptians believed that the fight between the (solar) bird and the serpent was generative of the cosmic moisture.[29] This tallies with the Nepalese belief that, when it rains heavily, the Nāgas and the bird (Garuḍa) fight and the image of the god *Cāṅgunārāyaṇa* gets wet.[30] Now, it is interesting to note how this motif of fight gets tinged with that of sex. We have seen the example from the Bhils above. In the ancient Egyptian belief about the fight between the solar bird, who is named Horus, and the serpent Set, both abuse each other of having allowed the homosexual act; but ultimately the truth comes out in the 'semen' of Horus coming out of the ear of Set,[31] in the form of rain. In a more polished account that we have in the Avesta, the fight between the white and the black horse (Tistrya and Apaosha respectively) in the mid-region ocean, called Vouru Kasha, causes the ocean to cross limit; and thence comes rain.[32] Tistrya is associated with Apām-napāt. Here there is no tinge of sex. But, here is another version of the fight-motif from a backward tribe, which, like the Bhils, combines sex with fight. Among the Pali people of Dinajpur, when the land is suffering from want of rain the women of the locality assemble at one place in the night; cover their bodies with some red dye (vermilion?); and they go naked through the village, swords in hand, dancing and singing obscene songs. Notice is given beforehand to the men in the locality not to leave the house. The song and the ritual as a whole is called "*hudmdyao*".[33]

It is to be kept in mind that what appear as symbols for the cloud, including the fiend or the zoomorph, were actual terrestrial forms of the cloud, fully animated, for the ancient people. Appeasing "him" in rituals by means of mimetic behaviour is the result of this faith. In certain cases appeasement takes the form of sexual rituals, and there is also a double motif: (i) appeasing by sexual symbolic rites; and (ii) getting rid of him if the water-controller is deemed to be a fiend.

In the Vedic tradition of beliefs, the controller of waters, or rain-waters, had passed the stage of the mere fiend; and Vṛtra, and the like, of the RV are only a passing phase. Here the belief has passed the stage of fight, or even of sex and fight; it has already reached the concept of the Bird that stays at the confluence of the waters and the light of the sun in the solar orb. Another very interesting and sophisticated stage is that of the Gandharva; and he is sometimes with the Gandharvī, thus forming the copulative pair, devoid of the fight-motif. However, the Gandharva is not, at all places, devoid of the motif of fight. Thus he is seen as the enemy of Indra at a few places (RV VIII. 77.5-*abhi gandharvam atṛṇad abudhneṣu rajaḥsv ā*; also 1.11); but such places are scanty. The Gandharva is not considered to be on par with any of the aquatic fiends, far less the notorious serpent. The Gandharva is somewhat mystic rather than fiendish. He is associated with the "gheeful milk" of the couple Heaven and Earth; and on this "gheeful milk" do the wise fix their minds (RV I.22.14-*tayor id ghṛtavat payo viprā rihanti dhītibhiḥ gandharvasya dhruve pade*). The essence of the cosmos (which was rain in the simple symbolism) has now passed into the realm of mysticism, but is controlled by Gandharva (cf. IX. 85.12; X.123.7, where the Gandharva and the principle called the Bird are associated with the solar waters). The Gandharva, thus, becomes the supreme seeder; he is the water-usurper turned benevolent to the seers and mankind as a whole. The next step is to make him the male in the *mithuna* (sexual pair); and he is conceived as the seeder of the Gandharvī (X.11.2, the word occurs only here in RV), who is the *apyā yoṣā* ("water belle"). The oldest reference to the Gandharva is in the family-book of the Viśvāmitras, where we have not one but many Gandharvas (RV III. 38.6 *gandharvān vāyukeśān*) and they are placed in the mid-region, as is indicated by the epithet *vāyu-keśan*. The Gandharva and the Gandharvī (or the *apyā yoṣā*) form the final cosmic *mithuna* and are the prototypes for the couples Yama and Yamī (RV X.10) on the one hand, where both are ficticious, and, on the other, for Purūravas and Urvaśī (RV X.95), where the former is real and the latter ficticious. A beautiful combination of all these motifs is presented by RV in the name of the Gandharva Viśvāvasu (actually *viśva-vasu*, "All wealth"); and it is said, "He (Indra) broke open the gates (of the waters) that were captivated in the 'stone-reservoir'; the Gandharva disclosed (to him) the nectars of the waters; Indra knew the sustenance of (or, held by) the serpents". (X. 139.6; esp. *prāsām gandharvo amṛtāni vocat, indro dakṣam pari jānād ahīnām*). In the previous stanza we have Viśvāvasu mentioned by name (v.5 *viśvāvasur abhi tanno gṛṇātu, divyo gandharvo rajaso vimānaḥ*), where he is said to be wandering in the mid-region (*rajaso vimānaḥ* above). Thus, we have the 'stone-reservoir' (cloud), the Gandharva and the serpents, all holding the waters (cf. *ibid. caraṇe nadīnām*). The point to be noted is that the reference to the one Gandharva (singular, not plural) appears in the later stages of RV (all in books I and X only, which are later on the basis of the language). Only twice is the Gandharva mentioned in book VIII: (1.11; 77.5); but the places can be taken as exceptions, or later. This will indicate that the Gandharva is the last to be added to the symbolic controllers of waters; and this was on the basis of the many Gandharvas that were believed to roam in the mid-region, as "hair-on-winds" (cf. *vāyu-keśān*), where the concept is more of the mystic creatures rather than of the clouds that roam on the wind. The earliest symbol is that of the serpent (*ahi*), that occurs even in the old family books (RV II-VII, and even in VIII). The concept of the female counterpart of the one Gandharva, the Gandharvī, occurs only in the later books. As both (as a *mithuna* now) control all fluids (including rain and the generative fluid), they are ushered in the marriage-hymn (X. 85.21, 22; 40,41), for fecundity; and later, they became symbolic for sexual laxity.

Before we take leave of this point and take up that of the relationship of Fire and Water entering into the symbolism of marriage, we shall do well to examine the symbolism of the Bird in respect of rain or waters. We have already referred to it earlier, and shall have more particular occasions of referring to it further. RV has the concept of the bird that stays in the orb of the sun. The origin of the concept is, obviously, that the sun is the bird as he moves from one end of the sky to the other. That he is the receptacle of the waters, which he gets evaporated with his rays, is the experience. The two actual experiences gave rise to the complex image of the Bird in the solar orb in the Ṛgvedic seers' vision. Yet, the concept cannot be said to be restrictively Vedic. For the ancient Egyptians believed the Horus hawk to be residing in the beam of light; and he is the solar hero.[34] RV has the bird *śyena* (hawk) bringing honey, which is the symbol for rain (IV.18.12; 26.4,5; 27.3,4,5) and which forms the basis of the later legend of the gain of nectar and also rain.[35] The Avestan bird of rain stays on the "tree-of-all-seeds" (called Harvisptokhm) which is in the mythic ocean Vouru Kasha, where there is a regular fight of the white and black horses as noted earlier. This bird is called Sinamru; whenever he flies off the tree, there grow out of it thousand boughs; and whenever he alights on it, there break a thousand boughs, the seeds of which are scattered about and "rained upon the world by the rain-god Tishtar".[36] The bird, without doubt, is the flash of lightning. In most cases the bird is the sun or the lightning that is believed to control rain. The winged disc that adorned the main entrance of ancient Egyptian temples was at once a symbol of the sun and the "Giver of the life-fluid". It was believed to give rain that nourishes the vegetables, and also represented the thunder-bird which slew the water-confining serpent; it also ensured immortality.[37] It comes very near to the concept of the *śyena* bird in RV.

With the serpent and the bird being used separately as the symbols for the cloud in RV, it would have been only a step to the combined motif of the bird-serpent in one. But RV, or the Vedic literature, does not show familiarity with this combined motif. We may, however, do well to compare the motif from Japan where we do have the serpent and the bird in one. It should be noted, however, that here also the original motif of the fire and the serpent lies at the base of this double motif, though a new element is ushered in. Thus, the Tengu, who is a kite, or an elephant-headed god according to *Shishishu* (a book of the Japanese Shin sect), once carries off the serpent in a miniature form and drops it in a deep-cleft rock. Now, the serpent cannot fly until it gets a drop of water. The Tengu, after a few days, sees a priest about to fill a jug of water, and carries him off to the serpent. There is a drop of water in the pitcher; and this drop, when drunk, strenghtens the serpent, who now assumes the form of a boy and flies through the air amidst thunder and lightning, with the priest on his back.[38] Here we have the motif of the flying serpent, though he assumes the form of a boy. The serpent, it is clear, is the spent up cloud-fire of the last season; and it is to be strengthened. The drop of water from the pitcher is symbolic of the water in the cloud. The presence of the priest is, probably, a later addition, and an influence of ritual. The serpent-boy is a case of fire-anthropomorphism. The flight of the serpent is also indicative of the bird-serpent combination on the one hand, and, on the other, the cloud-serpent motif. The motif is, thus, a mixed one: lightning-fire + cloud serpent + water-drop; (further) = boy + water jar. In both the boy and the serpent are flying, indicative of the bird.

We have seen earlier that the fire-water symbolism is the germ of the Gandharva-Gandharvī relationship, and that it shows a peculiar sexual relationship. It is interesting to see how the water-fire motif forms part of the beliefs and rituals regarding human marriage. It is noticed among other Aryan races beyond the Vedic pale. Among the Romans marriage was a union between the fire and the waters, the bridegroom being fire and the bride the water. The marriage was symbolically described as *aqua et igni*; and the marriage between Romulus and the captured Sabine women was *aqua et igni mariti uxores accibiebant*.[39]

Bride being water may be compared with the Vedic custom of carrying water from the river earlier to the marriage on the part of the bride; the custom obtains even later and is seen even today, among the Birhors and the Bengalis.[40] In the Vedic custom the water thus carried was supposed to destroy the evil of sterility in the bride.[41] It was customary among the Roman Aryans to carry the marriage-torch and the marriage-water in procession round the altar from left to right (cf. the Hindu *pradakṣiṇa* way). Among the Slavs it had been a fixed marriage rite for the bride to take bath and to dance round the household fire after she had stepped over a jar of water.[42] In such rituals the motif is the union of the fire and the water or the element of heat and moisture,[43] which was believed to be conducive to human fertility and fecundity. In the reverse way, make-belief marriages played an important part in rain-rituals as a sympathetic charm for the cosmic forces to unite and send rain (the semen of the sky), as we have noted. In a variant custom from Ain Sefra Tlemsen and Mazunawe we have the following ritual. When rain is wanted, people take a wooden spoon and dress it like a little doll. They take '*her*' to the tomb of a local priest in procession, singing a song which contains the following:

> Gonja!
> Gonja has uncovered her head!
> O Lord; thou wilt water her ear-drops;
> Her ear is thirsty.[44]

Here we have a unique *mithuna*, that of the Rain-god and the Spoon-bride. Taking her to the tomb of the local priest appears to be added later and may be compared with the Japanese story of the winged serpent and the priest. It should be noted that the spirit of the priest does not form the male counterpart; it comes only as a blessing-aid. The 'ear' does not suggest corn-ear. Probably, it is the symbol for the generative organ of the spoon-bride.[45] It may be compared with the 'ear' of Set, noted earlier, from which flows out the semen of Horus. Even devoid of the motif of the fight, and of the bird-motif, the sun is seen as the controller of rain. Thus in many parts of ancient Egypt the crocodile was the symbol of sun,[46] indicating the sun to be in the midst of the cosmic waters. The crocodile is also associated with the Mexican god of rain, Tloloc.[47] Though this god is not strictly the sun-god, it is to be noted that he has association of the solar motifs. Thus, he is said to be the god of the East, and the children offered to him were to be bedecked with feathers.[48] In some of the representations he is seen as just awakened and rising from his bed.[49] The fact that he also has a pot of water, from which a wasp is seen coming out need not be taken to mean that this god was believed to be the Nāga.[50] This is only suggestive of the cloud (potful of water) from which starts the flash of the serpentine lightning. Actually Tloloc seems to be the fiery principle in the mid-region that controls the rains. He is shown with the axe having the sun above, from which a stream of blood flows,[51] which indicates the belief of the sun being the animal on the one hand and, on the other, that the body-sap of the god is the source of fertilizing rain. In some of his forms the god Tloloc has a dragon-shaped axe and a serpentine thunderbolt,[52] which are the symbols of the lightning, and suggest the solar-fire nature of the god rather than his being the Nāga. In yet another representation, above or before him, there is a burning house, on which lies the flaming axe; and below it there is a stream of water with snails or fishes.[53] The burning house leaves no doubt about his being the embodiment of the lightning fire, the stream of water with the snails and fishes suggesting his control over the terrestrial water-places also. In this nature of his, he comes very close to the Indo-Iranian god Apām-napāt, who was not only the god of the lightning, after his incorporation in the Vedic pantheon, but also came to be regarded as the male spirit of the river Sarasvatī, being called *Sarasvant*; and further on he was localized at the confluence of the Sarasvatī and the Dṛṣadvatī.[54] Like Indra with the Maruts, the fiery Tloloc was helped by his band of assistants called Tloloque, who distributed rain from the pitcher that he smote with serpentine rods (lightnings).[55] In ancient China the rain-maker faced the East, indicating the association with the sun-fire.[56] The same belief appears to lie at the bottom of the ritual of looking to the sun and sprinkling oneself with water when rainy weather is desired, as obtained among the Lithuanians.[57] The Vedic belief that the sun is the reservoir of waters (RV I.23.17) is only a phase of this universal one.

Rituals of the sort mentioned above were for rain. But, it is observed, that they *become* the regular features of the society during the year with the expectation of timely rains, though, originally, they must have been occasioned by the failure of rain at a particular time. The yearly rituals of this sort came at the solstices as was the case of the Horse-sacrifice and the Mahāvrata. The same was true of the other tribes, including the Aryans at other regions. To give an example. In some of the Aryan tribes of Europe young men and women join at the Summer solstice. They put on wreathes of field-mapple with fragrant herbs, gird themselves with artemisia, and gather before sunset on the elevated place facing the river. They set up two figures, one of a man and the other that of a woman, formed out of a piece of wood with the attire of a woman (cf. the Gonja-figure). Then they kindle a huge fire; and, taking the figures in their hands they jump across the fire. This jumping is done in pairs — one boy and one girl. When all have done this ritual of jumping the figures are thrown into the river.[58] Here we have the double sex-pairing (*mithuna*, to use the Vedic term); one, the figures: and two, the young boy-girl. Such rituals were mostly performed at the Summer solstice. As noted above, in the Vedic Mahāvrata, which was replete with sex-symbolism, among other things, there was a huge fire round which the girls danced having pitchers, filled with water on head; at the end of the dance the water was to be poured into the fire, with the invocation to the "cows" (the clouds that pour the rain-milk). Rituals for rain at various places, thus, have a close similarity of concept. The

Vedic seer-sacrificers of ancient times used many of such motifs in their *mantra*-s, which were used by them for the gain of rains. In certain cases more complicated varieties were used, and were also innovated. They were never restricted to their own tradition; and indicate help from other ritual-traditions at times when the usual gods refused to do the needful.[59]

The gain of rain was one of the most dominant motifs in the varied speculations of the ancient people. The Ṛgveda shows various instances to that effect. Along with the speculations regarding the birth of the universe, the Vedic seers show various efforts for the gain of rain through some of their whole hymns, which are a beautiful blend of ritual and cosmological speculations. We shall refer to some in the pages to follow.

NOTES

1. On this point see Donald Mackenzie, *Myths of China and Japan*, London, pp. 66-72; also Rundle Clark, *Myth and Symbol in Ancient Egypt*, London, 1959, p.51ff.
2. Jaim Br., I.125-127; Kāṭhaka Sam. 37.14 etc.
3. See Jarl Charpentier, *Die Suparṇasage*, Uppsala, 1920, where he records the whole work and presents a critical study.
4. Sadashiv A. Dange, *Legends in the Mahābhārata*, Delhi, 1969, pp.1-153. *Myths from the Mahābhārata*, Vol. I, Aryan Books International, New Delhi, 1997, pp.1-150
5. D. Mackenzie, *op.cit.*, *loc.cit.*
6. The head of the serpent is mentioned in the Vedic ritual of *agnicayana* ("Piling of the altar"); Baudh. Śr. S.X.9; but this is not in connection with rain.
7. Ganesh Chaube, "Behir songs for Rain", *Bhāratīya Vidya*, VI, p.176.
8. Cf. W. Crooke in *Encl. Rel. E*, II. p.555b, for the Bhils offering cakes to Dharma-Indra.
9. Ganesh Chaube, *op.cit.*, *loc.cit.*
10. Many instances can be cited; but we may refer to a report from the *Hitavada* (A Daily from Bhopal), dated the 30th May, 1965; see also Waddel, "Frog-worship in Nepal",

Indian Antiquary XXII, p.293ff; Sharatchandra Mitra, "Frog in North Indian Rain-controlling rites", *Folk-lore and Tradition in India*, XIV, p.429ff.

11. *Indian Antiquary*, V, p.188.
12. Andrew Lang, *Myth, Ritual and Religion*, London, 1913, p.43.
13. D. Mackenzie, *op.cit.*, p.145.
14. K.F. Geldner, *Der Rigveda*, II, HOS, 1951, note on the passage; H.D. Velankar, *Ṛgveda Maṇḍala* VII, Bombay, 1953, p.225, note-8.
15. For the serpent motif in the Mb. see Dange, *Legends in the Mahābhārata*, Delhi, 1969, Ch.I; *Myths from the Mahābhārata*, Vol. I; for the frog in a different context and motif, *ibid.*, p.339ff; also Max Müller, *Chips from a German Workshop* (Vols. I-IV, 1896-1907) II, p.251ff.
16. They cannot be actual cows, as certain scholars (See note 14 above) believe.
17. D. Mackenzie, *op.cit.*, pp.132, 160; also by the same author, *Myths of Pre-Columbian America*, p.167.
18. Dange, Sadashiv A., *Pastoral Symbolism from the Ṛgveda*, Poona, 1970, pp.45-49.
19. For the sieve in non-Vedic rites see *Encl. Rel. E.*, XI, p.506a.
20. *Ibid.*, VIII, p.319, article by Macdonell, A.A.
21. *Ibid.* X, p.262a; also Chaube, *op.cit.*
22. *Encl. Rel.E*, Vol. II, p.40b, Schrader, F.O., "Aryan religion"; also III, p.419a.
23. *Ibid.*, IX, p.830; cf. the custom and rite of "*Hudmdyao*" ref. to further in the discussion; see note-33 below.
24. *Ibid.*, X, p.155; also Frazer, *Magic Art*, II, London, 1932, p.113.
25. *Encl. Rel. E.*, V, p.830; see Dange, *Sexual Symbolism from the Vedic Ritual*, pp.82ff, for the Vedic practice.
26. *Encl. Rel. E.* II, p.555b.
27. *Ibid.*, VIII, p. 257; we might compare the concept in the "honeyed whip" (*madhumatī kaśā*) of the Vedic twin-gods Aśvins; RV I.22.3.157.4; for a different interpretation of the "honeyed whip", see C.A. Blair, *Heat in the Ṛgveda and the Atharvaveda*, New Haven, 1961, p.153ff; however, the whip need not be the flogging hunter; it may be the strap that vibrates and sprinkles the drops... lightning. For another example of the sprinkling motif, Frazer, *Folk-lore of the Old Testament*, III, London 1918, p.66; Dange,

Pastoral Symbolism, p.45.

28. For stories based on this motif, *Folklore and Legend Oriental*, London, 1890, p.59f; A. Lang, *op.cit.*, p.42, 44.
29. Mackenzie, D., *Myths of Pre-Columbian America*, London, p.55.
30. Vogel, J. Ph., *The Indian Serpent-lore*, London, 1926, p.278; W. Crooke, *Popular Religion and Folk-lore of Northern India*, II, 1896, p.122. This fight is believed to take place on the day of Nāgapañcamī, which comes roughly in the month of August. It is called also Garuḍapañcamī in south India. According to the Chinese belief it rains when the dragons fight, D. Mackenzie, *Myths of China and Japan*, p.56.
31. Rundle Clark, *Myth and Symbol in Ancient Egypt*, London, 1959, p.150.
32. J. Darmesteter, Trans. of the *Avesta*, SBE XXIII, Intr. to the "Tir Yasht"; also p.9; for Tistrya as a horse, p.96. Apaosha as black horse, p.99f; see also Tir yasht, Zend Avesta, VIII.1ff. esp.VIII. 6.18-34, for fight.
33. G.H.Damant in *Indian Antiquary*, I, 1872, p.340a; the meaning of *Hudmdyao* is, according to John Beams. (*ibid.*, p.371), "naked women" or "loose women"; ploughing by naked women is practised even today, in north Indian villages, see news item: *Tarun Bharat*, Marathi Daily, Nagpur, 2nd May, 1963; also Chaube, *op.cit.*
34. Rundle Clark, *op.cit.*, p.150.
35. Dange, *Legends in the Mahābhārata*, Ch.I.
36. Darmesteter, SBE, IV, p.53; also note on p.54.
37. D. Mackenzie, *Myths of China and Japan*, London, p.71; Olcott, T.W., *Sun-lore of All Ages*, London, New York, 1914, p.292.
38. D. Mackenzie, *Myths of Pre-Columbian America*, London, pp.51, 55.
39. Schrader, F.O., *op.cit.*, p.49a.
40. Nilakshi Sengupta, *Evolution of Hindu Marriage*, Bombay, 1965, p.78; Dange, *Vedic Concept ...*, 1971, p.13; where he examines some of the opinions of N. Sengupta.
41. Dange, 1971, 14; also pp.73ff.
42. Schrader, *op.cit.*, *loc.cit.*
43. *Ibid.*
44. *Encl. Rel. E.*; II, p.510a.
45. Ear as the symbol for the female organ appears also

elsewhere. The demon Karṇāṭa, for example, is said to have been born from the ear of the Devī, see Skanda P.III.2.18.88f. See Dange, *Encyclopaedia of Puranic Beliefs and Practices* (vols. I-V), vol. II, New Delhi, 1987, p. 407. In the case of the spoon, the 'ear' is its frontal hollow, symbolising the generative organ of his 'bride'.

46. Olcott, *op.cit.*, p.294.
47. Donald Mackenzie, *Myths of Pre-Columbian America*, p.241.
48. *Ibid.*, p.251; feathers were invariably indicative of the solar aspect; see Olcott, *op.cit.*, pp.123, 153, 244, where the author gives instances of solar representations from the Melanesian, Egyptian and the Hopi Indian beliefs.
49. Mackenzie, *op.cit.*, p.252.
50. *Ibid.*, In another interesting representation, this god is shown as follows. A stream of water (rain) issuing from his body falls into a green vessel, in which are seated two images of Chalchiuhtlicue, one painted green and the other blue. Chalchiuhtlicue is the Mother and the jewel-water goddess, the controller of the water of life. The meaning of the name is "Jade-her-skirt"; she controlled all water-sources, see Frances F.Berden, *The Aztecs*, Chelsea House Publishers, New York, Philadelphia, 1989, p.82.
51. Mackenzie, *op.cit.*, p.248.
52. *Ibid.*, p.244.
53. *Ibid.*
54. Keith, A.B., *The Religion and Philosophy of the Veda and Upanishads*, London, 1925, p.352. Apām-napāt seems, primarily, to be the spirit of the waters and was distinct from Agni, Dandekar, *Vaidika Agni, Daivata śāstra*, Poona, 1972, p.45ff.
55. Mackenzie, *Myths of Pre-Columbian America*, p.243.
56. *Ibid.*, p.76; De Vesser, *The Dragon in China and Japan*, quoted by D. Mackenzie, op., cit., *loc.cit.*
57. Schrader, "Aryan Religion", at Encl. Rel. and Ethics, II, p.40b.
58. *Ibid* p.48a.
59. Dange, *Sexual Symbolism*, pp.161 ff, as an example.

Chapter 2

THE THUNDER AND THE AKṢARA

An important aspect of the contemplation of the Vedic seers is their vision of the fire settled in waters. In other words, they have contemplated a unit of 'dry and moist' (as the Śat. Br. I.6.3:23, clearly states, on the basis of the Ṛgvedic seers' tradition of thinking). In ritual it is seen in the continued association of the offering (Soma or any other offering) poured into the fire. On the cosmic plane it is seen in the waters in the sun (heavenly fire), the fire in the cloud, and the fire believed to be concealed in all terrestrial water-places, such as rivers, tanks, etc. that are holy. On the same analogy, the supreme Principle is seen as settled in water. It is the source of all nourishing fluids, the release of which is characterised by the thunder, which is the cosmic aspect of Speech. This Principle is seen variously as a Bird, and also as Akṣara, the word indicative of the Supreme 'Syllable', and is also associated with the 'flow', 'oozing out' (fr. the root *kṣar*). It is a complex image. Here, we take the vision of Dīrghatamas.

The thunder-cow that emits rain as its milk has been a favourite image of the Ṛgvedic seers; and this is balanced by the image of the sustaining bull that "sprinkles" (*vṛṣan* or *vṛṣabha*). It is interesting to see how this symbolism is used by Dīrghatamas, the seer of the "*asya vāmīya*" hymn (RV. I.164). The hymn has been studied by various scholars;[1] and it was the subject of a seminar, the results of which have been published by Norman Brown.[2] Professor Brown has shown the various aspects of the hymn, taking note also of the earlier scholars; and it is not quite necessary to repeat the opinions of those scholars. Brown's suggestions about the hymn, however, are worthy of note and further study. His main thesis is that the hymn is not merely a series of disconnected riddles; and, as he has shown, this view was already breathed out, though feebly, by such scholars as Haug, Henry, Deussen, Kunhan Raja, and V.S. Agrawala.[3] In trying to give a stylistic unity to the hymn, Haug looked upon the hymn as a series of riddles intentionally used; naturally these riddles were purposeful and, hence, connected. For Henry the hymn has a unity in primitivism, which fails to reveal much of the sacerdotal purpose of exalting the sacrifice, the sun, the fire and the speech. Granting Deussen's plea that the hymn is devoted to the exposition of monism, Brown suggests that in the hymn Vāc (speech) itself is the centre of monism and that the sun, Agni and the sacrifice are only secondary to it. Brown criticises Deussen for not bringing out the exact significance of the expression "*salilāni takṣatī*" said in respect of the Cow Vāc. He points out that Kunhan Raja did not demonstrate the clear unity in the various images of the hymn; and about Agrawala he says that he relied more upon the post-Vedic sources and ideas than the Vedic proper.

According to Brown the hymn, which has fifty-two verses, has to be divided into three parts. He suggests that the last three verses are added later on; and this is supported by the fact that the hymn, as it occurs in the Atharva-Veda (=AV), appears as two successive hymns, and the last three verses here are absent there in this connection.[4] From an analytical study of the hymn Brown has come to the conclusion that it tries to explain the cosmology and cosmogony, and presents Vāc as the origin of the whole cosmic structure. Even so, there are certain difficulties in the interpretation proposed by Brown; and it is, hence, necessary to re-examine the hymn in its main aspects, following its various images. We first take the most prominent one.

The Thundering Cow and the Oceans

The hymn starts with the mention of the Cosmic Fire and its three aspects. The Sun, the Lightning-fire and the sacrificial Fire; and, at a certain point, makes the mention of the Cow that thunders. This cow is said to be intrinsically associated with the waters. The expression is "*gaurīr mimāya salilāni takṣatī*" (v.41; AV IX.10.21 has *gaur in mimāya*), which means "the cow lowed fashioning the waters"; and it is further said that she got transformed into the "one-footed", "two-footed", "eight-footed", "nine-footed", and that it assumed the thousand letters at the highest heaven (*sahasrākṣarā parame vy'oman*). From her drip down the oceans which sustain the four (main) quarters; and then oozes the '*akṣara*', which nourishes the whole world.

There is no doubt that here we are face to face with the concept of the all-pervading speech, especially when it is said to assume the various forms which suggest the measured arrangement of syllables in metres; or it may indicate the various parts of speech as suggested by Sāyaṇa. Yāska (Nirukta, XI.40) suggests it to be the speech of the mid-region. She is one, due to her being alone in the mid-region, "two-footed" due to being with the sun, "four-" due to the four quarters, "eight-" with the quarters along with the sub-quarters, "nine-" due to the eight quarters and the sun, and "thousand-" being with the unlimited waters at the source in the highest heaven. Yāska, thus, connects the mid-region speech with the ultimate source of waters. Sāyaṇa also follows this interpretation and suggests the one which we have referred to above as an alternative one. The point to be noted is that both connect the mid-region speech, which is the thunder, with the ultimate source of water. This is, obviously, because of the presence of the word "*salilāni*" in the verse proper and "*samudra*" in the next verse. The water (*salilāni*, Plural) here and in the next verse (*samudrāḥ*) being so unmistakably associated with the Cow, the traditional interpretation, which sees here a mixed image of the mid-region thunder and the consequential rains, cannot be lightly set aside. It suggests that the thunder stands as the norm of all speech; but, that it is a mixed image of the Cow that emits speech and rain simultaneously. Brown understands "*salilāni*" as the "tumultuous chaotic floods", an expression rather difficult to comprehend, and compares it with RV X.129.3. But it has to be pointed out that the comparison is not sound; for at the latter place we have the expression "*apraketam salilam*", in the Singular, which rightly indicates the principle of fluid chaos (the abyss); but here it is "*salilāni*", in the Plural, which get connected with the "oceans that flow", in the next verse. The Ṛgveda presents the concept of two oceans, the upper one and the lower one; and when from the upper ocean the waters flow down to the lower one, it is rain; and nothing else—a fact that forms the motif of the hymn of Devāpi and Śantanu (X.98.5).[5] The mid-region Cow thunders in the *antarikṣa*, but has her conceptual abode at the highest heaven (*parame vy 'oman*). She has the essence of the principle called "*akṣara*"; and, that is why, she is called "*sahasrākṣarā*". The image is twofold. In the first place it indicates the various sounds in the mid-region that are the proto-types of all *mantra*-s and the human speech; and, in the second place, it indicates the multiple forms of the "*akṣara*" principle. It is to be noted that the "*akṣara*" is said to "flow" (*tataḥ kṣaraty' akṣaram*). This brings us to the concept of the "*akṣara*".

The Akṣara

The first mention of *Akṣara* in the hymn is in the context of the various metres as "*akṣareṇa mimate sapta vāṇīḥ*" (v.24) and the implication is that *akṣara* is the prime cause of all speech, measured metrically, or ordinarily. At a later stage, and in the context of the thunder of the Cow, we have the *akṣara* "oozing" (*tataḥ kṣaraty' akṣaram*), being the nourishment of all (*tad viśvam upa jīvati*); and this nourishment is closely connected with the idea of the down flowing streams from the upper oceans (v. 42). The next phase of the *akṣara* is to be seen in an earlier verse (39), where it is conceived as the abode of all the gods (*ṛco akṣare parame vy'oman yasmin devā adhi viśve ni ṣeduḥ*). Here the *akṣara* is conceived as being in the (sparkling) verse (ṛc), as also in the highest heaven. Conversely, it means that the verse (or better, the *mantra*) is itself, the abode of the gods—a well attested belief. The *akṣara* is not confined, however, to the verse; it is all-pervading. It is apt to flow; but it may not flow always. It may be heard in the thunder or in the various words; but it is not restricted to these. The concept, hence, is of a potent life-force that may ooze out or be heard, but is steady in the highest abode. Hence, the suggestion of Brown that it is the "sound including phonology, articulation etc." (*op.cit.*, p.216) is only partly true. It does not go suitably with "*kṣarati*", and goes against the clear mention of the down-flowing oceans in our hymn. It is clear, hence, that the *akṣara* is not only the "syllable" as Brown suggests, nor even the "creative syllable", as Van Buitenen understands and Brown follows; for even being a "creative syllable" he considers creativity to be restricted to the formation of sounds.[6] The creativity of the *akṣara* has to be seen in the context of the nourishing or the creative fluid, which is so clear in our hymn. In this connection it is interesting to note the traditional belief about the *akṣara*. The Jaiṃ. U. Br. (I.23.3) indicates that the god pressed the *akṣara*; and that, as the *akṣara* was being pressed, fluid oozed out (*sa etad akṣaram abhy' apīḷayat, tasyā-bhipiḷitasya rasaḥ praṇedat*). The concept of the fluid from the *akṣara* is referred to at another place also in the same context (*ibid.* I.i). Buitenen identifies this *akṣara* with *brahman*, and renders it only as "syllable", without explaining the concept of the fluid of creation. Though this fluid indicates the substance for the formation of the various forms of speech, it is, without doubt, the essence of all creation. And it is this concept of the oozing *akṣara* that Dīrghatamas sees in his vision of the thundering Cow releasing the oceans. Rightly does he question, "he who knows not this *akṣara*, what shall he do with the mere verse" (v.39, *yas tan na veda kim ṛcā kariṣyati*? cf. Bṛhadār. Up. III. 8.9,10).

Sometimes the *akṣara* is said to be luminous being born from the foot of the celestial cow (RV III. 55.1 *mahadvi jajñe akṣaram pade goḥ*), and comes close to the concept of the divine *madhu* that is hidden in the divine cow, being closely associated with water; for it is said to be hidden in the (cosmic) waters (RV. III.39.6 *madhu saṁbhṛtam usriyāyām... guhā hitam guhyam gūḷham apsu*). The association of the *akṣara* and the cow here does not indicate the syllable and the Speech-cow. Actually the cow-image goes far beyond that of the speech; and the concept behind *akṣara* is not restricted to the syllable. It is the highest luminous principle that sustains all life; and it is also the source of all nourishing cosmic fluids. On the first basis the cosmic fire is said to stay in the *akṣara*, which is the very womb of Ṛta. (RV VI. 16.35); and in its second aspect it is said to ooze. The Cow which causes the *akṣara* to flow is an aspect of the Sabardughā that "milks" rain;[7] and she is called "*sahasrākṣarā*" in view of the oozing oceans.

The Bird

With the concept of the flooding *akṣara* the seer uses another one; and that is of the Bird. These two get mixed up with that of the Cow in a variant image. In the Cow that thunders (*gaurī*) we have a single cow; but earlier the seer describes the sun with his manifold "cows"; and the image gets mixed up with that of the bird (v.3 *yatra gavām nihitā sapta nāma*, where the seven cows are the seven rays of the sun, corresponding to the seven "mares" or seven "sisters" at other places. Cf. VII. 66.15; I.50.8 etc.; and here v.7 *śīrṣṇaḥ kṣīram duhrate gāvo asya*, where we have the reference to the mystic Bird in *vāmasya nihitam padam veḥ*.). This verse, together with 45, 51 and 52 (which specifically refer to the rains), embodies the seer's theory of rain, as Brown also remarks (*op.cit.*, pp.205; 212, under v.7). The idea is that the solar rays (cows) drink the waters with their 'feet' (v.7 *udakam padā-puḥ*), and in these waters that stabilize in the solar orb, the "bird" stays. The bird is referred to here as "*vi*" (cf. *veḥ*), and is the same as the *suparṇa* (at v.52). Actually this is a very fond image of the seers; for elsewhere we have the deity Vena as the bird residing at the confluence of the sun and the solar waters (RV X.123.1 *apām saṅgame sūryasya*; and v.6 there, *śakunam bhuraṇyum*). As we have the sun-bird, which is the 'foetus of waters' ("*apām garbha*"), here, in our hymn, impelling rains (*vṛṣṭibhis tarpayantam*), so we have Vena, staying in the solar water (in the orb), impelling the waters in the mid-region ocean, himself being born in the mid-region in his variant aspect (X.123.2 *samudrād ūrmim ud iyarti veno nabhojāḥ*). The bird that takes its seat in the sun and also works on the mid-region plane is the potent aspect of the cosmic fire. The Vena 'bird' corresponds not only to the *apām garbha*, but to also the thundering Cow that "fashions the waters", and by which the oceans start to flow, causing the very "*akṣara*" to ooze. The *akṣara* thus corresponds to the Vena. Dīrghatamas puts a riddle, as it were, in the image of the bird here, and asks "Let him, who knows, say here the abode of this bird" (v.7). At another place Agni, the fire in its cosmic aspect, is said to protect the abode (*pada*) of the "bird", that is the sun (RV.III 5.5 *padam veḥ, pāti yahvaś caraṇam sūryasya*; Agni is the seat of the bird IV. 7.7). It will be seen that the concept of the "bird", that is the all powerful one, dominates the mind of the seer of our hymn also. This supreme One is ushered in by another word; and it is Suparṇa. The verse in which there is the reference to this supreme Suparṇa is quite famous; but as it has been differently understood by Brown it is necessary to quote it in full:-

indram mitram varuṇam agnim āhur
atho divyaḥ sa suparṇo garutmān /
ekam sad viprā bahudhā vadanti
agnim yamam mātariśvānam āhuḥ / / (v.46).

Brown takes this verse to suggest that the *ekam sat* (The ONE Real) in it refers to the all powerful Speech. This cannot be accepted. The reason is not so much that it goes against the earlier interpretations, as that it is structurally unsound. On the very face of it the gender of the *ekam sat* differs from that of Vāc, the former being the neuter and the latter feminine. Even Brown feels this difficulty, and tries to patch it up by a unique suggestion. It is necessary to quote him — "The 'One Real' is neuter, Vāc is feminine. Assuming that the identification of the two is correct, the inconsistency in gender may be explained by looking upon Vāc here as conceptionally mid-way between such personal creators as Prajāpati (RV. 10.121), Viśvakarman (RV. 10.81 and 82) and even herself (10.71 and 10.125) and the purely impersonal *tat ekam* (neut.) of 10.129" (*op.cit.*, p.217, note under v.46). The explanation that Vāc is conceptionally mid-way between the masculine and the neuter divinities is itself based upon the assumption that Vāc is the *ekam sat*, which itself has no sound support. The position, rather, is that in the verse under consideration the word *suparṇa* occurs as the symbolic name for the "Bird", that stays at the confluence of the sun and the waters, as we have seen. It is the same Vena, the double fire-principle that stays in the solar orb and works on the plane of the mid-region. There is also another point. If the last portion, which refers to the advent of rain, and the *suparṇa* who is "*apām garbha*" (vv.51, 52), is any indication (even if it be supposed to be a later addition), it is natural to presume that it was added in view of a common motif. It is necessary, hence, to see a close relationship between the *suparṇa* here and at the last verse. And if we remember that the hymn starts with the concept of the three fires, of which the sun is the first, there should remain no doubt that the *suparṇa* here is the same One Real principle that is seen as the sun-fire. Here the tradition, as shown by Yāska, is clear (Nir. VII.17-18); and there is no necessity of any other interpretation that would confuse matters due to lack of a proper comparative and analytical approach! Brown's contention that the *ekam sat* is Vāc suffers from another shortcoming on his own explanation. He translates the phrase "*ekam sad viprā bahudhā vadanti*" as "the inspired priests speak of the One Real"; but in the notes he has, "the priests speak the *ekam sat.*" This creates contradiction. If the priests speak of the One Real, it has to be different from Speech or the action of speech. The point is that the *ekam sat* is different from Speech. It has also to be noted that *suparṇa* is not a deity of the type of Indra etc. mentioned in the verse. He is separated by the word "*atho*"; he is in the nominative while the other deities are in the accusative, which is, probably indicative of the importance of the *suparṇa*. It is this principle that is referred to in the words "*ekam sad viprā bahudhā vadanti*". It is also not improbable that the words "*ekam sat*" indicate the accusative related to the *suparṇa* in view of its being the object of the sentence, if we take *sat* as irregular for *santam* (cf. for the masculine of *sat* RV.IV. 5.10 *adha dyutānaḥ* ... *mātuḥ pade parame anti sad goḥ*, which describes the all-pervading fire).

It would be, thus, clear that *sat* in the present context refers to the fire-principle that becomes manifest in the form of the sun, or, on the mid-region plane, in that of the lightning-fire. To stretch it beyond this concept into the realm of the later mysticism would be seeing beyond the legitimate image presented by the seer. If we stick to this image of the *sat* as the fire-principle, we get support. It is the fire that is Yama. In this connection we may refer to the concept of the solar fire that is himself called Yama (RV. I. 66.4 *yamo ha jāto yamo janitvam, jāraḥ kanīnām patir janīnām*) as the controller of all fertilizing fluids, whose abode (*yoni*) holds the "Bird" Vena (X.123.6 *yamasya yonau śakunam bhuraṇyum*), and which is indicative of the solar orb containing waters. Mātariśvan is already believed to be the aspect of the mid-region fire (III.5.9; —26.2; I; 96.4). We have also the identification between Agni and Mitra (III.5.9). Indra is associated with Agni more than any other god as he is the aspect of the mid-region fire (see *Vedic Index* under Indra; cf. also Nir. VII.5); and Varuṇa, along with Mitra, is identified with Agni (VII.12.3). Thus the *suparṇa* at our verse is the supreme principle; it gets manifest in the form of the sun-fire and the lightning fire; and is, as such, the "*apām garbha*" that brings rain (I.164.52). This is the place in the hymn (v.46) where the thought changes to the coming of rain; for in the next verse (which is taken to be original by Brown) we have a clear image of rain sprinkling the earth with the heavenly nourishing fluid (v.47); and so says also the tradition. (Āśv. Ś.S 2.13 uses it for the ritual for rains, *varṣa-kāmeṣṭi*). About this verse there is no doubt in the mind of Brown, as he takes it to support the image of rain. The whole thought of the seer, then, is the gain of rain; and all the images in the hymn converge on this point. As we have the "*divya suparṇa*" here, in the very next verse we have the "*suparṇāḥ*" (solar-rays) flying to the abode of the sun (called here the *sadana* of *ṛta*) in the yearly flight, and returning with the divine *ghṛta* (ghee), which is the rain-water (cf. *ghṛtena pṛthivī vy' udyate*).

Symbolism of Bull-cooking

We have seen that the main motif of the hymn is closely interwoven with the concept of the One that is the Fire-bird bringing rain, as he is the very controller of the cosmic waters. We have also noted how Dīrghatamas follows here the traditional beliefs as reflected elsewhere in RV. We now turn to another important concept he uses. It is the concept of the cooking of the bull. Here the seer turns auto-vertic, using the *ādhyātmikī* type of verse.[8] The picture he presents is that of the cosmic sacrifice. He declares that he sees the dung-smoke; and the smoke is far beyond the "lower moving one"; there the "heroes cooked the variegated bull; (for) they were the rites of yore" (v.43 cf. esp. *ukṣāṇam pṛśnim apacanta vīrās tāni dharmāṇi prathamāny' āsan*). The words "*tāni dharmāṇi prathamāny 'āsan*" occur also in a later verse in our hymn (v.50, in the portion supposed to be a later appendage), and also form part of the famous *Puruṣa-sūkta* (X.90.16) which it concludes. This suggests the cosmic sacrifice on the upper plane, the smoke of which only the inspired seer can see. The "lower one" indicates the cloud, and the one beyond is the realm of the upper invisible fire. In this upper fire the bull is being cooked. Before we see which this bull is, let us note how the seer uses a familiar motif. The cooking of the cosmic bull is a motif that obtains in RV at another place. Thus, we have the belief that the *suparṇa*-birds attack the dark-bull (cloud), as the clouds roar out their groans; then do Mitra, Varuṇa and the Parijman (Vāyu) squeeze and open up the hide of the bull at the abode of the "upper one" (I.79.2;3). Elsewhere we have the concept of the all-sustaining bull that sustains Heaven and Earth; beyond him there is none; and he makes his hide the sieve through which the nourishing fluid comes (X.31.8). This bull is compared with the sun (*ibid.*). The cooking of the bull far beyond the normal human perception, and in the realm of the cosmic, indicates the conceptual cooking of the sun-bull. It is to be remembered that the bull is said to be "*pṛśni*". This *pṛśni* bull has been understood by scholars as Soma.[9] Now, though Soma is often called *ukṣan*, nowhere in RV. do we have a tangible support to the cooking of Soma. Actually the root √*pac*, and its nominal formations, do not occur in the context of Soma. The word *ukṣan* also is not the exclusive epithet of Soma. This shows the difficulty in understanding the *pṛśni-ukṣan* here as Soma.[10] In fact it does not indicate Soma. In this connection it has to be remembered that the cooking of the bull obtains as a ritual fact. He was cooked as the very "*apām garbha*" (foetus of waters); and there is indication that its sap was sprinkled on the herbs for their growth (cf. Mait. Sam. II.5.10; 61.12-; Kāṭhaka Sam. XIII.9 *apām garbha oṣadhīṣu ny-aktaḥ*; and Sāyaṇa "*hutaḥ san megheṣu apām sambandhī garbhaḥ punar oṣadhīṣu ny aktaḥ*"; cf. also AV. IV 4.5). That the bull was "*apām garbha*" (foetus of waters) brings him conceptually nearer to the sun, called by the same epithet in our hymn; and also indicates that he was sacrificially cooked as a sympathetic spell for rain, suggesting the rain drops in the oozing drops of his sap. The concept is the same as noted above in the hide that is caused to ooze on the cosmic plane. In the passage noted above, that speaks of the bull as "*apām garbha*", he is also said to be "*vṛṣabhaḥ payasvān*" (*ibid.* v.1; *sthaviraḥ payasvān* at v.3). In the later times the *Śūlagava* ritual is an example to this effect. This will make it quite clear, that bull-cooking on the plane of the terrestrial ritual (cf. RV I.145.5. III.21.5) was a sympathetic act indicative of the imaginative cooking of the sun-bull to cause it ooze out the nourishing fluids (or rain) he contains. On this background we have to examine the word *pṛśni*. The word occurs as the unique 'epithet' among the gods, of the sun and Agni only in its masculine form, see (IV.3.10 Agni; X.189.1; cf. Nir.II.14). The sun is said to be the *pṛśni* stone in the mid-region[11] and he is also *ukṣan*, the ocean and the shining *suparṇa* (V. 47.3). The sun, as the *pṛśni*-bull is the male counterpart of all the female-*pṛśni*-s (Earth, cow, *antarikṣa*-the mother of the Maruts). As the store of all nourishing fluids he is ritually, and symbolically cooked for rain. Along with ritual-gambling (for symbolic success) the cooking of the bull obtains also in the ritual of the *agnicayana* (cf. Baudh. Śr. Sū. X. 9 *dīvyantaḥ ṛṣabham pacante*). Though the "*asya vāmīya*" hymn does not refer to the playing of dice, it is referred to in another hymn, which has the same motif, and has necessarily to be referred to (though unfortunately Brown does not even mention it). It is the hymn of Vasukra.[12] There we do not have the bull, but the cooking is in respect of the ram. We place the expressions side by side:-

> *ukṣāṇam pṛśnim apacanta vīrāḥ*
> (I.164.43 at Dīrghatamas);
> and *pīvānam meṣam apacanta vīrāḥ*
> (X. 26.17, at Vasukra).

This shows that the thought of the two seers is parallel. As we shall see presently, the parallelism goes even further. But sticking to the motif of the cooking of the bull, we note that Vasukra says something more. He adds that the "thunderers" come from all sides, and that the half of the (ram) gets cooked, while the other does not (X.27.18). Though here we have the ram being cooked, at an earlier verse we have the cooking of the bull (*ibid.*, 2), along with the pressing of Soma. The latter indicates the ritual on the terrestrial plane, in imitation of the cosmic cooking; and we shall not be wrong in believing that the two words, *meṣa* and *vṛṣabha* present the same motif, *viz.* the sprinkling or the oozing animals. In the Vasukra-hymn the "thunderers" that arrive (X.27.18, noted above) are undoubtedly, the Maruts, as a result of the charm of the cooking. The animal being cooked is the sun in the upper region, while it is the cloud in the mid-region. Mixed with the thought of the cooking of the *meṣa* is that of the "bow in the waters" in the same verse (*dhanum bṛhatīm apsu antaḥ*); and then we have the "purifiers with the sieve" (*ibid.*, 17 *pavitravantā carataḥ punantā*), the motif we have already seen in the case of the "one who makes his hide the sieve." The thunderers in the first Vasukra-hymn (X.27) give place to the "gods with the axes that come to cut the tree" in the next hymn (X.28.8). At both the places, the indication is that of the cutting of the cloud-trees. In the first hymn of Vasukra, after the mention of the "bow in the waters" and the arrival of the thunderers, the thought of the seer gets concentrated on the gain of rain. He asserts in the autovertic statement that he has seen the "band with the sustenance moving without the wheel" (cloud?); and further on we have the clear reference to waters and rain (vv.19-23).[13] The "*asya vāmīya*" reflects a similar composition of images. We have noted above the similarity between the two hymns as regards "the heroes" (Dīrghatamas) and the "heroes" (Vasukra) that cook the animal. In place of the "gods with the axes" and the "thunderers" of Vasukra, we have the "three haired ones" (*trayaḥ keśinaḥ*) at Dīrghatamas (v.44), which are the Sun, Agni and Vāyu. And, even here, the thought gets ultimately connected with rain (I. 164.48–52).

Gharma, Cow and the Lightning

We have noted earlier the symbolism of the thundering Cow, and how it indicates the gain of rain. At another place in the hymn, and earlier than the thundering Cow, we have a very interesting motif of the Cow. This motif is presented in a sequence of verses as follows:-(i) The Cow is "su-dughā", and is milked by the dextrous milkman; here Savitṛ is praised; (ii) The Cow is said to be "*vasu-patnī*"; she desires the Calf, and arrives with a '*hiñ*' sound; she is desired to be milked for the Aśvins, and to get fattened; (iii) The Cow is said to low at the Calf, which is characterized by the word "*miṣantam*"; she longs for the milk-dripping mouth ends of the Calf; she lows and fattens with milk; (iv) The Cow is enclosed by some one who snorts; resting on the "*dhvasani*", she annihilates the "mortal" with her "*citti-s*"; she throws off the covering (vv.26-29).

According to the tradition these *mantra*-s were used at the *pravargya* ritual. With this *pravargya* ritual the concept of the "*gharma*" is closely associated. The word "*gharma*" actually occurs in the verses mentioned above (v.26 and v.28). In this rite milk is heated in an earthen jar. The jar is also called Mahāvīra, and in shape appears as if three jars are kept one upon the other.[14] Brown does not go into the details of the *pravargya*; but suggests that the milk in the jar (*gharma*) is symbolic of the Dawn-Cow. This Dawn-Cow sniffs at the sun, the calf. This Dawn-Cow also gives milk to the Aśviṇs. He also suggests that the rite operates by sympathetic magic to bring about the rise of the sun and of the Dawn (*op.cit.*, p.314). Brown nowhere strikes an identification between the sun and the *gharma*; on the contrary, he says that the jar is the udder of the mother-Cow (Dawn). The image he presents is not very clear. If the milk in the jar is symbolic of the (Dawn) Cow, (taking the part as symbolizing the whole),[15] one fails to understand how the jar is again the udder. For the jar to be the udder, the milk has to be taken as milk only, and not as the cow. If the boiling milk (Cow) that reaches the fringe of the jar is to be taken to indicate the Cow kissing the Calf, the top of the jar has to be taken as the Calf. In the symbolism of the Dawn-Sun (Cow-Calf), the jar (-top), being thus kissed, will be the sun. But, for Brown it is only the udder. The real difficulty for the milk-Dawn-Cow hypothesis comes when the Cow is said to become the lightning (cf. *vidyud bhavantī at* v.29d). The interpretation which bypasses this point cannot be accepted as helpful; and has to be discarded as unsound. If by the expression "*sā cittibhir ni hi cakāra martyam*" (v.29c) we were to understand "she, with her hissing (pious thought) has felled the mortal (enemy)" (Brown, along with the brackets), we expect the clarification as to who this "mortal (enemy)" is! To suggest that this "mortal enemy" is the lid of the jar (*prati vavrim auhata*) is totally unsatisfactory. That we have in the throwing of the *vavri* (cover) the echo of the Indra-Vṛtra-fight is acceptable; but the "mortal (enemy)" cannot be seen in the actual lid of the jar (*gharma*). It is, hence, necessary to accept that the ritual of the *gharma* (*pravargya*) is a sympathetic spell for the cosmic act. The boiling fluid (milk, or *payas*, "the nourishing fluid") is enclosed in a "jar" of closed mouth; this mouth has to be opened up, so that the fluid may ooze out. The boiling fluid presupposes also the presence of the fire. With the mention of the lightning, there should be no doubt that the seer has the cloud in mind in presenting this image. The rain is already the "boiling fluid" that is to be released by Indra (cf. VIII, 69. 14 *bhinat kanīna odanam pacyamānam paro girā*) and the cloud is the "*cāru*" (I.7.6); it is also the "stone-mouthed reservoir" (II.24.4 *aśmā-syam avatam...madhu-dhāram*), broken open by Brahmaṇaspati. Elsewhere we have the image of the "stone-covered honey resting like a fish in scanty water" (X. 68.8 *aśna-pinaddham madhu...matsyam na dīnā udani kṣiyantam*). We have also the "sprinkling spring" (II.24.4d *utsam udriṇam*). The concept of the *gharma*, and the *pravargya*, have the cosmic reservoir with the boiling fluid as the image. The three-fold shape of the *gharma* (*mahāvīra*), which we have noted earlier, is also a symbol. The idea gets conceptually connected with the three-fold *gharma* in the cosmos, of which the *pravargya* is the ritual-reproduction. RV refers to the three *gharma*-s (VII.33.7), where they are indicated to be also full of *retas* (the nourishing manly fluid, a symbol for rain); and we have also the three-fold *gharma* that pervades the three worlds, where, further on, we have the concept of One *suparṇa* in the ocean (X.114.1 *gharmā samantā trivṛtam vy' apatuḥ*; and v.4 *ekaḥ suparṇaḥ sa samudram ā viveśa*). The concept of the *gharma*, thus, is closely connected with that of the nourishing fluid, which is rain—rain that comes from the highest ocean, wherein the Real One, conceived as the Bird, takes his seat. The three *gharma*-s are the sun (heaven), Vāyu or the lightning fire (mid-region) and the terrestrial fire. The term *gharma* itself has the threefold implication:-(i) the fire (at the three regions); (ii) the pot to boil the fluid, the cosmic water or milk; and (iii) the fluid itself. The milk in the terrestrial *gharma* in the *pravargya* rite indicates the solar fluid on the one hand, and, on the other, the water in the cloud. Both these fluids are conceptually hot, as they are in contact with the solar fire and the cloud-fire respectively. As the seething boiled milk crosses the limit of the boiling pot in the ritual, the fluid from the sun and the cloud is expected to have an easy flow. The cloud-formation is an important aspect of the sun's power; hence the seer of the "*asya vāmīya*" mixes the image of the sun and that of the cloud, using the traditional symbol of the Cow. With the mention of the lightning, there remains no doubt whatsoever, that the seer has, here, the cloud-Cow in view. And it is not necessary to put aside the traditional interpretation[16] in favour of a new one that is less plausible. The solar orb is the cover (*vavri*) and the conceptual Cow (the female counterpart of the male "*pṛśni-gau*" i.e. the sun) is the fluid therein (or the solar waters, which we have already substantiated; see again I.23.17). On the mid-region plane the Cow is the nourishing rain-Cow or the inner sap of the cloud; the cover (*vavri*), or the external "form", is the enclosure of the cloud that falls off. On the terrestrial plane the Cow is the milk (but not the Dawn); and the cover (*vavri*) is the lid of the pot. Though Dawn is associated with the rite of the *pravargya* (cf. also *trayo gharmāsa uṣasam sacante* at RV VII.33.7) and she is said to have the sun-calf (I.113.2) the Cow in the present context suits her less. This is clear from the fact that the root *mā*, "to low" (here *amīmet*) is not common with the dawn, while with the cloud-cow it is common (cf. I 38.8 *vaśrā-iva vidyun mimāti*, where the concept of the calf is present—*vatsam na mātā siṣakti*—indicative of the lightning-fire). The heaven is said to thunder for weal, as the Maruts sing and the treasure of the skies is released (indicative of the advent of rain), where the mention of the dawns (Pl.) is probably indicative of the ritual-time only; for there is a clear mention of the rains at an earlier verse (V.59.8 *mimātu dyauḥ a-acucyuvur divyam kośam*; and earlier v.5 *sūryasya cakṣuḥ pra minanti vṛṣṭibhiḥ*). In the cloud-cow we have a double symbol—that of the lightning-cow and the lightning-fire. The first lows after the *vatsa*, which is the lightning-fire and is characterized by the epithet "*miṣantam*" indicating the "winking of the lightning-fire (who is often called *śiśu*; cf.II.35.13). It may also indicate the sun at the rise who looks on like a child at the *pravargya*, as the milk (in the *gharma* pot), standing for the cow, makes the boiling sound (*mimāti māyum*); and the expression "*payate payobhiḥ*" may indicate the dawn "milking" the sunlight or the dew; but the image does not end here: it has to be connected with the next verse, which clearly states the lightning.

It is, thus, clear that the Cow is not so much the Dawn-Cow, as the thunder-Cow, that stays in the cloud (*dhvasani*) and flashes in the form of the lightning and "milks" the rain. She is the same as the cow that fashions the waters and, at the same time, generates the multitudes of sounds (vv.41;42). The *pravargya* is the charm for the boiling fluid of the upper region to ooze out as rain. There is another indication of a ritual to propitiate the mid-region cow on the terrestrial plane in the form of an actual cow (v.40). The stanza cannot be said to have been "uttered by the officiants of the first sacrifice, who were possibly the Ādityas" (Brown, p. 216), nor was the cow Speech (Vāc). In the event of her being Vāc, it is difficult to understand the address to her, "partaking of dainty fodder, eat good grass all times and, drink pure water as you graze" (v.40). The ritual works on the principle of sympathetic magic. We have support to understand that the actual cow here stands as the symbol for the mid-region Cow that is invoked, just in the next verse, as we have noted above. Thus, at the famous Mudgala-hymn (X.102) it is indicated that the bull in the pasture was sympathetically given sweet drink at the ritual for urinating in the field, indicative of rain.[17]

The Immortal One

The symbolism of the *pravargya* ends in the mention of the cloud-cow, which itself is a complex image of the fire (lightning) in the waters. The thought is immediately connected with the ever active fiery life-principle that stays in the "*pastyā*". It is referred to in the next verse which, being important, has to be examined:-

> *anat-śaye tura-gātu jīvam*
> ejad dhruvam madhya ā pastyānām
> *jīvo mṛtasya carati svadhābhir*
> *amartyo martyenā sayoniḥ* (v.30)

The first half of the verse we shall take first:-

> (Breathing lies the swift-moving One, the animated that vibrates and is (yet) steady in the *pastyā-s*).

This half shows that the animating principle of the whole universe lies in the *pastyā*-s, and that it is the most important principle that is called "*jīva*". This brings to our mind the subtle comparison between this principle and the "*ekam sat*" we have seen earlier. The word "*pastyā*" (in the plural) has been rendered variously as, "home", "people" and also as "water". Agni is said to be "*tri-pastyā*" (RV. VIII. 39.8).[18] The word occurs also in the singular; but there it is not clear what exactly it means—whether "home" or "waters". The "*pastyā* of the Cow" (X. 96.11) probably indicates the waters, from what we have seen about the symbolism of the Cow. In the plural the word indicates "waters" at various places (*Vedic Index*; also I.25.10 Varuṇa stays in; IV. 1.11 Agni born in; X.46.6 Trita in). In that case the "one staying in the *pastyā*-s" comes near the *apām garbha* of our hymn, and may be compared with the Haṁsa that stays in the waters indicative of the cosmic life-principle that is manifest in the form of the sun (X.124.9 *bibhatsūnām sayujam haṁsam āhur apām divyānām sakhye carantam*). Even if the word be taken to mean "home", it could be the "home in the form of the waters". In other words, the One in the *pastyā*-s indicates the fiery principle in the cosmic waters, as their seed or their foetus. It fertilises them; and yet, by another well set symbolism, it is also their child (cf. *vṛṣa-śiśu*, a favourite symbolic name for Apām-napāt-Agni—RV.II.35.13, and the Sarasvant-fire principle at VII. 95.3). The epithets indicative of activity in respect of this principle make it also the Bird that stands at the confluence of the waters and the sun. It is active, moving and yet steady (*ejad dhruvam*), indicative of its everlasting pervading nature.[19] This is only a counterpart of the One Real Bird; and is it not the same principle as is suggested by the term "*akṣara*"? The "*akṣara*" that stirs at times and streams into the fluid of nourishment!

We now take the other half of the verse:— "*jīvo mṛtasya carati svadhābhiḥ*"; and "*amartyo martyenā sayoniḥ*". The possibility of the rendering is twofold:— (i) The life-essence of the dead sustains with the *svadhā* (*mṛtasya jīvaḥ...*); and (ii) The life-essence (in general) is active through the sustenance of the dead. The first is the rendering of Sāyaṇa, and it is followed generally. Brown thinks here that the verse suggests the death of the one sun and the rise of the new (next morning's) sun, "the (immortal) life of the dead one (the sun that died the previous evening) fares according to his constituent nature" (*op.cit.,* p.214; brackets are Brown's). This is workable as far as it goes; and the belief in the death of the sun is supported in the Vedic tradition (cf. for example Jai. Br.I.7;8). But as far as RV is considered, there is hardly any place in it to support the belief of the death of the sun. There is, however, a doubtful place where Uṣas is said to waken "some dead one", also impelling the alive (I.113.8 *vy ucchanti jīvam... mṛtam kañ cana bodhayantī*). But one wonders if this place could be taken to indicate a clear belief in the death of the sun (Sāyaṇa takes the word *mṛta* as indicative of the sleeping one, as if dead; and Brown does not note this place at all, nor does he give any other reference from RV to indicate the death of the sun!). Actually the words *mṛta* and *martya* do not occur in the context of the sun in RV. The word *martya*, as a general rule, occurs for the mortal sacrificers; and it is Vṛtra who often lies 'dead', in the context of the release of the waters. The Maruts are said to have shattered the "*martya*", itching for a battle, and caused him to fall (to the earth) with the streams like a debtor (I. 169.7 *ye martyam pṛtanāyantam ūmair ṛṇāvānam na patayanta sargaiḥ*). This "*martya*" who falls to the ground is, without doubt, the cloud that streams out his "debt" of waters that are stored in it (cf. Sāyaṇa).[20] We have noted above the symbolism of the "oozing hide" which suggests the release of rain (cf. I.79.2, *tvacam pṛñcanti uparasya yonau*: and X.31.8, *tvacam pavitram kṛṇuta*). Elsewhere we have the same expression in respect of the demon(!) Araru. Indra is said to cause the hide of the Bull to fatten and smash the "*martya*" Araru (I.129.3), which is the symbolic description of the pressing of the cloud and the gain of rain, as Sāyaṇa rightly suggests. The *martya* at these places indicates the cloud, as it is smashed and set to naught. If the *mṛta* or the *martya* is the one who gets destroyed and falls to the ground, the "*martya*" who is annihilated by the lightning—Cow with her flashes, at our hymn, is the cloud (cf. *sa cittibhir ni hi cakāra martyam vidyud bhavantī prati vavrim auhata*). The *martya* who is annihilated (v.29) and the *martya* who stays at the same abode as of the "*amartya*" are, obviously, the same. The *martya* itself is the cover (*vavri*) for the *amartya*.

The *amartya* is the same as the moving, agile yet everlasting steady principle (*anạt...tura-gātu jīvam ejad dhruvam*); and its cover, the cloud, is the *martya*; and they are "*sa-yoni*" as they stay together not only in the "*pastyā*-s", but also in combination. The inner fiery principle is the "*jīva*", the outer covering (cloud) is the *martya*; it becomes "*mṛta*"; and by the "*svadhā*" sustains the former, i.e., the lightning fire (*vaidyuta agni*). How? The nourishing waters fall to the earth; they generate the crops; thence we have the material for the sacrificial offerings; those offerings cause the formation of the clouds, wherein the *vaidyuta* fire dwells, and also sustains the solar energy.[21] It is this way that the process gets connected with sacrifice; and that is why the seer ushers in the "*brahmodya*", i.e. dialogue about the nature of the sun and the universe, immediately after, intervened by the reference to the sun. The importance of the sun is because of his position in the cosmic order, and also as the one who forms the clouds. When the fire in the cloud is not seen, as the *martya vavri* (mortal cloud-cover) has fallen to the ground, it merges with the sun (for they are brothers). The expression "*jīvo mṛtasya carati svadhābhiḥ*" gets explained this way. It can also be explained the other way:-the "*jīva*" of the "*mṛta*" (who is not the sun, but the vanishing *vavri*, "cover") is sustained by the intrinsic sustenance. Being always endowed with this "*svadhā*", the life-principle (*jīvaḥ*) moves on, pervades the cosmos, sometimes with the *vavri*, but even without it (later v.38, which corresponds to the v.30). Thus, the principle underlying the scheme of the seer is that the cosmic fire-principle is the life-essence, while the *vavri* is the one that disappears. This is true in the case of the cloud, as also in that of the sun. The cover in the case of the sun is the orb—the Double—that holds the solar fire-principle and the solar waters. The cover (solar-orb; cloud) and the *jīva*-principle are often together and move together everywhere. Of these, one is seen (the *vavri*, "cover; orb"), the other is not seen (*jīva*; v.38 *tā śaśvantā viṣūcinā viyantā, ny anyam cikyur na ni cikyur anyam*). This is a cosmic fact;

and is true also of all moving bodies. This also shows that the moving sun and the cloud were on par, for the Vedic seer, with the earthly animated beings. Having presented this parallelism, the seer refers to the thundering Cow and the *akṣara* in the very next verse, the implication of which we have already seen. The One not seen (by the people) is, obviously, the same as the *jīva*-principle (cf. v.30); and it is the same as the *akṣara*, lying steady, yet full of the potentiality for activity; it is not Vāc; it is beyond it. It is stirred by Vāc, the first manifestation of which is in the form of the Thunder. And as it is moving, it is suggested by the seer in the word *suparṇa* which is a solar image together with the concept of the speech in her aspect of the metres.[22]

Cosmic Drama and the Seer's Vision

The hymn starts with the concept of the three fires closely related to one another, indicating the three to be three aspects of the Supreme principle of animation, conceived as the Fire-light principle. This principle is visualized in the form of the sun—the visual Double—in the heavenly region; but actually the solar orb is its residing place, being termed the "*ajasya rūpam*" ("The form of the unborn") (v.6). This principle is also symbolized as the Bird that stays in the solar orb; here the seer presents the complex image of the Cows (rays) that wear the covering (*vavrim vasānāḥ*) and drink water with their "feet" (v.7). This *vavri*, as we have noted, is the solar orb (and corresponds to the cloud-*vavri* of the lightning fire in the mid-region). In this image of the *vavri* itself the seer subtly suggests the *gharma* that he presents further on in the hymn. In both, the idea of the fire-fluid being the inner essence and the *vavri* being the container is the same. Then the seer presents the sex-image in the great Parents uniting: The Father (Heaven) planting the seed in the Mother (earth), that is characterized as "*garbha-rasā nividdhā*" (v.8). This is done in the context of the sacrifice with the help of the *mantra*-s, (*ibid.*, *namasvanta id upa-vākam īyuḥ*). This sacrifice is the cosmic one, and suggests the same on the terrestrial level. This sex-motif is further referred to in our hymn, where the Father is said to have planted his seed in his Daughter (v.33), and this motif obtains elsewhere in RV. Thus, at the Nābhānediṣṭha-hymn (X.61), we have the Father rushing towards his Daughter to release his semen; there the Daughter is the earth (X. 61.7); and at this act the gods are said to have created the *brahma* (*ibid*). The seer of the "*asya vāmīya*" further refers to the cosmic *garbha*, and the One principle that stays aloft, where the divine *mantra*-s are recited on the heaven's plane. The thought then glides into the image of the year (*sam-vatsara*). The *saṁvatsara-cakra* has the Great Father (deity of the year or Time) full of nourishing fluids (cf. *purīṣiṇam*). Then we have the image of the two birds on the same tree, the most famous one, and taken further by the Upaniṣads as the *jīvātman* and the *paramātman*.[23] But if we stick to the fire image, the two birds seem to be the two forms of the fire. The bird that is said to be eating is the mid-region lightning-fire (cf. v.1, *madhyamo asty aśnaḥ*), with the pun on the word *aśna* ('*aś* "to eat", and "to pervade"); while the non-eating one that simply gazes corresponds to the *Suparṇa*, the One Real, showing himself in the form of the sun. The sun's cows (rays) drink the juices, but the 'Bird' is always differentiated from them, as we have noted earlier. The mid-region fire eats (subsists on) the waters of the cloud—his mothers. The tree is the cosmic tree of light, which compares with the *stūpa* of Varuṇa (RV I.24.7). This *stūpa* of Varuṇa is said to have been erected in the ether (*abudhne*), with its light-shoots spreading downwards, ultimately reaching and staying in the human heart (*ibid*., *asme antar nihitāḥ ketavaḥ syuḥ*). The image of the tree is carried further; and now we have honey-eating birds resting on it (the sun-rays conceived as eating the essence of all juices stored in the solar orb). The vision of the tree where there is honey and the "Birds" (vv.20-22) is the culmination of the solar concept in the hymn. This indicates the solar orb to be the honeycomb, and without doubt, gave rise to the *Madhuvidyā* of the Upaniṣads.[24] The highest principle that has its seat in this tree is called the "*bhuvanasya gopāḥ*" "protector of creation") (v.21), and also "*pitṛ*" ("father") (v.22). And this principle is said to be present in all the forms of Speech; for the seer says that what is "*gāyatra*" in the *Gāyatrī* (metre), the "*traiṣṭubha*" in the *Triṣṭubh* (metre), i.e the essence of all the various metres is "THAT". One who knows thus attains *amṛta* (v.23). This principle is, thus, above all the metres; of it Vāc is only one aspect. It is the same as the Akṣara, the bright-fluid principle.

Communion with the Highest

We have seen above how the seer of this hymn presents certain images similar to that of the Vasukra-hymn, and also that of the Nābhānediṣṭha. The cooking of the bull is the motif that is common to the hymn of Vasukra and that of Dīrghatamas; and we have already noted the same. Likewise the symbolism of the sun and his rays is similar (I.164.13 and X.27.13; 14). So is the case with the "thunderers" and the "gods with the axe" at Vasukra and the "hairy ones" at the "*Asya vāmīya*". But beyond this there is something more important which underlines the thought of the seers of such hymns. And it is the concept of the communion with the Ultimate One Real. The idea appears to be that, unless this communion is established, the seer, or the priest who later used the hymn on the terrestrial plane, cannot work the wonder he is up to. This is clear from such references as we may call autovertic (*ādhyātmikyaḥ* in the words of Yāska, Nir. VII.1). The seer speaks about himself as if he were himself the deity (indicating that it is the deity itself speaking), or suggesting strongly that there is a close association between himself and the god. Thus, Dīrghatamas declares the Protector of the whole universe to have entered his own personality (v.21 *ino viśvasya bhuvanasya gopāḥ sa mā dhīraḥ pākam atrā viveśa*). Elsewhere he says, that the *gopāḥ* has been actually vizualised by him (v.31 *apaśyam gopām anipadyamānam*). Likewise, Vasukra presents the solar symbolism, himself being a personal witness to the march of the sun (X. 27.8 *gāvo yavam prayutā aryo akṣan, tā apaśyam sahagopāś carantīḥ)* where the rays, or clouds, are visualized as 'Cows', the sun being their leader protector; and further on he says that he "saw" the "multitude with the nourishment" (v.19), meaning rain-clouds. Likewise the seer at the Nābhānediṣṭha declares solemnly the close association between himself and the Ultimate, when he says, that it is his navel, and that he himself is All (X. 61.19). This association with the Ultimate cause of the universe puts the seer on a different, and decidedly on a much higher, level than of the ordinary men. It is from this state of elevation that he assumes to know the working of the universe, with the result that he can work to follow his own plan with the assured divine help. The superhuman faculty is attained by the seer, or the later priest, at the sacrificial level. Dīrghatamas says that the *pitṛ*, the Lord of the universe, has entered him (v.21); and later, with this superhuman vision, he sees the cosmic *gharma* and the thundering and milking Cow. He declares that the Earth is his Mother, and Heaven his father (v.33 *dyaur me pitā janitā nābhir atra* etc). He says that the sacrificial altar is the very end of the earth, and the sacrifice the very navel of the universe; the nourishing offering (Soma) is the very essence of the sun (v.35). Thus he controls the cosmos through the ritual at the terrestro-divine level, the divine speech helping him through the *mantra*-s. The "first-born of Ṛta" has, indeed, entered him; and has given him the aspects of Speech (v.37); thus is Speech different from the "first-born of Ṛta". With this aspect of Speech (*mantra*-s) he activates the *akṣara*; the Cow thunders and the *akṣara* oozes, as the oceans stream forth (39-40), bringing down the heavenly fluid, that is rain. For this, the cosmic ritual is contemplated wherein the Bull (sun; and in another aspect, the cloud-bull) is roasted (v.43), which is, without doubt, performed also on the terrestro-divine plane of the sacrifice. The "Birds" enveloped by waters (*apo vasānāḥ*) dash to the heavenly plane; and from that plane they now return; they sprinkle the earth with *ghṛta*, which is only another name for rain (v.47). The heavenly plane, where these birds (hymns) go, is called the seat of Ṛta. It is here, as at many other places in RV, that Ṛta gets associated with water; and, it is because of this belief, that the tradition understands also "water" by the term Ṛta (Nir. II. 25). The other meaning of the word *ṛta* in the Vedic tradition, is "sacrifice". This clearly indicates that the concept of the sacrifice was associated, as an important aspect of it, with the gain of rain. At least, the present hymn, and the two others noted (X. 61; and X. 27) have the formation of rains as the motif[25] expressed in symbolic language, with mystic images.

The concept of being the near-kin of the supreme in the case of the seer has been indicated and explained above. In line with it is the expression "*prathamajā ṛtasya*", which Dīrghatamas says has come to him (or entered him I. 164.37). The expression obtains at two more places, one of which being the hymn of Nābhānediṣṭha. Here (I.164.37) the "*ṛtasya prathamajāḥ*" (The first-born of Ṛta, the universal order), is said to have arrived at the sacrifice to be associated with the seer, while at the Nābhānediṣṭha-hymn the seer himself is the "*prathama-jā ṛtasya*", for whom the Cow milks (X.61.19). He is also said to be the "*dvi-jaḥ*", indicating second birth at the sacrificial plane. At the only other place where the expression occurs it indicates the fire (X.5.7). This would mean that the seer, who is described by this expression, is only the aspect of the cosmic fire. The concept of the fire being the "*prathamajāḥ ṛtasya*" is important. We shall do well to examine it. The Fire, which is said to be the "*prathamajāḥ ṛtasya*" (in the verse which also concludes the hymn) is said to be also the "One Ocean" that holds all nourishments (*ibid.*, 1 *ekaḥ samudro dharuṇo rayīṇām*). He holds the "udder" that lies at the bottom of the down-sliding ocean; this Agni is also said to be the "Bird", whose one foot lies in the spring of water (*ibid.*, *sisakty 'ūdhar niṇyor upasthe, utsasya madhye nihitam padam veḥ*). Now, we are quite familiar with this image of the Bird that lies at the confluence of the waters and the sun, and in our hymn, it compares with the Bird—the supreme principle that lies at the solar orb that confluences with (=holds) the waters. In the last verse of the "*asya vāmīya*", this principle is referred to as "*apām garbha*", and also as "*vāyasa bṛhat*", in addition to being the "*divya suparṇa*" that pacifies with rains (*vṛṣṭibhis tarpayantam*). Thus, when the seer says that the "*prathamajā ṛtasya*" has come to him, he, obviously, indicates that the "Fiery Spirit of the Cosmic Waters" has entered him. And, hence, he is sure of the divine fluid! This 'Fiery spirit in Cosmic waters' is known, later, as Nārāyaṇa (*nārā* = waters + *ayana*= movement). Its another image is: Viṣṇu in the cosmic ocean.

Androgynous Deity

We have noted above the concept of Agni, who is said to be the "*ṛtasya prathamajāḥ*", and who controls the waters of the upper ocean. Another important point to be noted is that the deity, described as the "*ṛtasya prathamajāḥ*", is suggested to be androgynous; for it is said to be both the Bull and the Cow (X.5.7d vṛ*ṣabhaś ca dhenuḥ*). This image of the bisexual Agni occurs at one more place (III. 38.7 *vṛṣabhasya dhenoḥ*), where it may be argued to refer to Indra, following the introductory remarks of Sāyaṇa. But in the hymn proper there is no reference to Indra, except for the typical last verse (*śunam huvema maghavānam indram*...). Under such a circumstance, and on the analogy of the expression "*vṛṣabhasya dhenoḥ*", which exactly compares with the one from the Agni-hymn (X.5) we have noted above, it is perfectly safe (and also proper) to take the deity of this hymn also as Agni—or, at the most as Indra seen as Agni. It is interesting to note how the other motifs of the hymn we have been discussing appear here. In the verse previous to the one that refers to the Bull-Cow, we have the (now) familiar autovertic reference to the seer's vision. He says, "Reaching mentally, I have seen here the Gandharvas, with their hair of the wind, engrossed in (their) sacrifice" (III.38.6 *apaśyam atra manasā jaganvān vrate gandharvān api vāyu-keśān*). They do not seem to be the guards of Soma (as Sāyaṇa thinks); but they remind one of the "three haired ones" (*trayaḥ keśinaḥ*) from the "*asya vāmīya*" (v.44). After this comes the reference to the Bull-Cow with whose name the sacrificers are said to have obtained the nourishment of the Cow (III.38.7 *ā nāmabhir mamire sakmyam goḥ*). The Bull-Cow image here and at the other place (X.5.7) is, obviously, the same. It is the potent seeding principle. The seed is generated because the deity is bisexual; and, if the mention of the Gandharvas with "wind-hair" is taken into account, the plane is, without doubt, the mid-region. It is with this mid-region sacrifice that the seed of the deity generates the Cow's nourishment (the nourishing fluid), by an auto-sex-act. The Cow-part of this deity is the waters, and the Bull-part is the Fire. The idea is the same as that of Apām-napāt (fire) and his females (waters), or that of the Sarasvant (spirit of the Sarasvatī, identified with the deity Apām-napāt) and his females (the waters of the Sarasvatī). We shall presently prove this point. Now, this motif of the bisexual deity is to be seen in the "*asya vāmīya*" also. This is where the seer says that "he snorts, who has covered the Cow" (v.29). Yāska is perfectly admissible when he says that here we have the bisexual deity (Nir. II.8 *tasmai devatā-ubhayaliṅgā prādurbabhūva*); and the purpose of the bisexual symbolism is, probably, to suggest self-copulation[26] resulting in the divine fluid (rain). This also explains another image in the hymn; it is the image of the river Sarasvatī. The seer mentions the "*stana*" of this river deity. The verse which refers to it (I.164.49) is not from the portion that has been doubted to be added later. Sāyaṇa takes here the "*stana*" (udder) of the Sarasvatī to indicate the various words (*laukika-vaidika-śabdarūpaḥ stanaḥ*); and Brown simply follows him. But, in view of the fact that in the last verse we have the sun being called *Sarasvant* and *apām garbha*, the possibility of the Sarasvatī being the goddess of speech in this context is remote. She appears here as the river conceived as the Cow whose "*stana*" gives the nourishing water. Even if it is conceded that the last verse, that refers to the *Sarasvant-apām-garbha*, is a later addition, it cannot be said to have been added without taking into account the general theme of the hymn, which concentrates on the sun and the gain of water, with the mixture of the idea of the fire and the cosmic waters. Moreover, we have the reference elsewhere, to the "*stana*" of Sarasvant (not Sarasvatī), which gives the idea of the bisexual deity (RV.VII. 96.6). The deity Sarasvant is, obviously, the male spirit of the Sarasvatī,[27] and is praised in the hymn to the Sarasvatī. This "*stana*" of Sarasvant nourishes the people. This clearly shows that the seer of our hymn works on a familiar image, according to which the Sarasvatī is conceived as the Cow that nourishes the people; and this is in her aspect of the river, and not in that of Vāc.

The "*asya vāmīya*", thus presents the picture of the cosmic Fire-principle that seeds the female waters. It is this principle that is shown in various aspects—the *suparṇa*, the *akṣara*—and it is the *ekam sat*. Its main visible forms are the sun and the mid-region fire. Both are the males that seed the waters, their union being aided by the cosmic sacrifice, where the thunder utters the *mantra*-s, and the "Cow" milks rain. For the gain of this milk the terrestrial sacrifice represents the Cosmic one.

Roar

We may note another point here. The cosmic activity of the release of the cows (waters and the rays of light), that marks the exploits of Indra, results in the freedom of other divinities such as the sun, the Dawn, Agni, Soma and others. Another marked characteristic of this Great Release, as it may be termed, is that the divinities "roar". Thus we have Agni roaring as soon as he is born in the *parama vyoman* (highest heaven). His roar is connected with the act of creation.[28] He is also said to resound the highest peak on the earth with powerful sweeps (RV.VII. 7.2a ā *sānu úṣmair nadayan pṛthivyāḥ*). He is said to arrive at the *vedi* with a roar from the heavens (I.128.3). As the child of Heaven and Earth, he roars as he is born from his mothers (X.1.2). The roar here cannot be said to refer to the crackling sound of the fire in the sacrificial altar; for, as we have noted, the roar is associated with him as he arrives from heaven. Again, such a roar is associated even with other deities who have no background of sacrificial "kindling". Thus the sun is said to make a loud noise as he traverses the high heavens (*kanikradat patayad ūrdhva-sānuḥ*, I. 152.5b). Earlier (*ibid.*, v.3) he is said to be the foetus of Mitrā-Varuṇā, thus getting his roar associated with his birth. As Brahmaṇaspati roars he is also associated with the activity of creation and the cracking of Vala.[29] Here the creation is the release of the waters (IV.50.5). Actually the roar of Brahmaṇaspati is the symbolic expression of his overlordship of the various *mantra*-s. At another place he is said to roar, being the Bull, his unique epithets being "*prā-gharma-sad*" and "*dvi-barha-jmā*", which show him to be having his abode in the mid-region, the *antarikṣa*. Even the sun-horse, that comes out of the primeval waters, is said to roar (I.163.1, *yad akrandaḥ prathamam jāyamānaḥ udyansamudrāduta vā purīṣāt*), connecting the roar with his birth or, in other words, with creation. The triple bound bull (symbolizing the sacrifice, or the sun) is also said to roar (IV.58.3). There is no question about Parjanya who is said to be roaring (V. 83.1; VII. 104.1) indicative of rainy advance. Soma comes roaring from his high abode as he glides along the path of *ṛta* (IX.97.32; 63.20). Though in some places it may be said that the roar of Soma indicates the resounding of the earth-drums at the pressing ritual, he stands as the impeller of Speech, which gives his roar the status of the arche Speech. It is to be remembered that it is Soma (with the only exception of Viśvakarman at X.81.7) that is called Vācaspati, bringing him on par with Brahmaṇaspati (he is actually addressed as Brahmaṇaspati at IX.83.1). In the case of Rudra his very name suggests that he is the Roarer. The roar of Indra is quite well marked (II.11.8f).

The references we have noted indicate that the roar is significant. It gets associated with the very activity of creation; and, as such, has to be treated as the expression of the primeval Speech. In the case of the sun, believed to be the horse coming out of the primeval waters, it is difficult to understand the roar as anything else than the primeval *speech associated with activity.* On closely following the concept, it appears that the roar is as necessary as activity itself. The most prominent concept of the combination of the roar with activity is to be found in Brahmaṇaspati, who appears to have smashed Vala by his mere roar (IV. 50.5 *valam ruroja phaligam raveṇa*). For this great feat his helpmates are the divine singers, the Aṅgirases (*ibid*). He is said to have dispelled the darkness by his roar (*ibid.*, v.4, *raveṇa vi saptaraśmir adhamat tamāṁsi*). Here the roar is magnified sevenfold, he being said to be *saptāsyaḥ* (seven-mouthed) in view of his having the seven Aṅgirases as helpmates; and elsewhere he is said to be "*sapta-gu*" (having sevenfold speech, X. 47.6) an epithet unique to him. The activity of smashing Vala (the enclosure of the divine water-cows or the light-cows), who is said to be "*phaliga*" is associated with Indra elsewhere, when he is said to accomplish it with his *rava* (I.62.4) and the Aṅgirases break the 'mountain' with *rava* (I. 71.2), which can be nothing else than a peculiar word-charm. The *rava*, thus comes to indicate the mental support to the physical activity; and this is borne by the fact that it is transferred from Brahmaṇaspati or the Aṅgirases to Indra; for he is said to have cut Vala with his *rava* as with the hand (X.67.6, *indro valam rakṣitāram dughānām kareṇeva vi cakartā raveṇa*). It is, thus, clear that the *rava* or roar, indicated by the word *kanikradat* (also *krandat* etc.) at other places, signified the mystic aspect of Speech which, with whom the word *kanikradat* is associated, is said to be or was believed to work out the result that was desired. The *rava* of Brahmaṇaspati was some mystic or magic power (Geldner, on RV. IV.50.5, Zaubergesang). We have also the word *ravatha* indicative of the power of the *mantra* (I.100.13; IX.80.1).

In the concept of the *rava* that we have been examining also falls the *rava* that has been associated with the exploit of Saramā, the bitch of the gods. It is said that she was the first to know the *rava* (III. 31.6, *agram nayat supady' akṣarāṇām acchā ravam prathamā jānatī gāt*). The idea is that Saramā knew the mystic aspect of Speech, which caused the release of the "cows". This is exactly the case with the Aṅgirases or Brahmaṇaspati, who effect the release of the "cows" with their *rava*. The force of the *rava* is seen to be present also in the combination of the metres in the sacrifice (VII. 33.4c), where the concept takes a new turn. In this new aspect the *rava* is necessary to create new strength in gods (cf. *ibid.*, *yac chakvarīṣu bṛhatā raveṇa-indre śuṣmam adadhātā vasiṣṭhāḥ*). At various places in the Ṛgveda one meets the idea that the gods require praise by the humans to acquire additional valour.[30] The belief is seen even today, and is well rooted in the tradition as indicated by the *saṅkīrtana* and other methods such as *ārātrikam* (*āratī* in Marathi or Hindi; but in the original concept, *mantra-jāgara*, song and praise throughout the night, *rātrī*).

What has been said above will prove that any study of *Vāk* (Speech) remains short of its mark if the concept of roar that is so well marked in RV remains out of its scope. The roar of the divinities and the presence of the speech in its various forms at the sacrifice, fall in the same line. As a matter of fact, the roar is the arch type of all speech-activity in the world, may it be in the ritual setting or in the secular sphere. In other words, it indicates the *universal symphony*. It is this belief that makes it necessary for a ritual to be accompanied by the speech-aspect called the *mantra*; and the meaningfulness of the *mantra*-s is borne out by this belief.[31] In the secular rites even, the aspect of speech is present in the form of the various ritual-songs. Where the song is not seen, it is often substituted by the notes from the musical instrument.[32]

NOTES

1. Kunhan Raja, *Asya Vāmīya Hymn. (The Riddle of the Universal), Ṛgveda* I.164, Madras, 1956; V.S. Agrawala, *The Thousand Syllabled Speech*, Vol.I, *Vision in Long Darkness*, Varanasi, 1963.
2. "Agni, Sun, Sacrifice and Vāc", *JAOS*, Vol.88, pp. 199-218.
3. *Ibid.*, p.200.
4. AV. IX. 14; 15 (Ed. Vishveshvarananda Instt. Hoshiarpur; acc. to Brown "AV. 9.9 and 10"). According to Satavlekar ed. AV. IX. 9; 10.
5. The hymn is the subject of the account, that for twelve years there was no rain in the kingdom of Śantanu; and Devāpi, the elder brother, became the priest at the sacrifice performed by Śantanu. He caused it to rain. See Nir. II.12. The story obtains in the later literature also. See A.A. Macdonell and A.B. Keith, *Vedic Index of Names and Subjects*, London, 1912, under Śantanu.
6. Brown, p.216; on *Akṣara* see Van. Buitenen, "*Akṣara*", *JAOS*, Vol. 79, pp.176-87. Buitenen renders the expression "*salilāni takṣatī*" as "building lakes" which is not quite happy; however, the difference between Brown and Buitenen is to be marked. Brown thinks the waters to be chaotic, while for Buitenen they are terrestrial.
7. RV X.61.11; 17; Dange, *Vedic Concept of 'Field' and the Divine Fructification*, University of Bombay Pbn., 1971, pp. 123-53.
8. For autovertism in the Veda see Mrs. Dange, Sindhu S., "Autovertism from the Ṛgveda", VIJ, Hoshiarpur, Vol. XIV, pt.i. (March 1976).
9. Sāyaṇa, Ludwig and also Brown
10. Only at RV IX 83.3 we have *pṛśni* in association with Soma; but Sāyaṇa rightly takes it as for Āditya, quoting Yāska.
11. In a ritual in the Brāhmaṇas a variegated stone was to be placed in between the Gārhapatya and the Āhavanīya fire-altars; it was *pṛśni* and indicated the sun.
12. "The Vision of Vasukra", Ch.4, *infra*.
13. *Ibid.*
14. See *Pravargya* monograph by J.A.B. Van Buitenen, Deccan

College, Poona 1968; also its criticism by C.G. Kashikar, "Apropos the Pravargya", *CASS* No. (1973), Poona University. According to Kashikar, the jar had originally five ascents, and later they came to be three.

15. This could be also supported from Yāska, Nir. II.I, "*kṛtsnavat-nigamāḥ*".
16. Yāska, Nir. II.9 and Sāyaṇa on the verse. Cf. Geldner, *Der Rigveda* I, note to the verse in question, "Danit 'er' der Stier Parjanya und die Kuh die Regenwolke".
17. Dange, *Vedic concept...* ("The Bull of Mudgala"), pp.108-22.
18. With Agni *tripastya* we may compare the concept in "*Try'ambaka*" *infra.*
19. Probably here we have the origin of the later account of the child Mukunda resting on the leaf of the banyan tree in the comic ocean, the motif being that of the life-essence of the cosmos in the primeval waters. It is also the germ of the later concept of Nārāyaṇa; *nārāḥ* = waters.
20. With the idea of the debt here may be compared the idea of the heroes with the "measure of grain" at the Vaukra-hymn (*sthivi-mantaḥ* X.27.15).
21. *svadhā* is the innate power; but in place it indicates the nourishing fluid; cf.I 33.11 *anu svadhām akṣarann āpo asya*; X 157.5 *svadhām iṣirām pary apaṣyan*; also I.144.2, *svadhā adhayat*, spoken of Agni etc.
22. In the later phase we have Gāyatrī, along with the metres called *Suparṇāḥ* or *sauparṇeyāḥ*, or even *sauparṇāni*, in the famous account of the bringing of Soma; see Kāṭhaka Sam. 23.10; Mait. Sam.3.7.8; etc. See Dange, *Legends in the Mahābhārata*, pp. 67-90.
23. Muṇḍaka Up. 3.1.2.
24. Cf. Chāndogya Up. 3.1.12; Bṛhadāraṇyaka Up. 2.5.
25. Dange, *Vedic Concept...*"Virgin and the Divine Seed-layer"; also "The Vision of Vasukra" *infra.*
26. For this motif cf. also Prajāpati in the primeval waters impelling creation by himself; cf. the principle of Atum in ancient Egyptian belief, Rundle Clark, *Myth and Symbol in Ancient Egypt*, p.41f.
27. Hapi was the god of the Nile; he was androgynous; see D. Mackenzie, *Egyptian Myth and Legend*, p.27.
28. RV. VII. 5.7, *sa jāyamānaḥ parame vyoman* and *tvam bhuvanā janayann abhikran.*
29. *Ibid.* IV.50.5 *valam ruroja phaligam raveṇa.* The word

phaliga has been understood variously by scholars. See *Vedic Index* under the word. Suryakanta in *Belwalkar Com. Vol.* (1957) p.44, takes it to be from *pari-ga*. More probably it appears to be a case of metathesis for *pari-gha* > *phari-ga* > *phali-ga*. The word *parigha* does not occur in the Vedic lit., but later it does occur and conveys the meaning of a weapon round in shape. In this context it indicates the enclosure, like *pari-dhi*, of the heavenly rain-cows. Vṛtra is said to be the *pari-dhi* of the rivers (III.33.6; cf. IV.18.6).

30. I.31.18; II.11.2; VII.19.11 etc.
31. Cf. Nirukta, I.16, *etad vai yajñasya samṛddham* etc.
32. See "The Vāṇa", *infra*. A detailed study of various aspects of Speech is made by Mrs. S.S. Dange, *Aspects of Speech in Vedic Ritual*, Aryan Books International, New Delhi, 1996.

Chapter 3

COSMIC FOETUS

We have had a fair idea of the images presented by the seer Dīrghatamas. Alongside them, we may note, that, for the Vedic ritual-philosopher-seers the cosmic activity of the formation and release of rain was the formation of a 'foetus' and its release at the proper time. This belief is seen also in later times. The belief centres round the conviction, that the liquid from the skies is not mere water; it is organic fluid. Like the *retas* (semen), the *garbha-rasa* had already become symbolic for rain. Rain was, hence, the liquid from the 'foetus', that gets formed in the mid-region. Being the organic fluid, it was procreative helping germination in the earth.

The word *garbha* (meaning foetus) occurs several times in RV. Apart from the flat meaning of the word as animal-foetus, or, to be precise, 'human foetus' which Tvaṣṭṛ, as Dhātṛ, is invoked to protect (X.184.1; cf.183.3), it came to be used symbolically. Thus Agni is said to be the foetus of the plants at various places (I.70.2; II.1.14; —10.3 etc.). He is also said to be the *garbha* of the churning stick (VI.15.1), which are said to be his mothers at several places. This is clear as the fire is born from the 'sticks' as they are churned, and the medicinal plants hold the fiery life-principle. The etymology of the word *oṣadhi* will bring this out (*oṣa* +√ *dhā* + *ki; oṣa* <√ *uṣ* 'to shine' or 'to make warm'; cf. Uṣas). Agni is also the *garbha* of *Ṛta* (I.65.2; I.156.3 etc.), which could be taken to indicate the position of Agni as the very centre of Sacrifice, which is the earthly aspect of *Ṛta*. Again, if *Ṛta* be taken to mean "water" as

Sāyaṇa does, following the tradition, at a number of places, (cf. Nirukta, II.25), Agni as the *garbha* of *Ṛta* is the same as *apām garbha*, which is his unique epithet, with the only exception of Soma at IX.97.41. Agni as the *ṛtasya garbha*, in this sense, corresponds to Apām-napāt. Apart from Agni, the Aśvins are associated with the word *garbha* as the generators of *foetus* in the creatures (I.157.5). Vāyu is said to be the *garbha* of the universe (X.168.4). The Ādityas are said to be the *garbha* of Mitra and Varuṇa (I.152.3), and Soma is said to be the "*garbha* of Pajrā" (IX.82.4), an expression said to be not very clear.

On closely viewing the references to the word *garbha* in RV. it appears clear that a concept of the cosmic *garbha*, associated with the advent of rain had developed at that period. At various places Sāyaṇa explains the references to *garbha* as being indicative of rain; and this is not arbitrary. It was believed that rain came from the *garbha* of the mid-region. Vāyu being called the *garbha* of the Universe (X.168.4) attaches to this mid-region god the potentiality to procreate.[1] Though said to be not clear, significant, in this context, is the expression that Soma is the *garbha* of Pajrā.[2] Scholars are at variance about the implication of the word Pajrā. There is another word, *pajrā*, which is rendered as "strong"; but the feminine word Pajrā is not easy. Sāyaṇa renders the word as meaning "earth" or "*mādhyamikā vāk*" (Speech in the mid-region). In the present context, where Soma is said to be the *garbha* of Pajrā, in the previous verse Parjanya is said to be the father of Soma (X.82.3a, *parjanyaḥ pitā mahiṣasya parṇinaḥ*). It is, thus, clear that Pajrā is closely associated with Parjanya. In the only other reference to Pajrā (fem.) she is associated with the Maruts, as a young lady borne by them in the assembly (I.167.6, *āsthāpayanta yuvatim yuvānaḥ śubhe nimiślām vidatheṣu pajrām*). Parjanya and the Maruts being of the mid-region, it is obvious that Pajrā[3] belongs to the mid-region as a close associate of the Maruts and Parjanya; and, in all probability, it denotes the thunder being the prototype of all types of speech in the universe.

The Maruts and Parjanya are themselves connected with rain.[4] RV reflects the belief that Soma came to the earth through rain, and the Soma-ritual had the gain of rain as an important motive.[5] The concept of Soma being "*pajrāyāḥ garbha*" appears to underline this belief, and is to be, probably, understood as suggesting the advent of *Soma* along with the thunder that accompanies rain on the cosmic plane; and, on the ritual plane, it indicates the oozing out of Soma-juice from the shoots as the *mantra*-s (ritual representatives of the cosmic *Vāk*) are chanted. Elsewhere the thunder, conceived as sevenfold, is said to have the (cosmic) fire as its *garbha* (III.1.6).[6]

The concept of Agni as *apām garbha* (I.17.2; III.1.12,13) is allied to that of Apām-napāt, which had been already developed as the lightning fire.[7] As a fire in the mid-region, in one of his forms, he creates foetus in the watery vapours; or, in other words, he impregnates the watery vapours and forms them into clouds to emit showers. The same concept is reflected in RV where he, as Apām-napāt, is described as staying in the unbaked sustaining fluids (II.35.6 *āmāsu pūrṣu*). Here the mid-region fire is the *garbha* in the sense that it causes the *garbha*. The word *āmā* has a subtle sense of pregnancy, as can be clearly seen from the expression "*yasyāḥ udaram āmayat*" (X.86.23), and implied elsewhere (I.180.3; III.30.14; and for the double imagery of the cloud and the cow cf. VI.17.6; —72.4; VIII.89.7 etc.). In the famous "*asya vāmīya*" hymn the supreme deity, conceived as the divine Bird, is said to be "*apām garbha*" that pacifies the earth with water-showers (I.164.52, *apām garbham...vṛṣṭibhis tarpayantam*). The concept of *garbha* is, here, directly connected with rain. In the same hymn, earlier, we have the expression "*pitā duhitur garbham ā dhāt*" (v.33) ("The father planted the foetus of the daughter") the place being in between two wide-mouthed bowls (cf. *uttānayoḥ camvoḥ*), representing the sky and the earth; and the space in between these two is the uniting place for the Father and the Daughter,[8] where the *garbha* is placed. In an unmistakably clear reference to the rain-waters we have the *garbha*-s oozing out from the darkness of the cloud (X.73.2, *dhvāntāt prapitvād ud aranta garbhāḥ*). Elsewhere, in a well-set punning style, the advent of rain and the sacrifice is suggested in one (III.1.8, *ścotanti dhārā madhuno ghṛtasya vṛṣā yatra vāvṛdhe kāvyena*), indicating that the sprinkler Bull (Fire) increases in the sacrificial assembly with *mantra*-s and the ladles of clarified butter, while the heavenly *ghṛta* (rain) is showered onto the earth as the fire in the mid-region rages with the divine Speech (thunder). There itself we further read that Agni nourishes the *garbha* of the Father (v.10 *pituś ca garbham janituśca babhre*). The Father is the same as the one who places the *garbha* in the mid-region. It is because of this belief, that the sacrificial fire, being propitiated by offerings, causes the *garbha* for rain-clouds in the mid-region, that he is called *apām garbha* in the same hymn (vv.12; 13), and is identified with the supreme Bird who is likewise described (cf. *apām garbham darśatam oṣadhīnām* at v.13 above = I.164.52).

The concept of rain being the *garbha* or connected with the *garbha* is seen also in the case of other divinities. Thus, Indra is known to the plants (fem.) as causing the *garbha* in them (III. 57.3, *namasyantīr janate garbham asmin*). At the advent of the Maruts the earth is said to bear the *garbha* as a wife does at the union with her husband (V.58.7; cf. VI.66.3). Parjanya, of course, is the sprinkler of the *garbha* for the plants and the cows (VII.101;—102.2). Soma causes the *garbha* in the *Vasatīvarī* waters[9] by mixing with them on the ritual plane (IX.19.5); and, by that sympathetic action, causes *garbha* in the mid-region, in the form of the clouds. In line with this belief of the *garbha* in the mid-region we have the earth described as "*garbha-rasā*" (I.164.8). There is indication of the *garbha* being formed every season, the wonder-workers being the Maruts (I.6.4 *ād aha svadhām anu punar garbhatvam erire*); and this was done through the agency of sacrifice (*ibid.*, c, *dadhānā nāma yajñiyam*).

From what has been said above, it will be clear that

the Vedic people believed the generation of rain to be by the formation of the cosmic *garbha*. The actual stages of this formation were—evaporation of the earthly waters by the Sun-fire and formation of the cloud-*garbha* in the mid-region by the mid-region fire. The clouds, conceived as the cows, are said to become *āmā* (pregnant), which is indicative of their being in readiness to ooze out the *garbha* (rain) for the sustenance of the earthly plants. The *garbhādhāna* (placing or generating of the foetus) is attributed to Agni prominently as the central god of the sacrifice; and, secondarily, to Indra, Soma and the Maruts, while *only* Parjanya is the Father that is invoked to implant the *garbha* (V.83.6, 7).

The belief that it rains when the mid-region forms the *garbha* continued, as is clear from the *Bṛhatsaṁhitā* of Varāhamihira.[10] We are not concerned here with the details of the time of the formation of the cloud-foetuses.[11] Interesting, and equally important, is the belief itself that the clouds (or, in the Vedic symbolism, the 'cows' in the form of the clouds) get pregnant. For, this belief stands as the basis of sex-rituals for the gain of rain, reflected in the Ṛgveda and later, as indicated by the legends of Sukanyā-Cyavāna, Vṛcayā-Kakṣīvant, Śāntā-Ṛṣyaśṛṅga and by popular practice.[12]

NOTES

1. With this may be compared the belief among the Malayan people that if women, after menstruation, stand astride naked on the peak of a certain mountain they will be conceived by the flowing wind-god, G.L. Gomme, *Folk-lore as an Historical Science*, London, 1908, p. 243. Cf. *Vāyu* and Añjanī's *garbha*. It may be remembered that the father of Hanūmant was Kesarī, but he was born from Vāyu.
2. The *Vedic Index* says that this word occurs only once in the Ṛgveda. That is as a name. But in addition to this place (i.e. IX. 82.4) see also I.167.6; also cf. *pajrā* at various places.

3. The word *pajrā*, which occurs about ten times in the Ṛgveda, is taken to mean "strong". In that case *Pajrā* would indicate a strong female. Might it indicate the strong thunder considered as a female? The word *pajrā*, though only once yet significantly, occurs as in an epithet of the twin gods Agni and Indra and is directly connected with speech. Read, VI.59.4, *joṣa-vakām vadataḥ pajrā-hoṣiṇā*. The word *hoṣa* means invocation or the roar (*ghoṣa>hoṣa*; cf.VIII.92.4, I.150.2), and *pajrā-hoṣa* would mean "having loud invocation" or "roaring". Yet with the association of Pajrā with the Maruts and Parjanya, one wonders if we do not have a case of metathesis here — *pṛñj>pṛj*, which would give Parjanya; and' *pṛj>parj/pajr>pajra/pajrā*, which would indicate the female counterpart of Parjanya (in other words, it will indicate *Parjanyā*).
4. At various places. But see RV. VII.101ff; V.83; V.57.4 etc.
5. See "The Advent of Soma", Ch.7, *infra*.
6. III.1.6, *ekam garbham dadhire sapta vāṇīḥ*. Sāyaṇa renders *sapta vāṇīḥ* as the rivers in the mid-region; but in comparison with vv.8 and 10 (which we shall refer to presently) they are, without doubt, the seven (meaning manifold) thunders of the mid-region Speech. Geldner "Speeches" (Stimmen).
7. Apām-napāt is, however, not restricted to the mid-region. He is also the deity of the terrestrial water-places, and compares with the concept of the *Payasvān* Agni. Originally he was purely a water-deity, or the deity of confluences of rivers. In the Avesta, he is the lord of the water-females (Yasna xxxviii.1[2]. He is the spring (*napāt*) of waters (*apām*).
8. For a detailed discussion on this point see Dange, *Vedic Concept of 'Field' and the Divine Fructification*, Bombay, 1971, pp. 123ff.
9. These waters are required at the Soma-sacrifice. Pressed out shoots of Soma are moistened in them for fresh-pressing. For this they have to be poured into the cup of the Hotṛ priest, whereby they get the name Nigrābhya. This water from the cup is now used for moistening. They are called Vasatīvarī as they are collected on the previous day and kept (√*vas*) overnight.

10. Bṛhatsaṁhitā XXI-5, *kecid vadanti munayaḥ kārttika-śuklāntam atītya garbha-divasāḥ syuḥ.*
The idea is that the *garbha* begins to form by the end of the bright half of the Kārttika. The commentator Utpala quotes from Sidhhasena—
Śukla-pakṣam atikramya kārttikasya vicārayet
garbhāṇām sambhavam samyak.
See also Meghamālā, Ms. No.844 of 1884-87, Bhandarkar Or. R.I., Folio No. 13, vv.13ff. This information is taken from Dr. A.M. Shastri's *India as Seen from the Bṛhatsaṁhitā of Varāhamihira*, Delhi, 1969.
11. A.M. Shastri *op.cit.,* for a detailed study as regards this point.
12. See Dange, *Sexual Symbolism from the Vedic Ritual*, Delhi, 1979.

Chapter 4

THE VISION OF VASUKRA

Three hymns from the Ṛgveda are ascribed to Vasukra (X.27;-28;-29). But the first of this group is the most interesting and is also full of obscure images. The hymn has been studied by scholars,[1] but the riddle about it remains undiluted. The second of the group also has a few obscure images, but they do not warrant a separate study; and will be referred to for comparison as the discussion advances. We shall jot important points and the whole translation of the hymn (X.27), and leave, as they are, those passages which need to be discussed further. The hymn is in the nature of a dialogue, and the parties are said to be Indra and the seer. They being easily discernible, are not mentioned as such. (Translation here and further on by the author.)

1. There is the eagerness of mind, O Singer! when I bestow (favours) upon the sacrificer, who "presses" (*soma*). I be the killer of the mighty tormentor, who hurts the Truth (*satya-dhvṛtam vṛjināyantam ābhum*) and is the non-giver of the offering (*anāśīrdām*).[2]
2. When, indeed, I challenge for war the non-godly hordes that spurt for the conflict, I would cook a fat bull; and I would sprinkle the strong "pressed out" (*soma*) that is "fifteen" (-fold) in preparation (*amā te tumram vṛṣabham pacāni, tīvram sutam pañcadaśam ni ṣiñcam*).[3]
3. Know I not any one (else than myself), that says he has killed in the battle the non-godly horde.

When he sees (my) fight, (he and) all the mighty ones will praise (me).

4. When I was engaged with unperceived adversities (*ajñāteṣu vṛjaneṣu*) all were the givers of offerings, as I was sustained (*viśve sato maghavāno ma āsan*). I do conquer the mighty one who holds secure (!); grasping by the foot, might I shatter him at the mountain (*jināmi vet kṣema ā santam ābhum, pra tam kṣiṇām parvate pāda-gṛhya*).
5. They, indeed, do not obstruct me in the battle, nor (do) the mountains, when I take to mind (*manasye*)! Of my roar the stone-deaf (*kṛdhu-karṇaḥ*) is afeared; thiswise, indeed, day by day, the '*kiraṇa*' stirs himself to activity (or trembles).
6. May they see, indeed, (*darśan*) the "non-Indras", that drink the offerings (themselves, and do not sacrifice)[4], the "strong-armed" (*bāhu-kṣadaḥ*, lit. "attacking or eating (!) by the arms"), that fall in for injury;-(Those) who, again, censured my friend (Indra); may the fellies (of his chariot) turn on them.
7. You have been; have grown (*aukṣīḥ*; but Sāyaṇa- "*kāle kāle tvameva pṛthivīm siñcasi*); You have attained '*āyuḥ*'. May the former cut asunder, may the latter cut (*darṣat nu pūrvo aparo nu darṣat*). The two covers (*pavaste*) cannot properly cover him. (*pavaste* are Heaven and Earth acc. to scholars).
8. Tho cows—*prayutā* as they are—have eaten the barley of the 'lord' (*gāvo yavam prayutā aryo akṣan*); I saw them moving in company with the herdsman. The calls of the lord have come forth, indeed, everywhere. How much will their own lord (*sva-patiḥ*) 'milk' his desire from them?
9. When we shall be the 'enjoyers of the pasture among the people' (*sam yad vayam yavasa-ado janānām*) — I be the 'barley eater' — Being engaged here (*atra yuktaḥ*) may he wish for the *ava-sātṛ*; may, indeed, the 'seeker' (*vavanvān*) engage the non-engaged (*ayuktam yunajat*).

10. Know here (this) to be truly said of me—I create the two-footed, the four-footed. I divide (among my people, or obtain) the wealth of him, being unvanquished, who might cause (employ) women to fight the mighty (Bull).

11. Whose daughter be 'eyeless' (*anakṣā*), how could he,—Know as he does,
Taunt her as 'blind' (*abhi-manyāte andhām;* for the sense cf. X.86.9);
Who (of the two) does the *meni* (?) accept[5]
He who carries, or he who marries? (*ya īm vahāte, ya īm vā vareyāt*).

12. How far can a woman,
Gladdened by a laudable gift,
Be for a virile wife-seeker (*vadhūyoḥ*)?
Bhadrā (auspicious) becomes the *vadhū*, well-formed,
When she chooses her 'friend' (*mitram*).
Indeed, among the people.

13. Through his feet he swallowed; (he) eats the 'facing one';
With the head he holds the protecting essence (*varūtham*).
Sitting on the 'Upper One' (female, *'urdhvām*), on the lap;
He emaciates her;
(And) down comes upon the earth,
That is prostrate (*uttānām*; lit. "on her back").

14. Great is the shade-less foliage-less 'courser' (*arvā*);[6]
The Mother stands; the released 'foetus' eats;
Licking another's calf did she bellow;
In what region has the Cow
Concealed her Udder?

15. Seven valiant ones came from the lower direction;
Eight came from the upper-they together;
From the back arrived nine, with the measure (*sthivi-mantaḥ*);
Ten from the front (the East);

They (all) reach the summit of the *aśna* (pervader).

16. *Kapila*, the common for the ten,
Him do they invoke for the accomplishment of the *kratu* (rite; deed; exploit);
The foetus well preserved and un-longing,
Does the Mother hold, in joy, along the 'streams' (*vakṣaṇāsu*; also 'wombs').

17. The valiant ones cooked the fat ram;
Cast were the dice on the (gambling) board;
Cleansing the great *dhanu* in the waters,
The two with the strainers move.

18. On came the all-pervading Roarers (*vikrośanāso viśvañca āyan*)
The half gets roasted; half, indeed, did not roast!
Unto me has the god *Savitṛ* said-
"The one having wood-as-food (*drv-'annaḥ*) would alone attain, — he that-has-ghee-as-food (*sarpir-annaḥ*)."

19. I saw the multitude being borne from afar, endowed with the wheel-less sustenance! The lord accompanies (supervises, serves, *siṣakti*) the eras of the creatures (*yugā janānām*), freshly shattering the *śisna*-s, ever-young as he is.

20. These two bulls of mine—Pramara's—are yoked;
Obstruct not! Indeed, again pacify (*mamandhi*);
Even the waters attain his destination (*vi naśanti-artham*);
And may the Sun — the *marka* (purifier; or "killer")—be the *upara*.

21. This thunderbolt that is manifoldly turned (waved),
Below the great sustaining moisture (*purīṣāt*; or from the water) of the Sun.
Beyond it is, indeed, another sustenance;
That the singers do attain—effortlessly (*avyathī*).

22. On every 'tree' fastened, may the Cow bellow (*mīmayad gauḥ*);
Thence may shoot forth (fly) the 'birds' — the *puruṣa-adaḥ*—

Might this whole creation be, indeed, afraid?
May one 'press' (*soma*) for Indra; and help the seer.

23. In the measure (respect) of the gods stood they foremost;
From their cutting the *upara*-s came forth;
Three 'Seeders' (*anūpāḥ*) heat the earth;
Two carry the nourishing fluid (*bṛbūkam vahataḥ purīṣam*).

24. She is your life-sustenance; and also, do know of Him;
Do not, thus, conceal (him?) in the battle;
(He/she) shows the light (*svaḥ*), (and) conceals the *busa*;
He, the "courser" (*pāduḥ*), never gets devoid
Of his form of lustre (*sa pādur asya nirṇijo na mucyate*).

Even a minute reading of the hymn is apt to baffle the mind; for the words in it do not readily reveal the images! The seer, clearly, is indulging in "wort-spiel". He declares that he has some unique experiences, as is clear from his word, "I saw...". But, in this he is not alone; and the Ṛgveda, and even the later ritual-literature, shows the tendency on the part of the seer, or the Hotṛ, to proclaim his (mystic?) experiences. The reason is that this person wants to place himself (or is actually emotionally placed) on the same plane as of the highest guiding principle of this Universe;[7] and, ritually, he represents the divine principle. His declared experiences, in this identification with the divine, form the vision. Vasukra says many things, as can be seen from the hymn; and all those need explanation; but they can be explained only on the basis of comparison with similar passages from RV., which we shall presently see. To start with, if we analyse the hymn, it shows the following clear structures:-

(i) The reference to fight (vv.1-6, v.7) and the success

of the god. This god may be Indra, or the Seer in his divine form, due to the unique identification;

(ii) the element of sex indicated by the references to women, the 'blind' (*anakṣā*) daughter, the *vadhū* and the wife-seeker, the *vadhū* finding her own 'friend'; and, as an extension of the same imagery, the ONE sitting on the lap of the *'Urdhvā* and coming down upon the prostrate Earth; and further the reference to the foetus; ...(vv.10-16);

(iii) mention of the valiant Roarers and the lord (vv.17-19);

(iv) the 'purifier', the thunderbolt, the "birds" and the three Seeders, in the imagery of Water... the nourishing fluid (vv.20-23).

Now, in this apparent conglomeration of ideas and images there are references to a probable ritual:- (i) "I would cook the fat bull and sprinkle the strong pressed out *soma*" (v.2); (ii) "the valiant ones cooked the ram," (v.17), which balances the earlier reference, and seems to be the cosmic phase of the earthly ritual, referred to at v.2, (iii) the one "having-wood-as-food", the one "having-ghee-as-food" (v.18); and (iv) faintly, "the two with the strainers", and "cast were the dice on the gambling-board" (v.17).

What the ritual might have been for is not clear; but there is a hint, that the ritual is closely associated with the fight, which is indicated by the words "unperceived adversities" (cf. *ajñāteṣu vṛjaneṣu*", which is "unknown fights" acc. to Sāyaṇa; Geldner "Unknown captivity"). Likewise the thought of challenging the non-godly hordes is closely associated with the cooking of the bull (v.2). In the context of the fight one thing has to be marked. There is no mention of any particular enemies as such, they being indicated only as *'adevayu'* and *'an-indra'*, being termed "*śṛta-pā*" (v.6). The only other case of the last word is in the context of the 'war-of-ten-kings'; but even there the exact identification of the *'śṛtapā an-indrāḥ'* (cf. *ardham vīrasya śṛtapām an-indram*, VII.18.16) is doubtful. Which of the kings defeated by Sudās, under favour of Indra, it refers to is unsure. Such passages present a purposeful mixture of the cosmic fight with the terrestrial (cf. also VII.18.10; 20; IV.26). Hence it will be only proper to take the case in hand as indicative of only imaginative enemies, and not any hostile tribes as such. RV has instances of such imaginary enemies where the idea is to redeem the locality from evil or the completion of a ritual for a particular gain, a trait to be clearly marked in later rituals,[8] which, thus, combines the fight-motif with sacrifice. In the present context also there is an association of the defeat of the adversaries and the offering. Indra's stay is in unknown (to men!) regions. There the fight continues (v.4). He is to be offered to, so that he could be strong. It is supposed that here Indra speaks, and it is perfectly right. But the point is of the exact implication of the words. Oldenberg adds, after taking this verse as the speech of Indra, that Indra felt, "then all were the '*maghavan*' like me"; and explains it as meaning that Indra was not, thus, like the others! (Sagt Indra damals waren alle "maghavan" *mir gleich, d.h.Sie* waren mir alle nichts wert). Geldner writes in the note to indicate that the others were ready and eager to be liberal, so that they could get Indra's help (...um meine hilfe zu haben). This would indicate that the offerings had a reciprocatory nature: Indra to fight and the 'liberal donors' to offer to him in order that he may help them, by showering favours on them. The rendering, "all passed for maghavan, though I existed" (Griffith) understanding an insult to Indra (cf. *sato...me*), taking it to be a case of genitive absolute, is non-Vedic; for in the Veda the uses of *satah̩* do not indicate dishonour. In fact this is the only case for *me satah̩* (cf. *te satah* only twice, I.36.3 and IV.6.6, where the meaning is normal). Geldner seems to be right; for, the thought of Indra being in the "*ajñāta vr̩jana-s*", and that of the donors' offerings,[9] directly get connected, in the same verse in the next line, with the *kṣema* (protection) by hurling (or shattering) the *ābhu* (?) on the 'mountain', grasping him by the foot. The *ābhu* is the same as referred to earlier (v.1). As such, he compares with another "one who was shattered by Indra, grasping him by the feet"; but there he is said to be the *pitṛ*, whose death makes Indra's mother a widow (IV.18.12; *prā tām kṣiṇām parvate pāda-gṛhya* at X.27.4, and at, IV.18.12. *prā-kṣināḥ pitaram pādagṛhya*). The *piṭr* (protector) and the *ābhu* who is hurled for the *kṣema*, or who controls the *kṣema*, of the people are clearly identical. In a later myth[10] Indra is said to have chased his father, Tvaṣṭṛ, who concealed *soma* from the former. Probably, we could connect *an-āṣīr-dām* (v.1) from our hymn with Tvaṣṭṛ concealing *soma*. From our hymn we have two aspects of the *ābhu*; one is the benevolent one, as is suggested by the words "*kṣeme ā santam*", the other being the malevolent one, as indicated by the word "*vṛjinayantam*" (v.1) which conveys the meaning of crookedness. The words *kṣiṇam* here and *akṣiṇāḥ* at IV.18-12 compare with another similar word in our present hymn in the expression "*āsīna ūrdhvām upasi kṣiṇāti*" (v.13). The exploit indicated by these forms of the root *kṣi* is thus associated with the upper region as is clear in the words *parvate*, *ūrdhvām* etc. Even in the case of VI.18.12, where the region is not mentioned, in the very previous verse the defeat of Vṛtra is mentioned (*athā-bravīd vṛtram indro haniṣyan*); and earlier, as is usual with the Ṛgveda, Vṛta's defeat is associated with the gain of waters (IV.18.7). The defeat of Vṛtra is usually believed to be accomplished on the *parvata* or in the *parāvata* region.[11] Taking into account the "son-father" relationship of Vṛtra and Tvaṣṭṛ in the later literature, it seems probable that the "mighty crooked *ābhu*" (X.27.1)—who is the same as the one shattered on the mountain—and the *pitṛ* convey the idea of a malevolent "controller" of waters. In the case of Vṛtra the control of waters is clear in the tradition. In the case of Tvaṣṭṛ it is Soma that is controlled. But, as water (especially rain), nectar and Soma are mostly associated and identified,[12] it is not improbable that the Soma of Tvaṣṭṛ was only a symbolic name for rain, as in the case of Vṛtra. Tvaṣṭṛ is said to be the father, in the later literature (and nowhere clearly in RV). The most prominent "father" in the RV appears to be Parjanya (cg. V.83,6d; IX.82; 3a etc.); and the myth of the "Father" copulating with his "Daughter" (earth) has the same bearing in the Ṛgveda.[13] Scholars differ about the nature of Tvaṣṭṛ;[14] but there seems to be no doubt about his being a mixture of the traits of the Sun and Parjanya, with an evil tinge, as the father of Vṛtra, in one of his aspects. The *ābhu* in the hymn under study shows the mixture of goodness and crookedness; and the seer skilfully shows it by his "wort-spiel": *vṛjinayantam ābhum* and *kṣema ā santam ābhum; kṣema* means 'protection of what is gained' or 'control' (√'*kṣi*) and also 'welfare'. Here, then, we have a very good case for "Vedic dualism"[15] indicating the good and bad (or kind and cruel) aspects of the deity. Fight with this *ābhu*—of double character—is the first stage in the hymn. The enemies suggested by the plural are ancillaries to this Great "foe", who is conceptual and supraterrestrial. He is the *an-āṣīrdā*, the non-giver of the 'sustenance' to the people. To vanquish him Indra is sacrificed to by the liberal donors. Thus, the cosmic fight gets associated with sacrifice for the good of the people.[16]

The position now is this. The verse which begins the hymn is an assurance of Indra that he would shatter the *ābhu*, and serves as the principal motif of the hymn, to be explained further. The second verse appears to be the speech of the seer, who says that when he challenges the enemies (the conceptual ancillaries of the *ābhu*) he offers a fat bull and *soma* to Indra so that he may succeed. Then proclaims Indra his unique strength, and assures that he would shatter the *ābhu*; for none obstructs him in the battle; and even the *kiraṇa* trembles (*kiraṇaḥ sam ejat*, v.5). Now the point is—what does this signify? Sāyaṇa understands *kiraṇa* as the sun (*kiraṇa-vān raśmi-vān ādityaḥ*), while Geldner understands it as "dust" (staub). The word occurs only five times in RV, out of which only twice in the plural (actually only once; for at X.106.4 the form is *kiraṇa-iva*, which should be taken to be the dual in respect of the Aśvins who are two; the other case is I.63.1, where the mountains are said to tremble like the *kiraṇa-s*). In the singular the instances are three including the present context. The Maruts are said to shake the earth like the *kiraṇa* (V.59.4); and the sun-horse, Dadhikrāvan, is associated with *kiraṇa* (IV.38.6). In the plural the word would not present any difficulty if it be understood as "dust"; but what about the singular or the dual forms? The Aśvins are like "*kiraṇa* (*u*)" for enjoyment (*bhujyai*); and Dadhikrāvan bites the *kiraṇa*. As he is the sun-horse, the *kiraṇa* indicates the ray. Likewise *kiraṇa* in the hymn under study suits more the image of the Sun. The two *kiraṇau* in the context of the Aśvins, probably, speak of their solar trait.[17] It seems better, thus, to understand the word *kiraṇa* as the sun, the other sense being that of the cloud (from √*kṛ* to spread), but the second does not suit the expression "day by day" (*anu dyūn*). The antagonism between the sun and Indra is attested by the Ṛgveda,[18] though at other places both come to be identified. The antagonism is due to the dual nature of the sun, i.e. as a life-giver and as a tormentor, the latter being in his role of imparting the scorching heat, whence he is shown in the concept of Śuṣṇa 'The Dryer' (fr. *śuṣ*). This also is a case of dualism. If this is remembered, the *kiraṇa* that trembles before Indra, has to be only another phase of the *ābhu*. This also helps explain another verse throwing light on certain epithets, which are considered to be obscure. The *ābhu*, and the *kiraṇa*, present the image of the vile tormenting power that has sucked up all nourishing fluids on the earth. They have to be defeated in the fight; and for this the singular benefactor, Indra, is to be strengthened. The enemies mentioned in the next verse are not, and cannot be, terrestrial. They are said to be *śṛtapā*, *an-indra*, and *bāhu-kṣad*. As we have noted earlier, the word *śṛtapā* occurs only once more (VII.18.16), and the exact identification is doubtful. More probably, there also the expression indicates the cosmic enemies; and they were referred to in the context of the actual terrestrial war, because the terrestrial war was believed to be only a phase of the cosmic phenomenon. Indra was identified with the terrestrial king and, thus, took part in the terrestrial wars on the side of the terrestrial king, according to a well set Vedic belief.[19] The word *an-indra*, more properly, indicates "non-Indra" rather than the "enemies who do not worship or believe in Indra"! Only one example in support of this would suffice. Thus, the *druh* (evil power) is said to be so (IV.23.7, *druham jighāṁsan dhvarasam an-indrām*; cf.I.133.1 *druhaḥ.. an-indrāḥ,* plural). The word occurs six times; and at no place does it have the implication of the terrestrial enemy. The word "*bāhu-kṣadaḥ*" has been posing a problem; and, admittedly, it is a difficult word. It has been rendered variously as "mean offerers" (Griffith), "parsimonious worshippers who offer the forelegs, or inferior parts of the sacrificial animals" (Roth quoted by Griffith), "who cut the worshippers to pieces with their hands" (Wilson, following Sāyaṇa), "who cut their arms" (Geldner, who also suggests a correction as *bāhu-sadaḥ* in respect of "*bāhubhiḥ śaśadānān*" VII.98.4, and *bāhu-śridhaḥ*, in respect of *bāhu-śardhī*, X.103.3). Though the verse may be taken to refer to actual enemies, in the context of *niniduḥ* (censured), there seems to be no doubt that the verse is intentionally darkened by the seer. The word *bāhu-kṣadaḥ*, most probably, is meant to be taken in the context of *kiraṇa* and the crooked tormenting *ābhu*. Again it may be compared with such expressions as "*patto jāgāra*" and "*pratyañcam atti*" (v.13) or "*vayaḥ puruṣa-adaḥ* ("man-eating birds"). This would indicate that the word *bāhu-kṣadaḥ* cannot be taken in the flat sense. Now, there is no difference of opinion about the meaning of the expression "*patto jāgāra*". It is the description of the sun "swallowing with his feet", i.e. "sucking by his rays". In view of the word *kiraṇa*, which indicates the sun (as we have examined above), the "*bāhu-kṣadaḥ*" (eating by arms!) appears to be the symbolic description of his rays. It has to be noted that the word ends in a root-formation where the meaning warranted is the "eating" (√*kṣad*) or of "attacking".[20] Hence the renderings noted above cannot be accepted. The rays (arms!) of the scorching sun, who is crooked in his aspect of the evaporator, appear to the seer as enemies "devouring" the juices. Hence, indeed, are they described by another rare epithet "*śṛta-pā*" (the drinkers of the essence of life—water and all juices). Hence they are seen as if they advance for killing the creatures (*śarave patyamānān*). This completes the battle phase of the vision of Vasukra, who visualizes the terrible sun emitting his killing heat as a fiend (and is the veritable Śuṣṇa!); and he is confident of remedying the conditions by an oral charm of the hymn and by the sacrifice to Indra; for, without sacrifice Indra cannot gain the required strength to help the people. He sees Indra to be the supreme power that stands beyond all (v.7).

The next stage starts with the advent of the cows, which have a clearer, and a known, connotation. The cows are the clouds and the rays of light, in Vedic symbolism. The relationship among the verses that follow is a difficult problem; yet certain points are to be noted. There is mention of the desire of "enjoying the pasture" (*yavasādaḥ*) and of the corn (*yavādaḥ*). The *avasātṛ* (*ava* + √*san* 'to win') is "one who gains"; and, in the context of the first half (v.9ab), he has to be connected with the gain of good pasture and corn. This also indicates the motive of the ritual—the gain of bumper pastures and corn. The sense probably, is that a person who engages himself in the ritual (*atra yuktaḥ*) gains the "attainer" (*ava-sātāram*), who, being the "winner" (*vavanvān*; fr. √*van*, "to gain") might bring about the desired effect. Though it is very difficult to say what exact implication of this verse (which is without the commentary of Sāyaṇa!) is, it seems to imply "joining some one who is not joined" (*ayuktam yunajat*). In line with the thought of the first half, which centres on the barley and the pasture, the "one who is expected to join" appears to be the divine agent who might accomplish what is suggested in the first half. The words 'pasture-eaters' and 'barley-eaters' (*yavasādaḥ* and *yavādaḥ*, v.9) are supposed to present a contrast as Geldner says (note to his Tr.) and indicate cattle and human progeny sustaining on the land. The next verse supports this as Indra declares that he would create the "two-footed" and the "four-footed", which indicates the weal of the creatures (v.10). The next half of the verse speaks about 'women in fight', which is the beginning for sex references leading to the mention of the cosmic *garbha* (vv.11-16).

When we come to examine the reference to the women as fighters and compare them with the fight against Vṛtra, we see that it forms a regular style in RV. Indra is the supreme lord in all fights, and his adversaries are eunuchs, or dependent on women. Vṛtra is often said to be the castrated bullock trying to be equal to Indra, the virile one (I.32.7; 33.7; cf.X.102.12). More pointed references to women occur in the context of Namuci and Kuyava. Thus Namuci is said to have employed women as weapons (v.30.9a); and Indra declares, "What could those feeble armies do to me!" (*ibid.*, b). And in the same context, where Namuci's head is said to have been cut off by Indra, the seer is said to have been made the associate, the exact expression being, "*yujam hi mām akṛthā ād id indra*" (v.30.8), which may be compared with "*ayuktam yunajat*" from our hymn, and coming immediately before the mention of the women. Kuyava has two females that are said to take bath with milk (I. 104.2). Various interpretations are given for these passages; but it appears that these enemies of Indra are only representations of the sun in his scorching phase. The support for this supposition comes from an interesting passage from the hymn which starts with "*asya vāmasya*" (I.164), which has parallels from the hymn under consideration. The rays of the sun are considered to be women; and the riddle is put forth in the following words:-

> 'Women' they are of mine, them do they call 'men';
> One having eyes may see, the blind discerneth not;
> The Son that is wise might recognize them;
> He who knows them (feminine) is the Father's Father.
> (I.164.16)

There seems to be no doubt, hence, that the "One who fights with the help of women" is the scorching Sun, whose "wealth" (*vedaḥ*), in the form of the waters, Indra would win. Namuci and Śuṣṇa get to be called Dāsa, in the image of the "tormentor" when the beneficial solar nature in them is extinct. Here that epithet is not used (at v.10) when the sun's "women" only are mentioned, but when his crooked aspect is visualized (in his concept of Tvaṣṭṛ)[21] he is referred to as "*vrjinayant ābhu*" v.1). The mixed concept (good and bad) is to be noted in "*kṣema a santam ābhum*" (v.4).

The image that is presented by the verse that refers to the "women" has to be seen from another angle; and that is very important. The inner meaning of "making the 'Bull' fight the women" (*strībhir vṛṣaṇam pṛtanyāt*) does not cease with the verse in hand alone. It actually is a motif at other places in the hymn; and the places are not far to seek. The motif is that the Vṛṣaṇa is the supreme god of this ritual—Indra—, and the "women" are juxtaposed with him. In other words, the motif is of suggested copulation, which is present at other hymns in the Ṛgveda supposed to be obscure.[22] The position is this: the "women" (scorching rays) of the other one (the sun) 'fight' with the Vṛṣaṇa (Indra); and the fighter (Indra) gains the wealth from the "other One". The concept of the one who is the owner, and one who is other than him, and yet has some association with the former's woman, is to be seen in the following two verses, which, hence, have the same motif as "the one fighting with another's women". The fight-motif, thus, gets associated with that of sex; and all this gets the setting of ritual. The motif we have hinted at is present in "*ya īm vahāte ya īm va vareyāt*" about the 'blind daughter' (v.11). The same is also present in "*maryato vadhūyoḥ*" and "*mitram vanute*" in respect of the *yoṣā-vadhū* (v.12). The '*mitra*' is different from the *vadhūyu*, and the one who is spoken of as "*vareyāt*" is different from the one who is indicated by "*vahāte*". There cannot be any difference of opinion about the fact that these verses have suggested sex in them. The next verse also indicates it in the expression, "*āsīna ūrdhvām upasi kṣiṇāti*" indicating the 'upper female' (in the mid-region), and "*uttānām bhūmim*" (the earth 'upon' which (or, whom!)

the *āsīnaḥ* (male) 'comes'! The next verse has an extension of the same idea in the foetus of two mothers. This shows that we shall be on safe ground if we expect the same motif in the context of the cows and the 'lord' (v. 8). We shall recall the verse here part by part, and try to fix the meaning:-

(i) The cows have eaten the barley;
(ii) They are seen moving ("grazing" cf. *carantīḥ*), and are in the company of the cowherd;
(iii) the *hava*-s (calls) of the *arya* (lord) have come forth;
(iv) their *sva-pati* 'milks' to his desire.

To take the first. The original expression is —"*gāvo yavam prayutā aryo akṣan*". Probably here we have to take the expression in two ways, (1) *aryaḥ prayutāḥ gāvaḥ yavam akṣan* (the *prayuta* (?) cows of the *arya* ate the barley); and (ii) *prayutāḥ gāvaḥ aryo yavam akṣan* (the *prayuta* cows have eaten the barley of the *arya*). Before we examine the probable implication of this expression, we would better note the difference between the *arya* and the *sva-pati*, which the verse appears to indicate. The *sva-pati* appears to be the owner of the cows, while the *arya* appears to be different from him. The eating of the barley by the cows seems to be intended for the *arya* while the fulfilling of the desire from the cows is the gain for the *sva-pati*. The problematic words used for the cows, in this verse, are —*prayutāḥ, yavam akṣan*; and the expression "*havā id aryo abhitaḥ sam-āyan*" (c). We examine the last first. The word *hava* is in the neuter in RV and is also, though only at a few places, in the masculine. The only other place in the RV which compares with "*kiyad āsu svapatiḥ chandayāte*" (d) is "*paure chandayase havam*" (VIII. 50.5), where "*havam chānd*" appears to mean "to like the praise, or, to accept the invocation". The expression, in the present context, "*havāḥ abhitaḥ sam-āyan*" has two possibilities: (i) "the shouts (*havāḥ*) of *arya* (lord) came all around", conveying the idea of the calling of the cows grazing in the pasture; and it tallies with that in the first half, which speaks of the cows grazing in the pasture with the herd; but (ii) the cows themselves came towards (*abhitaḥ*) the *arya*, bellowing (*havāḥ*). The latter meaning takes *havāḥ* as the epithet of cows (as Sāyaṇa has taken; and convincingly so), which exactly fits in with "*āsu*" (d) both being feminine. The image that we get this way is of the cows that graze with the herd, but run to the *arya*, and milk for the *sva-pati*, who is favoured by the *arya*. Which are, then, the cows? For the exact parallel to the concept of the "bellowing cows" here, we turn to the following verse of Babhru Ātreya:-

> Here did the cows bellowingly praise (*abhito navanta*),
> Scattered as they were, and separated (*vi-yutāḥ*) from their calves;
> Them did Indra with his exploits release,
> When the juices of Soma made him pleased. (V.30.10)

The running of the cows to Indra is a common theme in the RV. Here, in the hymn of Babhru Ātreya, just before the image of the bellowing cows, we are told of the "female fighters of Namuci" and Indra's success over them. The references just preceding are to the release of waters held by the serpent (*apo ajayaḍ dāsa-patnīḥ* v.5; and *ahim ohānam apa ā śayānam* v.6), which leaves little doubt about the bellowing cows being the thundering clouds! In the context under discussion, then, the *hava*-s are the thundering cloud-cows, the *arya* is Indra, and the *gopāḥ* (cf. *saha-gopāḥ*) is "the One who controls them" and is unwilling to release them! He is the same "*vṛjinayant ābhu*", who sometimes, turns crooked and is to be defeated at the far off region, beyond human perception. He is the scorching and tormenting aspect of the Sun. "Eating of the *yava*" by the cows (clouds!) is indicative of their getting fattened, and, hence, being prone to release the content. In other words, they are "with foetus" (rain), and thunder for 'delivery'. This Indra accomplishes and helps the *svapati* (performer of the ritual) to achieve bumper crops and weal of cattle (v.9). There is no reference to any particular sacrificer here as such; but in the hymn of Babhru (as at other places) there is clear reference that the 'cows' were released, and the (rains) waters were gained for the Ruśamas and their king Ṛṇañcaya (V.30.13ff). The eating of *yava*[23] and the epithet "*prayuta*", thus, have a causative relationship. They have 'eaten the *yava*' and, hence, are "*prayuta*". The word "*prayuta*" directly contrasts with "*vi-yuta*" from the Babhru context. There the cows are separated from the calves (?); but here they are "joined" (with calves, or with the foetus!). The idea in the word "*pra-yuta*", in this context at least, must be supported by the other implication we have noted; and it is that of 'pregnancy' (and if indolence, with Geldner, it is) due to the cows being "with the calf".[24] This also goes well with the element of sex in the verses that follow. Speculations about the exact meaning of these verses may yet be made; but there should be no doubt in the least, that the verses are of the nature of the oral sex-charm for added help for "fructification" of the "Cows". We have noted the difference that is sought to be made between "one who marries" and "one who carries" in respect of the *vadhū* (v.11); the same is true of the 'wife-seeker' and the "mitra" (v.12). If we view the verse minutely, the seer seems to uphold the thought that the '*mitra*' selected among the people is auspicious. Read in the context of the thought in the hymn which we have noted, the verse seems to indicate sex in the ritual-context, where the one who is not the real husband acts as the sex-partner. The motif is not solitary, and is distributed in the Vedic ritual-tradition. The concept is of the 'foreign seed' or '*patividya*'.[25]

The next verse (13) sets the image of the sun sucking earthly juices by his 'feet' (rays). This is expressed by "*patto jāgāra*" (*pad* + *taḥ*). The words "*pratyañcam atti*" have been obscure.[26] The clue appears to be, however, in the explanation of the concept of "*pratyaṅ*" (*pratyañc*). The word *pratyaṅ*, in the singular, comes mostly to indicate the fire, and, by implication, the sacrifice (I.144.7: II.3.1; — 10.5; V.28.1; X.12.1; 75.5 etc.), and also the sun, as an aspect of Vaiśvānara (X.88.16). The expression "*patto jāgāra, pratyañcam atti*" is, hence the description of the sun, who sucks up the moistures by his rays (=feet) and "eats the (earthly sustenance through the) sacrifice." The sacrifice faces him, and he "eats" it. The seer plays on the words and uses riddles to conceal his thought. He uses the same imagery in his next hymn (X. 28.4; 9), where the *lopāśa* (jackal according to Geldner; Sāyaṇa, "deer") is said to have challenged the lion, at the earlier place, and at the latter the *sasa* (hare ?) is said to have swallowed the "blade" (*kṣura*, Sāyaṇa "an animal as the lion or the tiger").[27] The sun sucks the moistures, and sustains on sacrifice (as is the case with Indra, v.4). He holds the sucked up moisture as the "protective helmet" (*varūtham*, with Geldner), which is actually the "essence that is sought by the creatures" (*varūtham*, with Sāyaṇa). He causes the "upper female" to get emaciated and comes down in the form of the rays, and later, through the water-streams, to "fructify" the prostrate Earth-lady. Next the sun is seen as the "courser" without shade or foliage.[28] He is the seeder of the "mother" that stands still (in the mid-region); and the foetus, that is released and eats ("*viṣito atti garbhaḥ*"), is the next phase of Agni. He is the atmospheric fire visible as the lightning. The mid-region Mother fondles and licks the foetus (lightning-fire); and she thunders (in joy), though it is not her own child; for the idea is that it is the same sacrificial fire (of the earth) transmigrated to the mid-region. She fondles him and feeds him; but her "udder", whence the "milk" of rain comes, is not visible! The concept works like this:— the sun sucks the terrestrial waters; his rays become waterful (cf. *Asya vāmīya*, I.164.7 *śīrṣṇaḥ kṣīram durhate gāvo asya, vavrim vasānā udakam padā-puḥ*. This creates the *garbha* in the mid-region in the form of the clouds— the *garbha* being a form of the fire—(cf. I.164.9 *atiṣṭhad garbho vṛjanīṣv-antaḥ;-vṛjanīṣu* may be compared with *vṛjaneṣu* at Vasukra 4 both indicating "beyond reach"). The cow-calf symbolism, indicating the rain-cloud and the lightning fire here, has convincing parallels (I.164.9; —28f; 41). But, what is interesting is the symbolism of the "lower mother" (the earth) and the "upper mother" (the mid-region), and the "upper one" licking the foetus of the "lower one". At another place the "lower one" (earth) is called *padyā*; and the "upper one" licks the calf—

> The *padyā* assumes multi-formed appearances
> The "higher one" stood on licking the (child) three-year old.[29]
> (III.55.14)

Just in the previous verse we read "*anyasyā vatsam rihatī mimāya, kayā bhuvā* etc. (III.55.13ab = X.27.14). The hymn of Viśvāmitra, referred to above has further on the image of the barren cow being fructified by the roaring Bull (a graphic picture of the clouds and the thundering lightning Bull). Vasukra indicates this thunder in the reference to the valiant seven, eight, nine and ten, which do not indicate any fixed deities as such, but appear to suggest the Maruts, or wind in general. The *kapila*, the "tawny one", is the name of the mid-region fire and is the same as the new red *garbha*.[30] This *garbha* is placed in the *vakṣaṇā*-s, which indicate the watery streams in the mid-region.[31]

Up to this point Vasukra mixes sex-symbols with the formation of the mid-region-foetus, indicating the formation of the clouds; and this is closely the pattern of the "*Asya vāmīya*" (I.164), which is also noticeable at other places as we have noted. He now builds the image of the cosmic ritual, where the valiant ones, spoken of earlier, are said to cook the "fat ram". This is the counterpart of the terrestrial ritual mentioned before (v.2) in which the cooking of a fat bull is mentioned. This means that the earlier cooking was the sympathetic spell for the cosmic "cooking". This expression parallels with "the sprinkler bull did the valiant ones cook" (I.164.43d) which further indicates the ritual-tradition in "such were the rituals of yore" (*ibid.*, d). This gets culminated at the end of the '*asya vāmīya*' in the concept of the "water-foetus" (*apām garbha*) which is the sun (I.164.52). The cooking of the ram or the bull was, then, a sympathetic ritual-act for the gain of the heavenly streams. The belief was settled in the Vedic ritual-tradition.[32] When Vasukra speaks of the dice being thrown he, probably, offers another ritual-symbol for success. Dice-playing at the ritual was symbolic of success in the undertaking;[33] and here the success that is sought is the gain of rain, about which there is no doubt now, and which is again symbolically described in the concluding verses of the hymn (21-24). In the setting of the cosmic activity, the "bull-cooking" indicates the "cooking" of the cloud (or the sun),[34] and the dice, the clouds that are scattered in the sky. The vision of the cosmic-ritual continues. He mentions "the two with the strainers" who cleanse the *dhanu* in the waters. The waters are the moisture in the mid-region; and the two are the sun and the wind. The sun is referred to as such in the hymn itself (v.20c āpaśćid asya vi naśanty artham, sūraś ca marka uparo babhūvān) and we shall turn to it again. Vāyu is said to make the strainer of his own body (X.31.8, *tvacam pavitram kṛṇuta svadhāvān*: see Sāyaṇa), or it may also be the mid-region fire. But which is the "*dhanu*" being cleansed in the water? Macdonell's suggestion that *dhanu* is a symbolic name for the cloud in RV (*Vedic Index*) is perfectly right and is amply supported (I.33.4; 144.5; VIII.3.19; 4.3). Moreover the waters are said to be *dhanutrī* (III.31.16) and being honeyed (or honey) are said to be purified by the strainers, that are said to be *kavi* (*madhvaḥ punānāḥ kavibhiḥ pavitraiḥ...dhanutrīḥ*), which means that the strainers are divine or cosmic. Probably they indicate the Sun, the Wind and the atmospheric fire.[35] The belief seems to be that the waters come through the divine strainers of the sun and the atmospheric wind. *Dhanu*, then, is a symbolic name for the cloud which is to be washed off (*punantā*) and is feminine. We may recall to our mind the valiant ones spoken of earlier (v.15). They are said to be *sthivimantaḥ* (having the *sthivi*); *sthivi* is a corn-measure (X.68.3); the *sthivi-mantaḥ* are the Maruts who carry the *sthivi* (i.e. the cloud containing rain-drops resembling corn, and producing corn later). They are again referred to as the "roarers" (*vikrośanāsaḥ*, v.18); and the cloud ram/bull is only half-roasted, the other half being yet unroasted. The roasting of the cloud-ram is based on the belief that the atmospheric fire heats the cloud, which, then, drips 'Ṛain'.[36] This is supported by the belief that rain is the *"pacyamāna odana"* (VIII. 69.14 "food being cooked" by boiling) and comes from the "cooked buffalo" (*ibid.*, 15). Vasukra uses the same symbols in *"pacāti nemo na-hi pakṣad ardhaḥ"* "half is getting cooked; half is not cooked", indicating the "unripe" clouds. The concept gets compared with the *"āmā"* cow or *"āmā pur"*, another cloud-symbol. And for the cooking of the Cloud-bull, offerings to the terrestrial sacrificial fire are necessary; for it is he who is ultimately to accomplish the ritual and, through it, the gain—so said *Savitṛ* (v.18)! Vasukra reverts to the image of the heating of the cloud, which he calls the *kṛpīṭa* and a tree (X.28.8, *vāṇa vṛścantā; vāṇa* is a mixed concept indicating the rain-cloud or water and the tree);[37] and there the valiant ones give place to "gods who carry axes" (*ibid.*, *devāsā āyan paraśūr abibhran*). Thus, "cutting the *vāṇa*" is symbolic of splitting the cloud.

Then we are at another aspect of the vision. Now, Vasukra says that he has seen a group being borne, from afar, moving with the "wheel-less sustenance" (*acakrayā svadhayā vartamānam*). The exact parallel, and the only one, for *"acakrayā svadhayā"* occurs in the hymn of Vāmadeva, in the context of the saga of Soma-gain (IV.26.4). There also the seer, Vāmadeva, identifies himself with Indra, as if in a trance, and describes the exploits of Indra as if they were his own! In the case of Vasukra, the seer is believed to be the son of Indra; and the reference to *"śvaśura"* (X.28.1) is supposed to be for Indra by Vasukra's wife. This shows that the seers had developed a style of identifying themselves, or showing close relationship, with the deity; and the purpose seems to be the accomplishment of a particular ritual. The bringing of *Soma*, and the *Soma*-ritual, get associated at various places, with the advent of rain; as such the *"acakrā svadhā"* at the Vāmadevīya hymn indicates the gain of rain. In the present context, where the association of waters is prominent as we have seen and shall further see, the "*acakrā svadhā*" is clearly symbolic of the clouds that are wheelless and carry the sustenance in the form of rain. The group with the "*acakrā svadhā*" has to be seen in comparison with the "valiant ones with the *sthivi*" (v.15); for, both indicate the same concept. The valiant ones there reach the sānu (summit) of the *aśna*. The *aśna* has been known as the symbolic name for the Mid-region fire,[38] who is all-pervading (√*aś*); he also indicates Vāyu, both being the "one with the strainer", that are believed to purify the waters that come to the earth.[39] The "*acakrā svadhā*" concept works on the fact that the clouds, being in the mid-region, move, but have no wheels! We may compare, in this context, the concept of the "moving city" of Śuṣṇa, which symbolizes the cloud[40] (VIII.1.28). The *arya* that is referred to here (v. 19c) is the same as, generation after generation (*si-ṣakti aryaḥ pra yugā janānām*),[41] but referred to earlier (v.8, twice) and is Indra. He is expected to favour the people, what is the implication of the expression "*sadyaḥ śiśnā pra-mināno navīyān*". *Navīyān* is Indra who is ever new,[42] i.e., ever young. "*śiśnā pra-minānaḥ*" has been a problem; and the word "*śiśna*" appears to be a purposeful knot kept by the seer, in view of the element of sex employed earlier. The plain meaning of *śiśna* is the "male-organ"; and in view of the enemies of Indra being considered as *vadhri* (castrated), the words would have the sense of "vanquishing the enemies completely," by cutting their organs, the enemies being only conceptual and thought to be thwarting rain, which is belated! But in view of the word-play the seer is indulging in, and not contrary to the general tendency seen in the Ṛgveda at places, it is probable that the seer uses a peculiar word which would be outwardly mistaken for a sex-symbol and yet be a symbolic name for the clouds. The word *śiśna* indicates the root √*śas* (to jump or to be active), rather than √*śnath* (to pierce) as is proposed by Yāska and followed in the tradition. In that case *śiśna* would indicate the "jumping" cloud that is shattered by the ever young Indra. RV uses the image of the jumping (or running) cows, that are barren and without milk, to indicate the yet non-raining clouds (III.55.16 *ā dhenavo dhunayantām aśiśvīḥ sabardughāḥ śaśayā a-pradughāḥ*); and we have the concept of the "*śaśayā*" being "milked" by the gods, which indicates the raining of the cloud (III.57.2); moreover, the udder (*stana*) of the Sarasvatī is said to be "*śaśayā*",[43] where it indicates the never-failing cosmic source of water, here Sarasvatī being the cosmic streams, looking to the nature of the "*asya vāmīya*". There is another reason to take *śiśnā* as symbolically indicating the flying or active clouds. In the next verse, and for the first time now in the hymn, we have a clear reference to the gain of waters by the seer, who calls himself Pramara, which, probably, is a mystic ritual name of the seer (v.20 ā*paś cid asya vi naśantyartham*); and the sun is said to have become the "purifier" at the upper region (d, *sūraś ca marka uparo babhūvān*), the significance of which we have noted already. The word *upara* (Pl. 22) occurs again shortly afterwards in the hymn and indicates the showers that come from the cutting of the clouds (v.23b).[44] The word Pramara, like *Marka* is solitary in the Ṛgveda. Possibly in Pramara the seer suggests his identification with Marka,[45] who is the "purifying" (√*mṛc* cf. Sāyaṇa) sun. Now what is the implication of the "two bulls" of Pramara expression "*atra yukto' vasataram icchāt*" and "*ayuktam yunajat*" (v.9). The word *yukta*, in any form, nowhere occurs in the hymn. Hence it could be said that these two verses balance each other. The first sows the seed of the motif, while this one actually indicates the harvest! A point that is worth noting here is, that the bulls of Pramara are two (*etau me gāvau pramarasya yuktau*). We have already noted that the seer refers to the two "having strainers" (v.17). Just later in the hymn we have the "two that carry or hold the nourishing water" (v.23 *dvā bṛbūkam vahataḥ purīṣam*). The seer seems, thus, to harp on the idea of "two", and he has a definite concept about them. Earlier he speaks of the one "*yukta*" employing the non-*yukta* (v.9) which, probably, indicates that the sacrificer (*yukta*) would successfully usher in the non-*yukta* (not yet favouring) Marka. Apart from whether the "two" are the sun and Vāyu, or the sacrificer and the sun, the expression indicates the success of the seer's hymn and the ritual accompanying it; for in the very next line the advent of the waters is mentioned (*apaś cid asya vi naśantyartham*).[46] What follows has clear reference to rain.

The thunderbolt is said to turn below the nourishing waters of the sun. This also supports the concept of the previous verse, where the sun (*sūraḥ*) is said to have become the "*upara*". The turning thunderbolt is the symbol of rain-gain; and the same idea is seen in the hymn of Kaṇva, where the *vajra* is said to lie in the cosmic waters that are said to nourish it (VIII.100.9). The turning of the thunderbolt below the waters of the sun, with the idea of his becoming *marka* (a word having double meaning:—"purifying" (*marc*) which connects him with the "strainer", and "death" (√*mṛc*), which indicates his defeat as a tormenting *ābhu-*) is clearly suggestive of the earlier declaration "*pra tam kṣiṇām parvate pādagṛhya*". Here the seer speaks of the sustenance (*śravaḥ*) beyond (the sun), an idea that obtains elsewhere (cf. 31.8, where verse 9 compares with v.13d from our hymn; cf. I. 64.17; 18;—43 all from the "*asya vāmīya*"; cf. also X.82.5; —125.8) and is culminated in the concept of the Indu *drapsa*—the source of all visible nourishing fluids.[47]

In the next verse Vasukra presents a complex image. He speaks of "the bellowing 'cow' that is fixed on every tree" (22a), "the man-eating (?) birds" that shoot from it (b); the fear of the world and the pressing of Soma for Indra, which is clearly a ritual-reference. Now, which is the Cow that bellows? This expression has been generally (and unjustly!) taken to convey the idea of a "bowstring twanging on the bow". The word *vṛkṣa* has been understood as the "bow prepared from the *vṛkṣa*" (by the maxim "*taddhitena kṛtsna-van nigama*" Yāska, Nirukta II.2); so is the case with the "cow", understood as the "bow-string prepared from the tendon of the cow". This is perfect as far as the word-formation is concerned. But the question is—what has the bow to do with the image of the streams of water that precedes and follows?—unless, of course, the bow is understood as the curling lightning..! And might it be that Vasukra intends the birds to be the shafts of the striking lightning that "kill men" (*puruṣādaḥ*)? Vasukra, without doubt, has a curve of smile on his lips, and a lining of art to his trance (!). He follows the general images, as we have compared; but here he has his own! The word "*puruṣādaḥ*" is deceptive; and Vasukra follows his earlier pattern in "*adaḥ*" (*yavasa-adaḥ; yava-adaḥ*, v. 9). The "birds" are not "the eaters of men", but, doubtlessly, "whom men eat" and subsist on (*puruṣaiḥ adyante*). The seer has used the image of the "kṛntatra" (cutting) in the context of the *bṛbūka-purīṣa*, which is the sustaining water, in the next verse. He uses the same image of cutting the forests (*vana*, a word indicative both of water and forest) (X.28.8) in the context of the shattering of Vṛtra (*ibid*., v. 7), which leaves no doubt about the context being of the gain of waters. The tree-image in the present context, then, is for the cloud. "*vṛkṣe vṛkṣe*" (on every tree), thus, means, "on every cloud that is to be cut" (cf. *kṛntatra* in the verse that follows; *vṛkṣa* fr. √*vṛsc*, "to cut". The cow is familiar to us. It is the thunder (cf. the "*asya vāmīya*" 28; 29; 41). The "birds"[48] that are described as "*puruṣādaḥ*", we have examined. We may add that the seer still has in view the "*purīṣa*" in the preceding verse; for in the next verse also he employs the word. It is not improbable that even in "*puruṣādaḥ*", he has in mind "*purīṣa-adaḥ*", which would mean "subsisting on the *purīṣa*" (in line with the *madhvadaḥ* birds from the "*asya vāmīya*", I.164.22). It is to be noted that the word is *vayaḥ* which really means "flying" (√*vi*). These "flying ones" are to be compared with the thundering cow and the clouds that are said to be *vṛkṣa* (etymologically, *vṛścyante iti*-"that are to be cut"; *vṛśc*). They are, thus, the showers "flying" from the cloud-tree, as the "cow" thunders. They are "subsisting on the waters" (*purīṣa-adaḥ* > *puruṣa* (!) *adaḥ*) or "sustaining the mortals". Hence the clouds were the first to receive the respect; and from their cutting came the "*upara*-s" (the above-ones i.e. waters).[49] The three (Agni, Sūrya, and Vāyu) heat the earth, but out of these three, two (Sūrya and Vāyu) hold and carry the waters from the upper region to the earth. They, indeed, are the "Two Bulls" yoked by Pramara. The hymn ends with the concept of the *Vṛṣabha-dhenu*,[50] the primeval sustaining male-female principle in one wherein cosmic union generates the *retas* that is rain, a concept that is quite common in the Ṛgveda. This twin principle is referred to in "she is your life-sap" (*sā te jīvātuḥ*, v.24a); and the male principle is referred to in "know of him" (*uta tasya viddhi*, *ibid.,* b). He is the highest step (*pādu*) as the resort of waters. This cosmic relationship of He and She (Bull-Cow in certain places) gives support to the element of sex; for the gain of rain is a cosmic sex-act, which warrants a ritual of a similar nature in which sex is present—verbal or actual! This is the vision of Vasukra; and in it are the various phases of the then current beliefs mixed.

To sum up. The hymn of Vasukra presents some symbols, which, if not understood, are apt to make the hymn obscure. These symbols are common at other places in the Ṛgveda where the motif is similar. Only at a few places Vasukra has his own symbolic expression, but that could be understood in the context of the general style of the Ṛgvedic passages under similar contexts. The context in these cases is the gain or rain, which is the kernel of the hymn, and is clearly referred to in the concluding verses. The gain of rain has been believed to be a cosmic sex-act in one phase; and, hence, the element of sex gets introduced in such hymns. Here the point is present in the "blind daughter"[51] and the reference to the gain of the "friend" by the maiden, as we have noted. The woman has two aspects in this hymn. As the "females of the fiend" (the rays of the terrible and tormenting sun) she comes as the fighting counterpart of Indra, while, in the ritual contexts she proves a sex-charm for the formation of the *garbha* in the mid-region, so as to facilitate the advent of rain. The formation of this cosmic *garbha* depends on the terrestrial rituals which also give the necessary strength to Indra to accomplish the gain. The sex-references in this hymn where the "daughter" is mentioned seem also to be due to a perfect plan, where the "daughter" represents the earth, a motif obtainable in the incest of the "father" (I.71.5; X.61.6-10). The vision of Vasukra, where he actually uses the words "I saw" (*apaśyam*), and at other places, does not seem to be anything special; it follows a definite pattern as is seen at the "*asya vāmīya*" and at other places in the Ṛgveda where the seer appears to be in trance. The vision, then, is a methodical one; in other words it is inherent in the ritual and the *mantra*-s that have a definite aim. The pattern of symbols used by Vasukra can be charted down as follows:-

HEAVENLY PLANE

SUN...

(A) Good and beneficial aspect

(i) Sucks up the earthly juices and stores them to give back.
(ii) Subsists on the sacrifice; is *Kapila.*
(iii) The Courser, without foliage and shade.
(iv) The "one with the strainer" (purifies waters; sends as rain).

(B) Tormenting aspect

(i) Śuṣṇa, (Kuyava) has "females" (rays) — as fighters — whom Indra meets in battle.

(C) Varied aspects

(i) Sits in the lap of the '*Ūrdhvā* (Sky-female). Comes upon the "lower one" (earth).. SEX.
(ii) Swallows with "feet" (rays); eats the *pratyañc* (sacrifice and offerings).
(iii) The fat ram, or the Bull that is cooked, conceptually

and ritually.

(iv) One who imprisons or controls the "cows" (*gopā*).

MID-REGION PLANE

(A) The atmospheric fire (lightning)

(i) Eats the "mothers" (waters), as the sacrificial fire licks/or eats his parents (the churning woods).

(ii) Child of the "Lower mother" (earth), being kindled in the sacrifice; child of the "upper mother" (mid-region), born on the earth (in the sacrifice) ascends to the mid-region.

(iii) Fostered by the "step-mother" (the mid-region), who thunders; her udder not visible to human eye; the wise know.

(iv) *Kapila*.

(B) Clouds

Wheel-less sustenance; the "Cow" that licks the child (fire in the lightning); "birds"; "*śiśnā*-s"; the thundering cows, the fat ram or the Bull; "*sthivi*" (corn-measure, or bag).

TERRESTRIAL SACRIFICIAL PLANE

(i) Offerings that sustain Indra.

(ii) Sex-"Blind" daughter (!); the concept of ritual "friend".

(iii) Bull cooking — as a sympathetic charm.

NOTES

1. Schroeder, L.Von, *Mysterium and Mimus im Ṛgveda*, p. 344ff; Oldenberg, *Noten,* Pischel and Geldner, *Vedische Studien*, etc.
2. The word *āśira* means "offerings" here; according to Sāyaṇa it has been associated with Soma I.23.1; VIII.95.7; it also indicates "the fruit" of the sacrifice X.128.3; and it also

indicates milk.

3. According to Sāyaṇa the leaves of the Soma-creeper grow, with the addition of one each day, in the bright half of the month and drop off in the dark half. Hence Soma is called "*pañcadaśa*".
4. Geldner differentiates as the "drinker of Soma" who is Indra, and the non-Indras who do not drink Soma, but milk.
5. The word *meni* is solitary; Oldenberg "Rache" (revenge); Geldner "zorn" (anger); does it indicate responsibility? √*man* > *meni*? = constant thinking? Sāyaṇa, "*vajra*". See note 51 below.
6. The *arvā* had been a difficulty. Oldenberg and Geldner take it to indicate "tree"; Oldenberg tries to connect it with '*mātā*' (Mutter) in the next hemistich and fails to see through the connection. Ludwig understands it as *arvāk* changed to *arvā* (?), or straight as *arvāk*. He is the "horse", a known symbol for the sun.
7. Cf. the concept of Nābhānediṣṭha; Dange, *Vedic Concept of 'Field' and Divine Fructification,* (pp.123 ff); also Vāj. Sam. VIII. 10, and RV. X. 183.3 etc.
8. *Ibid.*, pp.108ff.
9. The word *vṛjana* has been understood variously; Sāyaṇa, "*saṅgrāma*"; Geldner for, *ajñāteṣu vṛjaneṣu*, "Fremde aufhielt"; see *Vedic Index*. For the belief that offerings sustain the god—RV. VII.19.11; cf. The Zend Avesta SBE, Vol. 4, p.lxviii.
10. Śat. Br.I.6.3. 6ff; (Kaṇva, II.6.1.5).
11. RV. I.57.2;—32.2a; the Sarasvatī comes from the great heavenly *parvata* V.43.11; at some places the defeat of Vṛtra is accomplished on the earth also, cf. I.80.4.
12. The expression *madhva ūrmiḥ* is associated with all the three; on this point see Dange, *Vedic Concept of 'Field' and the Divine Fructification*, pp. 200ff.
13. *Ibid.*, pp.123ff.
14. He is said to be the sun, the god of rain, and the god of generation; See Macdonell, *Vedic Mythology*, under Tvaṣṭṛ.
15. Cf. Śuṣṇa, who is the demoniac aspect of the sun, whose other aspect is good.
16. Cf. such expressions as *bahave janāya* (X.102.8) etc.
17. X.106.4; there is another reference to the word *kiraṇa* in the dual; but the meaning has indication of sex. RV. Khila V.21. See "Kuntāpa Hymns", Ch.26, *infra*.

18. IV.30.5; 6; and *ibid.,* 8 where Indra is said to have killed the cruel woman (Uṣas acc. to Sāyaṇa); cf. the women Vasukra refers to X.27.10; IV.28.2.
19. "Aspects of War", Ch.13, *infra.*
20. Actually √*kṣad* seems to be formed from the roots √*ghas* and √*ad.* See Dange, "Root-germinants in the Sanskrit Language", *Indian Antiquary,* Bombay (Third series) V-i Jan. 1971. In this context a custom of sacrifice in south India may be noted. In this case the male buffalo is offered, and sacrificed to the goddess, by cutting the head of the buffalo. His right foreleg (*bāhu*?) is cut and placed in the mouth of the beast. One wonders if the Vedic seer knew of such a custom as prevalent among the non-Vedic people. In any case, here the description is figurative rather than actual. For the custom see, Henry Whitehead, *Village Gods of South India,* Delhi, 1976 (1921), p.51 and others.
21. See note 14 above.
22. For the motif of fight and the gain of rain, See also Dange, *Pastoral Symbolism from the Ṛgveda,* Poona Uni., 1969, p.15; also, *Vedic Concept of 'Field' and the Divine Fructification,* pp.108-22; 154-89.
23. The '*yava*-eating' comes as a sex-motif in the ritual of the Horse-Sacrifice; Dange, *Field and the Divine Fructification,* p.36, n. 15.
24. Velankar renders this word as to indicate "lying restfully" (Agni, III.55.4 and "lusty" cow. *Ibid.* 57.1, *Ṛgveda Maṇḍala, III,* University of Bombay, 1968).
25. Dange, "Field and the Ritual Husband", in *Vedic Concept of 'Field' and the Divine Fructification.* Thus "*svayam sa mitram vanute*", does not indicate Svayaṁvara (marriage by self-choice).
26. Griffith for *pratyañcam atti,* "He eats the man who meets him"; Ludwig—"the pious, after death go to the sun, and become the sunbeam"! These interpretations are unfounded, as they are not supported by parallels.
27. The *kṣura* actually gets associated with the sun at certain texts. Thus in the Somāharaṇa-account the sun-disc is symbolized as such. Mb. I.33.2 *sa cakram kṣura-paryantamapaśyad amṛtāntike*; Soma was in the golden enclosures, which were *kṣura-pavi* acc. to the Śatapatha Br. III.6.2.9. Soma as the sun-juice is a belief well-attested in the Vedic tradition. See Pischel and Geldner, *Vedische*

Studien, I.181f.

28. See note 6 above. The image is a mixed one. In the sacrifice it shows the fire (*arvā*) darting forth from the wood (*araṇi*), while it is the sun or the lightning fire above.
29. The word is *try'avi* which, according to Sāyaṇa, indicates a calf that is three "lamb-year" old; the duration of the pregnancy in the case of the lamb is six months. Tryavi would also mean the "protector of the three worlds", Velankar, *op.cit.*
30. Geldner compares the saga of the birth of Kapila at Śvet. Upaniṣad, 5.2; Oldenberg, *Noten*, takes it to refer to Agni or Soma churned by ten fingers (*daśānām ekam kapilam*). Geldner-Brahmaṇaspati or Agni.
31. On *vakṣaṇā* see Pischel and Geldner, *Vedische Studien* I, 175-81; the word conveys also the meaning of the womb, √*vah*, to carry, or hold.
32. See Dange, *Pastoral Symbolism from the Ṛgveda,* p. 45f.
33. It formed a part of the Rājasūya and the Agnyādhāna, *Vedic Index* under *akṣa*. The dice are the stars acc. to Ludwig. The motif is seen later in certain Festivals and Vratas, Kane—*Hist. Dharma,* V-i, Poona, 1974, p.25.
34. For the sun as the Bull, IV.3.10, is *pṛśni* (male) V.47.3; VI.56.3.
35. Cf. the concept of the three *gharma*-s VII.33.5; X.114.1 etc.
36. Cf. X.28.8.
37. Cf.III.9.2, where we have the mixed image, *kāyamāno vanā tvam yan mātṝr ajagan apaḥ*; I.54.1 *akrandayo nadyo roruvad vanā*; 5.
38. I.164.1; at certain places *asna* (not *aśna*) occurs as a power that covers the "cows" (waters)—IV.28.5; X.68.8; *aśna* is also the enemy of Indra, II.14.5; —20.5; VI.4.3. This also shows the dualism, *aśna*, in one phase being the all-pervading divine fire (or Vāyu), and, in the other, the "all eater", the enemy of Indra; cf. the discussion on *vṛjinayantam ābhum*.
39. Cf. *pavitra-vantā carataḥ punantā* at X.27.17; also X.31.8.
40. The concept obtains even later; cf. the *pariplava nagara* of the Gandharva Trisīrṣan, Jaiminīya Br. 1.125.
41. Cf.*mānuṣa yuga* II.2.2; I.144.4; V.52.4.
42. Cf. Indra as *kanīna* III.48.1; VIII. 69.14; X.99.10, and is also *vṛṣabha*; the concept may be compared with that of *vṛṣa śiśu* which is the marked epithet of Agni.

43. RV. I.164.49; on the etymology and the meaning of *śaśaya*, see Velankar, *Ṛgveda Maṇḍala III*, Bombay, 1968, p. 133, n.16.
44. Yāska, Sāyaṇa and also others. There is no dispute about this interpretation.
45. Marka is understood by Sāyaṇa as the "purifier" (*marko mārjayitā sarvasya śodhakaḥ*); Oldenberg rightly remarks that Marka here is different from the Marka, who is the priest of the *asura*-s and comes along with Ṣaṇḍa. Taitt. Sam. 6.4.10.1; Śatpatha Br. IV.2.1.4. In the passage "*suraś ca marka uparo babhūvān*", *sūraḥ* is understood as the Genitive by Oldenberg and Geldner (hinter der Sonne). They see Marka as different from Sur (?). The form is, however, the nominative of Sūra; cf. I.34.5 *sūre udite*; I.50.2. *sūrāya*; I.163.2 *sūrāt*. Marka and Sūra are the same but signify different aspects. Oldenberg has no comment on the word Marka; Geldner renders it as "Vernichtung zuruckgeblieben." Oldenberg compares V.31.11 *śuraś cid ratham pūrvam karat uparam*; but even here it could well be the Nominative. Even if Marka signifies the "deadly one", the sense seems to be that even the deadly sun (*marka*) became the "upper" one (cloud, with Sāyaṇa). In the Avesta Marka signifies the evil tormentor.
46. For a similar method we may compare the hymn of Nābhānediṣṭha, where, after sex and other riddles, we have "*apaś ca vipras tarati sva-setuḥ*" (X.61.16). For full discussion, Dange, "Virgin and the Divine Seed-layer" at *Vedic Concept of 'Field' and the Divine Fructification.*
47. *Ibid.*, last ch.
48. According to the Avesta (Vendidad), SBE, Vol. 4 (1965 reprint), p.54, note 2, there is the "Tree of all Seeds" in the mid-region-ocean (Vouru Kaśa). On it there lives the divine bird "sinamru". Whenever he flies off the tree, there *grow* out of it a "thousand boughs". Whenever he alights on it there break a "thousand boughs", the seeds from which are scattered about, and rained down upon the Earth by the star-god Tistar (Tishtrya)-the rain-god (also Bundahis, xxvii; also Fargard xx.4ff). The "thousand boughs" are obviously the shoots of the lightning.
49. We may compare the Hindi word *olen* (hail)-*upara* > *uvara* > *uvala* > *ola* > *olen* (plural); *upara* > *upala* = *stone* = hailstone.

50. Cf. RV III.38.7; X.5.7.
51. The word is *anakṣā*. The surrounding is full of sex. After all; does the word have the sense of *an* + *akṣa* ("without an axel"), axel being intended as a Sex-Symbol? Ritual employment of words warrants this. Thus at the dialogue at the Horse-sacrifice, instead of "*āhanti bhage śapaḥ*," the actual words used are "*āhanti gabhe paso*" (with letters changed in position! Vāj. *Sam*. XXIII.20). In that case the words *anakṣā* and *andhā* are only seemingly similar; really there is only play on words, the inner meaning being-"one having a daughter without axel" (i.e., not yet sexually used), how could he call her "blind"? For he is *Vidvān* and knows what "*anakṣā*" really means!

Chapter 5

THE SON-HUSBAND

One of the most fascinating and equally intriguing concepts of the early Vedic period is that of the son who is himself the Husband of the "Mothers." The deity is the son as it is born from the female, while it is the Male as it impregnates the female. On a larger application of the concept (cosmic as well as terrestrial) the females are the waters in one aspect, while they are the flames of the fire in another. The first is the case where the Male impregnator is the Water-god, while the other is the case where the Male is seen as the Fire-god. The water-god is Apām-napāt, "The foetus-of-waters," while the fire-god is fairly understandable. In the Vedic tradition the god Apām-napāt is completely identified with the fire-god (RV II.35.9-12); and there is mostly agreement among Vedic scholars on this point. Whether Apām-napāt, as he appears in the Vedic context, was originally a pure water-god or he was an aspect of the fire-god, has been already discussed by older scholars in the beginning of the study of the Ṛgveda.[1] The belief that the fire-god is the spirit of the waters obtains in the Ṛgveda where he is called *payasvān* (I.17.23 *payasvān agna ā gahi*); and this belief is corroborated by the myth that the fire-god went away from the gods due to pressure of the load of carrying sacrificial offerings, and hid himself in the waters. This myth is told and retold in the ritual-texts.[2] The same motif obtains in later times where the fire-god is said to have married the rivers.[3] Actually he is the chosen husband of the rivers, according to the accounts from the Purāṇas. In the ritual tradition the husband-wife relationship of the fire and the waters is clear from the establishing of the 'Praṇītā' waters as the wives of the fire-god to be kindled and established in the altar. This is the first and foremost 'couple' (*mithuna*) in the Vedic sacrifice.[4] Yet, the husband of the rivers is not the fire-god in the Ṛgveda; he is Apām-napāt. It is the latter who is termed "*nādyaḥ*" (belonging to the rivers, which word occurs only once in the Ṛgveda II.35.1).

There is no doubt in the assertion of Oldenberg[5] that the Water-god was a separate entity, and later got identified with the fire-god that was believed to be residing in the waters. But, even beyond the separate existence of Apām-napāt one trait of his is to be marked — a fact left unnoticed by most Vedic scholars. Apām-napāt, and also Agni, the fire-god after this identification, is said to possess a double character, which is also uniquely interesting and interestingly baffling for common understanding. He is at once the "seeder" (impregnator) and the child-son of the mother-females. Thus, it is said:

> The three goddesses offer him food, him the unshakably strong god. They approach him as they are *kṛtāḥ*; he, the child, sucks their milk, of them who are freshly made Mothers (RV II.35.5).

The word "*kṛtāḥ*" has been variously rendered, as "wet nurses," "those who had sexual union" and so on. However, the point, that the god is both the impregnator and the child that sucks them, whom he makes mothers, is clear. The point is further stressed, when it is said that,

> He, indeed, is the "seeder" — bull; he generated the foetus in them. He, indeed, is the new-born son; he sucks; they lick him (*ib.*, 13, mark *sa īm vṛṣā-janayat tāsu garbhaṃ; sa īm śiśur dhayati tam rihanti*).

The poet works on a fond image from agriculture life, making the god the "Bull" of the 'cows' (=water) and also the calf whom the 'cows' lick. The god (Apām-napāt) is fixed in the mind of the Vedic seers as the lord of the waters, as is clear from another context, where the seer-poet is Kavaṣa Ailūṣa (X.30); at the place noted above the poet is Gṛtsamada. Kavaṣa's charm to cause floods in the river Sarasvatī at the time of drought is famous, where he visualizes the god as sporting with the water-females (*ib.*, 5), as does the god Soma. It is the imagery of sexual union of this god (and also of Soma) with the cosmic waters that forms the basis of the floods, indicating that the female watery spirits "deliver" the nourishing and fertilizing waters. But, here the water-god is identified with Soma, another important god in the Vedic pantheon. This is a further step.

One more point to be noted here is that Apām-napāt is localised in the Sarasvatī, actually. Though the earlier seer does not clarify this localization, there is no doubt about it; for, a regular sacrifice to Apām-napāt came to be accomplished yearly at the bank of the Sarasvatī, or, to be exact, at the confluence of the Sarasvatī and the Dṛṣadvatī.[6] His localization in the Sarasvatī renders possible a shift in his name; for, this way, he is termed Sarasvant (Sarasvān) by Vasiṣṭha (RV VII. 95). It may be of some interest to know that Vasiṣṭha praises this new god Sarasvant with the same attributes that are characteristic of Apām-napāt, and yet nowhere calls him by the name Apām-napāt though the latter god is known to him; he refers to Apām-napāt, elsewhere only in a casual way (RV VII.35.3; 47.2) as the conventional lord of the waters. He describes Sarasvant as follows: "He, the virile one, grew strong among the females — he who is the "seeding Bull" and "the child-son" (RV VII.95.3 *sa vāvṛdhe naryo yoṣaṇāsu, vṛṣā śiśur vṛṣabho yajñiyāsu*). The concept of the Son-Husband in one is the same. But, here, one more trait has been added. Sarasvant has also his 'breast' (*stana*, *ib.*, 96.6), indicating that he is a bisexual deity. At another place the Sarasvatī, who is the supreme river-goddess of the early Vedic pantheon, is characterised by a *stana* (RV I.164.49). In later mythology, Sarasvant is said to be the son of the Sarasvatī from Dadhīca, where he is called Sārasvata. It is said that Dadhīca practised penance on the bank of the Sarasvatī. When Indra sent a nymph named Alambuṣā to disturb him, the sage emitted semen which fell in the waters of the river, where it turned into a foetus. The son born from it was Sārasvata, the mythical ancestor of the Sārasvata clan (Mahābhārata, Śalya, 51-5.21). He is also said to be the son born to the Sarasvatī from Purūravas (Brahma P.101.9ff). These later accounts do not revert to the older version of making the son again the husband; for, here a real mortal comes in the picture as the "seeder." Again though Vasiṣṭha sees in the Sarasvatī her male spirit also, making him the bisexual god, the latter is not her child. This means that the image of the Son-Husband got diluted in the later period. A closer look at the references to Apām-napāt reveals that, though the god is known in the Vedic pantheon, it is only the seer Gṛtsamada of the older Ṛgveda who refers to the Son-Husband motif about this water-god, while Vasiṣṭha, also of the older tradition, transfers the image to the new god Sarasvant, whereafter the image loses trail. If we remember that Apām-napāt is the god of the Indo-Iranian period,[7] it becomes clear that into the Indian field he came, but lost foothold.

It is to be noted that the concept of a male river-god is generally absent in the Vedic and later Hindu pantheon.

We have noted above that the great water-god is believed to be both a male spirit and the female, as is indicated in the image of Sarasvatī-Sarasvant. Also we have noted that he is the Son-husband of the waters. Both these traits are very ancient and are not restricted to the Vedic belief. As on the Indian side we have Brahmā who is the androgen, being a combination of a male and a female, the latter produced from himself as his daughter, or as Śiva is the Ardhanārīśvara ("Half-woman-god"), or as Viṣṇu is the woman in relation to Siva[8] and also in the episode of the churning of the ocean where "she" distributes the divine elixir to the gods, in the aspect of Mohinī, we have the Lybian Neith and the ancient Egyptian Isis. Neith is the mother-goddess, who is also known as androgen; and Isis, the female, has also the beard indicating her male-hood. The Persian Mithra was a goddess and god in one; and Herodotus appears to know Mithra only as a female deity. This deity was known, according to him, to the Assyrians as Mylitta and was a goddess.[9] In the Vedic ritual-belief Varuṇa, the older male god and lord of cosmic order, is virtually the female who takes in the semen from Mitra, the solar male deity.[10] The ancient Persians had the goddess Urania, who can well be compared with the Vedic Varuṇa in his aspect noted above. The typical concept of the bisexual deity is the result of the ancients to solve the mystery of creation through a compact male-female unit. A further stage in this ancient philosophy (which may be termed proto-philosophy) is the concept of the Son-Husband in one.

The Son-Husband motif has to be understood in a wider context, than the Ṛgvedic itself, before we take examples from elsewhere. The Ṛgvedic seers' attitude to bestow all epithets upon a particular god while invoking him, a method named Henotheism by Max Müller, is based on the belief that all gods are ultimately in the One; hence all epithets are in One. There is already an indication of this trait in the hymns of the Ṛgveda (cf. I.164.46 *ekam sad viprā bahudhā vadanti*; also III.55.1-22d from the new and the old portions respectively). The statements of interchangeable relationships where the same deity is the sister and the wife or mother (for example between the sun and the dawn-goddess) of a god, or the concept of the gods being born of each other (as is the case in the Purāṇas, where Śiva is born of Brahmā and *vice versa*)[11] are instances of this ancient belief of ultimate Oneness, even leaving room for cultish superiority. Hence the daughter could be termed also sexual partner (cf. Prajāpati and his daughter; later Brahmā-Gāyatrī, Sarasvatī etc.). Conversely, the son and the husband are on par. But, care has to be taken not to misunderstand these ideas as indicative of a real social structure; for, that would be a presentation of ignorance. These seemingly curious relationships are true only as an explanation to solve the mystery of creation; in other words, they are true only in myth, and also in ritual where the myth is enacted for aiding creation or procreation and fertility.[12] This motif is seen elsewhere, as noted above, where the principle of "All-into-One" and "One-in-all" is seen.[13] Thus, the Cretan god was the son of the Great Mother and also her Husband. The Assyrian Tamuz was the son and spouse of the goddess Ishtar. The Greek Adonis was the son and lover of Aphrodite; and we may compare the case of Oedipus who had to espouse his own mother. The ancient Egyptian Osiris was the son of Isis (and also of Nepthys) and also her husband.[14] The concept of the husband being born as the son is only another, and a refined, aspect of the same motif.[15] However, the earliest experience for the Son-Husband motif has to be understood as being from the agricultural context. The seed goes into the Mother Earth; it makes 'her' pregnant. It is 'born' from her; it is the son. In appearance it is the same. Hence, the simple, and yet perfectly true, equation for the ancient thinker is that the same seed is the impregnator. It is this twofold nature of the seed that enters the mythical realm as the wonderful divinity. The next step is to connect the motif with all spheres that answer procreation or abundance. When more water is required, a deity with this dual nature is associated with it. This is exactly the case with Apām-napāt. As a next step, the motif comes to be connected with the Vedic cult of fire, who, with its constant association with its flames, cannot be thought of as separate from them. The sacrificial fire, the very spirit of the Vedic sacrifice, is more important than the abstract godheads. It is he that brings prosperity, through rain, by being propitiated. Hence he is associated with the dual motif. And He became the Son-Husband in relation to the flames, as was Apām-napāt, in relation to the waters, the Son-Husband.

NOTES

1. See A.A. Macdonell, *Vedic Mythology* under Apām-napāt, last paragraph. See also R.N. Dandekar, *Vedic Mythological Tracts*, Delhi, 1979, his essay on Agni Mythology.
2. For ex. Śat. Br. I.2.3.1ff.
3. Brahma P.144.5 ff; Matsya P.51.11-15 etc. More information is collected by Dange, *Encyclopaedia of Puranic Beliefs and Practices*, Vol. IV, New Delhi, 1989, p.1183, under "Rivers".
4. Śat. Br. I.1.1.18 *yoṣā vā 'po vṛṣā' gniḥ*; for detailed study see Dange, *Sexual Symbolism from the Vedic Ritual*, Delhi, 1979.
5. *Die Religion des Veda*, Berlin, 1894, pp.118-20.
6. Pañcaviṁśa Br.35.10.13-22; also A.B. Keith, *The Rel. and Philosophy of the Veda and Upaniṣhads*, London, 1925, Vol.II, p.352.
7. *The Zend Avesta,* pt.I in SBE, Vol. 4, p. lxiii, n.4; "son of waters" on main page; see also pt. II, p.6, 12,14,20,etc.
8. Kūrma, P. II. 37.9 ff; also Dange, *Towards Understanding Hindu Myths*, p.284ff; also O'Flaherty, W.D., *Sexual Metaphors and Animal Symbols in Indian Mythology*, p. 283ff.
9. Mackenzie, D., *Myths of Crete and Pre-Hellenic Europe*, London (year, not mentioned), p.169.
10. Śat. Br. II,4,4, 9 *mitro varuṇe retaḥ siñcati.*
11. Śiva P.II.9.17; also 56-57. Cf. Aditi and Dakṣa, RV X. 72.4
12. On this see Dange, *Vedic Myths in Social Perspective* (Vishvabandhu Memorial Lectures), Panjab Uni., Hoshiarpur, 1982.
13. D. Mackenzie, *op.cit.*, *loc.cit.*
14. According to a myth, when Osiris is killed and dismembered by the evil Set, Isis tries to search for and collect the various limbs of his body that fell at various places; she found all but his generative organ; Rundle Clark, *Myth and Symbol in Ancient Egypt*, London, 1959, p.105; we might compare the cutting off of Śiva's penis, a populr Puranic myth.
15. Aitareya Br. VII.13=33.1

Chapter 6

THE CRYING WORLDS
(krandasī)

The Ṛgveda mentions two words which are conceptually related to each other, but never come together. They are *krandasī* and *rodasī*. The concept of crying is inherent in both, etymologically; and Sāyaṇa actually connects them at two places while commenting on the word *krandasī*, rendering it as *rodasī* (II.12.8, *krandasī rodasī śabdam kurvāṇe*) at one place, and giving the general meaning of the word *rodasī*, which is Heaven-and-Earth at another, explaining that the heaven and earth are called *rodasī* as they are associated with the crying (weeping) of Prajāpati when he found himself alone in the primeval waters (on RV, X.121.6). He quotes the passage from the Taitt. Br. (II.2.9.4) to the effect that Prajāpati wept in the space that stands as the void between heaven and earth (*kranditavān roditavān anayoḥ prajāpatir iti krandasī dyāvāpṛthivyau*). At the other two places where the word *krandasī* occurs (VI. 25.4; X.38.1; at the latter place it is not *krandasī*, dual, but *krandasi*, loc. sing.), though the reference to heaven and earth is not present the idea of tumult or noise is clear (fr. √*krand*). At certain other places, the word *rodasī* is understood as 'the wife of Rudra' in spite of the dual in the *padapāṭha* (cf. V.46.8; *rodasī* at I.167.5 and V.56.8 with a different accent should be left out in this discussion), which does not seem to be right. The combined concept of the words *rodasī* and *krandasī*, indicating the two worlds, needs more consideration than it has received so far from scholars.

(i) RV X.121.6

Yam krandasī avasā tastabhāne
abhyaikṣetām manasā rejamāne
yatrādhi sūra udito vibhāti
kasmai devāya haviṣā vidhema

Here the *krandasī* are obviously the heaven and the earth; and there are no two opinions about it among scholars. The image of the seer in this verse is of the two worlds being held at their respective places, for their protection, or for the protection of the creatures, as Sāyaṇa understands. But they are said to be trembling (*rejamāne*). Sāyaṇa and Mahīdhara (on Vāj. Sam. XXXII.7) understand it to mean "shining"; but that cannot be accepted. The exploit of separating and supporting heaven and earth, after they are thus separated, is common to certain other gods also. Thus Indra is said to accomplish it (II.12.2: *yo antarikṣam vi mame varīyaḥ, yo dyām astabhnāt*); so does Viṣṇu (I.154.1bc) and also Mitra (III.59.1b). The exploit of separating the heaven and earth has to be understood together with the fear in these primordial parents (cf.II.12.1c *yasya śuṣmād rodasī abhyasetām*), and their resultant cry of despair at being away from each other. This cry is hinted at in the word *krandasī*. Though the word *krandasī* is not associated with heaven and earth, indicated by the word *rodasī* in the RV, the AV (IV.2.3 ab) has the word *rodasī* in this same verse recorded with a slight change;

yam krandasī avataś caṣkabhāne.
bhiyasāne rodasī ahvayethām

where the image of the heaven and the earth getting terrified and afraid (*bhiyasāne*) at their being separated and held apart is clear.[1] There also the hymn has Prajāpati as the deity as in RV. Apart from who is the deity of this exploit, it has to be noted that it hints at the belief pertaining to creation; and, in this act of creation, the separation of the two worlds forms the most primordial motif. Before we examine other parallels of the exploit, it is necessary to point out that *krandasī* in the original image indicated the two worlds, groaning at their separation, and that *krandasī* can be nothing other than the *rodasī*, which also has the concept of crying or making noise (√*rud*). The same is the case with other references of the word, *krandasi* or *krandasī*, where the seers mix it up with the description of two tumultuous armies. Let us examine.

(ii) RV. II 12.8

Yam krandasī sam-yatī vihvayete
pare'vara ubhayā amitrāḥ.
samānam cid ratham ā tasthivāṁsā
nānā havete sa janāsa indraḥ

(AV XX.34.8)

Here, commenting on the word *krandasī*, Sāyaṇa understands it as *rodasī*, and yet explains the image as that of two armies closing in and clashing with each other (*sam-yatī*); and, not being able to comprehend which these two armies are, he says that they are the human and the divine. Almost all translators of the Ṛgveda[2] betray their confusion here, as they take the two here as two armies. But the point is, why should the seer feel it necessary to refer to the mutual enemies (*ubhayā amitrāḥ* in the plural), again, when he has already referred to the two enemies in the first half (*krandasī sam-yatī*)? Obviously, the translators are as confused as the commentator who brings in the image of the *rodasī* due to his traditional training and yet strays away; this is, obviously, due to the reference to the enemies (*amitrāḥ*) in the latter half. But, now, they find it difficult to coordinate the dual of the first half in (*krandasī sam-yatī*) with the plural of the next half (*amitrāḥ*). The fact is that in *krandasī sam-yatī* the seer ushers in the traditional concept of the crying worlds, and in the rest of the verse he brings in the image of the warriors of the opposite sides calling upon Indra for help. The common factor is the cry. In the first image, it is the cry of the worlds, being stretched in the opposite directions — the heaven or the sky upwards and the earth downwards.

The method is not uncommon to the seers; for, often, the terrestrial activity is mixed with the cosmic one, the latter being described first as a base to the terrestrial one.[3] A very important point in the present context is that the epithet *sam-yatī* never indicates a conflict in the language of RV. This will be clear from the fact that the epithet comes elsewhere for the day-and-night (V.38.5 b *ubhe vṛtau sam-yatī*) and for the heaven-and-earth in a similar exploit of Soma (IX.68.3 *vi yo mame yamyā sam-yatī*). The image of the worlds being called *sam-yatī* has to be understood along with their being *yamyā* (the joined up twins), which is about the same as *vṛtau*. Gift is *saṁyadvīrā* (RV, II.4.8), which goes against the idea of clashing. The concept is that of the two worlds joined up in a unit, in a close clasp; and when, at the beginning of creation, they are sought to be separated, as the first ever signal of creation, they are believed to groan or grumble, and invoke Indra, being disturbed in their clasp. The idea is carried in the words *vihvayetām* (RV) and *ahvayetām* (AV) noted above. An important point that deserves to be noted in the connection is that the implied clasp of the worlds prior to their separation is attested by a regular myth in the other Vedic texts. Thus, it is said that "the worlds were joined up; they languished" and that Indra removed their langour by means of the laud called *Traiśoka* (Pañcaviṁśa Br., VIII.1.9). This is rubricating an already existing myth into ritual-context as an *arthavāda* (a statement of praise or censure in respect of a particular act in ritual). Here the purpose is to praise the laud. The clasp of the worlds is mentioned in other places also (Jaim. Br., III.72 *ime vai lokāḥ saha āsan*, where the three worlds are indicated, including the mid-region). The Śat.Br. (I.4.1.22), which states that all the three worlds were close together, mentions that heaven was so near that it could be touched (*unmṛśya haiva dyaur āsa*); and it employs the myth in the praise of a verse from the Ṛgveda, wherein the word *vītaye* occurs, stating that it is because of the utterance of the word *vītaye* that the worlds got separated[4] (also cf.

Taitt. Br. I.1.3.2: *dyāvāpṛthivyau sahāstām*).

It will be clear from what has been said above that the word *krandasī* never has any other connotation than that of the two worlds in the two passages from RV and AV examined above. In one passage (RV VI. 25.4) *krandasī* has no direct connection with the cosmic activity of Indra; but the two worlds (*krandasī*) are invoked to bless the sacrificer in his desire for the gain of various things including sons, water (i.e. timely rain), ploughable field and cows. This indicates that the *krandasī* are elevated from their dependent status to that of minor deities. But, here also there is no connotation of war. At the last place (X 38.1) *krandasi* is clear locative of the word *krandas*; but it is an adjective of another word meaning "battle", *pṛtsuti* (the form in locative, *pṛtsutau*), and indicates tumult or cry that marks a battle.

We have seen that in the words *krandasī* and *rodasī* there is the reflection of the belief in the worlds being closed in a clasp, and that they are separated. The two worlds, as indicated by these words, appear to be both females. But the evidence of the occurrences of the word *rodasī* shows that the word has in it the concept of the male implied. The same appears to be the case with the word *krandasī*. Both indicate the primordial couple in one mass without distinction or clarity of form. It is the separation that gives them a distinct form; and this separation marks a distinct duality that is necessary for further creation. In the Vedic ritual texts, the separated worlds are again sought to be brought together by a ritual, so that they should sexually unite for the creation of rain.[5] Thus, there are three distinct stages: 1. No separate identity, the worlds being in a mass; 2. Separation of the worlds, that marks the beginning of creation and 3. Re-union of the worlds, Male and Female — Heaven and Earth, for the gain of rain. The last stage is marked by the ritual-marriage of the worlds.[6]

It is to be noted that the separation motif is not unique to the Vedic mythology. It obtains elsewhere and at various strata of society — from the ancient sophisticated Egyptians to the tribal Maoris and the rustic Indian villagers. According to the ancient Egyptian belief, Shu, the god of the first light/air, gave birth to two children: Nut (the Sky-female) and Geb (the Earth-male; also pronounced as Seb). The children lay in a close embrace, and the father Shu felt jealous. He separated them, lifting Nut with his hands. Being separated, the two meet only at their feet and hands, in a face-to-face lying posture. The concept behind the myth is that when the light-principle is dormant, everything is in a mass undistinguished; but the moment the light-principle is expressed it marks the difference between the two worlds and gives rise to space.[7] In the Vedic context, the myth is only half-developed and ends at the exploit of separation. Its latter part, the clear image of the ray shooting up forth from the mass of moist darkness is recorded in another mythical hymn (X. 129; cf. 3 and 5), where the upright ray of light brings in the concept of 'the one below' and 'the one above' (*adhaḥ* and *upari*). According to the Maori belief, the two parents — Heaven and Earth — were in a close clasp; and children got created. But, then, a time came when the children got suffocated for want of room; and they decided to separate the parents. At a council of the children, the Forest-god (the Tree-god) decided to take up the responsibility. He fixed his head on the chest of the Mother (Earth) and, with his feet pushed up the Father (Sky). He stands thus for ever, lest the parents should again close in. It is also said that the Father occasionally sheds tears due to the grief of separation; and they become morning dew or drops of rain![8] Here, the separating god is not the god of light, but the Tree-god, suggested from the visual experience of the tree standing in between the sky and the earth, and due, probably, to the denseness of the forest the light being less striking. But, the quest for the beginning of creation is clear; and the answer is the same — the separation! Like the Vedic 'parents' the Maori myth has the Mother below and the Father up; their position in the Egyptian myth is reversed due to other factors.[9] Near home, there is a story current among the villagers in the Vidarbha region of Maharashtra that formerly the sky was very close to the earth; and it actually touched the roof of the hut of the primeval Old Woman (who, like Indra or the prime Hero, must always precede the cosmic act of creation!). Once she got angry as she could not have sufficient room for her movements, and hit the sky with her broomstick. Instantly the sky went up and stands there permanently. Now, let us take an ancient Japanese belief. According to it, the Old Heaven and Earth were not yet separated; likewise the YIN and YO[10] were also not separated. They formed the chaotic mass like that of an egg. When separated, the purer part went up and became the sky; the soild one remained below and became the earth.

It will be noted that the separation motif cannot be isolated from the general concept of creation, wherein the widening of the space between the two worlds forms an important link. Likewise, the Vedic exploit of the separation of the worlds has to be understood in the context of the wider implication thereof, as it obtains in other thoughts. It hints at the primeval image of creation that throbbed in the human mind, irrespective of the tribe to which the humans belong. In conceptual development, it appears, the separation of the *krandasī* or the *rodasī* is only a forerunner of the cosmic egg which is said to break into two, the upper half becoming the sky and the lower one the earth. The myth of the *krandasī* has to be taken as the first step in the proto-philosophical myths of creation. The mention of the sunrise in the exploit (X.121.6c noted above) indicates the advent of the first streak of light, as a result of which the worlds are seen to be separated.

NOTES

1. At the verse in AV the *krandasī* and the *rodasī* are associated with two different actions; but they need not be taken as mutually different, in view of the traditional identification.
2. K.F. Geldner, *Der Rigveda*, I, Leipzig, 1951, p.290; H.D.

Velankar, "the two shouting (armies) arrayed for battle, both enemies" (brackets are his), at *Ṛgveda Maṇḍala* II, Bombay Uni., 1966, p.34; he takes *sam-yatī*, like Geldner, to mean "clashing together." At his subsequent translation, *Ṛksūktaśatī*, Bombay, 1972, we read, "the shouting armies which clash together as also the mutual enemies:" but see his notes to RV., X. 121.6; Ram Gopal mentions the various opinions, without adding his own; *Ṛgveda Vyākhyā Vivecana*, Delhi, 1979, pp.96f. and pp.230f.

3. Cf. VII. 83, where the exploits of Indra precede the actual description of the battle; such is the case also at other places.
4. The verse is RV VI. 16.10; *vītaye* is understood here as *vi(viruddham)* + *iti*, indicating separation, by the ritual thinker on the basis of sympathetic magic.
5. As noted in earlier chapters, the creation of rain has often the imagery of a sex-act in the Veda; see also Dange, *Sexual Symbolism from the Vedic Ritual*, chapter on "Cosmo-sexualism."
6. *Ibid.*, chapter on "The Marriage of Heaven and Earth." The ritual texts shift the original image to the marriage between the Sāmans (lauds), Rathantara and Bṛhat. For Dange's reply to the objection by Bodewitz regarding this contention, see *Towards Understanding Hindu Myths*, p.32, n. 14.
7. Rundle Clark, *Myth and Symbol in Ancient Egypt,* London, 1959, p.45; Shu is also the Eternal One in the Old and Middle Kingdom; in a later phase Shu is said to be helped by the spirits of the Wind-god, p.48.
8. George Grey, "The Creation according to the Maori", in A.L. Croeber and Waterman, T.T.; *Source-book in Anthropology*, New York, 1931, p.444 ff. A fuller study of Separation-myths is done by A. Seidenberg, "The Separation of the Sky and the Earth", *Folk-lore*, 1959, Vol.70, pp. 477-82.
9. Actually the sky is the Cow called Hathor with her belly studded with stars; it is always feminine; Rundle Clark, *op.cit.*, p.87 ff.
10. Mackenzie, D., *Myths of China and Japan*, London, p.348; this is from the translation of a passage from *Nihongi*, as translated by Aston, according to Mackenzie. YIN and YO correspond to the Chinese primordial principles of YANG and YIN, the passive and the active. Later they came to be distinguished as Izanagi (the Male who invites) and Izanami (the Female who invites), p.347.

Chapter 7

THE ADVENT OF SOMA

Much has been said about the Vedic Soma. Well known is also the controversy on the point whether Soma was identified with the moon even at the Vedic times. Hillebrandt went so far as to say that all the Soma-hymns of the Maṇḍala IX, and a few from other *maṇḍalas* are addressed to the moon-god.[1] The myth of the bringing of Soma from heaven by a divine falcon, has also been interpreted variously, the notable interpretation being of Bloomfield who sees in it the bringing of rain from the clouds (= the iron-fort) along with the flash of lightning.[2] Not accepting this hypothesis, Oldenberg points out that there is no positive proof to see any physical phenomena in the 'bird' that brings soma.[3] It has been shown that this myth of 'a bird bringing divine drink' obtains in other mythologies also.[4] On examining the material available to him Macdonell concluded that the idea of the 'sweet drink' was a creation of the Indo-European period and that, in India, it gave rise to the idea of Soma, as in Greece to 'mead'. Oldenberg seems to be quite right in pointing out that the physical (or natural, we may say) phenomenon is not warranted. Taking into consideration the existence of the myth in other mythologies the 'natural' method of interpretation would not be well applicable here. The 'iron-fortress' from which the bird 'Śyena' is said to take away *soma* need not again be the cloud. There seems to be a constant quest for the immortal liquor or the 'water of life' in the mind of the ancient man recorded by various mythologies.[5]

Opinions regarding the identification of the Moon and Soma (the juice) originated from such passages where Soma is said to be married to the Sun's daughter,[6] where Soma is said to be in the midst of stars,[7] and the saying "none eats of the Soma that is known to the Brāhmaṇas", and which is said to be different from the one that is pressed.[8] Here, Soma that is different from the one that is pressed, is believed to be the moon-god by some scholars,[9] while according to one opinion it indicates 'Corporeal' Soma *viz.* the inner physical power which could be utilised for meditation (*samādhi*).[10] It is possible that Soma, when drunk, caused a state of hallucination leading the drinker to fanciful imagination which might have been referred to as another Soma.[11]

Apart from the point of the identity of the twofold Soma, we shall confine ourselves to see if there is a definite scheme in RV about the conception of the advent of Soma, comparing it with a similar conception in other mythologies. Soma is described as '*maujavata*' i.e. growing on the Mūjavat (RV X.34. 1 *somasyeva maujavatasya*). The same is the implication of the expression where he is said to be residing in the mountain.[12] Macdonell says that the word *giri* or *parvata* here refers to the terrestrial mountain. Soma, as we know, is also the '*juice*' of the Soma-plant. Looking to the etymology of the word Soma, it seems to be clear that the name of the plant (Soma) is suggested from the 'juice'; and that the word 'Soma' was applied to the juice primarily and to the plant only secondarily.[13] It should be noted that the word generally used for the juice of the Soma-plant is *indu* or *drapsa* which hits at the original conception of the first oozed out 'drop'.[14] This '*indu*' i.e. the 'drop' is said to be the god.[15] This would mean that the Soma juice at the sacrifice embodies the first drop (*drapsa*) that is divine, which is mystically pressed from the plant which is *hence called* Soma. This *drop*, that is divine, is invoked at the sacrifice with the same honour as other gods. It is this drop that is called *andhas* (nourishing food) and is said to descend from heaven, upon the earth,[16] naturally in the sacrificial Soma-plant on the mountain top.

We now turn to another point in the saga of Soma. Very often Soma is said to be 'milked', connecting it with a cow-symbol. Thus, the shoots of this miraculous plant are said to 'milk' like the udder of a cow.[17] The fountain (*utsa*) of Soma is said to be in the midst of cows.[18] Soma is identified with the cow when it is said to be bound with ten straps (*valgā*). It is said to be a 'milking branch' that is being chewed by the pressing stones.[19] It would, thus, indicate that the divine drop is full of milk and is said to be mystically gathered in a branch, i.e. the Soma plant. To complete the identification of the Soma and the cow, as it were, we have a ritual in the brahmanic sacrifice according to which, in the rite of the purchase of Soma, a cow is to be given as the price of Soma, and the colour of the cow is prescribed to be white or ruddy, because Soma is also of the same colour.[20] It will be interesting to note that the stones that are used to press the shoots of the Soma-plant are laid on the hide of the cow.[21] This indicates that the Soma juice is thought to be the essence from the cow. Connecting this idea with the one where the divine drop or the fountain is said to be in the midst of the (heavenly) cows, we get the conception that the divine drop that lies in the midst of the heavenly cows, is to be mystically gathered in the terrestrial cow.

We have already noted that, while talking about Soma, the Vedic sages have imagined a well or a fountain (*utsa*) of Soma in the midst of the cows(=stars). This fountain (of honey) is also said to be in the highest step of Viṣṇu (RV I.154.5), where there are multi-horned cows.

Which are these cows? Commenting on the passage where the word *bhūriśṛṅgāḥ* (multi-horned) occurs (RV I.154.5), Yāska takes it to mean 'the rays of the sun'.[22] Peterson, following Sāyaṇa, takes it to mean the stars with myriad rays.[23] The fountain (*utsa*) is said to be in the highest place[24] which clearly means the sky, though Sāyaṇa takes it as the sacrificial place. Even if we accept Sāyaṇa's interpretation, it could be so done only secondarily, taking the terrestrial sacrifice to mean the ritualistic representation of the heavenly phenomena on the earth. The gods are said to be born of the cows (*gojātāḥ*).[25] Aditi is called the cow[26] and she is identified with the sky and is said to give milk to the gods.[27] Elsewhere Soma is compared with the milk of Aditi,[28] thus helping their identification. In sacrificial ritual the consecrated cow is said to be Aditi[29] —the very sky-goddess symbolically represented on the earth at the sacrifice. Now, the 'divine fountain', in the midst of the cows, whence *Indu* or the *drapsa* (the divine drop) oozes, can be nothing but the mystic 'well' in the midst of the stars, or in the very lap of the sky-cow, Aditi.[30] Soma that is gathered from the shoots at the sacrifice represents the 'drop' that comes from the divine fountain that lies closely associated with the cow-of-the sky. The descent from heaven of the divine 'drop' is the first stage in the advent of Soma. This 'drop' is fertilizing, generative and invigorating. It is the very life-essence, which has the potentiality to give heavenly life of immortality to those who might taste it. It is represented in the sacrifice by Soma which is a drink of restricted distribution, and is offered very sparingly. Even some of the divinities (like the Aśvinau) have to qualify for its gain zealously.

This reminds one of similar beliefs in the fertilizing 'drop' from heaven or from the stars elsewhere. An emperor of China is said to have constructed a huge and high tower on the top of which he would keep a pot to get the morning dew directly from the stars for gaining long life.[31] From ancient Egypt obtains a belief in the fertilizing ray that oozed from the moon. Osiris, who is said to be the son of the sky-mother (in the form of the cow), is said to have been conceived from the fertilizing ray of light that fell from the moon.[32] According to the Japanese mythology the drinker of the dew of immortality was a moon-girl who drank from the bowl of the moon.[33] The 'drop' (*drapsa*) that is said to descend from heaven, comes very close to the fertilizing ray of the moon or the first dew from the stars, both connected with heaven (or the sky). If the cows with multiple horns are to be taken as rays or stars as we have noted from the authorities, the *drapsa* would mean the first divine drop from the heavenly rays, or from a fountain amidst the stars. This fountain amidst the stars gives out the drop-*indu*. *Indu* seems properly to mean the 'drop' from the moon, which, in later periods, gets to be called both Soma and *indu*. It seems probable, hence (though it may be said that the Ṛgveda does not have a clear identification between the moon and the Soma-juice) that in the Ṛgveda-period itself the conception of a divine drop from the moon was cultivated. This 'drop' from the moon is invoked as the god and is lauded like other gods in the sacrifice. It is the very essence of the moon-god, who is on a different plane from the other gods; for he is 'killed' (pressed. The word used in the context is *ghnanti*) and eaten for nourishment by other gods, and is undying in the real sense of the word. It only changes the form which vanishes to give sustenance to the gods and is reborn (juice-form) in sacrifice, as in the heaven (moon-form), very much like Osiris who gets killed and is brought back to life in the famous Osirian ritualistic drama.[34]

The next point is the absorption of the 'drop' in the plant (called Soma) as it reaches the earth. The plant, as we have noted, is identified with the udder of the cow. Thus the plant oozes from the fountain among the 'cows' in heaven and gets absorbed in another 'cow' (in the form of the plant). This is the second stage in the advent. The 'drop' reaches the mountain, a high place on the earth and, as it were gets changed into the plant.[35] This could be clear from the RV where Soma is addressed as follows:-

> O Soma of divine abode, that art generated high in heaven! of thy juice the earth doth procure.

Further we have,

> "(What) excellent (juice) of thine was procured in the navel of heaven, that same sprouted upon the summit of the earth (the mountain), being sprinkled

thereupon. The pressing stones eat of thee on the hide of the cow. Thee did the wise ones milk with their fingers in the water".[36]

The latter clearly brings out the principle underlying the descent of Soma, as we have already noted.

The close association of the *utsa* (the fountain/well) and the plant that takes the 'drop' from it on the earth is to be noted outside India also. The Chinese 'dragon-well' is usually situated inside a deep mountain-cave. It flows from a cave called 'golden well-spring'.[37] In the Chinese mythical tale of the 'Blue Boy' we have the Blue Boy residing in a well in a high mountain. He darts to heaven from the well and disappears in the clouds that rain heavily to the utter amazement of a certain Wang Shu, who was wandering to obtain the herb of immortality. When the rain subsides, the Blue Boy returns to the well and disappears. Now, on the bank of the mountain well, Wang Shu finds a peculiar herb sprouting out. He takes it away; for it is the herb of immortality.[38] The herb is generated from the drop of the divine cloud, which itself is formed from the divine well high in the mountain. Similarly, in the legend of Gilgamesh we have the 'plant of life', and the 'well of immortality' associated with the adventures of the hero.[39] The 'well of immortality' that sends the 'drop' and sustains the herb of immortality can be seen, in the sacrificial ritual of the Aryans in ancient India, to be represented by the 'Vasatīvarī'—waters, where the pressed out shoots of Soma are placed for getting re-swelled, the indication of which is to be found as early as the RV.[40] Here is a clear indication of the belief in the 'living waters' that are apt to give immortality, and which represent the heavenly *utsa*. Now here is an interesting phenomenon. The 'drop' is restored in the pressed out shoots of the Soma-plant by the '*Vasatīvarī*' *Nigrābhya* waters, and at the same time, by this ritual, the 'drop' of Soma is said to swell the waters. Soma is elsewhere said to be the lord of the waters—both the oceans and streams,[41] both the cosmic waters and the terrestrial ones. The cosmic waters give place to the actual rain drops, and Soma is said to impel rain (RV X.30.9) and cause the waters to expand in the form of rain and the streams on the earth. The heavenly 'drop' that is said to be in the celestial *utsa* (well) in the midst of the cows is represented in the sacrifice by the Soma-juice as going to the tub (*kalaśa*) of Soma which also is called *utsa*.[42] Thus from the divine 'well' to the high peak on the earth and thence to the *utsa* (*kalaśa*) in the sacrifice is the advent of the 'drop'. The whole purpose of the Soma-sacrifice is thus to bring the divine 'drop'—the *indu* which is the essence of the moon or the starry region and is invoked as a divinity — to the sacrifice. When it is symbolically brought forth after the pressing of the Soma-plant, which is gathered from the mountain, the constant flow of life, food and water is ensured-water in rivers, food in the plants and the cows, and continued life in the sacrificer and those who partake of the juice.[43] Hence this divine drop (now Soma-juice) is ritually mixed with water, milk (whence *gavā-śira*) and barley (*yava-śira*) representing prosperity in plants, milk, water, and grain. Milk represents the cows, and Soma-juice (the divine-drop) mixing with milk gives fertility to the cows. Hence this 'drop'-now sacrificial Soma — is described as a youth in the midst of cows.[44] Without the ritual of sacrifice this was not supposed to be accomplished. The 'drop' that is so potential in swelling the earthly flood,[45] and gives immortality, figures prominently, in the Brahmanic tale of '*Somāharaṇa*' (the bringing of Soma), where the Ṛgvedic bird Śyena-Suparṇa gives place to the metres and the *mantra*-s, obviously to *establish the importance* of the sacrificial ritual and the efficacy of the *mantra*-s, thus connecting the myth to the magical symbolism in action. It is here that the myth gets transacted into ritual.[46]

It would be, thus, clear that the 'bringing of Soma' by the Śyena-Suparṇa is only a phase of the general saga of the 'Advent of the divine drop'. Once the conception of the divine drop oozing out from the sky is rooted in imagination, it is natural to have a myth of some powerful personality to get it from such a forbidden place. This personality will naturally be super-human, and more probably, a great bird that could fly aloft right up to the high region on the earth or right into the domain of the sky. As we have seen, rain is only a phase of the 'divine-drop'. In the same way the bird that brings it could only be a mythical bird, and it is not necessary to suppose that the bird is the lightning or any other natural phenomena, as Bloomfield has done. The desire for longevity and immortality in man is great and the myth is the product of that desire. Hence the expression of this desire in a number of folk-tales widely spread in the world. The bringer of this ('drink of) immortality' sometimes is a man, like the Babylonian Gilgamesh or the Chinese Wang Shu or the bird Zu who stole the tablets of immortality,[47] or the Śyena-Suparṇa of the ancient Indian Aryans. It is this conception of a celestial 'drop' or 'divine drink' that could be found in the wide—spread belief in the 'island of the Blessed,' or the 'floating island' where nobody dies—the very 'Svarga' that is known to the Ancient Indians, with its secret of immortality. The secret of the most invigorating 'drop' could naturally be as well guarded as the drink itself. Hence it could be said to be in the very interior of forts which the hero, whosoever he might be, has to destroy. This fort need not be the 'cloud' as the adherents of the Nature-theory would have us believe. The conception of the 'divine-drop' and that of the 'bringer' of it are closely connected. Hence it is usual to find in the tales of the 'cultural hero', the fetching of a plant of life or the water of immortality as one of the exploits, that necessarily gets associated with the killing of the guards and destroying of the 'prison' that holds the 'divine food or drink'.

NOTES

1. A. Hillebrandt, *Vedische Mythologie*, Vol. I, Breslau, p.309.
2. M. Bloomfield, *J.A.O.S.* Vol. XVI, pp.1-24.
3. H. Oldenberg, *Die Religion des Veda*, Berlin, 1894, pp.177,

180. For the oldest account of the bird bringing *Soma* see RV IV, 26 and 27

4. Macdonell, A. A., *Vedic Mythology* (Hindi Tr.), p. 216. Oldenberg, *op.cit.*, p.176.
5. We shall note a few examples further on; see for example the Zu bird from the Babylonian Mythology; Wang Shu from the Chinese Mythology mentioned further on.
6. RV X.85.
7. *Ibid.*, 85.2.
8. *Ibid.*, 3.
9. Cf. Macdonell, *op. cit.*, p.214, also Sāyaṇa on RV. X.85.3.
10. Cf. T.R. Kulkarni in *Proceedings of the Indian Science Congress*-1961, pt. IV, pp.119 to 121.
11. It may also be noted that Soma is said to reside in every part of the body, cf. RV VIII.48.9; but this probably refers to the effect of Soma when actually drunk and not Soma as an inner fluid of the body.
12. RV. IX.46.i. *kṣarantaḥ parvatāvṛdhaḥ*: also-95.4 *amśum duhanti ukṣāṇam giriṣṭhām*'. For the origin of the *Soma* plant see Roth, ZDMG 38, 134-39; Max Müller, *Biographies of words,* London, 1888, pp.222-42.
13. From √*sū* "to press", 'Soma' would mean 'the pressed one' or the (plant) to be pressed; (√*hu*.. > *homa).*
14. RV IX.89.2—*apsu drapso vāvṛdhe*; also for '*drapsa*' see—IX.85.10, 78.4, IX.51.3-*tava tya indo andhaso devā madhor vyaśnate*; also-77.4.
15. *Ibid.*, IX.51.3; X.115.3-cf. *svāyudhaḥ pavate deva induḥ.*
16. RV. IX.61.10 *uccā te jātam andhaso divi sad bhūmi-ādade*; for *andhas* meaning nutritious food see RV VIII. 32.28; X.94.8.
17. *Ibid.*, VIII. 9.19 *gāvo na durha ūdhabhiḥ*; VIII.98.1.
18. *Ibid.*, V.45.8; VI.44.24.
19. *Ibid.*, X.94.3-*vṛkṣasya śākhām aruṇasya bapsataḥ.*
20. Taitt. Sam VI.1.6.7; Śat Br. III.3.1.13 f; for the colour of Soma RV. VII.98.1.
21. RV. IX.79.4
22. Nirukta, II.7.
23. *Hymns from Ṛgveda*, Bombay Sanskrit Series XXXVI, 1924; cf. Sāyaṇa *raśmayaḥ*. So also Velankar *Ṛksūktaśatī*, p.126, n. to the verse; Geldner understands as 'stars', *Der Rigveda*, I, p.213, note to the verse.
24. V. 45.8 *utsa āsām parame sadhasthe.*

25. *Vedic Mythology* (Hindi Tr.) p.286.
26. Vājasaneyi-*Sam*. XIII.43-49.
27. RV X.63.3
28. *Ibid.,* IX 96.15.
29. Macdonell, *op.cit.*, p.206; Aditi being the cow, See VIII.101.15.
30. It is the 'sky-cow' (studded with stars) that is symbolically killed for offering at the sacrifice. Clearly, the sacrifice of the cow was for mystically imbibing the essence of the sky-cow and ensured good crops and cattle. This sky-cow is, doubtless, Aditi. In ritual she was the spotted cow; see note 32 below.
31. Mackenzie, D., *Myths of China and Japan*, London, p.138.
32. *Ibid.*, p.150. The name of the cow-sky-goddess is Hathor. She is said to have star-speckled belly which reminds us of the Vedic sacrificial cow described as having prominent spots; cf. *sthūlapṛṣatīm anaḍvāhīm ālabheta.* For Hathor having a star-speckled belly, Rundle Clark *Myth and Symbol in Ancient Egypt*, London, 1959, p.87.
33. Mackenzie, D., *op.cit.*, p.152.
34. For which see Rundle Clark, *op.cit.*, and Mackenzie, *op.cit.*
35. It could be seen how the usually understood meaning of '*giri*' as the 'cloud' is unnecessary; and could be only a secondary one.
36. RV IX.79.4 *divi te nābhā paramo ya ādade pṛthivyāste ruruhuḥ sānavi kṣipaḥ.*
    adrayaṣṭvā bapsanti goradhi tvacyapsu hastair duduhur manīṣiṇaḥ. In ritual the apparatus for pressing the shoots of *soma* was placed on a cow-hide.
37. Mackenzie, D., *op.cit.*, p.55.
38. *Ibid.*, p.80; there is also another herb called the 'Red-cloud-herb' p.79.
39. *Ibid.*, p.109
40. Cf. RV IX.89.2 (and Sāyaṇa's note thereon) a*psu drapso vāvṛdhe;* Sāyaṇa, *apsu vasatīvarīṣu*. Actually in their aspect called *Nigrābhya*.
41. *Ibid.,* 86.33 *rājā sindhūnām pavate patir divaḥ*. cf. also 15.5; 89.2, 85.10.
42. X.30.9 *madacyutam auśānam nabhojām pari tri-tantum vicarantam utsam.*
43. The famous tale of the advent of the Gaṅgā is only a phase of this motif. The river drops from the star-path (called

Ākaśa-gaṅgā) on the mountain Kailāsa, and thence flows upon the earth. Mark the name 'Tripathagā' (going along three paths) given to her.

44. ṚV V.45.9; IX.9.5.
45. Compare with this the idea of a tear from Atum swelling the Nile. Rundle Clark, *op.cit.*, p.84; also a drop from the star Sirius (sky-cow and the mother of the sun-god) flooding the Nile, Mackenzie—*Myths of China and Japan*, p.64.
46. A similar conception can be seen in the present day Hindu festival of 'kojāgirī'— which is held on the first full-moon day of the Autumn. At night milk in a big cauldron is boiled with cardamom, saffron and other ingredients, in the open, *so as to get the reflection of the moon into the vessel.* The idea is to get the nectar from the moon in the milk. This seems exactly similar to the idea of the 'fertilizing ray' or the '*indu-drapsa*' from the moon, mixing with the milk, and reminds one, of the actual mixing of the Soma-juice (the terrestrial form of the *drapsa*) with milk, in the Vedic sacrifice. This heated milk is then distributed for drinking.
47. Mackenzie—*Myths of Babylonia and Assyria*, p.74.

Chapter 8

SYMBOLISM IN THE RITUAL OF SOMA

When Soma is said to arrive, through rain and gets the form of the plant, it has to be noted that rains for the Vedic people were light-waters (cf. *svarvatīḥ apaḥ*, i.e. Sunful waters), a concept which enters the ritual use of waters in the touch thereof to the immolated victim, and in sprinkling over (with the palm up).[1] The association of Soma with rain-waters is only a phase of the association of Soma with the sun. On the one hand, Soma is said to be brought by the daughter of the sun through rain-waters to the earth (*ib.* IX. 113.3 *parjanyavṛdham mahiṣam sūryasya duhitābharat*); and on the other, waters are said to be resting in the sun, or being in constant company of the sun (*ib* I. 23.17; cf. Taitt. Ār. I.8.1 *āpaḥ sūrye samāhitāḥ*). In ritual, the sun-association of waters, is strictly followed by collecting the ritual waters while the sun is still shining; or if the sun has set, by holding near them a piece of gold,[2] a well-set symbol for the sun and also fire in ritual.[3] As resident among the stars, Soma in the form of the mystic drop gets controlled by the sun, like other stars. It is hence easy to understand the seer saying that, when Soma is pressed in the ritual context, "he" is released by the Sun at the heavenly plane (RV. IX. 27.5 *eṣa sūryeṇa hāsate pavamāno adhi dyavi)*. The control of Soma by the sun, and his subsequent release, is a constant heavenly drama, which was used by the Vedic ritualists in the ritual-context at the Agniṣṭoma, the principal Soma-sacrifice. Here the Śukra cup (of pure Soma) stood for the sun and Indra, and the Manthin cup for the moon (a later phase of Indu-drapsa Soma). The latter was eaten and released by the former involving the principle of complementation in rivalry and seeming enmity, with a step further — Indra = Sun = Śukra, the eater; and Soma = Moon = Vṛtra, the eaten.[4] This, in itself, is the cosmo-ritual drama of sacrificing Soma = Moon (in a later symbolism) to Indra = Sun. That Soma anthropomorphosed as the wise god is to be sacrificed, is already set in the Ṛgveda when the seer says, "Indu is squeezed and made to drip (RV IX. 27.1; 109.22 *tośate*, and Sāyaṇa *hanyate*). In the later ritual texts the pounding of Soma-shoots is clearly described as the "killing" of Soma; and the ritual details, of tying the shoots, in the shape of a man, leave no doubt of the "king" to be "pounded" for its juice.[5] The divine victim's juice-the fiery liquid-is ultimately thrown as offering into the fire-the Āhavanīya, some of it being drunk by the chosen priests and the sacrificer. Thus the circle is complete. From the light-abode, through the control of the sun, to the earth through rain, to the sacrifice-and into the fire to revert to the gods—the light principles (*devāḥ*) is the main theme in the Soma-ritual.

The concept of complementation between the fiery juice and the sacrificial fire is not so very prominent in the Ṛgveda. The later texts, however, express it clearly in the Śukra and the Manthin cups specially, and in others, faintly (Śat.Br.IV.2.1.1ff). Thus, when all the cups are to be filled in and offered to, the Adhvaryu holds the Śukra-cup and the Pratiprasthātṛ holds the Manthin cup. After many details, and after offering into the Āhavanīya fire the juice in the Manthin cup that remains after the offering, is poured into that of the Śukra, wherefrom also offering is made earlier, expressing that the eaten (Manthin = moon) has done justice to the "Eater" (Śukra = Sun). It is to be noted that the Śukra cup is with pure Soma, while to the liquid in the Manthin cup, *mantha* (a mixture of malt) is added to give the semblance of the moon (Śat. Br., *loc. cit.*, 2). After the residue from the Manthin (moon) - cup has been poured into that of the Śukra (= Sun) - cup, the whole is offered into the cup of the Hotṛ who had earlier offered the liquid from his cup, likewise, into the Āhavanīya. The Hotṛ drinks it (*ib.*, 29f). Though it is not specially mentioned here, from another context we learn that the "eating" and again letting out of the moon by the sun is a monthly drama in the cosmos, which is enacted at the Soma ritual, with the belief that the "eater" and the "eaten" are complementary to each other, suggesting the ultimate wholeness of the two. It is with this ultimate basis, "the swallowing-disgorging" drama is enacted at all rituals of initiation.[6] The ultimate oneness of Soma and its partaker is brought home by a myth—where Vṛtra is said to have been created by Tvaṣṭṛ from the drops of Soma that rolled into the fire (√vṛt> Vṛtra). The sacrificial (Āhavanīya) fire being only another aspect of the sun (=heavenly fire), Soma offered into the fire forms one whole with it to create something unique (here Vṛtra)—the symbolic whole-unit of creation!

The ritualists of the later Vedic age, undoubtedly forged a new image of Vṛtra, who symbolised a creative whole.[7] The myth tells us that when Vṛtra was split open by the thunderbolt of Indra, Soma and Agni got separated and Vṛtra was lost into oblivion! (Śat.Br. I 6.3.1ff). Pouring of Soma, the sacred juice, into the holy fire was, thus, an act of creation; for in the cosmos there is no other principle except these two—moisture and heat! The Śat.Br. very clearly states this ultimate basis of all creation, "This (cosmos) comprises a dual; there is no third-the Wet and the Dry. That which is Dry pertains to the fire; that which is Wet pertains to Soma."[8] That is why a unit of these two deities was extremely important in the sacrifical set-up. Thus, at the Agniṣṭoma (the norm for all Soma-sacrifices), the victim to this dual was offered as the first offering (*agniṣomīya paśu*); and, out of the context of the Soma-sacrifice, in the case of the Darśapūrṇamāsa i.e. New moon and Full moon rites (especially the Pūrṇamāsa *iṣṭi*), where a beast was not sacrificed, a *puroḍāśa* to this dual was offered (prepared on eleven potsherds: eight indicating Agni and three Soma). The ultimate oneness of the victim and the god, to whom it is offered, is another aspect of the offering of Soma in ritual. It should, however, be noted, that the *indu drapsa* concept of the RV shifted to the moon-liquid in the period of the Brāhmaṇa-s, prior to its ritual enactment in the Śukra-Manthin cups. Other cups, such as the Upāṁśu-Antaryāma, Aindrā-Vāyava, Maitrā-Varuṇa and Āśvina (for the two Āśvins) preceding the Śukra-Manthin are modifications of the last, which has to be taken to be the norm indicating the ultimate unity of the "eater" and the "eaten". The ritual tradition identifies the cups with dualities, and with vital breaths (Śat.Br. IV.1.1.1;18; Ait.Br. VIII.3 etc.), which has to be taken as a secondary phase of Soma-symbolism. A pertinent difference to be marked between the other cups for the dual deities and Śukra-Manthin is, that the former cups mention specific deities, while Śukra and Manthin are no deities but two types of Soma itself, maintaining their nature as offering, though one of them is identified with the sun or Indra. And, identification is a later phase! With this, we go to other phases of the ritual of Soma.

The important rites in the ritual of Soma, prior to the offering of the juice into the fire are: (i) The purchase of Soma, the king; (ii) Bringing "him" in a cart and depositing in the sacrificial chamber, which is the old (Darśapūrṇamāsa type of) structure (=*Prācīnavaṁśa*), and thence to the Havirdhāna shed. (iii) Reception given to Soma as a special guest; (iv) The fetching of the waters called Vasatīvarī, on the previous day prior to sunset; the Ekadhanā waters on the next day in the morning; placing them finally in the shed called Havirdhāna, where earlier Soma shoots are led and deposited from the old sacrificial hall; and (v) Pressing of Soma and offering from various cups.

The purchase of Soma has some interesting details; there is a fusion of myth and ritual. It could be said that the ritual enacts the myth, which says that Soma was in the third heaven; which vibrates with the *indu-drapsa* concept, saying that Soma was far beyond the reach of the humans (or even gods) who wanted to sacrifice with it as offering. To indicate that Soma has been brought from that far, purchase was a necessary rite. The Śat.Br. says that a person who performs with Soma that is not purchased, performs with Soma that has really not come as a guest (III 2.4.7 *anāgatena ha vai sa somena yajate yo'krītena yajate*). In this context the Ait. Br. states, that it was purchased from the thirteenth month, which is symbolised by the Soma-seller who is to be duped and driven away. It states that, as the thirteenth month is non-existent; so the Soma-seller is non-existent (I.12). It is difficult to know the significance of the thirteenth month; but probably this is to indicate that Soma is not usual; that it is mysterious-like the *indu-drapsa*! This practice implies that Soma should be purchased in a year having the intercalary month, and then kept for the sacrifice; or better, the Soma-sacrifice was itself to be performed in such a year. Later this practice was probably dropped; so in place of the eight verses fabricated to twelve at the rite, which has been a common practice, the Kau.Br. (VII.10) (of the Ṛgveda tradition) enjoins nine verses to be fabricated to thirteen, thus keeping the memory of the thirteenth month.[9]

In the actual purchase, *soma* is bartered for a cow. Though the ritual texts are unanimous regarding this point, reading between the lines, and shifting the evidence, indicates that, prior to the cow, an actual woman figured in the ritual, this woman, in all probability being a public woman. The Air.Br. (I.27=5.1) mentions the Mahānagnī, which actually is in the form of the cow. The Taitt. Sam. (VI.1.5) mentions that the Gandharvas from whom Soma was to be bartered were "desirous of woman" (*strīkamāḥ*); hence the gods turned Speech into a one-year old cow. One wonders how the cow could serve the desire (*kāma*) of the passionate Gandharvas! The Śat.Br., which like the Taitt.Sam., gives some details in this context, prescribed that the wife of the sacrificer should be made to look at the *Somakrayaṇī* cow. It explains that Soma is the male and the sacrificer's wife his female (*yoṣā*); that here the *Somakrayaṇī* cow stands for Soma (male); and that the sacrificer's wife and Soma make a procreative couple — *mithunam prajananam* (III.3.1.11). It may be noted in this connection that the Jaim. Br. (II. 117), speaks of a stud-Bull (*gauḥ* soma*krayaṇo bhavati*) in the Sādyaskra sacrifice, which has the norm in Agniṣṭoma and in which the rites of purchase of Soma and the pressing are to be done on the same day, unlike the Agniṣṭoma, where Soma is purchased on the previous day (cf. Śat.Br. III 5.1.17). What appears to be original is that the guest Soma and the "wife" form a symbolic procreative couple, and the cow symbolizes the "wife". If we probe the details further the following pattern gets surfaced-a woman exchanged for Soma, but taken back. When Soma is brought as a guest to the chamber, the sacrificer's wife symbolically acts as his female associate. The employment of a cow is a later phase, when pastoralism gave prominence to the bull and the cow. This phase is suggested even in the RV when in addition to the starry abode of *indu-drapsa*, Soma is described in the cow-motif. This liquid is said to be milked like the udder of cows (VIII. 9.19 *aṁśavo gāvo na durha ūdhabhiḥ*); it is also called 'tawny milk' (VII.98.1 *aruṇam dugdham*). But, in spite of this mixture of images, the one of woman lingered, in such words (in spite of the cow) as *yoṣit*, *yoṣā* (which indicate a fully-grown woman, capable of uniting for procreation), *strī*, and *mahānagnī*. But, the texts are one in saying that the cow has to be such as has not been yet impregnated. The original idea seems hence, to be of sexual charm to bring Soma from the far-off region.[10]

It is necessary to note that in concept, and also in ritual, one trait of Soma was that he was seen as an androgen, having a bisexual nature, a prominent trait in Vedic ritual symbolism. It is very well known that the main god and sacrifice incarnate, Prajāpati, is himself seen as an androgen.[11] Reverting to Soma, we may note a detail mentioned above, which shows that Soma, though a male, is seen in the form of the cow. The imagery works on the lines of the famous concept of Vṛṣabha-dhenu (RV III. 38.7; X. 5.7). Another instance of androgynic expression is where Soma is the procreating male advancing through rain and getting changed into the Soma-creeper, the female (RV II.3.1). But, somehow the androgynic nature of Soma was not as prominent as his nature as the "seeder" of waters, who is said to stay in them, to impregnate them; as a result of this union comes rain. In ritual, this association of rain is indicated by the contrivance of the holes called *uparava* - four in all-over which the pressing apparatus is arranged in the shed called Havirdhāna. These holes are one arm deep and long inwards; and when the pressing goes on, the sound produced is in the likeness of thunder; however, this is not specifically said to be a rain-charm! But, when Soma-shoots are brought in the cart, according to one of the practices, if both or one of the bullocks is of black colour, there would be good rain (Śat.Br. III.3.4.11). Then Soma-shoots are placed in the *prācīnavaṁśa* as mentioned earlier. From here, they are to be taken to the Mahāvedi when it is constructed; and there too ultimately in the Havirdhāna shed. This completes the process of bringing the heavenly *indu*-drop into the sacrificial precincts.

The Vasatīvarī waters, fetched on the previous day and the Ekadhanā waters, ritually brought on the morning of the pressing day, are mixed up in the cup held by the Maitrāvaruṇa priest. In a variant method, the two cups are only touched together, indicating mixing. Both types of waters are, at a later stage, collected into the trough called Ādhavanīya (used for washing the shoots of Soma).

At the pressing, the upper stone called *upāṁśu savana* is said to be sun, which "kills" Soma (*ib.,* 7ff). In this, the image is the same as in the cosmos,-the sun "eating" the moon or the Śukra-cup "eating" the Manthin (referred to earlier, and to follow, in actual ritual when the juice is collected). The meting out of the shoots is done five times, to conform to the concept of "Five" in the sacrificial symbolism (*pāṅkto yajñaḥ*).[12] When the shoots are being pressed, the Nigrābhya waters (a portion of the Vasatīvarī waters, poured into the cup of Hotṛ) are poured thereupon for rejuvenation, each time, totalling four times, The fully pressed out Soma-shoots are placed into the cup of the Nigrābhya waters as an alternative method. While the shoots of Soma are pounded, Soma is addressed-"Be not afraid, nor tremble. I strike so and so, not you, O Soma", *ib.* 18; Vāj Sam. VI. 35). Further, the quarters are invoked to resort to Soma, so that Soma could consort with them as their lord; and he is requested to enjoy the longing waters that run from all quarters[13] (Śat. Br. *loc.cit.* 21; Vāj. Sam VI. 36; cf. Taitt. Sam. I 4.11.6-8). This completes the pressing and taking out the juice to be offered into various cups.

The last prayer dwells on the union of Soma as the male on one hand, and the quarters and the waters as females, on the other. Conversely the Vasatīvarī represent these waters, from the quarters. They help Soma to be "killed" and also rejuvenated, they being termed "ambā"[14] a collective epithet. If we compare the heavenly aspect of Soma among the cosmic waters, and his ritual aspect of being "killed" and rejuvenated with the help of waters, together with the concept of Soma being their lord, and also they being his "Mother", the picture that the ritual of Soma (with the various added-details set aside) presents is that the heavenly Lord is brought on the plane of the sacrifice through the mid-region, in the form of a divine herb to be sacrificed as the main *havis* (offering) and partaken thereof for all prosperity. This is the Ultimate basis of the whole imagery and rituals of Soma. The coupling of the male Soma and the female waters, with the androgynic nature referred to earlier, is a charm to get the male *par excellence* to the sacrificial plane for the symbolic sacrifice. This pattern goes to take other forms where the victim is a male beast. His female counterpart as a charm, is seen and symbolized by the wife of the sacrificer,[15] and in yet another phase, by the Neṣṭṛ who only, among all the priests, is said to represent the wife (*patnī-bhājana*).[16]

Another important aspect, as has been indicated

above, is that, rain is the result of the ritual "killing" of the heavenly *indu*, anthropomorphically described in the ritual setting. The basic idea is that the holy liquid, when sacrificially united with the principle of heat, activates rain. This aspect, together with the sexual charm about Soma has been perennial in the Vedic ritual tradition, right from the RV, which speaks of Soma enjoying in the company of the cosmic waters, as does a young man with auspicious women (X. 30.5), which image is transferred to the ritual context in the union of the Vasatīvarī-Nigrābhya waters and Soma, as cited above. He is at once the child of the Mother waters and their lord (IX. 93.2), which image works on the basic Vedic (and even ultra-Vedic) belief of the "Child-husband".[17] About rain, his image is clear in such words as *ap-tura* (IX. 63.5), *apsāḥ* (65. 20); and he is invoked to bring rain at various places (39.2; 41.3; 49.1 etc.). There is, hence, a very clear basis for the ritual of Soma in the Vedic ritual tradition, with a firm belief in a sexual pairing at various levels. This is but the enactment of the cosmic relationship between the principles of Moisture and Heat, on the basis of Complementation.

NOTES

1. Śat. Br. I.2.4.16 *śāntir āpaḥ tad abhiḥ śamayati.*
2. *Ibid.*, III 9.2.5. *divā gṛhṇīyāt...; hiraṇyam upari dhārayan.*
3. Cf. also oblation of ghee on a piece of gold at the foot-print of the cow, *ibid.*, III. 3.1.3.
4. *Ibid.*, III 9.4.2; *ibid.*, I. 6.3.17; 2.1.3ff; Jaim. Br. I. 82.
5. On this symbolism, see Dange, S.A., *Legends in the Mahābhārata*, Delhi, 1969, pp. 171-83.
6. *Ibid.*, pp.194 ff. for other tribes. By the same author, *Encyclopaedia of Puranic Beliefs and Practices*, Vol. III, Delhi, 1987, under "Initiation."
7. Cf. Śat.Br. III.9.4.2 where even the mountains are said to comprise the body of Vṛtra., cf. also Mait.Sam.III.6.3; IV.6.5 etc.
8. Śat. Br. I. 6.3.23. *dvayam va-idam na tṛtīyam asti, ārdram*

caiva śuṣkam ca yac chuṣkam tadāgnyam, yad ārdram tat saumyam

9. The fabrication, or arrangement, is known by the term *sampad*. In almost all texts, in this context, eight verses are prescribed, to be made into twelve by reciting the first and last thrice each. Where the verses are nine, it will give thirteen verses:
   1 + 6 + 1 = 8; by *sampad*, 3 + 6 + 3 = 12; and
   1 + 7 + 1 = 9; by *sampad*, 3 + 7 + 3 = 13.
10. An extension of the same belief is where nude women plough for the gain of rain; cf. G.H. Damont, "Some Account of the Palis of Dinajpur," *Indian Antiquary* I (1872), p.340; the rite called *Hudmadyao*, among the Palis, requires nude women roaming at that particular night in the village, sword in hand; males are prohibited from seeing them; cf. a news item, *Tarun Bharat* (Marathi Daily), Nagpur, 2nd May, 1969.
11. Pañc. Br. XIII 11.18, where the two lauds, having the words *ghṛtaścut* and *madhuścut*, are said to be his two breasts. He is a self-couple, Mait. Sam I. 9.6.
12. For various units of "Five", see Ait Br. 8.6 = II. 24.
13. See Eggeling J., SBE, Vol. 26, p.245.
14. Śat Br., *loc.cit.*
15. On this point see Dange, *Sexual Symbolism from the Vedic Ritual*, Delhi, 1979, p. 71ff.
16. Cf. Ait. Br. 26.3 = VI.3.
17. RV.II.35.13.

Chapter 9

THE RITUAL OF SOMA AND KĀVYA-RASA

We have examined the concept of the advent of the sacred Soma-the divine light-drop (*indu*)—from heaven to the earth.[1] The importance of this heavenly drop of liquid-light,[2] which sustains all aspects of life, lies in the fact of a detailed ritual associated with it. At the sacrifice this heavenly liquid is placed in various '*graha*'-s.[3] Drinking from these '*graha*'-s (wooden cups), symbolically means the gain of life-breath, heavenly light and immortality. This 'drop' (*drapsa*) of the '*indu*' (the shining one) sustains the sun and the moon and the luminaries,[4] and is to be gathered on this earth through the medium of the sacrifice. This act of the gain of the light-drop from heaven is supported by the *mantra*-s. The *mantra*-s are an expression of the inner personality of man and hence they are said to fully accomplish the ritual act.[5] Without the *mantra*-s, hence, no ritual can ever be said to be complete. To keep up the faculty of the creation of the *mantra*-s is necessary; and for this Soma is very efficacious.

Soma and the Poetic Faculty

As an impeller of the *mantra*-s Soma is directly connected with Speech. Thus he is said to kindle Speech (RV. IX.50.1c). At the very sight of the pressed Soma Speech gets released (*ibid.*, 2). He is invoked, not only to stimulate the speech of the Vedic poets, but to modulate it in its oscillations, being called the very oscillator (RV. IX.101.5).[6] Here the concept is of the speech that swings and forms into rhythm and rhyme, in the effect of the juice of Soma. It is to be particularly noted that, of all the deities of the RV, Soma alone is said to be *Vācaspati* (lord of Speech),[7] with the only exception of Viśvakarman (X. 81.7). At the third and the last place where the epithet occurs, we are not sure of the deity (X.166.3); for the deity is said to be the "meaning which is the Defeat of the rival". With Soma the case is quite clear-*vācaspatiḥ* (at IX.101.5), and *patim vāco adābhyam* (IX.26.4c).

Soma, being the impeller of Speech, is conceived of as a poet himself. He is the divine *kavi* (IX.47.4;.64.24;.30 etc.). He is the generator of poetic speech—not only the rigid *mantra*-s, but also imaginative poetry. He is rightly called "the begetter of the poet's speech."[8] Soma produces Speech (IX. 62.26). As he oozes from heaven, he is invoked, being the leader of Speech (on the tongue!), to kindle speech, and cause it to ooze out,[9] thus establishing a cause-and-effect relationship between Soma and poetry. This would indicate, not only the birth of poetry (or the *mantra*-s) as accompanying the pressing of the juice from the plant but also, the flow of poetry being impelled by the intake of the juice. The close association of Speech and Soma is attested by tradition which believes that Speech resides in Soma.[10] Hence it is that Soma is to be purchased with speech.[11] It is interesting to note that Soma is said to reside at the point of the tongue[12] of Varuṇa. The Vedic seers or the poets are to gain it by their mental activity-an act said to be beyond the power of an ordinary man and for which a '*dhīra*' (one of stable intellect) is required. At another place it is said that the tongue of the sacrifice causes the lovable sweet drink to ooze out, and the speaker (of poetry) is the master of Speech (IX.75.2).

That the effects of Soma cause the birth of poetry is further suggested from the fact that Soma is called *Brahmaṇas-pati*, when the former is said to be the lord of the body of the singer (*ibid.,* 83.1). What the singer, or the composer, of the hymn does when he utters the word is, that he only re-produces the juice of Soma in the form of Speech. Thus Soma is said to be the '*foetus*' of the thunder-speech (*pajrā*) and is invoked to wake up and move in the utterance or the poetic composition.[13] This is supported by the fact that, in the famous hymn of Speech, she declares that she bears Soma in herself (X.125.2). The close association of Soma and the poetic expression is further clear from the fact that Speech is said to be Soma-*vatī,* i.e. mixed with Soma (X.113.8), an expression that comes only once more and is applied to a healing herb (X.97.7), which is so called because it has the healing qualities of Soma.

The next point worth noting is that Soma's place is often said to be the heart (he is said to be *hṛdamsaniḥ*-IX.61.14; also cf. I.91.13; I.168.3;.179.5, where Agastya addresses Soma that is drunk and is residing in the heart; also VIII.2.12;49.12). He is also given the unique epithet "lord of the mind",[14] which no Ṛgvedic god shares, the only other case being of the deity of dreams (X.164.1) which is not clearly defined in the Vedic pantheon. The fact that Soma is the lord of the mental or the imaginative faculty goes well with the conception of Speech being "Soma-*vatī*", which means it to assimilate the effects of the juice of Soma when taken in. The concept that the speech of the poet is full of the juice of Soma is clearly to be seen in the following expression:

> He partaketh of all that is pure and sweetened by Mātariśvan who doth meditate upon the *Pāvamānīs*, that are, verily, the juice of Soma collected by the *ṛṣi*-s (*ṛṣibhiḥ sam-bhṛtam rasam*).
> For him doth Sarasvatī[15] milk the elixir *kṣīra*, ghee and sweet water, who doth meditate upon the *Pāvamānīs*. (IX.67.31-32).

The *Pāvamānīs* are the hymns associated with pressing of Soma; *Pavamāna* is flowing Soma. Hence the verses praising it are called *Pāvamānī*; and the idea is that these hymns act as a charm for the easy oozing out of Soma from its high abode in the heavens. Now, in these hymns the *rasa* of Soma is said to be collected by the *ṛṣi*-s. How? We have seen that Soma-juice is said to be the lord of the mental faculty. It acts on the mind to help produce poetry. Hence it is that the hymns are said to be full of Soma. The juice of Soma, as it were, resides in the hymns. Thus the idea, clearly, is that the in-taken Soma gets expressed as the poetic expression. Now, because the expression is full of the juice of Soma, it causes, sympathetically, the '*indu*' to ooze out from its high abode and arrive in the sacrifice in the form of the *rasa*. When the in-taken Soma gets expressed in the form of the *Pāvamānīs*, it is obvious that the utterance is full of Soma, as it bears the juice as a foetus. The utterance (speech) is, hence *somātmaka*, which is clearly suggested in the words—"collected juice" (*saṁbhṛtam rasam*). We, thus, get the conception of the '*rasātmikā Vāṇī*', which at once reminds us of the famous maxim "*vākyam rasātmakam kāvyam*" (Sāhitya-darpaṇa I.3) which has become the banner of the *rasa* theory.

Soma, Rasa, Brahma and the Ānanda

A further comparison of the poetic concept of the Rasa-vādins and the psychic image behind the ritual of the pressing of Soma is apt to be interesting. The experience (*anubhūti*) of the poetic sentiment (*rasa*) is likened to the realization of the highest Self, the *brahman*, as it is said to be non-worldly (or, properly speaking, heavenly).

It may be urged that the word '*brahma*' associated with the *rasa* in a poetic composition has the philosophical set-up. It should be noted, however, that the philosophical concept of *brahman* itself is rooted in the ritual of Soma-pressing. The ritual concept of *brahman* is twofold: it applies to the physical activity at the sacrifice on the one hand; and, on the other, indicates the mental activity. Thus, it indicates the sacrificial act as also the *mantra*.[16] The juice of Soma—the receptacle of all juices (*rasa*, IX.113.5) is said to ooze out when the plant is purified in pressing by a *brahma*, i.e., a *mantra*. At another place Soma-juice is itself said to be the *brahma*, as we hear the seer invoking Soma to purify him with the *brahma-sava*-s (IX.67.24). We have here a clear identification of the ritual juice of Soma and *brahma*. Drops of Soma are said to attend with zeal every brahma at the sacrifice (IX.77.3), an expression used exclusively for Soma. The identification of the ritual juice of Soma and *brahma* is complete when the knowers of *brahma* are said to purify the pure *brahma*, i.e, Soma collected in the *Pāvamānīs*,[17] that are said to lead to the heavenly world[18] which corresponds to the '*alaukika*' experience of the *rasa-vādins*. Soma is, indeed, the fluid *brahma*, and also the bright flash[19] (Khila. III.10).

That the concept of the liquid *brahma*—the ritual drink of Soma—gives rise to the philosophic concept of *brahma* is clear from an interesting account found in the Vedic texts. It is well known that the initiate gets the *brahma* at the initiation ceremony (*upanayana*); and, thenceforth, he is said to be the *brahma-cārin*. This *brahma* is conferred on him through the *mantra* Gāyatrī-Sāvitrī, which stands at the threshold of the whole Vedic study. Only the knowledge of the Gāyatrī-Sāvitrī is enough for a person to be called a *brahma-cārin* (Manu. II.118). It is after the initiation that the boy gets the advantage of being called *saumya* (Manu. II.125). Now according to the Vedic tradition it is Gāyatrī that brings Soma that lies in the highest heaven.[20] In other words, the *brahma* that is conferred on the initiate by the Gāyatrī corresponds to Soma, giving the '*saumya*' (initiate) the right to study the Vedas. It is the same *brahma*, in the liquid form that is partaken of in the sacrifice, denoted by the self-expressive term '*brahmasava*'. This heavenly liquid is said to be placed in the Soma-plant by the Daughter-of-the sun=*Savitṛ* (IX.113.3) which is clearly the *Sāvitrī* embodied in the Gāyatrī metre. A further support to this belief is found in the fact that *brahma* is said to be *Gāyatra* (i.e. belonging to Gāyatrī) and that Jamadagni gets inspirated by partaking of the *brahma* in the form of Soma.[21] The concept of the liquid *brahma* in the form of Soma is thus at the basis of the philosophic concept of the highest principle. In this light, it is easy to appreciate the maxim which lays down that the highest principle is only the liquid (*raso vai saḥ*, Taitt. Up. II.7). When the *rasā-vādins* talk of the poetic *rasa* being *brahma-sahodara*, we shall do well to understand this background of the ritual of Soma, which though forgotten, cannot be set aside.

It is to be particularly noted that the earliest mention of *ānanda* is in the ritual of Soma. The *pāvamānīs* which are infused with Soma, are said to be teeming with NANDANA (Khila-III.10.6). The authority of the Khilas may, rightly, be questioned. But, it should be noted that in the RV itself the word *ānanda* never occurs in any other context than that of the pressing of Soma. Says the *ṛṣi*:-

> Whither doth Brahma utter the metrical Speech, being honoured in the ritual of Soma-pressing, evolving *ānanda*, thither, O PAVAMĀNA, ooze for Indra (IX.113.6, *somenānandam janayan*)

and to clarify what this *ānanda* is, from the very next verse we have the description of the heavenly world (cf. the poetic *alaukika*), where there is the continuous unquivering flame—the immortal world of bliss with the sun and nectar. The hymn ends with an invocation to the *pavamāna* Soma- "Whither abide the multitudes of *ānanda*—thither lead me O Pavamāna"(IX.113.11).

It is, thus, clear that the Ṛgvedic concept of the liquid *brahma* (the Juice of Soma) giving *ānanda* lies at the back of the philosophic *brahma*, which has been conceived as *rasa* which again, has been so well adapted by the *rasa-vādins*.

Rasa and Bhāva

Though there have been opinions as to the number of *rasa*-s,[22] it has been accepted that *rasa* is really one,[23] and gets various names. New experiences give rise to new names of the *rasa*. Thus, there have been additions to the number of *rasa*-s and the *sthāyi-bhāva*-s. No *rasa* can be without a *bhāva*; no *bhāva* without a *rasa*.[24] This means that the *rasavādin*-s believe that there is an archetype of the *rasa*-s and the *bhāva*-s. In other words, there is originally only one *bhāva* and one *rasa*. This is corroborated by the comparison of the poetic *rasa* with the *brahma* which is one and without the second. The relation of this *bhāva* with the *rasa* is that of STABILITY and ACTIVITY. The *rasa* implies movement; there can be no *rasa* without movement.[25] It is the task of a piece of art or poetic expression to cause a stir in this stable *bhāva* for the experience of *rasa*, its variety depending on the various situations. Now the concept of this fluid in man obtains in the RV and this fluid (*rasa*) is said to be Soma; for it is said, that the seers of *mantra*-s (*brāhmaṇāḥ*) know of another Soma of which nobody partakes. It is said to be well concealed and hears the rumbling of the stones which press the other Soma (from the plant) (X.85.3; 4).[26] It is to be noted that this expression occurs at the beginning of the famous hymn of marriage, and as such the concealed Soma, probably, is the body-fluid of procreation, the very essence of the personality. We have another reference to the body-fluid (*rasa*) that is the essence of a living body and creates a son (I.105.2). This *rasa* depends upon Soma as do all fluids (VIII.48.9; IX.30.3; 66.18; 61.4; 86.28; and Sāyaṇa). The fluid that remains in the body as its very essence suggests also a fluid that is formless and subtle, the movement of which is felt and experienced through an outside impact. It is this concept of the subtle fluid that is expressed in the words 'He indeed is RASA' which ritually gets connected with the juice of Soma—the fluid *Brahma*—the archetype of fluids, both visible and subtle when they do not move, are not particularly experienced and are stable, though dormant, in a living body. This is the concept of the *Sthāyi-bhāva*. According to the *rasavādin*-s this is stirred by the poet's efforts. In the *dṛśya* form of poetry (drama or *dṛśya* dance) it is accomplished by the various actions of the actor and the scenic situations. In the other forms of poetry—*śravya*, or we may say '*hṛdya*' which is only enjoyed by the *rasika* in seclusion by reading the piece (which Abhinavagupta names "*mānasa sākṣātkāra*") where no such aids are forwarded, the realization of *rasa* is through the *visualization* of the efforts of the poet by the reader *in his own way*.[27] Though the word *rasika* is apt to make us believe that the realization of *rasa* is in the reader or the spectator, it should be noted that the poet has already gone through this stage when he first experienced the impact which roused him, prior to putting to pen his experience. In this way the poet is the first *rasika*; for, the experience causes the stir of his personality, to produce the piece of art which is the cause of the stir of the later *rasika*-s.[28] The same is true of any other person who produces any piece of work. It is he that first gets the stir. The idea is clear in the case of the juice of Soma. The *rasa* (juice) causes a stir in the poet, for it captures his very heart, making him the *rasika*. This *rasa* the poet reproduces in the *mantra*-s, making them *rasātmaka* to cause a stir in others who may meditate upon the *Pāvamānīs*, by their influence, bestowing *ānanda*, the *alaukika* bliss.

It is, thus, probable that the theory of RASA in poetry has its base in the ritual of Soma.

We have seen that the word *ānanda* never occurs in the RV in any other context than that of the pressing of Soma. It should be of no little interest to note that the only verbal form of the root √*nand*, occurring in the RV, comes in the context of the ritual of Soma. Thus, in the midst of the hymn of Speech we have a *ṛc* which, in ritual, is enjoined to be sung at the sight of the flow of the *Soma-rasa* (X.71.10; see Sāyaṇa thereon). This *ṛc*, which leads three others from a Soma-hymn (I.91.9-11) says:-

> All friends (of Speech i.e. Poets) get filled with bliss at the advent of the friend (in the form of the *Soma-rasa*) in the sacrificial assembly.
>
> *(sarve nandanti yaśasāgatena)*

This shows the height of close association between Speech and the advent of Soma which marks the success in sacrifice. It clearly shows the highest aim of the whole effort of the friends of Speech (the poets or those who are the knowers of Speech, being its appreciators). As expressed in ritual it is the victorious flow of the sparkling *rasa* of Soma by which they get filled with BLISS (*nandanti*).

NOTES

1. See 'Advent of Soma' Ch.7, *supra*.
2. RV IX.29.2;.86.10;.97.39; etc. Unspecified references are all to RV.
3. Śat. Br. IV.1.2.;3 and further Taitt. Sam. VI.4.5-10; B.G. Tilak, *Orion*, Poona, 1955 (1916), p.162.
4. RV IX.23.2;63.7.
5. Nirukta 1.16 *etad vai yajñasya samṛddham* quoted from Ai. Br. 1.4; I.13=3.2; also Nirukta I.3 *karmasampattir mantro vede*.
6. Also IX.101.6b *vācam īṅkhayaḥ*; cf 35.5a. The expression occurs only at these two places in the RV. The idea will be clear from another expression, where Soma is said to cause tremor in the speech, *ibid.*, 96.7[a] *prāvīvipad vāca ūrmim*.
7. IX.101.5b *vācaspatir makhasyate*
8. IX.67.13a, *vāco jantuḥ kavīnām*. The word *jantu* does not mean 'the one created', but the creator. See Sāyaṇa.
9. IX.62.25: also 84.5; 92.3.
10. Sāyaṇa on IX.73.7, *some vāk tiṣṭhati iti*.
11. Speech is represented by a cow in this ritual; see Sāyaṇa (*ibid.*): also Mahīdhara on Vāj. Sam. IV.18. This cow (=Speech) is called Soma-*krayaṇī*; Ai. Br. I.27=5.1. There is, at many places, identification of Speech and the cow in RV.
12. IX.73.9 *jihvāyā agre varuṇasya māyayā*; or, it may mean, 'at the tip of the tongue of the human, through the magic of Varuṇa'.
13. *Ibid.*, 82.4 where he is addressed as *pajrāyāḥ garbha*. Sāyaṇa's rendering of the expression as the "Speech in the mid-region" is acceptable. see Ch.3, note 3 *supra*.
14. IX.11.8; also 28.1. The idea that Soma is the lord of the

mind can be compared with the conception that the moon was produced from the mind of the Puruṣa, X.90.13.

15. Sarasvatī is not taken to be the goddess of Speech in RV, by scholars. However, she is often connected with the mental faculty (VII.35.1; II.3.8 etc.). Later she is clearly identified with Speech (Śat. Br. III.9.1.7; Ai. Br. III.1=11.1). Sarasvatī was, quite early, associated with the sacrificial ritual (cf. the Āprī hymns) and hence, with the *mantra*-s; and this formed a natural basis for her later identification with Speech. The process, however, began in RV itself with her association with the mental faculty.
16. Cf. VII.28.4; 71.6, and Sāyaṇa's explanation.
17. Khila-III.10.1 & 4 *ṛṣibhiḥ saṁbhṛto rasaḥ*. For the concept of *rasa* in metres, see ch. on Kuntāpa.
18. IX. 113.7-11; Khila-III.10.6.
19. The word '*indu*' itself has the concept of the light drop or flash. For Soma as the light-liquid see IX.71.8; 74.7, etc. With the light-liquid (Soma) that causes (or is in) poetic expression cf. Vāmaṅa *dīptarasatvam kāntiḥ* (III.2.24). Soma is said to have been released by the Sun, IX. 27.5a *eṣa sūryeṇa hāsate.*
20. Śat. Br. III.2.4.1; Ai. Br. III.25=13.1; Tāṇḍya Maha. Br. VIII.4; Mait. Sam. III.7.8; Kāṭhaka Sam. XXXIII.10 etc.
21. Khila. V.3.1, *tubhyam gāyatram ucyate*; and 4 *rājñaḥ somasya bhakṣeṇa brahmaṇā.*
22. For which see Kane's ed. *Sāhitya-darpaṇa*, Bombay, 1951, the portion of History of Poetics, p.350.
23. *Ibid.*, p.353. Opinions differ about the name of this *one rasa*, Bhoja saying that it is the Sṛṅgāra, and the grandfather of Viśvanātha (Nārāyana) saying that it is *Adbhuta*; cf. Bhavabhūti saying it to be the Karuṇa, Uttararāmacaritam, III.47.
24. Nāṭya Ś. VI.36
    na bhāvahīno' sti raso
    na bhāvo rasavarjitaḥ
25. Cf. Rasataraṅgiṇī VI, *sthāyibhāvo rasyamāno rasaḥ*; and Rudraṭa XII.4 *rasanād rasatvam eṣām.*
26. According to Sāyaṇa it is the moon; but the word 'concealed' goes against it.
27. The reader or the spectator enjoys the piece of poetry in his own way. The experience of the poet and of the reader

etc. cannot be the *same* (cf. *samāna*; Bhaṭṭatauta). The poet creates a world from his own experience, while the reader his own on the basis of the poet's. They are similar, but not necessarily, the same.

28. We have noted that the RV suggests the fluid in the body that is the essence of the personality which can be excited by impact. In the subtle existence, this fluid gives the concept of the '*rasa*'—the highest principle. This concept of the fluid can be compared with the 'humour'—concept of Hippocratus (400 B.C.) who believed in four moist permanent currents in the body.

Chapter 10

THE EYE OF PRAJĀPATI

The eye has often been associated with the light in the cosmos; and there is a well-founded myth which tells us that the sun and the moon were produced from the eyes of the primordial Man, or that his eyes are the same as the said luminaries (RV X. 90.13b *cakṣoḥ sūryo 'ajāyata*). The highest step of Viṣṇu is identified with the sun (RV I.22.20 *divīva cakṣur ātatam*), who is also called the 'eye' of Mitra, Varuṇa and Agni (I.115.1); and when Atri is said to have restored the 'eye' of the sun in the sky, it indicates the orb of the sun (V.40.8). The same is the image when the seer speaks of the 'eye' of the sun that releases the *rajas*, which is the fluid of fertility (*ib.*, 59. 3b *sūryo na cakṣū rajaso visarjane*) or the 'eye' of the sun is said to be covered by the *rajas* (I. 164.14). The 'eye' is said to be fixed in the sun (VI.11.5) which has the same image, that of the orb. In an interesting image, the sun is said to be spreading the 'eye' of Mitra and Varuṇa, which is said to oversee the worlds (VII.61.1), where the image is complex; for, it has the twin shade: (i) The 'eye' is the sun; and (ii) The sun spreads the 'eye'. The gait of the eye is suggested from the sun traversing the sky. The RV seems to make a difference, generally speaking, between the *akṣi* and the *cakṣu*, though the point cannot be stressed too far—the former indicating the human or the individual eye and the latter the cosmic one. On the cosmic plane, in the image of the sun, two things get clear: (i) The fertilizing fluid; and (ii) the gait. It is the first one that gets associated with fertility-myths in the later literature, the second one being the usual quality of the sun, there being nothing very new or particular about it.

The concept of the 'eye' of various divinities, which supervises and which has also the fertilizing fluid, gets associated with the new god Prajāpati who dominates the ritual-field, as is seen from the Brāhmaṇa texts; and the difference between the *akṣi* and the *cakṣu* is set aside. A development of the concept of the fluid in the sun, or the orb of the sun, is the eye of Prajāpati that releases the fertilizing tear, or the fertilizing fluid. Thus, it is said that the left eye of Prajāpati got swollen; the drops that fell from it turned into rain (Mait. Sam. IV.6.3, *tasya vai prajāpateḥ savyam cakṣur aśvayat; tato ye stokā avāpadyanta tair idam varṣati*). This is a clear development of the belief that all waters get stored up in the 'eye' that is the sun (orb), whence they get released in the form of rain (RV. I.23.17; cf. Taitt. Āraṇyaka I.8.1). But, the belief goes a step further and says, that the pupil from the eye of Prajāpati fell down; from it was produced barley (*ib., tasya yā kanīnikā parāpatat sa yavo 'bhavat*). Here there is no attempt at etymology; but, here is a passage from Śat Br. according to which Varuṇa pressed the eye of Soma; from it was produced the horse; as it was created due to pressing and swelling, it was called (*aśva*=horse; IV. 2.1.11 *tad yac cchvayathāt sam-abhavat tasmād aśvo nāma*). Here the root √*śvi* is connected with *aśva* (horse). But the explanation from the Mait. Sam. noted above appears to be more appropriate in view of the direct association of *aśvayat* (also from √*śvi* = "to get swollen") with *aśvaḥ*, though it is not given there. The Śat.Br. further says in the same context that the tear from the eye of Soma became barley. It is to be noted that Mait. Sam. has the pupil of the eye connected with barley while at Śat. Br. it is the tear, *aśru* (*tasya aśru praskandat*). On comparison, it seems that the version of the Śat. Br. is more polished, as it employs the double etymology: (i) √*śvi*; and (ii) √*aś* "to pervade", the latter getting both forms-*aśvaḥ* and aśru; aśru would indicate not only the tear, but also the "pervading fluid" (*aś*, "to pervade"), which is the same as *rajas*, which is the characteristic fluid of the sun as noted above. The eye, or the tear that is shed by the eye, in such myths, thus reverts to the orb of the sun. The 'tear' has developed to further heights in the Vedic symbolism, when it is said that it is the 'tear' that lies at the base of all expansion of creation, but not as a simple tear; it is in its aspect of the pervading fluid, the *aśru*, a unique image from the fertile and apt imagination of the ritual-thinker of Śat Br. It is said that Prajāpati formed a sexual pair of himself as fire, and the earth as the female. Thence was produced an egg; from its solid portion was produced the air in the mid-region; and from the *aśru* were produced the birds. Then there was the second pair between the air and the mid-region; it produced an egg; from its *aśru* was produced the *pṛśni-aśman* ("cloud" according to the commentator, Sāyaṇa). Further it is said, that from the next pair, which is the sun and the sky (female), an egg was produced; from the solid the moon was produced; and from the *aśru* were produced the stars and the constellations (Śat. Br. VI. 1.2.1-8). It will be seen that in this account the belief regarding the procreative faculty of the eye-fluid gets mixed with the belief in a primeval egg, about which there is already a well-attested and popular myth. The *aśru* here leaves the precincts of the eye and enters the wider concept of the cosmic egg; it indicates the fluid of the 'egg', the pervading cosmic fluid! Both are now controlled by the Great God, the lord of all creatures — Prajāpati. The eye and the tear have, thus, a gradual and polished development in the Vedic sphere. It should, however, be noted that the beliefs regarding the eye and the eye-fluid giving rise to creatures and water are not restricted to the Veda. In fact, these beliefs here are only an aspect of such floating beliefs. We may do well to note some below, where the role of Prajāpati is attributed to the High God there.

The belief in the 'moving eye' obtains from ancient Egypt, where the eye of Atum is said to have been sent in search of his twin children Shu and Thefnut, in the primeval waters of the Abyss, Nun.[1] The eye is the sun; but, the ancient Egyptian belief has the moving eye developed into the rearing cobra,[2] which is not the case with the eye in the Vedic context. In another Egyptian myth regarding the eye of Atum, the primeval High God, it is said that Atum wept in the primeval waters; and from the drops mankind was produced.[3] The words for tear and mankind show phonetic affinity: Remeyet = "tears", Romech= "men".[4] The eye remains confined to the mythical domain in the Veda, whereas, in the Egyptian belief, it became a regular female deity.[5] The procreative eye in the Vedic context is already considered as the organ of generation in the myths noted above; but, it is not the female, nor is it actually identified with the female genital organ. The shade is seen in another tale, where the thousand female genital organs on the body of Indra, due to the curse of Gautama for seducing Ahalyā, become the 'eyes'.[6] The conceptual similarity of the eye and the female genital organ must have been lurking at the back of the detail. The 'eye' was believed by the Egyptians to be the most ancient Female in the world. The creative tear of the Egypitan sun-god Ra was believed to cause the Nile to be flooded.[7] Fertility is directly associated with vegetation in the Vedic belief as noted above; but, this also is a widely found belief. In Babylonia, Assyria and ancient Egypt alike, corn-deities were "weeping deities" that shed fertilizing 'tears.'[8] The belief entered rituals in certain cases, as, for example, among the Aztecs children were sacrificed at the altar of the rain-god, Tloloc; and, if they wept, it was believed to be a good sign, indicating good rains and crops.[9]

The eye of the High God, or Prajāpati, being the sun has a mixed conceptual base. It is that of light and water together. This differentiates the 'eye' from other limbs of the body that release the fluid. This is a step further than that of mere creative body-moisture. The Hindu concept that comes close to the 'eye', in this aspect, is that of Tryambaka = *tri* + *ambaka*, the god with three eyes, where the eyes get associated with the fire in the waters at the three regions.[10] A popular Hindu myth that connects the eye with waters is that which occurs in connection with Śukra, the priest of the Asuras. According to it, when the dwarf incarnation of Viṣṇu asked Bali to give him land measuring his (the dwarf's) three strides, the preceptor tried to persuade Bali not to accept the request. When Bali did not desist from his promise given to the dwarf, the preceptor is said to have taken his seat in the beaked pitcher, to thwart the flow of water that would fall on the hand of the dwarf indicating the completion of the gift. Though this is said to have been done by the preceptor without anybody's notice, the dwarf knew of the trick. He asked Bali to take a blade of *darbha*, the sacred grass, and insert it into the beak. This was done with the result that along with water blood came out. What actually happened was that the blade injured the eye of the priest. The point to be noted is that when the eye is pricked, water gets oozed out, though along with blood. The water, then, is the 'eye-water'! The name of the priest of the Asuras is Śukra; and the sun is also termed Śukra, due to his heat (*śuc*). In the ritual-context, the term Śukra is common for the sun (cf. *idam śukrasya purorucam kurvanti*; etc.).[11] In that case, even here, the popular myth of the priest Śukra reverts to the solar orb, which contains waters as we have noted. In ritual-symbolism, the cups called Śukra and Manthin are said to be the two eyes, as they are identified with the sun and the moon respectively.[12] The eye-myth of the priest Śukrācārya does not occur in the Mahābhārata or in many Purāṇa texts (only at Nārada, P.I.11); but, there can be no doubt that it was floating in popular belief. And it has the same motif, that of the solar 'Eye' of Prajāpati, that sheds the fertilizing fluid.

NOTES

1. Rundle Clark, *Myth and Symbol in Ancient Egypt*, London, 1959, p.84; for Nun, p.36.
2. *Ibid.*, p.224; also p.51ff.

3. *Ibid.*, p.72.
4. *Ibid.*
5. *Ibid.*, p.224.
6. The story is very old; but this trait is not attested in the Vedic literature or in the *Mb.*, Śānti, 266.47-51; but cf. Anuśāsana, 41.153, see also Brahma P.87.35ff.
7. Rundle Clark, *op.cit.*, p.84.
8. Mackenzie, D., *Myths of Babylonia and Assyria*, London, p.81.
9. Mackenzie, D., *Myths of Pre-Columbian America*, London, p.251.
10. See Ch.11, infra.
11. Śat Br. IV.2.1.8.
12. *Ibid.*, IV 2.1.4.

Chapter 11

TRY'AMBAKA

The word *try'ambaka* occurs only once in the Ṛgveda; and it is clear that the verse in which it appears (VII. 59.12) is a later one, though it is very popular in the Hindu ritual-*mantra* tradition. The verse is:

> *try'ambakam yajāmahe su-gandhim puṣṭi-vardhanam*
> *urvārukam-iva bandhanān mṛtyor mukṣīya mā'mṛtāt*
> (also Ṛgveda Khila IV. 11.28; Taitt. Br. I. 6.10.5 etc.).

It is customary to explain the word *try'ambaka* as, "*trīṇi ambakāni yasya*", where the word *ambaka* is taken to mean—the "eye", the whole expression taken to mean "one having three eyes", this God being Śiva. There is no question about the first part which is "*tri*". About the exact implication of the word "*ambaka*", however, the meaning given above is not the only one. The commentary (not Sāyaṇa's, but included in that of Sāyaṇa on the Ṛgveda) on the word *try'ambaka is "trayāṇām brahma-viṣṇu-pitāmahānām ambakam pitaram"*, understanding the word *ambaka* as "father". Scholars, including Grassmann (*Wörterbuch*) and Manfred Mayrhofer (*Kurzgefaztes Etymologische*), render it as "drei Mutter habend", ("having three mothers") understanding in it "mother". There does seem to be similarity of concept in the two views, though the meaning appears to show a difference in the gender. The concept seems to be of "parenthood" or "supervision". Mayrhofer takes the word to have been formed with *ambā* as the second part of the compound. At another place, under *ambaka*, he gives the meaning as 'eye'. Thus, he does not think that the word *ambaka* (eye) has anything to do with "*try'ambaka*". Mayrhofer does not show how the word *ambā* is changed to *amba* (with the last vowel shortened), nor is it in the scope of his work mentioned above!

The word *ambā* (meaning mother, lady or a woman) being at the end of a compound word (of the *Bahuvrīhi* type) gets shortened, the new hypothetical form being "*try' ambaḥ*" (Masculine, Pāṇ. I.2.48). We may get also the forms *try'ambāka* or *try'ambaka* (Pāṇ. VII. 4.13;14;15). The forms *try'ambaḥ* and *try'ambāka* are never found; and in the form *try'ambaka* we have the "*puṁ-vad-bhāva*" (masculine-like formation) which indicates the "father" (√*amb+a* = *amba* (masc.); *ambā* (fem) + *ka* (suffix); reverting to *amba* + *ka* > *ambaka*. The form *ambikā* is arrived at from *ambā* (by Pāṇ. VII.3.44). The point is, who are the three mothers and who the *tryambaka*? If the word *tryambaka* denoted Śiva, what could be the implication of his three mothers? The feminine form *try'ambake* (vocative) found in "*śaraṇye try'ambake gauri nārāyaṇi namo'stu te*" (RV. Khila, II.6.30), and showing the feminine *ambakā*, cannot be taken to support the form *ambakā* independently; for it occurs only in the compound and is obviously suggested from the masculine form "*try'ambaka*". Now, the word *amba* and *ambaka* are of peculiar connotation in the Sanskrit language. Both mean "father" and also "eye"; and the feminine *ambā* and *ambikā* mean "mother" (and are naturally expected to mean the "*female eye*"!). Another important point to be noted is, that the same word *amba* denotes "water". Now, though the word *ambā* does not mean "water" and means only "mother" (or a woman commanding respect, or a "gentle lady"), it is interesting to take another similar word—*ambi*. This word means "mother" and also "water". Thus the position is:-

1. *amba* / *ambaka* = < father/water
eye

2. *ambi (ambī)* = mother (woman)/water / Female eye?

and

3. *ambā / ambikā* = mother / water?/Female eye?

The word *ambi* denotes a river in the Vedic language, which is in accord with its meaning "water". It also denotes "woman" and "mother". This will show that there is a fusion of the meanings of 'father' or 'mother' and 'water' or the river in the word "*amba*" "/*āmbaka*'/*ambi*", and to this fusion is also added the concept of the "eye". This "eye" appears to have in itself the idea of "supervision" (and not only *vision*!) which is in accord with the concept of the "father" or the "mother".

If we go to root-meaning, the word "*amba*" (or *ambaka*) would indicate the "roarer" (from √*amb*), which will suit its variant *ambi* (river) like *nadī* (from √*nad*, to roar); but it should also indicate the "eye" (the seer), which is not, however, supported directly by the root-meaning. We may, however, take the meaning of the "seer" or "supervision", from the other meaning of √*amb viz.* "to go". Or, otherwise we have to take the meaning of "seeing" in √*amb* as lost to the Sanskrit language. The word *amba*, indicating "water" may be compared with the words *ambhas*, *ambu* and *ap* / (*abh* / *ab*), *apas* and *āpas*. Out of these *ambhas* and *ambu* have the senses of both "water" and "roar" (from √*amb* and √*ambh*, which originally appear to be one and the same root, later giving a reflected form). The concept of the all-pervading Speech being the daughter of *Ambhṛṇa* may be recalled here. The idea appears to be that Speech is the daughter of the divine principle that manifests itself in the Roar in the mid-region. It is of interest to note that Speech, called *Āmbhṛṇī* in the tradition, has her birthplace in the Ocean (RV, X. 125.7), which is nothing else than the atmospheric ocean of water-vapours often referred to as the *uttara samudra* in RV. Thus the concept of water and roar are fused together, both being all-pervading. It seems more than probable that this belief in the all-pervading nature of the waters, together with their all-nourishing quality gave them the status of the "mothers" in the belief of the ancients. This is reflected in RV where the waters are called the "mothers" (VIII. 89.4; 96.1; IX. 86.36; X. 17.10), and the terrestrial rivers are said to be *mātaraḥ* (X. 64.9) and also *aṁbayaḥ* (1.23.16), while the Sarasvatī is "*ambitamā*" (II.41.16) which indicates her to be the best of the mothers and also the best of the rivers.

The concept of the three roaring river-mothers is further enhanced by the belief that the three regions of heaven, mid-region and the earth are full of the watery streams, a concept that further gets developed into the idea of the Gaṅgā having three paths. The point, then, is that the three abodes of the waters (or better, the waters in the three abodes) are called *ambā*-s and "mothers". But, who could be the *try'ambaka*? Corresponding to the concept of the three *ambā*-s (water-mothers) we have, in RV, the concept of the *tri'mātā*. The word occurs only once (III. 56.5) in RV; but it is of unique importance. The hymn in which it occurs is believed to be having the All-gods as the deity according to Sāyaṇa; and this particular verse has the waters (or Rivers) as the deity; for, the vocative *sindhavaḥ* clearly shows it. The god, who is said to be *tri'mātā* (*trimātṛ*), is taken by Sāyaṇa as the Sun, or Saṁvatsara (the year), who is the "creator of the three worlds" (*trayāṇām amīṣām lokānām nirmātā*). But, it appears that the word *tri-mātā* has to be taken as indicating "one having three mothers" (cf. Sāyaṇa himself on III.55.6); and this is Agni, as the unique epithet "*vidatheṣu samrāṭ*" indicates (cf. the only other place III.55.7a). This would indicate that Agni has three mothers, though he is said to be *dvi-mātā* at other places (I.31.2;-112.4; III.55.6; 7) only. These three mothers of Agni are the abodes of water as we have noted above. A reference to a passage in a hymn (a riddle-hymn?) will be exactly suiting here. The hymn is no riddle if we note that it only brings out the coordination, by means of sacrifice, between the fire in the mid-region and that in the terrestrial plane, the resultant rain from the mid-region, where the atmospheric fire is at work, being a step further. This coordination is brought out with an extremely fine image. The seer, Haryata—the son of Pragātha—describes, that the singers catch the "*sasa*" (sleeping one, i.e. Agni) by means of their "tongues" (i.e. the verses in his praise) and want to place him in the midst of mortals. This Agni is also said to be Rudra (VIII. 72.3). Now Rudra has been mainly associated with the mid-region and the rain therefrom, a fact finely couched in the belief that the Maruts are the sons of Rudra (RV. I 39.7; 64.3 etc.) and from the *Raudra brahma* (X.61.1) which is for the gain of the "lost" cows(=rain-clouds), with the help of Nābhānediṣṭha. It is, hence, clear that Agni who is praised here (VIII. 72.3) is an aspect of Rudra. At another place the word *sasa* (X.79.4; here it is *gṛbhṇanti jihvayā sasam*) has been explained by Yāska as, "the one sleeping is the middle fire, not always visible" (cf. Nir. V.3, *svapanam etan mādhyamikam jyotir anitya-darśanam*); and, probably, we have a subtle reference to the cloud and the mid-region fire in "the butter-full hide of the sleeping one" (III.5.6 c). In the present case, when the "sleeping one" has been aroused by means of the "tongues", he himself uses his "tongue" to smash the "rock" as the terrible "bow flashes", out in the "forest" (cf. VIII. 72.4 *jāmy' atītape dhanur vayodhā āruhad vanam / dṛṣadam jihvayā'vadhīt*). Here the "forest" is clearly the cloud; and elsewhere we have the cloud symbolized as the "*kṛntatra*" (X. 27.23) or the "tree" (*vṛkṣa*) on which sounds the "cow" (*ibid.*, 22).[1] Now as soon as the "sleeping one" smashes the "*dṛṣad*" (rock; or, in fact, the tree-dweller, meaning the cloud), he is said to approach the "mother". The word for the mother is *ambi* (actually *ambyam*, which is the accusative; see v.5. c, cf. Pāṇ-VI.1.106). Here the concept of the *ambi* (or *ambā*), i.e. the Water-mother is closely associated with that of the fire. The close association of the waters and the fire, and their relationship as the "mothers" and child is as old, and as clear as RV. As there are three abodes of the waters, there are three abodes of the fire; and this triple fire is in the waters in the three regions. Thus, the sun is full of waters (I.23.17) and is the heavenly fire. The mid-region fire is sleeping in the waters of the clouds; and the terrestrial fire is equally in the waters and is called "*payasvān agni*" (I.23.23). Thus, the fire has three water-abodes in the three regions; and they are his mothers. This means that he is the "one having three mothers", which is exactly reflected in the unique epithet "tri-mātā", which also tallies with the concept in *try'ambaka*.

The most original concept in the word *try'ambaka*, thus, is that of the triple fire fostered by the triple water-mothers. This concept appears to be the most dominating one, and was later transferred to Rudra—Śiva, in one of the aspects of the cosmic fire. It is to be noted that the goddess praised as *try'ambaka* is not necessarily the female counterpart of the god generally known as Śiva. She is also called Nārāyaṇī and is mainly Lakṣmī, thus keeping her close association with the cosmic nature of the water-goddess (*nārā*=water). The fire is also prominently associated with Śiva in his form as *try'ambaka*, being present in his third eye on the fore-head. This brings us to the concept of *ambaka* as the eye.[2]

From what has been stated above it will be clear that, with the concept of the water-mothers (or mother-waters), Agni is closely associated, as the child. In other words, Agni is the light-principle that is constantly associated with the waters. It is not improbable that this gave rise to the concept of the shining or "seeing" water-principle-the *ambaka*. It has to be remembered that, though the word *ambaka* came to signify the eye, it is never used for the human eye. The belief seems to be of the pervading or moving eye, the cosmic light-principle. The sun is the eye of Agni, Mitra and Varuṇa, as he is also the heavenly fire (I.115.1, VI.51.1 etc.); and the eye of the sun is said to be full of moisture (1.164.14). Agni is the eye of the gods (V.

8.6; cf. X. 8.5). The sun holds aloft his *cakṣu* (eye or brilliance) at the release of rain (V.59.3; cf.5). (These images are already examined in the earlier chapter). In this way *try'ambaka* (one having three eyes) will be the cosmic supreme principle with the three fire-eyes in the three regions pervaded by the cosmic waters.

NOTES

1. See "The Vision of Vasukra" ch.4, *supra*.
2. According to an account (Skanda Purāṇa VI. 153.3-28) once Pārvatī closed the eyes of Śiva with her palms, and would not take them away even when repeatedly requested by Śiva to do so. So, Śiva opened up a third eye in his forehead. It is said that three skulls having three eyes each, are offered to him; hence he is called Tryambaka. Also a *puroḍāśa* (a sacrificial cake) prepared in three potsherds is offered to him. This *puroḍāśa* is called Tryambaka. See Dange, *Encyclopaedia of Puranic Beliefs and Practices*, Vol. IV, p.1308.

Chapter 12

SASARPARĪ : A WAR-SPELL

The Ṛgveda records various rites prescribed to be performed at the advance of the army.[1] One such rite appears to be enshrined in the word *Sasarparī* which occurs twice in RV (III.53.15, 16) and nowhere else in the Vedic literature.

Various interpretations have been offered for this word. According to tradition it indicates the 'moving' Speech (*sarpaṇasīlā vāk*) which helped Viśvāmitra gain a point over his rival Vasiṣṭha in a wordy conflict. It has also been said to indicate the cow and the war-trumpet. The interpretation of *Sasarparī* as cow might suit its description 'roared loudly' (*bṛhan mimāya*), but goes against its 'having wings' (*pakṣyā*). The war-trumpet has obviously been suggested from *Sasarparī* being said to have roared loudly.[2] But, as we shall see, the words *bṛhan mimāya* need not suggest the war-trumpet. Velankar, suggesting that it indicated the 'winged devil' (cf. *pakṣiṇī hetiḥ,* RV *X.* 165.2, 3) himself doubts the suggestion, for *Sasarparī* is said to have been given to Viśvāmitra by the Jamadagni-s who were respectable and, so, could not be said to have given a devil (*yātu*).[3] It is necessary to note the difference between *pakṣiṇī hetiḥ* and *Sasarparī.* The former is the epithet of the bird *kapota* which, along with the owl, is said to be the messenger of the goddess of Death (*dūto nirṛtyāḥ).* *Sasarparī is not* said to be an evil-doer. The traditional interpretation suggesting a wordy conflict between Viśvāmitra and Vasiṣṭha is obviously based on the word *amati* which is taken to mean 'lack of mental faculty'

(III.53.15a *amatim bādhamānā*).

While attempting to suggest a fresh interpretation of the word *Sasarparī* it is important to note that the word occurs in the context of the sacrificial release of the horse of Sudās; and, so, its employment has to be taken as an integral part of the ritual. The ritual starts with the consecration of the horse by the Kuśika-s and ends with the note of the advance of the Bharata-s. It is the same horse that is earlier said to have been consecrated for the glory of king Sudās, who is blessed for his conquest over his enemies in the eastern, western and northern quarters, and to sacrifice on earth.[4] The occasion is, thus, the horse-sacrifice of Sudās, as Velankar points out convincingly.[5] A thorough examination of the epithets of *Sasarparī* would go well to solve the riddle surrounding this word.

The Destroyer of Amati

Sasarparī is said to be the destroyer or expeller of *amati (amatim bādhamānā)*. This expression has been understood to mean 'warding off of ignorance' (cf. Sāyaṇa). The Bṛhaddevatā, narrating the story of the wordy conflict in which Viśvāmitra lost his mental faculty and was helped by Jamadagni, obviously sees a contrast between *mati* and *a-mati*, or the negation of *mati*. A closer examination of this word, with the same accent however, shows that the contrast is unwarranted. It can be shown that it has the connotation of evil. Thus, the Āditya-s are invoked to remove *Śaru* (the dart) and *amati* (RV VIII. 18.11). The contrast seems to be between the visible cause injury *(śaru)* and an invisible or, better, an unthinkable one. The evils of *a-vīratā* (sonlessness) and *amati* figure together (VII. 1.19; III 16.5). Sin and *amati* are spoken of together (IV. 11.6). The expression *amatim bādhamānā* has a parallel in the book of the Viśvāmitra-s, in the invocation of the *yūpa* (III.8.2, *amatim bādhamānāḥ*); and the *amati,* there, is indicated to be something not inherent in the person but which could infest him. That is why it is desired to be away (*āre asmad*). The *yūpa* (sacrificial pole) is invoked to be hoisted for great prosperity (*mahate saubhagāya*) keeping *amati* away, thus striking a clear contrast between *amati* and prosperity. The mind is said to tremble and dread from *amati* (V. 36. 3, *vepate mano me bhiyā amateḥ*). The word *amati,* thus, has the sense of 'evil', and, it is this belief of *amati* being something to be dreaded of that is reflected in the Ai. Br. (II.2). RV associates *amati* not only with the lack of food or clothes (VIII. 66.14; X. 43.3) but also with Death (X. 76.4). *Amati* being, thus, inauspicious, is to be kept away or avoided. *Sasarparī* wards off *amati* and, as a result, immortal fame is gained among the five tribes (*śravaḥ pāñcajanyāsu kṛṣṭiṣu;* see also, *śravo deveṣu amṛtam ajūryam*). On the occasion of the release of the sacrificial horse, the evil that might infest him is sought to be driven away by *Sasarparī.*

The Winged Daughter of the Sun

Sasarparī is said to be the daughter of the sun and also one having wings (*sūryasya duhitā* and *pakṣyā*). *Sūryasya duhitā* appears to be the most important and suggestive epithet of *Sasarparī,* connecting it with a well founded belief current among the Vedic people, according to which the sun has wings. The prominent example of this belief is the hymn used at the horse sacrifice (RV I.163), where the sacrificial horse, representing the Sun, is praised as having the wings of the hawk (I.163.1).[6] That the Ṛgveda reflects the belief in the beneficial energy having wings is proved by another example, *viz.*, the boat that is fashioned for Bhujyu (I.185.5). Now, if the sun has wings, the daughter of the sun could well be believed to have them. Who could this Daughter-of-the-Sun be? RV makes mention of the belief that the Daughter-of-the-Sun is associated with the ritual of Soma. She is said to be cleansing Soma (IX. 1.6) and to have restored Soma that was stolen by the Gandharva-s (IX. 113.3). It is this belief in the Daughter-of-the-Sun bringing Soma, after defeating the obstructing Gandharva-s, that gets developed into the legend of *Somāharaṇa* in the other Vedic texts, where she is said to be the *Gāyatrī*.[7] According to another Vedic belief, the rays of the sun are called *suparṇa-s* and the metres are called the *Sauparṇa-s*,[8] and the birds. They fly to fetch Soma.[9] Of all the metres, it is the *Gāyatrī*, *that is termed Sāvitrī and which flies* to fetch Soma in the form of the bird *śyena* (hawk) whose wings the Sun-horse is said to be endowed with. The concept of *Sasarparī,* the Daughter-of-the-Sun having wings, is thus exactly the same as that of the *Sāvitrī-Gāyatrī.,* both indicating the Solar energy conceived in the form of a bird. This gets support from the fact that the *Sāvitrī-Gāyatrī*, is traditionally believed to be the most remarkable contribution of the Viśvāmitra-s to the Vedic ritual of *upanayana.*[10]

The Bestower of New Life

Sasarparī is said to bestow new life (*navyam āyur dadhānā).* In this she conforms with the *Sāvitrī-Gāyatrī,* which is said to give new life to the initiate when he becomes a *dvija.* This epithet of the *Sasarparī* is particularly suitable in the context of the advance of the army for the protection of the sacrificial horse, where battles are expected and life is in danger, prior to final victory. Vedic tradition believes in the metres saving one from death.[11] In the legends *Gāyatrī* is associated with the bringing of Soma, the nectar-juice of immortality, and bestowing new life at the ritual. In the *upanayana* the initiate is supposed, ritually, to die and is brought to life by *Gāyatrī-Sāvitrī.*[12]

Sasarparī and the Gāyatrī-Sāvitrī

Sasarparī and *Gāyatrī* have one important point in common. The former has been said to be the gift of the Jamadagni-s to Viśvāmitra (cf. *Jamadagni-dattā,* RV III.53.15, and *Palasti-Jamadagnayo daduḥ,* III. 53.16). Now, there is reason to believe that the famous *Gāyatrī,* which, according to tradition, pertains to the Viśvāmitra-s, pertained originally to the Jamadagni-s. The hymn in which the famous *Sāvitrī-Gāyatrī* occurs (RV III.62) ends with a verse which mentions Jamadagni as the seer though it occurs in the family-book (*maṇḍala*) of the Viśvāmitra-s. There appears to be some doubt about the composition of the entire hymn. Following the tradition, Sāyaṇa says that the last three verses were composed by Jamadagni while the rest were by Viśvāmitra. It is to be noted here, that nowhere else in the family *maṇḍala* of the Viśvāmitra-s does such a combination of these two seers occur. The affinity between the families of Viśvāmitra and Jamadagnī is attested by Vedic and later literature. RV mentions Indra favouring Viśvāmitra and Jamadagni (cf. X. 167.4, with the dual, *Viśvāmitra-Jamadagni).* The Taitt. Sam. mentions Viśvāmitra and Jamadagni jointly as the antagonists of Vasiṣṭha (III. 1.7 3, *Viśvāmitra-Jamadagnī vasiṣṭhena aspardhetām;* also, *ibid.* V. 4.11.3). These two sages are said to have been born from *caru*-s given by the sage *Ṛcīka* to his own wife and to her mother (cf. Mahābhārata-Mb Anu., 4.20 ff., *Śānti.*, 49.9 ff., Bhāgavata P.IX. 15.8 f.). This intimate relationship between the two families gives rise to the suspicion whether the entire hymn, and not the last three verses only, was composed by Jamadagni. The Anukramaṇī quoted by Sāyaṇa is not clear on this point. Again, out of the eighteen verses in the hymn, the first three are in *Triṣṭubh,* while the rest are in the *Gāyatrī,* the verse in praise of *Savitṛ* (i.e. Sāvitrī) being the tenth. That all the verses and hymns in the family *maṇḍala* are not exclusively composed by the Viśvāmitra-s is proved by yet another example. Hymn III. 23 is composed by two seers Devavāta and Devaśravas who do not hail from the family of the Viśvāmitra-s, but from that of the Kṣatriya Bharata-s. In the same manner, it may be that the entire hymn (III. 62) was composed by Jamadagni but came to be inherited by Viśvāmitra, and found its place in the family collection of the latter, due to the close affinity between the two families, which would mean that the famous *Sāvitrī-Gāyatrī ṛc* which occurs in this hymn is by Jamadagni, though it passed into tradition in the name of Viśvāmitra.[13]

The tradition recorded by the Anukramaṇī says that *Sasarparī* is the 'moving' speech (*sarpaṇāsīlā vāk).* From the context of the release of the 'solar' horse (for the *Aśvamedha* of Sudās) that phase of the *vāk* or *mantra* could naturally be expected to embody the 'solar' energy, having the potentiality of bestowing success to an undaunted advance. The case of *Gāyatrī* is similar, though she is nowhere called *Sasarparī*. When the *Anuṣṭubh* and the *Jagatī* metres were unsuccessful, it is the *Gāyatrī* that fetched Soma, defeating the Gandharva-s (RV. IX. 113.3). The belief in the efficaciousness of *Sāvitrī-Gāyatrī* in giving success recommends its being chanted as the army advances. According to Mb, *Gāyatrī* was the binding cord of the chariot of Śiva when he advanced against the Tripuras (see Mb., Karṇa, 34.35; Droṇa., 202.75). Even among the Vasiṣṭha-s a *Sāvitrī* seems to have been current, and was to be recited for success at the start of the journey etc. (Mb., Anu., 150.10 ff., esp. 68).[14] It is interesting to note that in the hymn which mentions *Sasarparī* and the release of the horse of Sudās, a *verse in the Gāyatrī metre* occurs just after the command to the Kuśika-s to release the horse. The order of the verses in the *sūkta* III. 53 is as follows:

> v.11. Release the horse of Sudās for glory, Kuśika-s! May the king vanquish his enemies in the eastern, western and northern quarters.
> v.12. It is the *brahma* of Viśvāmitra that protects the Bharata-s.
> v.13. The Viśvāmitra-s have imparted the *brahma* to Indra, the *vajrin*. May he bestow prosperity upon us.

This verse is in the *Gāyatrī* metre, the only one in this hymn; and the next verse which marks the spirit of the advance says:

> v.14. Of what avail are the cows in the Kīkaṭa-s?... Bring to us the wealth of Pramaganda etc.

Immediately after, *Sasarparī* is praised in two verses. Then follow verses which indicate the consecration of the chariot and a spell to protect the bodies of the guards of the horse. The last four verses of the hymn form part of the general ritual of the advance of the sacrificial horse and could better be taken as directed against the enemies in the path of the march,[15] rather than against the Vasiṣṭha-s.[16]

The Roar of *Sasarparī*

Sasarparī is said to have roared aloud (*bṛhan mimāya*) which gave rise to its being equated with the war trumpet. But here, again, the belief that the loud chant of the *mantra*-s is necessary for the desired effect, helps one to arrive at the correct interpretation. Thus, the Daughter-of-the-Sun is said to utter a roar in the ritual of the pressing of Soma, which the latter surpasses (RV IX. 113.3, *sūryasya duhitus tiro ravam*). This roar of the Daughter-of-the-Sun is, obviously, the loud chant of the *mantra* which is believed to help Soma ooze out easily, thus blending the legend of *Somāharaṇa* by *Gāyatrī-Sāvitrī* with the ritual. The loud chant of the *mantra-s* was believed to create new vigour, and appears to be a well marked method. Thus, the Vasiṣṭha-s infuse Indra with valour by the loud chants of the *Śakvarī-s* (RV VII. 33.4), and the chants go roaringly up to pacify the gods at a time when (in war) life is in danger (RV VII. 23.2). Indra is said to have got success by a chant of a *mantra* in the *Triṣṭubh* metre (RV V. 29.6). This would show that the roar of the *Sasarparī* need not be the sound of an instrument. On the contrary, it is the loud chant of the *mantra*, and, in this particular context, the chant of a *mantra* in the *Gāyatrī* metre.

It is, thus, clear that *Sasarparī* is neither the war-trumpet nor the cow, nor even the winged *yātu* employed by Viśvāmitra. It was, no doubt, a mysterious power[17] of the sun. It was given to Viśvāmitra by the sagacious Jamadagni-s who were closely associated with the family of the former, and who also gave them the famous *Sāvitrī-Gāyatrī*. There does not seem to be an actual argument between Vasiṣṭha and Viśvāmitra in this connection, as stated in the tradition recorded by the Anukramaṇī. The occasion appears to be the horse-sacrifice of king Sudās where Viśvāmitra had full sway in the beginning. The horse was duly consecrated by the Viśvāmitra-s with the help of the famous chant *Sasarparī,* which had given them immense success and had raised their prestige. (Cf. verse III.53.15, which indicates the traditional use of the chant by the Viśvāmitra-s.) It was expected that the advancing spell of *Sasarparī* would bring easy and great glory to their royal patron, Sudās, among the five clans (cf. verse 16).[18] All this was done with a clear mind and without fraud by the Viśvāmitra-s, who enjoyed the goodwill of the king and banked upon their own confidence on the spell. But the expedition met with defeat at the banks of the Paruṣṇī, endangering the horse, and, as a result, the Viśvāmitra-s had to lose their position at the royal court.

They had to vacate, leaving the stage clear for the Vasiṣṭha-s who were immediately summoned by the perplexed king, since his army forming the guard of the horse was being slashed (RV VII. 33.6). It is to be noted that the Vasiṣṭha-s boast of their prowess that saved Sudās in the War-of-ten-kings (RV VII 33.33,46). In all probability, the horse-sacrifice itself led to the War-of-ten-kings[19] which was a decisive event in the life of Sudās. That the defeat of *Sasarparī,* with which the Viśvāmitra-s consecrated the horse, coincides with the War-of-ten-kings is clear from the fact that there is a clear mention of the horse in the Vasiṣṭha-*maṇḍala.* It is the Vasiṣṭha-s that carry the horse to a safe advance.[20] The Vasiṣṭha-hymn (RV. VII. 33), which glorifies the family of Vasiṣṭha-s, marks a clear-cut division. The first six verses refer to a great occasion when the Vasiṣṭha-s had to rush Indra to the help of Sudās,[21] and this great occasion appears to be the War-of-ten-kings, as the verses indicate.

A few parallels between the Vasiṣṭha-hymn (VII. 33) and the one having *Sasarparī* (III. 53) may be noted here:

1. The Vasiṣṭha-s (VII. 33.1-4) as against the Kuśika-s (III. 53.11).
2. The consecration of the chariot at VII.33.4 and at III 53.19.

3. The *Śakvarī* (VII. 33.4) and the *Sasarparī* (III.53.15-16).

The Vasiṣṭha-s infuse strength in Indra with the loudly chanted *Śakvarī*-s, as the Viśvāmitra-s tried the *Sasarparī*. We have noted how *Sasarparī* tallies with the *Gāyatrī*. The *Śakvarī-s* are so called as by the employment of these, Indra could vanquish his arch-enemy Vṛtra.[22] It is to be noted that the *Śakvarī* is also a chant composed with the *Gāyatrī*.

NOTES

1. See Ch. 13, "Aspects of war", *infra*.
2. For these interpretations see H.D. Velankar's translation of the hymn in *J Bombay U,* 23, May 1955 note on the verses; also his *Ṛgveda Maṇḍala III*, University of Bombay, 1968, p.120, his remark "whatever it is". Ludwig renders it as *Kuh (Der Rigveda,* II, *Prag,* 1876, p.651) and Grassmann as *Stromende Kuh (Rigveda,*I, p.583). Bohtlingk and Roth, *Worterbuch,* have *Kriegstrompete.* See also Geldner, *Der Rigveda,* I. pp.394-95.
3. Velankar, *op.cit., loc.cit.*.
4. RV III.59.11, *rājā vṛtram janghanat prāg apāg udag atha yajate vara ā pṛthivyāḥ.*
5. "Viśvāmitra and Vasiṣṭha in the Ṛgveda"; *Mirashi Fel. Volume,* Nagpur, 1965, pp.1-6.
6. Compare the Egyptian belief of the sun-hawk Horus, Rundle Clark, *Myth and Symbol in Ancient Egypt,* London, 1959, p.150.
7. Taitt. Sam. VI. 1.6. 1; Mait. Sam III, 7.7; etc. The sun is conceived as a bird; cf. RV. I.191.9; X. 177.1; 2; red bird V. 47.3
8. Nirukta 4.3, commenting on RV X. 73.11, Ed., V.K. Rajwade, Poona, 1940, p.56.
9. Kāṭhaka Sam. XXXIV.3; Taitt. Sam. VI. 1.6.1, etc. See J. Charpentier, *Die Suparṇasage,* Uppsala 1920; Dange, *Legends in the Mahābhārata,* Chapter I.
10. Śat Br. XI. 5.4. 6 enjoins the *Sāvitrī-Gāyatrī;* see also Gobhila Gṛ. Sūtra, II.10.34; Āśv. Gṛ. Sūtra I.21.4 etc.
11. Mait. Sam. III. 16.51; Gopatha Br. (*Uttarārdha*) V. 1 etc.

12. See Dange, *Legends in the Mahābhārata,* pp.194 ff; *Myths from the Mahābhārata,* Vol. I, pp.165ff
13. Other instances of non-Viśvāmitra hymns in this family book appear to be hymns 38, 54 and 36.10.
14. The Mb. quotes the *Sāvitrī* according to the *Parāśara-mata* and as originating from Vasiṣṭha. It mentions Viśvāmitra in v.38 among the sages who honoured it, but in a later verse which enumerates the sages (v.79) drops him.
15. Oldenberg's view that the last four verses form a destructive charm against an enemy can be accepted; but the view that the charm is conducted rightly in some parts and wrongly in the others is not convincing. The whole charm looks to be quite right, and customary at the advance.
16. See Geldner, *Der Rigveda*, I, pp. 394-95, note on the verse. These last verses are called Vasiṣṭha-*dveṣiṇyaḥ* and the Vasiṣṭha-s do not utter them. This is probably because they form a part of the Viśvāmitra-charm with *Sasarparī.*
17. Cf. H.D. Velankar, "Viśvāmitra and Vasiṣṭha in the Ṛgveda", *Mirashi Fel. Vol.,* p.4.
18. Cf. III. 53.16 *Sasarparīr abharat tūyam ebhyaḥ adhi śravaḥ pāñcajanyāsu kṛṣṭiṣu.* See Sāyaṇa who rightly renders *abharat* by *bharatu,* "may bestow glory".
19. See Velankar, "Viśvāmitra and Vasiṣṭha in the Ṛgveda", *Mirashi Fel. Vol.,* p.4. Though Prof. Velankar suggests the possibility of the horse-sacrifice leading to the War-of-ten-kings as a *conjecture,* the suggestion is highly significant. See note 20, below.
20. Cf. VII. 18.9 *āśuś caned abhipitvam jagāma.* See Sāyaṇa whose rendering appears to be correct. The mention of the horse *(āśu)* is important. It is difficult to account for the horse in any other way. Its apparently sudden mention in an otherwise smooth hymn shows it to embody a fresh event, *viz.,* that of its release at the sacrifice. The hymn is replete with sacrificial similes, and yet refers to the War-of-ten-kings. This gives support to Prof. Velankar's suggestion. Doubtless, Vasiṣṭha is the freshly appointed officiating priest at the horse-sacrifice which is closely associated with the said war.
21. Leaving the sacrifice of one Pāśadyumna Vāyata (RV. VII. 33.2).
22. Nirukta, I.8, Ed. V.K. Rajwade, Poona, 1940, pp.22-23; Kauṣitaki-Br., 23.2.

Chapter 13

ASPECTS OF WAR

War activity in the Ṛgveda does not get restricted to the sphere of the cosmic. Under the garb of a well formed mythopoetic style we have descriptions of the terrestrial war at many places. In the finely fashioned blending of the cosmic and the earthly war activity, the psychological set-up behind war is discernible and presents an interesting study. War, in its fierceness, is finely described against the background of the *war of ten kings* (RV. VIII. 18; 83). It is not always a happy affair; on the contrary it is dreadful. It appears that the ends of the earth would fall asunder (VII.83.2); and the tumult reaches heaven (*ibid*., 3). The arrows are said to shoot like tuft-less children.[1] The bow vanquishes the desire of the enemy and defeat is expected (VI.75.2). The bowstring, being stretched, reaches the ear and embraces it, as does a damsel her lover; 'she' (the string) whispers softly and darts on her target (*ibid*., 3). The ends of the bow are two mothers and take the arrow on their lap (v.4). The hero, going to war, wears the armour and resembles the cloud (*ibid*., 1), which indicates that it was made of black leather or plates of dark metal.[2] The chariot roars as it is driven by the mighty horses. The soldier is, thus, materially well prepared for war; and his body is protected by various appliances[3].

A general survey of war in ancient India has been taken by scholars.[4] But the whole approach is of historical or chronological interest. In the following pages we shall attempt to study the aspects of war from RV taking note of the possible beliefs associated with them.

The Divine Leader

The RV shows the belief in the divine leader. The king going to war is said to be protected by the *pitṛ-s* (ancestors; manes) and various deities such as Varuṇa, Agni, Brahmaṇaspati, Soma and Pūṣan (VI.75; X.173.5; 6.174.3); but he is identified with Indra. Out of the five war hymns that are traditionally enjoined at the consecration for war by the *Āśvalāyana Gṛhyasūtra* (III.12), two are dedicated to Indra. In one of these we have a mention of the fine qualities required by the leader. The king (Indra) should be of stiff command and the wielder of a terrible bow (X.103.3). He should have good assessment of the strength or the might of the enemy. (*ibid.*, 5). He should be the bestower of weal in war and not the bringer of calamity (X.152.2). The belief in divine leadership is clear in the fact that Indra, with Varuṇa, is said to be in the forefront of the army (VIII.82.9). This goes well with the belief that gods placed Indra in the vanguard of their army (VIII. 12.22; also, *ibid.*, 25). There is also a hint in RV as to why Indra was placed in front of the army. It is because Indra is said to be immune to death (VIII.93.5). This motif of Indra being actually present in the field of battle is fully exploited by the RV which believes, not only in a constant contact between the human hero and the divinity, but also in the annihilation of the enemies of the human hero directly by the god. Sudās is, thus, said to be directly assisted by Indra (VII.18). It is Indra who is said to have killed the sons of Varaśikha while helping Cāyamāna (VI.27.5). Indra figures prominently in the wars on the bank of the Paruṣṇī, the Yamunā and the Hariyūpiyā (VII.18.8; 9; VI.27.5). It is because of Indra that the scattered armies of Sudās again rallied together (VII.33.5). There is another point. Sometimes Indra is said to help Sudās; but, at other times, he helps his enemies. He helps Sudās against Druhyu, Turvaśa, Puru, Yadu, etc. (VII. 18.13; 14;6 etc.), while he helps also the latter (1.174.9; IV.30.17; V.31.8, etc.) This suggests a belief among the Vedic people that the one who gets success is impliedly helped in the battle by Indra while the defeated one is forsaken. It is because of this belief that both the armies are said to invoke Indra for protection (II.12.8). There appears to be a regular competition for winning over Indra to one's side. Vasiṣṭha is actually said to have won over Indra from the side of one Pāśadyumna Vāyata (VII.18.2). In the wake of this belief in the divine leadership, it will be good to examine the point whether this presence of the god was only a spiritual affair, or it had also a place in the ritual-practice. Out of the hymns for the consecration of the king for war,[5] two (X. 103 and X. 152) have Indra as the deity, while the other three (VI.75; X. 173 and X. 174) are directly associated with the king, the deities being invoked to sustain him who is the central figure. As regards the Indra-hymns (X. 103 and 152) it can be said that these identify the king and Indra; and, when the king proceeded to the battlefield he was consecrated as the very Indra. But, then, this would not go very well with the fact that the king is *helped* by Indra, which differentiates the two. As on the spiritual plane Indra would be invoked to assist the king, it would be natural to have a depiction of him carried in battle, or at the advance of the army. It is granted that it is difficult to find a pointed reference to the custom of carrying the image of Indra in front of the army; but the possibility cannot be entirely ruled out.

The Banner and Indra

That RV knew war-banners is beyond doubt. It refers to war-banner as *dhvaja* (VIII-85.2a; X. 103. 11a); and we also get a reference to the *ketu* with the war-drum (VI. 47-31), which is said to be the fist of Indra (*ibid.*, 30). At another place, and in a different context, we have a reference to the effect that Indra is "hoisted" like a pole[6] (I.10.1) which, probably hints at the erection of the representation of Indra in some form or other. Now in the very next verse (I.10.2) we get the expression that, when Indra climbed from top to top, he shook in the company of his followers.[7] The followers of Indra are, undoubtedly, the Maruts. The expression would, then, indicate Indra's movement at a height along with the Maruts, the wind-gods. This, with the idea of the hoisting of Indra, would give the image of a high staff fitted with a flag at the top, fluttering in the wind. The custom is clearly hinted at in the expression that compares Indra with the pole (*yūpa*) erected at the door of a house.[8] It is likely, hence, that some representation of Indra was customarily used on auspicious occasions. The banner of Indra (*Indra-dhvaja*) has an ancient tradition and its erection was enjoined as a mark of royalty. The famous account of Vasu Uparicara bears testimony to this fact.[9] The high position of Indra, as on a pole, is yet elsewhere suggested in RV. Thus he is desired to be bent as a container in a well (IV.17.16). Even generally accepting that idol-worship was not prevalent among the Vedic Aryans,[10] it cannot be said that the Ṛgveda does not support some kind of representation of the deity. The erection of the pole at the door and the hoisting of sacrificial posts which are said to be the banners of the sacrifice (III.8.8), and are hoisted for great prosperity (III.8.2, *mahate saubhagāya*), no doubt, contributed to the later custom of the Indra-dhvaja. War being the event of great importance, and an occasion for prosperity and the establishment of supremacy, it is natural that the *Indra-dhvaja* was associated with it later. As the custom of hoisting poles obtains in RV it is not improbable that some representation of Indra—the war god—was erected and carried at the advance of the army, like that of Agni.[11] At another place we have a reference to a horse carrying a deity.[12]

The practice of hoisting the banners or poles of Indra, which is, thus suggested in RV, is prominently seen in the later literature; and we have reason to believe that the war-banner was prominently an embodiment of Indra. The banner of Aśvatthāman is said to be like that of Indra,[13] thus showing the continuity of the belief. The Viṣṇudharmottara Purāṇa refers to the erection of the Indra-banner for the purpose of victory and protection of the soldiers in war.[14] Though it may be taken to refer to the *Garuḍa-dhvaja,* the praise starts with the address to and the invocation of Indra; and here we have a clear case of the identification of Indra and Garuḍa. This would only show that, though the banner shows Garuḍa on it, its former deity was Indra. From the Kāśyapa Saṁhitā we know that at the preparation of the *Garuḍa-dhvaja* a *mantra* from the Indra-hymn, traditionally used at the consecration of the king for war, is used.[15] This would not only show that as the symbol of victory, Garuḍa was accepted by a later tradition, but would also indicate the banner to be an emblem of Indra in the earlier tradition. It is to be noted that the *Garuḍa-dhvaja* is to be hoisted in the month of Bhādrapada according to the Kāśyapa Saṁhitā,[16] which is precisely the month for the *Indra-mahotsava.*[17]

The above discussion will show, that the banner with the Garuḍa on it was an aspect of the *Indra-dhvaja*. It was not only an indication of royalty[18] and prosperity in peace, but also a harbinger of success in war as can be seen from the Viṣṇu-Dh. P.The identification of Indra and Garuḍa as regards the banner has its seeds in RV itself, where Indra is often said to be the bird *śyena* or *suparna.*[19] Though Garuḍa never occurs in the RV he is, later, identified with *suparṇa śyena.*[20] In this connection the banner of Arjuna poses an important point and appears to be only another form of the banner of Indra. Arjuna is said to have a monkey on his banner.[21] It is important to note that, in spite of the account of how Hanumant took his position on the banner of Arjuna,[22] the latter is never called *Hanūmat-dhvaja*, the usual epithet being only monkey-bannered. Now looking to the close association of Arjuna with Indra,[23] it will be well to see if there is any connection between the monkey and Indra. Indra is actually said to have assumed the form of monkey, when he stole *soma* from the sacrifice of Naimiṣa.[24] He is also said to have been propitiated with an oblation when he ran away with *soma* and *sat* upon a tree.[25] Now the banner of Arjuna has more than the monkey. It is said to be having a tail of a lion, and a fierce face.[26] This tallies with the description of the banner of Aśvatthāman which also has the tail of the lion and is said to be like the banner of Śakra.[27] The epithets *ugra* and *bhīma* are primarily used in RV for Indra, with the few exceptions of Brahmaṇaspati and Agni who are also war-gods. He is also often compared with the lion (X.180.2; IV.16.14 etc.). It seems probable, hence, that the idea in the war-banner of Arjuna or of Aśvatthāman is that of the *Śakra-dhvaja*. The same can be said of other war-banners, though in later times various figures appear on them.[28] The smaller banners—the *ketu*-s—represented Agni symbolically.

Being the representation of Agni or Indra, the banner was more than a mere mark of distinction for the army. It can be gathered that the banner was for the protection of the army. This will be clear from the fact that the *mantra, svastidā viśaspatiḥ* etc. (RV X.152.2), in which Indra is praised and which occurs in one of the hymns for war-consecration, is directly preceded by another in the Taittirīya Br. (III.7.11.3) which invokes Indra for protection from one who would cause fear (RV VIII. 61.13). The verse does not occur in the traditional war-hymns; but suggests the war atmosphere. In the verse just preceding (i.e. VIII 61.12) the terrible Indra is said to be *employed* in war as he is the destroyer of the enemies.[29] Probably, this *employment* refers to the actual ritual of hoisting some sort of an image—possibly on a banner—prior to the advance. The Atharvaveda has the same *mantra* (*svastidā* etc.)[30] and, according to Sāyaṇa, it is used as a charm of safety prior to starting on a journey and so on. This belief in the banner being for protection in war is clearly seen in the verses from the Viṣṇu-Dharmottara-P.[31] we have already noted. It is easy to understand that it is not the banner, in itself, that protects; it is the deity that it represents! The deity in the banner, thus, has a twofold purpose:-(i) to protect the army; and (ii) to keep defeat away. In the second is the germ of the custom of making the banner look fierce, or imposing, by means of various figures. We have already noted how the monkey and the bird Garuḍa are associated with the war-banner. We learn from the Mb. that the banner of Arjuna was not merely *kapi-dhvaja;* but, also, it was terrible. It had a terrible face and a tail of a lion. It is said to protect the army of Arjuna causing fear in the minds of the enemy.[32] The same idea is reflected in the speech of Hanūmān who says that he would roar terribly from the banner of Arjuna so as to cause death in the rival army (Mb. Vana-149.17, 18). This belief in the divinity, that the banner represented, is to be marked from the account of the army of Porus, according to which it was an offence punishable by death to discard the image in the field of battle; for it was the god that would take revenge if so insulted.[33] The point gets support in RV in the fact that the arrows or the weapons were directed at the banners (*dhvajeṣu didyavaḥ patanti*-VII. 85.2), obviously to smash the banner and nullify the divine support of the enemy.[34]

The Ritual Drink and Offering

There is an indication that prior to starting on the expedition, the king offered to Indra and other gods. It is clearly said that the king is supported by the offering, and Indra supports him. It is said that, as the offering is *stable,* it will make the king firm in battle, thus establishing a cause-and-effect relationship.[35] The king is said to partake of the same *haviḥ* as was partaken of by Indra (X. 174.4). This would make the king the victor and render him without any enemy. While partaking of this *havis* the king is enjoined to say that he has become the enemy-less victor (*ibid.*). There is another epithet applied to the *havis.* Besides being stable (*dhruva*) it is said to be *abhivarta* (*ibid.,* 1), obviously because it is expected to give success as it did to Indra by advancing further (*abhi* + *√vṛt*). The king himself becomes *abhivarta* by partaking of this offering (*ibid.,* 4). The word, or any other word of similar formation, never elsewhere occurs in RV; and its occurrence only in the hymn for war-consecration leaves no doubt about its special use. The idea, obviously, is to infuse the king with some kind of power so that he could stand the onslaught of the enemy, and return victorious. Further, there is the suggestion of a ritual of touching *soma* (X. 173.6), which is said to be stable *(dhruva)* by the *havis* which itself is *dhruva* (*ibid.*). This ritual of touching the *stable* things would magically make the king firm and advancing (*abhivarta*). If Indra has been the main protector, and the ideal leader of the army, we may not be wrong in taking his war-preparation as a norm for that of the king. The ritual touch and drinking of *soma* by the king goes well with the special liking of Indra for the drink. There is reason to believe that *soma* was drunk by the king as a war-ritual; for Indra, the norm of the king, is said to partake of the drink of *soma*, as a rule before war, whether it is the cosmic one or the terrestrial one, when he is said to help the human counterpart. Elsewhere it is said that Indra's infatuation (due to *soma*) is needed in war (VIII. 46.8), and that drinkers of *soma* are said to be invulnerable to the enemy (VIII. 48.3; X.26.9). It is this belief that makes Soma the *Senānīḥ* (leader in army), next only to Indra (IX. 96.1).

It is useful to note in this connection, that it is not only the drink (*soma*) which is said to be efficacious in rousing the might of Indra; the chanting of *mantra*-s is also equally important. RV abounds in expressing this belief,[36] and shows the trace of the later belief that enjoins *mantra*-s to be chanted, not only at the war-consecration but also at other rituals, as the support to the physical activity, which is believed to be incomplete without them.[37] The warrior, thus, is prepared both mentally and physically and goes to war well protected. This protection is further aided by the wearing of various ornaments and by adornment.[38]

War and Sacrifice

The presence of Indra and Agni symbolised by the *dhvaja* (the banner) and the *ketu* (smaller banner or the flag) in the war at once suggests it to be equal in motif to a sacrifice. It will be seen that the Ṛgveda-concept of war is based on that of the sacrifice. This is clear from the fact that

Turvaśa—one of the kings that rose against Sudās—himself "became a *puroḍāśa,*" though desirous of sacrificing a victim (VII.8.6), and Cāyamāna, the wise, became the "sacrificial victim" (*ibid.*, 8). Indra is said to uphold the banner in the war when Agni is said to be sacrificing to the god like a powerful sacrificer (VII. 30.2). The mixing of the sacrificial atmosphere and that of the war is clearly seen from the fact that, the loud call (*ghoṣa)* for Indra is said to go aloft in the battlefield when sacrificial food is kept ready; and Indra is to be highly praised, as the span of one's life is not known.[39] Indra is said to lead the sacrifice so that war may be won (IV. 20.3). Brahmaṇaspati is said to collect debt (from the enemy) in the battle (i.e., help the king win the war) when the priest pours the offering in the fire in the sacrificial assembly (II.24.13).[40] The victory in war is said to be the direct result of the sacrificial performance of the priests. Thus Vasiṣṭha is said to invoke Indra and Varuṇa in the sacrificial assembly to accept the praise so that Bheda, the enemy of Sudās, might be vanquished in the battle (VII. 83.4). This would suggest that sacrifice and war were mutually connected in the Ṛgvedic belief. This also shows that sacrifice was a continuous ritual as long as the war lasted, and gave sympathetic support to the war activity, a custom clearly testified in the later scriptures.[41] There is a clearer testimony to this fact in RV itself; for, the Tṛtsus are said to be propitiating Indra and Varuṇa, where (i.e., in the battlefield) these gods were engaged in protecting king Sudās, who was surrounded by the armies of the enemy.[42] The close association of war and the sacrifice will be clear from the fact that Indra is said to be protected by sacrifice when he went to kill Vṛtra (III.32.12). The belief in the close association, and the cause-and-effect relationship between war and the sacrifice, results in having the common terms for both.[43]

Aspect of Ṛta

War being only another form of sacrifice, it gets connected

with the most important conception in RV, the Ṛta. The Vedic Ṛta is the principle of *Arche Action,* as the very name shows.[44] It is generally understood as the name for universal order. But it should be noted that the order does not imply inaction. It stands for continuous action, also hinting at steadiness. It is in this Action (that is Ṛta), *satya* is said to be established.[45] The whole idea behind sacrifice is that of connecting the earthly activities with the divine realm. It is through the ritual of sacrifice that the earthly actions are set into the cosmic sphere.[46] War, being closely associated with sacrifice, gets to be a phase of the Universal Action. Thus, Brahmaṇaspati (in the context of war, the presiding deity of the war-chants), has a bow with the string of *ṛta* (II.24.8). His chariot is of *ṛta* (*ibid.,* 23.3) and he is the punisher of the *brahma*-haters (*ibid.,* 4). He is said to bestow wealth upon the sacrificer (warrior), who upholds *ṛta* and kills the enemies (23.17). This activity on the part of Brahmaṇaspati, of helping the warrior-sacrificer, is connected at the end of the hymn with the cosmic exploit of the release of waters, one of the most common and the most fundamental indications of *ṛta*.

It is this close relationship of war with the cosmic order that validates the belief in the gods helping the human hero or the king, his enemies being the earthly forms of Vṛtra (*vṛtrāṇi;* cf. VII-19.4;-83.9). The word *vṛtrahatya,* thus, comes to be a common noun for war.[47] As the earthly war becomes the aspect of *ṛta*, and also of sacrifice, it is but proper that, not only Soma, Agni or Brahmaṇaspati but also, the *dakṣiṇā* and the very sacrifice are said to lead the advancing army, which is not, now, the earthly army, but the veritable *devasenā* (X. 103-8), and the king is praised as the leader of the army as Indra in his cosmic exploits (X.103.6, 7ff).[48] It is pertinent to note, in this connection, a famous ritual which presents the unique fusion of war and the cosmic activity of the release of the sun. It is the Horse-sacrifice. The horse is said to be tethered by straps that are said to be of *ṛta,* thus giving the idea, that the king who releases the horse performs a ritual that is a phase of *ṛta*—the cosmic action. The horse that starts on his march to make the king, who sits sacrificing the whole year round, the lord of the earth, is supposed to be mounted by Indra (I. 163.2), which shows the horse to be the *deva-vāhana* (cf. note 12). It is, thus, clear that the horse-sacrifice establishes a par between the cosmic order and the ritual of the march for the overlordship of the earth, not without a probable war during the course of the march.

The complete identification of sacrifice and war helps another belief which forms into an oft-employed motif in mythology. As the king, who sets out for war, is brought on par with Indra, the former is believed to have the power to go to help the god in the battles against the *asura*-s.[49] The epic descriptions of the divine help, and the free interaction between the human heroes and the divinities, are, thus, not simply fantastic; they are based on a belief having a long history. This belief does not teach resort to fate. On the contrary, it reflects the firm conviction that the hand of the human is backed by the divine power.

NOTES

1. RV VI.75.14. Cf. *kumārā viśikhā iva*. The word never again occurs in the RV. But this image of clean-shaven boys in the description of the arrows is interesting from another point of view; *viśikhā* means an arrow; in later Sanskrit viśikhāḥ may also mean "having loosened tufts".
2. VI.75.1, *jīmūtasya iva bhavati pratīkam*
   yad varmī yāti samadām upasthe
3. The hand-guards, quivers etc. See RV. VI.75. The attire of the Maruts is to be noted; from it one gets a fair picture of an early Vedic warrior.
4. E.W. Hopkins, "Position of the Ruling Caste in Ancient India", *JAOS,* XIII, p. 57 ff. For weapons see *ibid.* ,235; also see Keith, The *Religion and Philosophy of the Veda and Upanishads,* p.288; Ram Gopal, *India of Vedic Kalpasūtras,* Delhi, 1959, 184 ff; V.M. Apte, *Social and Religious Life in the Gṛhyasūtras,* Bombay, 1954, 50 ff.

5. VI.75; X. 103; 152; XX.173; X.174; also partly VI.47.29ff.
6. RV I.10.1 *ud-vaṁśam-iva yemire.* Sāyaṇa-"as do the pole-dancers hoist the pole".
7. *yat sānoḥ sānum āruhat bhuryaspaṣṭa kartvam /*
tad indro artham cetati yūthena vṛṣṇir ejati.
8. I.51.14, *indro aśrāyi.....duryo na yūpaḥ.*
9. Mb. Ādi 63.18 ff; Bṛhatsaṁhitā, 43. The *Indra-mahotsava* seems to be a social form of the original royal rite. See also Mṛcchakaṭika V; Raghuvaṁśa IV.3.
10. Keith, *The Religion and Phil. of the Veda and Up.,* Vol. I, p.31.
11. The banner is often said to be like fire. Cf. Rām. VI. 43.2; 44.7; Mb. Droṇa, 105-3 etc.
12. RV III 27.14, *aśvam na deva-vāhanam.* The word *deva-vāhana* occurs only once in the RV., and has to be differentiated from *havya-vāhana* (an epithet of Agni) in spite of Sāyaṇa's rendering. See Geldner, "wie ein Roz die gotter *fart"—Der Rig Veda,* I. Cf. *indraḥ pura etu naḥ* in the famous *mantra* (X.152.2) used for the erection of the banner. That Indra was the leader of the army on the terrestrial plane is clear from the fact that he alone is called *senyaḥ* (I.81.2; VII.30.2). He is also *senānīḥ* (VII.20.5), an epithet shared only by Soma (IX.96.1) among the gods and Manyu (X.84.2), who is Indra himself.
13. Mb. Droṇa-105-11, where we have the expression *pavanoddhūtam śakra-dhvaja-sama-prabham,* which shows that the *Indra-dhvaja* known to Mb. was fitted with a flying flag. Cf. RV I.51.2.
14. Viṣṇu Dh, P.II.160.10 ff-
śatakrato mahāvīra suparṇas-tatsutāśritaḥ (tu tvadāśritaḥ?)
patatrirāḍvainateyas tathā nārāyaṇa-dhvajaḥ
kāśyapeyo'mṛta-hartā nāgārir-viṣṇu-vāhanaḥ
aprameyo durādharṣo raṇe caivārisūdanaḥ
garutmān māruta-gatis tvayi sannihitaḥ sthitaḥ
sāśvavarmāyudhān yodhān rakṣāsmān mahadripūn.
It can be seen that the praise is that of Indra (*śatakratu*) and Garuḍa is said to be on the flag.
15. J. Gonda, *Aspects of Early Viṣṇuism,* Utrecht, 1954, p.246. The figure of Garuḍa with stretched hands and in the *vīrāsana* position is painted on the banner as the *mantra* "*svastidā*" etc. is recited. Gonda notes the *mantra* as from

the Taittirīya Brāhmaṇa. The earliest source, however, is the Ṛgveda (X. 152.2).

16. Gonda, *op.cit.,* p.247.
17. Bṛhatsaṁhitā, 42; we have mention of the small staffs called Śakrakumāri-s, in this context, 42. 30-40.
18. J.N. Bannerjea-*Development of Hindu Iconography,* Calcutta, 1956, p.103 note.
19. RV IV.27.1; 4; 26.4. As a *śyena* Indra takes away Soma from the mouth of the demon Śuṣṇa (Kāṭhaka Saṁhitā, 37.14).
20. The first notable identification is in the Suparṇādhyāya. The account in the RV Khila (II.1) is obviously later; it resembles Mb.
21. Mb. Bhīṣma, 25-20; Droṇa, 105.8; 29.
22. Mb. Vana, 151.17.
23. As the generator of Arjuna (Mb. Ādi, 63.116); helping Arjuna by depriving Karṇa of his earrings (*ibid.,* 67.144) etc.
24. Jaiminīya Br.I.363.
25. Śat. Br. I.6.9.18.
26. Mb. Droṇa, 105-8, *siṁha-lāṅgūlam ugrāsyam dhvajam vānara-lakṣaṇam.*
27. *Ibid.,* 10.11.
    tathaiva siṁha-lāṅgūlam droṇaputrasya bhārata
    dhvajāgram sam apaśyāma bālasūryasamaprabham
    kāñcanam pavanoddhūtam śakra-dhvajasamaprabham
    With this compare RV IV. 16.14, where Indra is said to shine like the lion in the vicinity of the Sun. With the concept of the tail of the lion in the banner may be compared the banners on Hindu temples in actual use even to-day, having a ball of wool or cotton at the end.
28. Mb. Droṇa, 28 ff, for various figures; Varāhamihira, Yogayātrā, VI.Iff. An image said to be of Herakles was carried before the army of Porus; see McCrindle, *Invasion of India by Alexander the Great.,* pp. 208-9. The image is also said to be of Śiva. But Śiva is usually associated with the skin of the tiger or the elephant while Herakles is associated with the skin of the lion and a staff. In view of the references from the Mb. we have noted, the image appears to be that of Indra as Bevan thinks. See *Cambridge History of India,* Delhi, 1955, p.328. It cannot be, however, of Kṛṣṇa as alternately suggested by Bevan. See A.M.

Shastri, *Varāhamihira and His Times*, Jodhpur, 1991, pp.80-90.

29. Cf. *ugram yuyujma pṛtanāsu sāsahim.*
30. AV I.21.1 (RV X.152.2). The *mantra is—svastidā viśaspatir vṛtrahā vimṛdho vaśī vṛṣendraḥ pura etu naḥ somapā abhayaṁkaraḥ.*
31. See note 14. See also Yogayātrā VI.3 which enjoins the following *mantra* from the RV (IV. 31.3) when the image of Indra is being carried if the army advances to the eastern direction—
abhī ṣu ṇaḥ sakhīnām avitā jaritṛṇām
śatam bhavasy ūtibhiḥ.
The word *ūtibhiḥ* is to be marked. The idea of protection in war is clearly seen in RV. VII.27.1; 2; 4; 28.4; 30.1; 2 etc.
32. *siṁha-lāṅgūlam ugrāsyam dhvajam vānaralakṣaṇam* and *trāsayāmāsa tat sainyam dhvajo gāṇḍīva-dhanvanaḥ.* The word *trāsayāmāsa* is interesting. Though in later Sanskrit, it means 'terrified', in the RV. it has the connotation of 'protection'; see RV I.128.5; 7; V.62.6; 41-1; VIII-62.4; IV.55.1.
33. J. W. McCrindle, *op.cit.*, p.208.
34. For banners destroyed in war see Mb. Karṇa V.50; 15.39; Rām.VI. 44.7 (monkeys tearing the banners). A more interesting reference is where Nīla—the monkey-chief—is said to dart directly at the banner of Rāvaṇa (VI.79.79 ff). The fall of the banner indicated the death of the king (Bṛhatsaṁhitā-42.74); The Romans carried the banner in front of the army; but in actual battle-action, it was at the rear of the army, Hastings, *Encl. Rel. & Ethics,* Vol. II, p.349[a], probably to save it from dishonour, and to avert an evil omen. The Assyrians had in the banner a deity placed within a disc at the top of the pole. Layard, *Monuments of Nineveh*, I series, 1849, pp.14, 27; also Ragozin, *Assyria*, 1888, p.252. The banner of the Hasmonaens was identified with Jahweh and had the inscription—' Who is like Thee among the mighty, Jahweh", Hastings, *op.cit.,* p.349[b].
35. X 173.3; *imam indro adīdharad dhruvam dhruveṇa haviṣā.*
36. Cf. *somasya tā mada indraś cakāra,* the famous refrain (II.15); also II 12.14; VI 44.; 15; 17; VIII. 17.18 etc.
37. V.29.6 where Indra is said to have got success by the

mantra in the Triṣṭubh metre. Soma and praise (in *mantra*-s) madden Indra for valour (IV. 42.6; VII.19.11); for *mantra*-s helping and completing the physical activity, see Nirukta, I.16; Ai.Br.I.16=3.5 where the *ṛk* is said to be *abhirūpa*.

38. See, Dange, "Adornment as a Protective Measure", Dr. Mirasi Fel. Vol. Nagpur, 1965, p.87 ff.
39. VII.23.1 & 2. For interpretation, see Velankar, *Ṛgveda Maṇḍala* VII (Bharatiya Vidya Bhavan) Bombay, 1963.
40. *utāśiṣṭha anu śṛṇvanti vahnayaḥ / sabheyo vipro bharate matī dhanā*
vīḷudveṣā anu vaśa ṛṇamādadiḥ sa ha vājī samithe brahmaṇaspatiḥ
The next verse makes the point clearer, when Brahmaṇaspati is said to go to war and collect *ṛṇa,* i.e. the booty.
41. In the Horse-sacrifice the sacrifice goes on for the whole year. Keith, *op.cit.,* p.344. Cf. Rāmāyaṇa VI 84.13,14 where Indrajit is said to return to the sacrificial chamber *nikumbhila* during the course of the battle to gain renewed valour. The place appears to be right in the vicinity of the battlefield. Cf. RV VII.83.8, where the sacrifice in the vicinity of the battle-field is hinted at.
42. VII.83.8 Cf. *dāśarājñe pariyattāya viśvataḥ*
sudāsa indrāvaruṇavaśikṣatām
śvityañco yatra namasā kapardino
dhiyā dhīvanto asapanta tṛtsavaḥ
The word *yatra* is to be noted. The Tṛtsus are said to be the Vasiṣṭhas. For various opinions see *Vedic Index.*
43. Cf. *samarya; samitha; samat;* more pointed is *havīman* (VII. 83.4), also *deva-vīti* (*ibid.,* 19-4), where many enemies are killed; the word also means sacrifice (V. 42.10; IX.96.14; 97.2 etc).
44. For other interpretations of this term, see Velankar, *op.cit.,* p. iv, also Guillemin, J.D., "Heraclitus and Iran", *History of Religions*, Chicago Uni., Summer 1963, Vol. III, No. 1.
45. Velankar, *op., cit.,* p.6 ff.
46. A. Bergaigne, *La Religion Vedique,* Vol. I. 1878, pp. vii-viii. For this concept in ritual, see the Vājasaneyi-Saṁhitā (I.10; II.11 etc), where the human acts are said to be accomplished by divine hands.

47. So is also *ahi-hatya;* cf. I.61.8; 165-6; III.32.12; 47.4. For *Vṛtrahatya* see I.52.4; IV. 19.1 etc.
48. The hymn is traditionally used at consecration for war, as already notcd.
49. Keith, *op.cit.,* p.346, note 3.

Chapter 14

DRUM AND THE DANCE (KRĪḌĀ) OF INDRA AND CHĀYĀ

In the context of the praise of the drum, the Atharvaveda (AV) makes a reference to Indra as "playing" with the gods in company with Chāyā (V. 21.8). The beating of the drum (*dundubhi*) has the background of an advance for war and the destruction of the enemy (V.20 and 21). The war-drum has been a necessary aid and is mentioned also in the Ṛgveda in the context of war for the purpose of causing terror in the ranks of the enemy and final victory (RV I. 28.5; VI. 47.29). It was addressed as the "fist" (*muṣṭi*) of Indra (*ib.*, 30), a detail which obtains also in AV (VI. 127.2); and he, alone, is associated with this expression (does it indicate the shape of the drum?). Among other details, the war-drum is described as having the roar like that of a lion or a bull and its vigour is said to be the same as that of Indra (AV V. 20.2 and 3). Its thunder is said to be divine (v.4). As the army advances, and battle rages, various gods are invoked to bless the army of the advancing king, among them being Indra, Āditya and the Maruts, particularly, who are invoked to pound the enemy-ranks (vv.10,11). The advancing armies of the king are termed "armies of the gods" (v.12 *devasenāḥ*). Taking into account the pattern of Vedic expression, it is evident that Indra has a twofold connotation here: (i) The god who leads the army of the gods, especially of the Maruts who are cast in the attire of the warriors in the Vedic period; and (ii) The human king, identified with Indra, who leads his army of human warriors.[1] But the mention of Chāyā in the context of war is unique to the AV. It does not occur in the Veda elsewhere. Chāyā is, here, conceived as a female power—as divine as Indra and the Maruts. The translation of the verse where it occurs is:

> With whom Indra 'plays' steps resounding, in the company of Chāyā, by them may our enemies be terrified-they who advance against us in rows (AV V.21.8).

The exact expression that would be under examination here is:

yáir indraḥ prakrīḍate pad-ghoṣaiś chāyayā *sạha*

To know the full implication of the passage, we have to give thought to each of the two parts in which the expression has to be divided: (i) Indra with Chāyā (*indraḥ* chāy*ayā saha*); and (ii) 'plays' with sounding steps (*pra-krīḍate pad-ghoṣaiḥ*). The point is, who is Chāyā? It must be remembered that the context is of the battle and the advance of the army. Though the word Chāyā occurs in the Ṛgveda and later, it does not indicate a deity associated with war. Another point is that it generally (or rather, mostly) indicates" "shade" or "shadow" which would suggest the dark colour. This is clear when a person desires to go to Chāyā from the heat of the sun (RV II 33.7; VI. 16.38). When Chāyā is spoken of being in the water (*ib.* V 44.6),[2] it refers to the reflection of a person and it is dark. But, when Mṛtyu, the god of death, is said to be the Chāyā of Ka (Prājāpati, RV X. 121. 2c)[3] the indication is of the belief of Death being of dark complexion; but, when it is said that even nectar is the Chāyā of Ka (*ib.*), darkness cannot be taken as indicated; on the contrary, we have to take the word as meaning "lustre". According to a myth in the Gopatha Br. (Pūrva I. 1-6), Brahma (Neuter; the primordial principle) was alone prior to creation (a pet motif in creation myths all over; cf. Prajāpati and, later, Brahmā of the Purāṇas). He heated himself (in *tapas* as a step to create), with the result that he perspired into streams (a common motif in Hindu myths), which formed the primeval ocean. He peeped into these waters (which must be assumed to be serene and motionless) and saw his own reflection in them (*ib.* 3 *svasya chāyām apaśyat*). He got sexually excited and his semen got ejected into the waters. (We are not concerned here with the rest of the account.) This mythical account suggests, that (i) the Chāyā was dark; and (ii) "she" was the female counterpart of Brahman (a male, though the term has the Neuter gender), which would also show that the primordial principle (like Prajāpati and Brahmā) was conceived as androgynous, being a bisexual whole able to create by itself. Even independent of creation, some important gods are said to possess this trait; and Indra is no exception.[4] About the word *chāyā* it is observed that it had the connotation of darkness, lustre and also of appearance.[5] However, that of darkness is more common and, especially so when it is related to a person or a solid object. As such, the expression *chāyayā saha* in the present context, would mean Indra, with the dark complexioned Chāyā, who is his own counterpart seen as a female divinity.

Now, we come to the other part of the expression, 'plays' with sounding steps (*prakrīḍate pad-ghoṣaiḥ*). In the context of war, and with the accompaniment of the drums, this 'play' can be nothing but a dance — a war-dance. Those who are said to accompany Indra in this dance (*krīḍā* or *prakrīḍā*), apart from Chāyā have to be understood as the Maruts, his constant companions as a group. The epithet *pra-krīḍin* is solely applied to them, among the gods (RV VII.56.16; the only other place is IV. 41.11 where the weapons are said to be *prakrīḷinaḥ* in battles, 'dancing weapons' showing the dexterity and quickness with which they are wielded). More particularly, *krīḍinaḥ* (cf. RV. I 166.2 where they are described as *krīḷāḥ*) came to be their unique epithet in a pseudo-myth related to the Sākamedha, a division of the seasonal sacrifices (Cāturmāsya-s). It is said that when Indra dealt a blow to Vṛtra with his thunderbolt, the Maruts sported (danced) round in front of him. Likewise, it is said, they (Maruts) dance before him (the sacrificer) in circular movements as he is about to destroy the enemy who hates him.[6] That is why, it is explained, he (the sacrificer) offers to the Maruts, the *krīḍinaḥ*, a cake (*puroḍāśa*), prepared on seven potsherds (Śat. Br. II 5.3.20). This dancing is said to be a glorificatory rite (cf. *parikrīḍante mahayantaḥ*). From the text it would appear that this glorificatory dance was performed at the beginning of the march against the enemy.[7] There is every probability that it was performed also in the fields of battle when the opposite armies faced each other. The purpose of such a dance was, without doubt, to infuse the warriors and the king, who was believed to be on par with Indra,[8] with strength and confidence. The Taitt. Br. (I 6.7.4ff) has a similar account, which could be taken as a variation of the same myth; and the context is the same (Sākamedha). According to it, when Indra smote Vṛtra he hurried to the farthest end; but he was not quite sure if he had really dealt a heavy blow. Hence, he said, "Who will know of it?" (i.e. if really Vṛtra was hit). The Maruts, who were his companions, said that they would know and tell him, on the condition that the first oblation in the rite Sākamedha would be offered to them. Indra agreed. (So, the Maruts went searching and found Vṛtra.) They, then, sported (danced) before him (*adhyakrīḍan*). As they did dance (*akrīḍan*) thus, that is the essence of their being *krīḍin*-s. This text does not say anything beyond this.[9] If we compare the pseudo-myth from the Śat. Br. noted above, the implication seems to be that Indra was apprehensive of the result of his blow; hence, he ran away in fear. The indication of the remark, "who will know of it" would be either: (i) who would verify if Vṛtra is really smitten; or (ii) who will know if he (= Indra, himself) shall be able to smite Vṛtra, completely? The word *hatvā* in *vṛtram hatvā* does not mean absolutely "killing". Its meaning is 'having smitten' (given a blow). The Indra-Vṛtra combat is a continuous affair. The word *vṛtra-hatyeṣu*, occurring at various places in the Ṛgveda, is an indication to this meaning. The dance of the Maruts, before Indra (and in a circle; cf. *pari-cikrīḍuḥ* at Śat. Br.) is to remove the apprehension and fear and to restore confidence. The *adhi-krīḍā* (Taitt. Br.), *abhitaḥ, parikrīḍa* (Śat. Br.) and the *pra-krīḍā/krīḍā* (RV and AV) are, hence, not indicative of a simple "play", but of a ritual dance. There is hardly any doubt, that the source of this *krīḍā* of the Vedic gods is the actual dance in ritual; and pseudo-myths got formed from actual practices, where the humans act as gods in the aura of ritual. An examination of the words indicative of dance (√*nṛt*; *nṛtū*) in RV shows, that they occur only with Indra, Maruts, Aśvins and Uṣas. Out of these for the Aśvins and Uṣas it occurs once for each. For Indra it occurs eight times[10] and for the Maruts twice, but in a special way. They are, at one place, said to have danced (*nṛtuḥ*) for Gotama to the tune of the metres (and lauds), for the release of waters (RV V. 52. 12).[11] The word *nṛtū* occurs only for Indra (RV VIII. 68.7), the Maruts (*nṛtavaḥ* VIII. 20.22), the Aśvins (*nṛtū* VI. 63.5) and Uṣas is compared to a dancer (*nṛtūr iva* I 92.4). This would indicate, that the dancer was a necessity on some important occasions in the Vedic society. The dance of the Maruts, along with Indra and Chāyā was such an occasion, which was advance for war. There is every probability of a ritual-dance at the advance of the army, where a dark woman figured along with some of the warriors or professional performers to enact the pseudo-myth; or, the myth itself might have been suggested and coined from such a practice.

We have suggested, earlier in the course of this discussion, that Chāyā was the female counterpart of Indra and that she came to be conceived as a female deity of prowess independent of the shadow. In later mythical terminology we could say, that she was the Śakti of Indra—a terrible one as against his popular counterpart, Indrāṇī who was the benevolent one. We have other benevolent female goddesses, a trait already seen in RV, namely Varuṇānī who is mentioned more often like Indrāṇī, though not as popular as the latter (RV I.22. 12; II. 32. 8; VII.

34.22), Agnāyī (I 22.12; V. 48.8) and, Aśvinī (V. 46.8). This would indicate that the concept of a female counterpart of a male god was already getting formed at the period of the Ṛgveda. But, the war came to require a terrible and ferocious goddess later. Chāyā met the requirement as a female counterpart of the prominent war-god, Indra. Contemplated as dark in complexion for the reasons mentioned above, she was the source of such later goddesses as Kālī and Bhadrakālī, which need not be traced to any source beyond the Vedic. Kālī, though not mentioned in the early Vedic Saṁhitā texts, appears to have been suggested from the name of one of the flames of the fire-god, Agni, being originally an epithet. The fire-god has Agnāyī as his female counterpart earlier; but when the Muṇḍaka Upaniṣad (I.2.4.) names the flames Kālī, Karālī, Sulohitā and Dhūmra-varṇā (black, cruel, clear red and smoky respectively), all with a common term Devī, we have an extension of the same trait. Though Kālī, as the dark goddess and a phase of the fair Gaurī, both being aspects of Pārvatī, appears later in the Puranic literature, the concept of the dark goddess named Kālī has to be taken as far back as the Muṇḍaka Upaniṣad. That the concept of the goddess Kālī was popular far early, and independent of the Śiva-myth is clear from the name Kālidāsa (the poet). Even before him, Kālī seems to have been popular. This is clear from the fact that one of the names of Satyavatī was Kālī (Mb. Bhīṣma 20.2), and Bhadrakālī is mentioned as one of the goddesses to whom a daily offering was prescribed by the Manusmṛti (III.89) and even earlier by the Śāṅkhāyana Gṛ. S. (SBE, Vol. 29, p. 86). But, as shown earlier, Kālī has to be taken even earlier—to the Muṇḍaka Upaniṣad. It is to be particularly noted that Mb. mentions various goddesses propitiated in the context of war by Arjuna, Kālī and Bhadrakālī included (Bhīṣma 23.4). This would indicate that the name of Satyavatī was not so much due to her (probable) complexion but on the basis of the popularity of Kālī, Kālī hereself being suggested from the "dark" flame of Agni. The position of Kālī in her invocation at the war is just the same as of Chāyā at AV, noted above. Even in the Śiva-myths his dance with Kālī forms a contrast with his relationship with Pārvatī, the former associated with strife and war.[12] An interesting development of historical value may be noted in this context. During the Pallava-Pāṇḍya period in south India (A.D. 550-850 and further), in place of the two girls who constantly attended on the king to sing his praise, and were called Virali and Patini, the former gave place to Mātaṅkī (Mātaṅgī, Mātaṅkī being a Tamil pronunciation). The Mātaṅkī had the function of swinging the sword, in addition to that of singing the praise of the king.[13] As the "swinger of the sword" she was named also *vālvici* (*vāl* means "tail" in Tamil; and as the curved sword resembles the tail, the latter gave its name to the former; cf. Sanskrit *karavāla* = 'hand-tail'). Yet another function for her was the beating of the drum (called *tannumai*, which is a Tamil pronunciation of *dundubhi*, due to the paucity of alphabets for all oral sounds).[14] A Tamil text of this period (Purapporulven-pamalai) mentions the Virali as singing the praise of the king and dancing behind the chariot of the king with a demon-anklet. This is in imitation of the dance of the goddess Korravai[15] (an aspect of Mātaṅkī? which is a borrowal from the Sanskrit Mātaṅgī?). The Mb. mentions Mātaṅgī as a ferocious goddess born from the wrath of the female demon Krodhavaśā (Ādi 66.61 and 66). The Atharvaveda may well be taken as providing the prototype for such myths and practices, and of goddesses, in the *krīḍā*-dance of Indra with Chāyā.

NOTES

1. Cf. RV. VII.18 where the exploits of Sudās Paijavana and Indra get fused; esp. verse 19 where the river Yamunā is said to have protected Indra. Such instances are frequent; cf. also the coronation of a king, X. 173; AV VI. 87-88. Such descriptions are the basis for later accounts of gods coming to earth and heroes going to heaven temporarily for mutual help.

2. *chāyayā dadhire sidhrayā-psu-ā*; Śāyaṇa renders *apsu* as *vyāpikāsu stutiṣu* and also *apsu* (in waters). Geldner, *Der Rigveda* "Abbild im Wasser" is more to the point.
3. *yasya chāyā-mṛtam yasya mṛtyuḥ*. According to a myth in Mb. from the fire in the body of Brahmā, a damsel was produced. Her body was dark, red and yellow. Brahmā named her Mṛtyu, Droṇa-parvan 53.17ff.
4. Indra is said to have become a girl called Menā, RV I.51.13
5. For lustre cf. Raghuvaṁśa IV.5 where *chāyā-maṇḍala* could indicate a circle of lustre, but, as compared with *ātapatra* in the same verse, it could also indicate shade. In the case of *Chāyā-Sītā*, born from the fire as Vedavatī it could be both similarity in appearance and lustre, Rām. XVII (Uttarakāṇḍa) 17; cf. also about the boy to be adopted, *putra-chāyā-vaham*, quoted by Nīlakaṇṭha in Vyavahāramayūkha, Ed. P.V.Kane, Bombay, 1926. p.110. Chāyā, the substitute for Sañjñā, is said to be *savarṇa* may be dark yet similar in appearance; the myth does not occur in Mb., but the Harivaṁśa gives it,I.9; Viṣṇu P.III.2ff has Chāyā-Sañjñā as the name of the look-alike.
6 Śat. Br.II.5.3.20 *vṛtram haniṣyantam* and *bhrātṛvyam haniṣyantam*. Eggeling J., renders *abhitaḥ paricikrīḍuḥ* as "sporting around" which leaves away the meaning of *abhitaḥ*; see SBE, Vol.12, p.416. On p.417, n.1 he has, "They sported and, in the bracket,"danced about", which is exact.
7. Like the Nīrājanā, which was a yearly rite; but it was always followed by a mock military march against an enemy represented by a clay figure; cf. Bṛhatsaṁhitā, 46.8 ff;21.3.
8. RV VII.33.4;esp. *indre śuṣmam adadhātā vasiṣṭhaḥ*.
9. Eggeling, *op.cit.*, p.417, n.1 has "They sported (danced about) on him (Vṛtra, and thereby found out that he was dead)" (brackets are his). This is not exact; *adhi* does not mean 'on'; and the dance is in front of Indra (cf. Śat.Br.); this is in line with the usual practice.
10. Nom. Sing. RV VII.68.7;92.3; and Voc. at I.130.7 twice; II.22.4; VI.29..3; VIII.24.4;12.
11. *chandastubhaḥ kubhanyavaḥ*; Geldner leaves away *kubhanyavaḥ* unrendered. In the note he compares it with *udanyavaḥ*, V.54.2. Sāyaṇa understands a root, √*kubh*, meaning 'release waters' (*undanakarmā*). However, the Paninian list of roots mentions the root √*kub*, and alternately √*kubj*, but meaning 'to cover'. M. Monier-Williams follows Sāyaṇa.

12. Wendy D. O'Flaherty thinks this dance to be "dangerous", *Sexual Metaphors and Animal Symbols in Indian Mythology*, Delhi, 1981, p.143.
13. Saskia C. Kersenboomstory, *Nityasumaṅgalī-Devadāsī Tradition in South India*, Delhi, 1987, p.22.
14. So, *t* stands for th,d,dh; hence *dundubhi-tantupi-tannumai* the ending being commonly *ai*; cf. *dosai*; *Yātrā-yāthirai* etc.
15. Saskia C. Kersenboomstory, *op.cit.*, p.23.

Chapter 15

THE VĀṆA

The word Vāṇa occurs six times in the Ṛgveda, and is also referred to in other Vedic texts. As regards the meaning of *vāṇa* in the other texts there seems to be no difference of opinion or any doubt, and it is rendered as "musical instrument." Thus, it is said to be an instrument having one hundred strings.[1] It also is said to be a kind of *Vīṇā;*[2] and it was customary for the Hotṛ priest to play on this instrument while he was made to oscillate in the swing in the ritual of the Mahāvrata.[3]

The difficulty about the original concept of *vāṇa,* however, comes in studying the passages from RV and AV. Here the word has been variously rendered, as "music" and "arrow". Here, then, is a point for investigation. We may jot down the passage from RV.

dhamanto vāṇam marutaḥ sudānavaḥ
made somasya raṇyāni cakrire (I. 85.10)

The word *dhamantaḥ* (blowing) would indicate that originally it could not have been an "instrument with strings", though it came to be so in the later times. This appears to be the reason why Zimmer renders the word, in this context, as "flute",[4] which answers the sense of "blowing". Sāyaṇa's rendering here, as "a musical instrument fitted with one hundred strings" (*vāṇam śatasaṅkhyābhistantrībhir yuktam vīṇā-viśeṣam*) cannot be accepted as it is influenced by a later practice. Moreover, he renders the word *dhamantaḥ* as "*vādayantaḥ*" (playing upon), which belies the exact sense of the word and brings in the stringed instrument. Geldner's,[5] "Ihre Musik blasend haben" (playing on, or blowing, their music) is not quite clear, in view of the fact that he renders the word *vāṇa* as "Stimme" (sound) at other places. Max Müller[6] renders the word here, as at another place (IX. 97.8) as "speech". We now take up the next passage, where we read—

> *āṅgūṣyam pavamānam sakhāyaḥ*
> *durmarṣam sākam pravadanti vāṇam*
> (IX. 97.8)

Sāyaṇa renders the word *vāṇam* as "musical instrument", and takes the word *pra-vadanti* to mean *"pra vādayanti"* (play upon), but adds, "by implication, they sing" (*tad upalakṣitam gānam kurvanti iti śeṣaḥ).* This clearly shows that he is not quite satisfied with his rendering as *"pra vādayanti"*. The idea in the expression *pra vadanti vāṇam* clearly appears to be of the loud chant, especially in the presence of the word *āṅgūṣyam* (commonly raised aloft). Geldner is perfectly right in rendering it as, "erheben sie ihre stimme", and Max Müller again renders *vāṇa* as "Speech". The *āṅgūṣyam pavamānam-vāṇam* is clearly indicative of the loud sonorous notes which are qualified by the suggestive epithet *"durmarṣam"* (unbearable). This also shows that originally *vāṇa* is not indicative of any instrument as such. It has a clear association with speech or the voice. The point will be borne out by the next passage. Thus we have, Soma being praised:

> Thy powers rise forth like the roar of the ocean-waves. Accelerate the edge of the *vāṇa* (IX 50.1).

Here Sāyaṇa gets into confusion in rendering the expression, *"vāṇasya codaya pavim"* as "make the sound like that of a shooting arrow" (*visṛṣṭa-bāṇa-sadṛśam śabdam kuru ity' arthaḥ"*), though he renders the word *pavi* as "speech". He renders the word *vāṇa* as "a musical instrument", and also as "arrow". The rendering does not bring out clearly the meaning of the word *codaya* (accelerate). Max Müller takes the word *vāṇa,* here, to mean "arrow", which is rather surprising! Geldner has in his main rendering, "Scharfe die Spitze der Rede"; but just after it he puts in the bracket the words "des Pfeils"!, adding in the notes that here we have a case of double meaning viz, "arrow" and "voice", referring to Sāyaṇa to support his point.

The point is an interesting example of "wortspiel". But it has to be remembered that, in spite of the interchange of /v/ and /b/ (*vāṇa-bāṇa)* giving apparent legitimacy to the rendering as "arrow", the dominating idea is of Speech; for in the same verse we read about the rise of the threefold Speech, which goes aloft with the advent of Soma (v.2, *prasave ta ud-īrate tisro vāco makhasyuvaḥ)*. There is also another point to be noted. The special invocation to Soma to impel the 'edge' of the *vāṇa* suits more to Speech, than to any arrow as such. It also ill suits the instrument of music. Even as Bṛhaspati is believed to be the lord of the speaking faculty, Soma has a direct control over Speech; for he alone, among the gods, except Viśvakarman, is clearly the *vācas-pati* and *vācam-īṅkhayaḥ* (RV IX.101.5;-6; cf. 35.5). Even in the case of the Maruts, who are said to "blow" (*dhamantaḥ)* the *vāṇa,* effects of Soma are referred to (*made somasya*), thus establishing a close association between the *vāṇa* and Soma.

But this association of *vāṇa* and Speech does not in any way whatsoever, guarantee the identification of the *vāṇa* and Speech. And here we have to think of *vāṇa* not, after all, different from Speech. Though the *vāṇa* is clearly associated with the vocal activity, as different from the instrumental one, in the most original concept as vouched by the RV, the difference between the *vāṇa* and *vāṇī* has to be taken note of. This does not mean that we can readily believe the *vāṇa* to be the instrument and *vāṇī* to be the Speech. The difficulty about the expression *vadanti,* in respect of the *vāṇa,* we have already noted. Let us consider another expression about *vāṇa,* which would help throw some more light on the point:

gobhir vāṇo ajyate sobharīṇām (VIII. 20.8)

The Sobharis are a sect of the Kaṇvas, and do not appear in any other *maṇḍala* than the VIII, which is the family *maṇḍala* of the Kaṇvas. Here the word *vāṇa* has been rendered as "arrow" by some scholars.[7] Geldner renders this portion as follows-

> "Mit Kuh (milch) wird die Stimme der Sobhari's gesalbt" (with the milk of the cow is smeared the voice of the Sobharis).

He adds in the notes a very interesting suggestion that the word *gobhiḥ* goes well with the idea of Soma, and compares it with IX. 50.1 where Soma and the *vāṇa* are associated. He suggests that the song of the Sobharis simultaneously accompanies the mixing of Soma with the milk. The exact implication of the remark, "der sanger glattet seine Stimme mit Milch oder Soma" (The singer smoothens, or polishes, his song with milk or Soma) is, however, not clear. If he means that the effect of Soma impels the faculty of Speech (*vāṇa!)* as at IX. 50.1, one can understand; but then, the point is—can we take the word *gobhiḥ* to indicate Soma, neglecting its first meaning as 'milk'?[8] That is exactly the difficulty before Geldner; for he says "Milk or Soma". Ludwig takes a flatly literal sense of the expression and renders it as, "mit der milk gesalbt den Sobhari der zapfen am wagen', thus taking the word to mean the pivot (zapfen) of the chariot which according to him, is smeared with milk. Griffith follows him.[9] It is difficult to accept this rendering; and we do not quite get the idea in the absence of any custom to that effect; and, moreover, it is not clear why only at this place the word *vāṇa* should indicate the pivot! Geldner rightly remarks that the *ratha* referred to in the expression "*rathe kośe hiraṇyaye*" is metaphorical, indicating the sacrifice (Der wagen ist der Opferwagen) and the "golden vessel (*kośa*)" is the tub of Soma (Der Soma-gefaz). Thus the act of anointing the *vāṇa* gets accomplished in the sacrificial ritual where Soma is being pressed. But one wonders if the anointing refers to the actual partaking of Soma which, thus, figuratively anoints the voice of the singers. Moreover, the word *gobhiḥ* has to be taken in an indirect sense to indicate Soma. We, therefore, have to seek resort to some other explanation. We may note, however, that Sāyaṇa renders the word *vāṇa*, here, as "*marud-vīṇā*".

We now take up another passage, which is a bit more obscure:

dīnā dakṣā vi duhanti pra vāṇam (IV. 24.9)

The context is of a barter in which a person gets a thing of lesser value in exchange for that of higher value; and the seer remarks, "the poor and the rich[10] *milk the vāṇa*". Sāyaṇa renders the word *vāṇa* as "*vacanam*". Macdonell and Keith (*Vedic Index*) do not note this passage while commenting on *vāṇa,* as they cite references from other scholars. From the context of the expression Geldner renders the word *vāṇa* as "Handel" (trade). In fact the idea appears to be of a wordy exchange between the person who purchases and one who sells; and this is figuratively expressed as "milking the *vāṇa*", as Sāyaṇa indicates. It appears more probable that the word *vāṇa* has, even here, an association with the faculty of speech.

Before we take the last passage of *vāṇa* we may recapitulate what we have discussed. Out of the total number of six passages in RV there are three clearly connected with Soma. They are: (i) vāṇ*asya codayā pavim;* (ii) *āṅgūṣyam pavamānam pravadanti vāṇam;* and (iii) *dhamanto vāṇam marutaḥ... made somasya.* Taking into account the relationship between Soma and Speech, it will be only proper to take *vāṇa* as having relationship with the faculty of Speech, as Geldner and Sāyaṇa have done in most cases, barring the latter's rendering as the "musical instrument" in some places. The most suggestive word, apt to be misunderstood, is *gobhiḥ*. Sāyaṇa renders the word as "*śabdaiḥ"* as one of the two alternatives, which appears to be quite correct and in keeping with the fact that Speech is often praised as Cow (*go).* The idea will, then, be that the words anoint the *vāṇa*. In other words, the *vāṇī* anoints the *vāṇa,* in the sacrificial assembly. The *vāṇa* cannot, however, be the musical instrument with strings in these places, as we have already observed above. This *vāṇa*, in the most original concept, then, can be nothing else than the vocal apparatus through which the words of the *mantra*-s flow, as if anointing the former. It is also likely that in the word *ajyate* the seer purposefully indulges into a pun, meaning (i) gets anointed, and (ii) gets impelled, the meaning, in the latter case, being that, the vocal apparatus (*vāṇa)* of the Sobharis gets impelled by Speech in the form of the *mantra*-s. It is in this sense that the expression *pra vadanti vāṇam* holds good. In the edge of the *vāṇa* being sharpened (or the edge [*pavi*] of the wheel of *vāna* being impelled, as another meaning) we have the sharpening effect of Soma on the human vocal apparatus. In *dhamanto vāṇam* the idea appears to be of roar, which, in the case of the Maruts, is the thunder before the storm. This may be compared with the *dhamani* of Indra (II. 11.8), which is his terrible speech. The symbolic identification of Speech and the cow being a settled fact, the expression *vi duhanti pra vāṇam,* in all probability, refers to the 'quarrelsome bargain' of the seller and the purchaser,[11] susggested in "milking the vocal organ" (=arguing and counter-arguing).

It is, thus, clear that the most original meaning of *vāṇa* is the vocal apparatus, i.e., the oral cavity which actually produces the sound. This apparatus is called *vāṇa* from the fact that the root √*van* means to produce a sound. In the secondary meaning *vāṇa* came to be the sound produced from the *vāṇa;* and in this way the expression *āṅgūṣyam pavamānam pra vadanti vāṇam* means, "They express the flow of sounds (in the form of the *mantra*-s*)* that is loud and accompanying the pressed out Soma." The root √*van* from which the word *vāṇa* (a flow of oral sounds, or the oral apparatus) is derived may be compared with √*pan*-√*paṇ* (to praise) and the similar √*bhaṇ (*to talk), which gives the word *bhāṇa* being a one-act play, Middle English *bannen* (to curse) which gives the English √*ban* (to exile by a proclamation), the Swedish *bann* (English, ban) and the Old German √*pannen* (to summon) associated with the Teutonic strong verb √*bannen* (to proclaim), which is phonetically akin to the Sanskrit *van*. On the other hand √*van* and √*pan* are comparable with the Germanic word for the oral sound, *phone*. The Vedic *vāṇa* is, then, the oral apparatus, in the most original concept. In an allied concept it is the flow of the oral sound, getting further recognized as the *vāṇī*. It will be, rather, interesting to note that, of the total number of six places where the word *vāṇa* occurs in the RV., it is associated only with the Maruts among the gods. According to the belief of the ancient Hindu grammarians the vocal breath, which produces the different sounds in the mouth, is controlled by the Maruts and is called *Māruta*. It is only natural that, on the basis of the human vocal organ (*vāṇa*), the next step would be of an instrument that would produce a similar sound or notes by blowing through. It is not improbable that RV refers to this type of an instrument when it describes the Maruts as *"dhamanto vāṇam"*. The stringed *vāṇa* of the later *saṁhitā*-s is an adaptation of the vocal *"vāṇa"*. There does not occur any clear reference to it in RV. Where the word *vāṇa* occurs with humans in the passages noted above, it only stylistically indicates the faculty of speech, i.e., roaring, arguing (*vi duhanti pra vāṇam* at IV. 24.9), singing (*vadanti vāṇam* at IX 97.8;-50.1 *vāṇasya codaya pavim*; and VIII. 20.8 *gobhir vāṇo ajyate*). We have already observed, while passing, that it is not improbable that in the last expression the poet is indulging in a pun on the word *ajyate*. The word may indicate the act of smearing (anointing) the vocal apparatus (*vāṇa*) on the part of the *mantra*-s (*gobhiḥ*) as also the act of impelling. With the second sense we may compare *"gāyatreṇa sam-ajyate"* in respect of Agni (I. 188.11) or *"kratvā hi droṇe ajyase'gne vājī na kṛtvyaḥ* VI.2.8), where 'smearing' is accomplished with a praise-formula.

We may refer to another passage, now from AV which leaves little doubt about the fact that *vāṇa* is, in the origin, the voice or the human vocal organ. Thus it is:

> *medhām ko asminn adhyauhat*
> *ko vāṇam nṛto dadhau* (AV X 2.17b)

This passage occurs during the description of the human body and its wonderful structure, and the seer asks himself—"Who established in it the Intellect, who the *vāṇa* (and) the gesticulations (including the dances)?". It is clear that *vāṇa* is the part of the human body capable of singing, or the vocal power. This whole part is quoted in the *Vaitāna sūtra* (37.19) along with the *Puruṣa-sūkta*. The human origin of the *vāṇa* continued in belief, as is seen from the psychological basis of the preparation of the stringed *vāṇa* of the later times and its *animation* in ritual. Thus when the stringed *vāṇa* is ready at the Mahāvrata, the following *mantra* is recited:

> For the *prāṇa* thee, for the *apāna* thee, for the *vyāna* thee do I strike (*prāṇāya tvā apānāya tvā vyānāya tvā ullikhāmi)* (Ai. Ār. V.1).

With this *mantra* the *vāṇa* was struck thrice with the branch of the *uduṁbara* tree, fresh and leafy. According to the Taitt. Sam. (VII. 5.9.2) the *vāṇa* is endowed with one hundred strings, *because* man is endowed with one hundred years of life. The concept of the actual life-sound is presented in a slightly different way by the Śāṇk. Śr. S. (XVII. 3.1-11), which lays down that the *vāṇa* may be covered with the skin of a red ox, with hair outside, probably indicative of the identification of Speech and the cow. Similar is the case for the lute (*vīṇā*) (Ai. Ār. III.2.5; Śāṇk. Ār. VIII. 9). The vocal giving place to the instrumental is clear in the word *vāditra,* as also in the words *vādanam* and *vādya,* which are causal forms of √*vad* (to speak) which denotes the human faculty. From *vāṇa* comes *vāṇīcī,* the musical instrument of the Aśvins (RV. V.75.4) as does the instrument *vāṇa.*

With this we now come to the last passage of *vāṇa* from RV-"*vāṇasya sapta-dhātur ij janaḥ*" (X.32.4). The whole *mantra* is as follows:

> *tad it sadhastham abhi cāru dīdhaya*
> *gāvo yac chāsan vahatum na dhenavaḥ*
> *mātā yan mantur yūthasya pūrvyā*
> *'bhi vāṇasya sapta-dhātur ij janaḥ*

The seer is Kavaṣa Aliūṣa, who is the seer also of the two preceding and equal number of the following hymns. The hymn immediately preceding is mystic in nature, and it has been accepted as such by scholars. This hymn is also mystic and the verse, which we have quoted, is not exactly clear. It is, however, accepted that we have here a description of the sacrifice, where Indra is to arrive. The cows *(gāvaḥ)* are the *mantra*-s that eagerly expect him, as the other natural cows (*dhenavaḥ*) expect the (homeward) path (according to Sāyaṇa). Though Geldner understands the "Somakuhe" (see his note) by the word *gāvaḥ,* there is no difference of opinion as to the sacrifice. The "mother of the group" (*yūthasya mātā)* is taken to be *iḷā* by Geldner on the basis of the only similar expression (V. 41.19, *abhi na iḷā yūthasya mātā*) indicating the other offerings. He renders the word "*mantuḥ*" as "sorgende" (anxious). Grassmann renders it as "Lenker", "Walter", "Rath", i.e. the "ruler", "guide", "counsel" (Wörterbuch), while Sāyaṇa understands it as the genitive of *mantṛ,* rendering it as "*arcakasya mama*" (of me, who am the worshipper). The probability is that, as Iḷā is the "*yūthasya mātā*", we have here the *female deity of the mantra*-s as the Mother (or the Measure). The word is not an adjective; it appears to be a noun from *man+tu* (cf. *gātu,tantu, jantu* etc. where *tu* is the formative suffix). We have, thus, a twofold concept of the "*yūthasya mātā*" : i) Iḷā, and ii) Mantu. The former is the deity of the offerings, while the latter is that of the *mantra*-s. There is no other occurrence of the "*mātā yūthasya*". Even if *mantu* cannot be taken as a proper noun, in view of *mantavaḥ* (I.15.21; IX. 73.6; X.63.8) there cannot be any doubt that the *mātā* here is not Iḷā; for the word *mantu* indicates the faculty of the *mantra* as different from the offerings. It is in line with this that the mention of the word *vāṇa* comes in the verse. The expression "*vāṇasya sapta-dhātur ij janaḥ*" has been taken to mean "the sevenfold folks of the voice" (Geldner, "das siebenfache Volk der Gesangesstimme"), "the chorus of seven parts" (Grassmann, "der sibentheilige Musikchor (?)"). Geldner is acceptable with a slight modification, as at all other places of his rendering of the word *vāṇa*, that it is not so much the voice of songs as the vocal apparatus. What could be the "sevenfold folks" of the voice? The rendering is not quite clear. The rendering of Grassmann leaves away the word *janaḥ,* or at least it does not render it as "folks"; and he obviously doubts what the expression could mean; for he puts a question mark at the end. Ludwig is more or less the same as Geldner with, "herum des chores sibentonig volk," taking *vāṇa* to mean the combined song or the chorus of seven persons. The difficulty is on account of the word *janaḥ*, and the awkward expression *vāṇasya janaḥ,* which is *sapta-dhātuḥ*. Grassmann accepts the awkwardness of the expression, as indicated by the question-mark and the omission of the word *janaḥ* in his rendering. It is not quite improbable that the word *janaḥ* is not at all intended to mean *folks!* Though it is difficult to find a similar case, in all probability, the seer desires to convey the meaning of "birth" by this word (fr. √*jan)*. The meaning, in that case, will be "indeed *(it)*, there is the sevenfold birth (i.e.,expression) of the *vāṇa!*" And this sevenfold expression is the *yūtha,* the Mother of which has already been alluded to in the word *mantuḥ*. This, probably, refers to the sevenfold recitation, by one individual, of the same *mantra,* or *mantra*-s in seven lauds. An actual practice at the time of the preparation of the *vāṇa* in the Mahāvrata may be compared here. The Hotṛ took the hundred-stringed *vāṇa* in his hand as he was swung in the swing. He produced, in turn, notes in seven metres; and, after this, the *vāṇa* was struck thrice for animation, as we have noted earlier (Ai. Ār. V. 1.4). In an earlier practice, when the stringed instrument was yet to make its appearance, this would naturally be accomplished with the vocal activity, which was the *vāṇasya saptadhātuḥ janaḥ* (sevenfold birth of tones from the *vāna*).

NOTES

1. Taitt. Sam. VII; 5.9.2; Kāṭhaka Sam. XXXIV, 5; Pañc. Br. V. 6.12; XIV. 7.8; etc. See *Vedic Index* under *Vāṇa.*
2. *Ibid.*
3. *Ibid.*
4. *Vedic Index* under *Vāṇa.*
5. *Der Rigveda* I, p. 110; for other references, vol. III, on the verses above.
6. SBE, vols. 32 and 46 for the respective verses.
7. See *Vedic Index.*
8. The word *go* is not generally used for Soma, though the latter is mixed with milk and the mixture is called *gavaśira; go* as milk or any of the produce of the cow is common, Nir. II.1.
9. *Hymns of the Rigveda*, (vols. I & II) Benares, 2nd ed. 1963; He quotes Ludwig; Max Müller has, here also "arrow"; but we have no other proof for the arrow being anointed with milk. Grassmann, *Der Rigveda*, "Durch Milk-trank wird der Sobharis Muṣik belohnt."
10. Sāyaṇa, *"samartha-asamarthasśca";* Ludwig, "Dumme und Kluge"; Grassman renders the line as, "geringe Einsicht melkt ganz das Euter aus" (d.h. Thoren wollen den hiochsten vortheil ziehen).
11. If the word *vanij* is really derived from *√van,* the original sense must be of *√van=* to sound (or *√van,* to praise), the word indicating "one who talks much and praises his things." Cf. *√pan-√pan* (to praise, Vedic). If *vāṇa* is trade (following Geldner) it, probably, is in the sense of "much talk." In Marathi *√van* means a "commodity." Can it be *varṇa > vaṇṇa> vāṇa* or from *√vaṇ > vāṇ?*

Chapter 16

THE BIRTH OF VASIṢṬHA
(A Motif of Divine Birth)

In dealing with the topic of the birth of Vasiṣṭha, we will do well to concentrate on the account from RV. It occurs at RV VII.33. The panegyric of the Vasiṣṭha family is woven against the background of the famous victory of king Sudās over ten kings.[1] After stating that the Vasiṣṭhas knew all the secrets of life, and that their greatness was like the sun and the sea, the poet goes on to narrate the birth of the first ancestor of the Vasiṣṭha family. The birth of the high sage is said to be twofold. The first is celestial and the second is sacrificial. The celestial is the one which was in the very form of light, when the two gods Mitrāvaruṇā saw him, and Agastya brought him among the people (as a child) (v.10). This would mean that the first birth was when Vasiṣṭha left the light of the lightning. The very sight of Mitrāvaruṇā (Mitra and Varuṇa) caused the lustre to shoot forth from the lightning. This was the first birth. At the same time, this birth was entirely without the semblance of any material cause; for, he was born likewise from the mind of Urvaśī.

urvaśyā brahman manaso-dhi-jātaḥ

This would indicate that the birth of Vasiṣṭha is (v.11 ab) entirely free from any personal cause. The whole purpose seems to be that it is not yet the "sexual intercourse" on the part of Mitrāvaruṇā and Urvaśī, that has brought about the birth of Vasiṣṭha. Such an intercourse is quite against the underlying idea of the hymn. The intercourse is only of the "seeing" and the "wishing" on the part of the celestial couple. It is only in this context of the celestial birth that the word *drapsa* is used.

> *Drapsa* was collected by the gods with a divine exploit, in a blue lotus (v.11).

The word *drapsa* is tempting and is apt to be rendered as the 'semen' of Mitrāvaruṇā.[2] It should be, however, remembered that the word only means 'drop' in the RV and with *'indu'*, it means "a shining potent drop." The whole idea in the first account of the birth of Vasiṣṭha could be analysed on the following lines:

(i) Vasiṣṭha was in the mass of lightning whence he broke;
(ii) This was when Mitrāvaruṇā glanced at him; hence he is Maitrāvaruṇa (son of Mitra and Varuṇa);
(iii) Urvaśī also gave birth to him from her mind, i.e. she saw the drop and longed for it. Hence *manasaḥ;*
(iv) The 'drop' that fell from the lightning was collected in a *puṣkara* (blue lotus).

This description of the celestial birth of Vasiṣṭha ends at the verse, where he is said to have been born from Urvaśī. At the next verse, it is said that these gods ejected semen in a jar, at a sacrifice (*kumbhe retaḥ siṣicatuḥ samānam).* Here the scene shifts to the sacrificial place wherein Vasiṣṭha is said to be born, along with Agastya, from a jar into which the semen of Mitrāvaruṇā is said to have fallen. The birth in this sacrificial setting is, thus, purposefully differentiated from that of the celestial plane.[3] The purpose is simple and obvious. The first birth was purely a celestial one without the idea of any physical cause, while the second account mentions the physical cause, i.e. the semen, though the plane is not entirely terrestrial. The second birth has the background of the sacrifice—a motif commonly found to be present in many accounts of divine or supernatural births. It will be interesting to note that the difference between the two births is clearly expressed by the employment of two separate words, *viz. drapsa* and *retas.* The psychic image behind the whole description seems to be that Vasiṣṭha is created from the very divine drop that oozes from heaven. The Ṛgveda attests the unique importance of this drop, *drapsa.* It is *indu-drapsa* that is said to arrive at the sacrifice and is said to be present in the pressed Soma. When the *soma*-juice is ritually mixed with milk, with the barley-flour or with the curds in the sacrifice, it is really this *indu-drapsa* that is mixed, being the very drop from heaven—the drop of immortality. When it is mixed with milk the cows would be full of milk; when with the barley, corn will be in plenty. And when taken inside the body it will bestow immortality. Now *retas* is only another, but a gross form of *drapsa* as Soma is a visible form of the mystic *indu-drapsa* that is present in the pressed out Soma. The idea of the hymn is, hence, that Vasiṣṭha was born from the 'drop' which is the very sustaining principle of the world, and which is divinity incarnate. On the sacrificial plane it is '*retas*' but on the celestial plane it is the very drop of immortality. The sacrificial level is, on the other hand, the purest level on the terrestrial plane and has the idea of the purest birth on the earth. The idea clearly is that, if the birth is to be for the benefit of the earthly people, it has to be in the sacrificial atmosphere. But even here the birth is far from a purely earthly one though it shows, partly, the semblance of an earthly cause,-*viz.* the *retas*; for, the physical *yoni* is absent, its place being taken by the jar (*kumbha).*

Having, thus, marked the difference between the celestial and the terrestro-sacrificial birth of Vasiṣṭha, we now are well at a point to understand the gradual mixing of the celestial birth with that on the terrestro-sacrificial plane. Now, the *puṣkara* had come to signify the highest point on earth touching the sky, and the first sprout on the earth. It also signifies the first connecting link between heaven and earth—the ancient parents. It is the first glimpse of life that sprouts out of the dark mystery of the abyss. It will be good to see if, in this particular context, the *puṣkara* (blue lotus) signifies anything else in RV itself.

In the sacrificial setting the word *puṣkara* signifies the front part of an offering ladle.[4] It is to be noted, however, that it signifies at various places the birth-place or the divine womb. We have already seen how it stands for a divine womb in the first account of the birth of Vasiṣṭha. At another place in RV (V. 78.7) it is closely associated with the womb that is full with foetus:

Yathā vātaḥ puṣkariṇīm samīṅgayati sarvataḥ
evā te garbha ejatu niraitu daśamāsyaḥ

[As doeth the breeze gently tickle
The Buddy blue lotus-bed on all its sides
So may thy foetus inside throb
May at the tenth month outside glide].[5]

The verse in question forms part of the '*garbhasrāviṇī-upaniṣad*' according to Sāyaṇa, who mentions an anecdote of the sage Saptavadhri. According to it, the sage was entrapped in a box by his kinsmen, hostile to him, who would not allow him to have sexual intercourse with his wife. The sage at long lost, hit upon an idea and praised the twin gods *Aśvinau* who released him from the miniature prison every night to have union with his wife. At day dawn, however, he would resort to the confinement of the box for fear of his hostile captors. The box itself is conceived as a *yoni* (womb) as is clear from the verse.[6] Here we have noted how the gods *Aśvinau* are invoked to facilitate conception. The same gods figure in yet another place in the RV (X. 184.2). Their description as the wearers of blue lotus-garlands (*puṣkarasrajau*) appears to have meaning in this background of conception and birth. At RV VI.16.13, Agni is said to be churned out of the *puṣkara* by Atharvan. This *puṣkara* is nothing but the lower *araṇi* which is the birthplace of Agni. It is the very womb of the sacrificial fire. It is of importance to note that this and the next verse are enjoined to be chanted at the sacrificial kindling of the fire.[7] At this place the *puṣkara* is said to be the head of all things, from which Atharvan kindled the fire.

tvām agne puṣkarād adhi Atharvā nir amanthata
mūrdhno viśvaṣya vāghataḥ[8]

This uniquely high position of the *puṣkara* is maintained in the later literature, where it is said to be the womb of creation. Thus, it is on the *puṣkara* that Prajāpati is said to have supported the earth.[9] The Taitt. Sam. mentions that Agni was first found on the leaf of the *puṣkara.*[10] It is this psychic image of *puṣkara* that gradually develops into the fully blown myth of the lotus-born Brahmadeva of the Purāṇas. This same motif of the lotus-leaf gets changed into the *vaṭa-patra* that stands as the support of the divine child Viṣṇu. The divine child of the later Hindu mythology is only the manifestation of the divine light-drop—*drapsa.* The lotus is regarded as the very womb of Agni, in the context of the *Agni-cayana* rites.[11]

The description of the birth of Vasiṣṭha from the *puṣkara* marks a tradition of symbolisation that was, undoubtedly, present in the Ṛgvedic times. The *puṣkara,* thus being the symbol of the divine womb, came to be employed when the birth of an eminent person was to be described, and he was to be deified.

The birth at the sacrifice or from a jar, also has many parallels in mythology.[12]

Having noticed the nature of Vasiṣṭha's birth in the RV we shall now turn to the next point in our discussion. What is the place of this birth in the hymn where it occurs? In other words—is the aim of the hymn to describe the birth of Vasiṣṭha or is the account of the birth of Vasiṣṭha of secondary importance? The whole hymn could be divided into two parts. The first part forms the praise of Vasiṣṭha, i.e. the family of the Vasiṣṭhas as priests of high eminence who brought about the victory of king Sudās by their supernatural powers. This praise concludes at verse 9. Then the description of the birth of the first Vasiṣṭha follows. In this connection it will be well to compare two verses, *viz.* the ninth and the twelfth. The ninth verse is:

ta inniṇyam hṛdayasys praketaiḥ
sahasravalśam abhisaṁcaranti
yamena tatam paridhim vayanto
apsarasa upasedur Vasiṣṭhāḥ

[Verily by the innate wisdom of their heart they divine the thousand tapered secret (of creation). Weaving (within) the frame fixed by Yama, the Vasiṣṭhas approached the *apsarases*].[13]

The twelfth is:

sa praketa ubhayasya vidvān
sahasradāna uta vā sadānaḥ
yamena tatam paridhim vayiṣyan
apsarasaḥ pari jajñe Vasiṣṭhaḥ

[He, the sagacious one, the knower of both (the worlds), the one endowed with thousand gifts-what more? being always with gifts, Vasiṣṭha was born of the *apsaras* desirous as he was to weave the outline established by Yama.]

It could be readily seen that the two verses are just similar. Comparing these two it appears that the plural in the word 'Vasiṣṭhāḥ' is purposefully kept. The idea is that the whole family of the Vasiṣṭhas is as powerful as the first of them. Hence, the innate knowledge of all the Vasiṣṭhas, as it were, balanced with that of the great first sage. It is not necessary, as Sāyaṇa does, to take the plural 'Vasiṣṭhāḥ' (in verse 9) as the plural to indicate respect for the first Vasiṣṭha.[14] The whole hymn, is thus the panegyric of the whole Vasiṣṭha family and the account of the birth of Vasiṣṭha-the first of the family—is only brought in as a support. It should be noted, however, that this account of the birth of the first Vasiṣṭha is not a later addition[15] as Roth suggests, though it is, in appearance, perfectly Puranic. It is the other way round, and it is clear that the Puranic manner of description developed from such accounts in the RV, as we have other similar accounts in the RV, e.g. of Vena (X.123) and of Vāmadeva (IV.26).

The line of thought in the present hymn seems to be this: Indra was at the beck and call of the Vasiṣṭhas as such, being on their side always, due to their hymns. Hence, the family of the Vasiṣṭhas could provide excellent priests. As an example is cited the case of the Vasiṣṭha who saved king Sudās in the war against the ten kings (vv.5 & 6). This was natural as the Vasiṣṭhas were wise and knew all secrets including the very secret of life and creation (vv.7-9.). It is their greatness that could give success to their patrons; for in their family was born the great Vasiṣṭha of divine birth.

NOTES

1. RV VII.33.
2. Geldner renders the passage thus "Und du vasiṣṭha, bist der sohn von Mitra und Varuṇa, von der Urvaśī "indicating a 'union'. H.D. Velankar, clearly uses the word 'semen'. Cf. Geldner, *Der Rigveda*, vol. II and H. D. Velankar, *Ṛgveda Maṇḍala* VII.
3. Geldner marks this point when he says "Eine andere version". The combination of Mitra and Varuṇa presents another point of interest. Their union (without Urvaśī) could produce Vasiṣṭha, as is clear from what we have noted. Though the Ṛgveda does not clearly state about the union of Mitra and Varuṇa as that between two sexes (both being treated as male), in the Śat Br. it is stated, where the waning moon is said to be Mitra (male) and the waxing moon Varuṇa (the female), Śat. Br. II.4.4.18.
4. Cf. Ai.Br. VII.5=32.4; *sṛcam prāgdaṇḍām pratyak-puṣkarām.*
5. Translation by the author.
6. V.78.5. "*vi jihīṣva vanaspate yoniḥ sūṣyantyā iva.*"
7. Cf. Sāyaṇa who quotes from the Āśv. Śr. S.
8. I follow Sāyaṇa here. See Geldner- "(dich) die Priester aus dem Haupt der ganzen welt."
9. Taitt. Br. I.13.6; Taitt. Ār. I.23.1.
10. Taitt. Sam. V.1.4.4.

11. SBE, Vol. 12 p. 215, also Śat. Br. V. 4.1.8. In this rite the dug up clay is spread upon the lotus leaf, which is itself spread upon the black antelope-skin, thus reminding us of the idea in the Taittirīya Āraṇyaka (note 19 above). The lotus leaf is said to be the womb and that clay the seed. The lotus leaf is further said to be the sky, signifying that it is yet unearthly and a divine womb. The dug up clay is not earthly either; for, it is said to be the divine seed.
12. Cf. the Birth of Rāma and his brothers from the *pāyasa* from the sacrificial fire. Also of Draupadī from the sacrificial altar. Mb. Ādi. 166.39 ff. The birth of the sage Śuka from the semen of Vyāsa on seeing the nymph Ghṛtācī, at the sacrificial altar, Mb. Śānti, 329.94
13. The translation of *paridhim vayantaḥ* is variously done by scholars. Sāyaṇa takes *paridhi* to mean a cloth. Professor H.D. Velankar follows him (*Ṛgveda Maṇḍala*, VII Bharatiya Vidya Bhavanā, 1963, p.86 notes. Wilson points out a mistake in the rendering of Sāyaṇa, Tr. and notes, Vol. IV. p. 328), stating that the latter takes *vayantaḥ* with *apsarasaḥ*. In fact, Wilson misunderstands Sāyaṇa, the misunderstanding being due to the full stop, the subject, Vasiṣṭhāḥ being kept in the previous sentence. For *paridhi* and its possible meaning in RV cf. RV I. 126-7; III.33.6, X.90.15, IV. 18.6, X.18.4, etc. It is better to take it to mean (as we have done) 'a frame' or 'envelopment' as Muir has done; for it is difficult to understand the 'weaving' of a cloth that is already spread (*tatam*) by Yama. The weaving of the cloth in the outline could well be understood to mark a limit, for life. See specially X. 18.4. in this context.
14. Cf. "*atra Vasiṣṭhā iti bahuvacanam pūjāyām*".
15. Cf. note by Griffith on the verse, where he refers to Roth.

Chapter 17

DVIBARHAS : A WONDER-WORKING PRIEST

The word *dvi-barhas* occurs quite a number of times in the Ṛgveda though in later literature its use is scarce (Śat.Br. IV.3.3.18=RV VI.19.1; and quotes only RV). The word *barhas* never occurs alone, and the only parallel to the word *dvibarhas* is *adri-barhas*, which occurs only once, as an epithet of Aditi (RV X.63.3). The word *dvi-barhas* is found used as an epithet of some of the deities like, Indra (RV VI.19.1; X.116.4), Agni (1.71.6; IV.5.3), Soma (IX.4.7.; 40.6; 100.2), Rudra (I.114.10), Uṣas (V.80.4) and Bṛhaspati (VI.13.1). It is also found applied to such nouns as *śarman* (I.114.10), *sāman* (IV.3.5), *manas* (VII.24.2) and *vāc* (VII.8.6).

The word *dvibarhas* is generally rendered by Western scholars as 'doubly strong' and by Yāska and by Sāyaṇa as 'grown at both the domains' (*dvayoḥ sthānayoḥ parivṛḍhaḥ*). That the word posed a problem even at the time of Yāska is indicated by his taking it as *anavagata* (VII.74). About the portion *dvi* there is no difficulty; but the word *barhas* has been understood variously, though about the root-meaning there appears to be no substantial difference. It is understood as indicating growth or strength (√*bṛh*- √*vṛh*). Mayrhofer (*Kurzgefazte Etymologische*) compares the word with *bṛhan* and takes the roots noted above. By the word *barhas* he understands "tall, great, high", and compares the Khotanese word *bulsya* with *barhas*. The word *bulsya* means 'long'. Probably, we have to connect the word *bulsya* with the Vedic word *vaśa*, indicating the branch of a tree or a scion of a family. The word *barhas* has close affinity with words like *barhis*, *barhaṇa* and *brahman*,[1] all indicating 'growth'. This is the reason why Yāska and Sāyaṇa render the word *brahman* as "a ritual that has grown on all sides" (*parivṛdham*). *Barhis*, *barhas*, or *barha* indicate some kind of growth. The *barhis* shoots forth from the earth, while *barha* grows from the body of a bird, and indicates 'wing'. The rendering of the word *dvi-barhas*, thus, rightly indicated 'double' growth. With a person or a god, the word would indicate 'the one who has control of both strata', indicating the earth and heaven, as Sāyaṇa understands. The wealth (*rayi*) that is *dvibarhas* may indicate the heavenly wealth and the terrestrial one.

In the most important reference to the word *dvi-barhas* in the Ṛgveda (X.61.10) it indicates a person of mystic powers whom the Aṅgirases are said to resort to for the gain of the cows. Here, this person is described as *dvi-jāḥ*, as also *dvi-bhandhuḥ*. He declares himself as being connected with heaven and earth. All these epithets fit in with his being the *dvi-barhas* and help in understanding the concept behind the word under study. He works the wonder of causing the unmilked cows ooze the 'milk' (*acyutā dudukṣan*), which is rain.[2]

Parallel to *dvi-barhas*, we have another word *adribarhas*, which is an epithet of Aditi (RV X.63.3). In keeping with the root-meaning of *barhas*, it is better to take it to mean 'grown with clouds' with Sāyaṇa, rather than "firm as the mountain" (Geldner), particularly in view of the fact that Aditi is Dyauḥ, 'heaven' and that she is said to 'milk' the *pīyūṣa*, which is rain. The idea behind *adri-barhas* appears to be that which would show *barhas* to be an external attachment. This conjecture gets support from yet another passage where Dawn is described as a female deer (or, the white deer, RV V.80.4, *eṣā vy'enī bhavati dvi-barhāḥ*). She is *dvi-barhas* as she appears in the east at her advent. This may be taken to indicate her brilliance 'touching heaven and earth,' which would explain the word *dvi*; but the expression has a deeper meaning: 'She becomes *dvi-barhas*' (mark the word *bhavati*). This will mean that one could get "to become" *dvi-barhas* on certain occasions; and yet, it was a distinction for only some, as noted above.

In this connection, it is important to note another (and the only) variant of *dvibarhas*, or, in fact of *barhas*; it is *barha*, in the word *dvi-barha-jmā* (RV VI.73.1). There is hardly any doubt about the fact that *barha* is a variant of *barhas*, both indicating the same concept. The word *dvi-barha-jmā* has been rendered as 'double-pathed' (Geldner, doppelt Bahn) combining the sense of *barhas* with that of *jmā*. But, evidently, the rendering is short of the mark, since it does not bring the concept behind the word *barha* to the fore. Geldner gives an interrogation mark after it. In the notes, he quotes Sāyaṇa, "having his gait heightened at both places" (*dvayoḥ sthānayoḥ bṛṁhita-gamanaḥ*). Oldenberg takes the whole expression to be separated as *dvibarhajmā prā* and *gharma-sat* (the first on the analogy of *antarikṣaprā* and *rodasī-prā*); but his rendering is about the same as of Sāyaṇa (doppelterfullend). The portion *jmā* (originally *jman*, from √*gam*- √*jam*, 'to go'), indicates movement (cf., *pari-jman*). But, this has to be in association with *barha*, the meaning of which has not been fairly brought out by the rendering so far. As we have seen *barha* means 'wing'; and it is so as it shoots out (√*bṛh*) from the sides. The *dvi-barha-jmā* hence would indicate the same thing as 'moving with the wings in both places (heaven and earth).' The word is an epithet of Bṛhaspati. At another place in RV Bṛhaspati is referred to as *śata-patra* (RV VII.97.7a), giving the picture of a bird. The image of the bird was favourite with the Vedic seers, and the Great Principle is described as *Suparṇa* (RV I.164.46). The goddesses are said to have whole wings (RV I.22.11, *acchinna-patrāḥ*), which may be taken as the earliest reference to the concept of the winged nymphs or angels. We have also the concept of the supreme god that blows the worlds with his wings (RV X.81.3).

That the concept behind the word *dvi-barhas* was that of working wonder is clear from at least two places, where the reference is to the gain of rain referred to above, the one being of the Aṅgirases resorting to the *dvibarhas* and the other that of Bṛhaspati. In both, we have reference to the gain of the heavenly fluid. The first (X.61) has it in the 'milking of the cow *Sabardughā*', while in the other, Bṛhaspati, described as *gharma-sat* (sitting at the *gharma*), is said to control the cosmic fire-principle (*gharma*), and exhibits also characteristic roar which indicates the thunder in the cosmos (cf., *ibid*., *ā rodasī vṛṣabho roravīti*). Looking at the very special, and also restricted use of this epithet *dvi-barhas* or *dvi-barha-jmā* (in the case of Bṛhaspati in this citation), the *barhas* appears to have some mystic-ritualistic importance. The case is about the same as that of the word *śipre*, with its variants *su-śipra* etc. In fact, the *barhas* appears to be a sort of an extra attachment, like the *śipre* may be on the helmet or to the sides. The first was for social status, while the other for ritualistic wonder. The first was a horn-like drinking-cup, which also served as a head-ornament worn on the helmet.[3] This surmise is supported by the fact that in ancient tribes wearing of feathers for ritualistic purposes was prevalent, as will be seen from the following examples.

The American Indians used feathers in imitative magic. Feathers were attached to prayer-sticks among the people of the south-western states of the United States, and among the Zuni Indians, for addressing the supernatural powers.[4] Feather-dress symbolised the clouds and sometimes, the gentle breeze[5] (we may compare *adribarhas*, above, said of Aditi). Among the Pawnee Indians, feathers were tied to the ear of the corn with a view to get rich crop; for, the feather symbolized the Creator-spirit, called Tirava. Most Egyptian gods wore two feathers, symbolizing the twin powers of goodness and knowledge.[6] Did *dvibarhas* symbolize some such thing to the earlier Vedic people? The probability is strong. In the Vedic rituals, the use of things is often substantiated with the help of etymology; and there are innumerable examples of things used due to their names indicating some sort of mystic quality or virtue. Thus, barley (*yava*) is used as it joins (√*yu*, 'to join'; also 'to separate' in certain cases). The *barhis*, a cognate of *barhas*, is thus addressed to: 'You are *barhi*, the one that goes to the gods' (Mait.Sam.IV.1.2.3), where the root-meaning of movement is clear. As the root-meaning of the word *barhas* is about the same (from √*bṛh*, as noted earlier), it is not improbable that in very early rituals the feather was used to signify a wonder-working priest, and that *dvi-barhas* enshrines a custom of wearing the double-feather.

NOTES

1. See S.K. Belvalkar, "Brahma, Baresman, Bright, Bhrāj," *Proceedings of the All India Oriental Conference*, Allahabad, 1926.
2. For a detailed study, see Dange, *Vedic Concept of 'Field' and the Divine Fructification*, Bombay Uni. Pbn, Bombay, 1971, pp.123-53.
3. See Ch.18, "Śiprin And Śipiviṣṭa", *infra.*
4. See Gertrude Jobes, *Dictionary of Mythology, Folk-lore and Symbols*, New York, 1962 under "Feather".
5. *Ibid.*
6. *Ibid.* On the Vedic side, the feather of the peacock was already noted by the seers. The horses of Indra had tails like that of the peacock (RV III.45.1); and the peacock and its feathers were used in the charm against snake-poison (RV I.191.14; AV VII.56.7;8).

Chapter 18

ŚIPRIN AND ŚIPIVIṢṬA

The words *śiprā* and *śipiviṣṭa* have been considered to be of uncertain connotation by scholars. *Śipr:a* has been rendered variously as nose, teeth, cheeks, nostrils, lips, chin and even the helmet. It rather appears to be queer that the word would have such varied connotations, though in different contexts. Some of these meanings are accepted by the traditional commentators like Veṅkaṭmādhava, Sāyaṇa, and Skandasvāmin. Modern scholars including Ludwig, Geldner, Grassmann, Griffith, Macdonell, Keith and others have followed the traditional interpretation; and yet a doubt regarding the exact implication of the word persisted. The suggestion of Frisk, that *śiprā* indicates a wagging-tail, helmet,[1] is also not satisfactory; for it does not satisfy all references to this word in RV. A fresh investigation is, hence, necessary taking into account all such references.

About the word *śipiviṣṭa* also the same difficulty persists. The word has been taken to indicate a sober as well as a vulgar sense. Hence it is necessary to examine it afresh.

We shall start with *śiprā*, taking the following passage:

> *ā te hanū harivaḥ śūra śipre*
> *ruhat soma na parvatasya pṛṣṭhe.* (RV V.36.2)

It will be seen that the passage has both *hanū* and *śipre* in one; and naturally *śipre* (dual of *śiprā*) cannot mean the *hanū* (i.e. chin). The idea in the passage is of the rise of the *soma*-plant on the mountain, and is accepted by all scholars, eastern and western. It is, also believed that Soma is to rise up to both the *śipre* and the *hanū*. Geldner renders the passage as follows.[2] "On your cheeks (*hanū*,"Backen") O valiant (god), on your opened up lips (*śipre*, 'geöffneten Lippen') would the Soma (drink) mount, as does the Soma-plant on the slope (back, 'Rucken') of the mountain."

Now the question is, how can we imagine the word *śipre* to mean "geöffneten Lippen". The verse has no word for warranting this rendering. And, even if we are to suppose *śipre* to indicate the *Lippen* (lips), how to account for "geöffneten" (Open)? Even granting that the word conveys the meaning of "opened up lips", it is difficult to imagine the *soma*-drink (cf. "trank") rising to the lips "as the Soma-plant (planz) rises on the mountain." The position of the *soma*-plant is at a height and erect, while such can never be the position of the *soma*-drink. Further, this rendering requires Soma to be taken twice—once in the *upameya* sentence; and again in the *upamāna* sentence. In short, Soma is compared with Soma itself, but in two different positions. Moreover, how could *hanū* be understood as "Backen" (Cheeks)? RV does not support it.

Geldner takes the word *hanū* here to mean "Backen", i.e. cheeks. It is highly doubtful if *hanū* ever means the cheeks; and even if we accept Geldner's rendering of the word as "cheeks" we could take the inner side, where there will be the actual contact of the drink. And the utmost surprising thing with this rendering is, that we have to understand Soma (drink) reaching the "Backen" (cheeks) first, and then the "geöffneten Lippen". This rendering, hence, cannot be accepted.

The rendering of Griffith is similar to that of Geldner and requires no comment. Ludwig renders *hanū* as "jaws" (kiefer); and it is acceptable; but *śipre* as "backen". Otherwise there is no change. Sāyaṇa, obviously, is in difficulty with both *hanū* and *śipre* being side by side; for he often renders the word *śipre* as *hanū* or the *nāsike* (nose openings) following Yāska. He seeks to surmount this difficulty by rendering *hanū* as *'hanana-sādhane'* (instrumental in cutting or killing), and commenting that though the word *hanū* is itself indicative of *śipre* it is subordinate as the word *śipre* is uttered again, expressly (*yady 'apy 'ayam śiprā-vacanaḥ tathāpi punaḥ śiprābhidhānād gauṇoyam vaktavyaḥ*). He, thus, takes *hanū* as an epithet of *śipre*, suggesting that the latter is something like an instrument. But they cannot be exactly the jaws, which is difficult to understand as *hanana-sādhana* in the case of a human being (or a god, if he is anthropomorphic like Indra) and not a demon! Let us examine the word *hanū*. The word *hanū* (in the dual) occurs only thrice more (IV.18.9; X.79.3; 152.3) and it has the meaning of "shattering" though it indicates the jaws. Once it occurs in the plural with (VIII.60.13 *hanavaḥ*) the fire (Agni) and indicates its destroying flames. Sāyaṇa wavers, however, as regards the *na* in "*somo na parvatasya pṛṣṭhe*", taking it as a negative particle rendering that Soma rises on to the *hanū śipre* (shattering jaws) and not on the top of the mountain (*na ruhat na arohati tatra na tiṣṭhati ity 'arthaḥ*), and also remarks that the particle *na* may indicate a simile, "though it is placed before *parvatasya*" which he believes to be the *upamāna*. Normally in simile *na* follows the *upamāna*. Sāyaṇa is, hence, not clear in his mind about his rendering; and his effort appears to be at random. The fact is, as has been rightly followed by all other scholars, that the *upamāna* is Soma; not *parvata*. So Sāyaṇa's hesitating alternative, "*parvatasya na pṛṣṭhe*" is out of question, though his suggestion that *hanū* is the epithet of *śipre* is perfectly admissible.

The main difficulty about the interpretations noted above is about the exact image. How could the *soma*-drink be imagined to rise to the lips or even the shattering jaws, in the way as the plant stands or sprouts on the mountain? We are in the bounds of legitimacy in expecting *śipre*, which are *hanū* (i.e. shattering or pointed), to be erect like the plant taking its rise on the mountain. This precludes the possibility of the *śipre* being either nose, nostrils, moustaches, jaws, lips etc. In other words, both *hanū* and *śipre* are to be taken as the nominative forms and *not* the accusative. To be clearer, these words are the Subject, being on par with Soma. Both Soma and *śipre* (having *hanū* as the epithet) are connected with the verb *ruhat*. Though the expected form of the verb in the case of *śipre* is *ruhataḥ* (dual), the form *ruhat* is due to the influence of Soma which follows.

We take another expression—"*vi ṣyasva śipre vi sṛjasva dhene.*" (I.101.10). Here Sāyaṇa renders the word *śipre* as the "jaws" (*hanū*), and *dhene* as "*jihvopajihve*" (tongue and lower tongue). Geldner takes *śipre*, in this context, to mean "set of teeth" (gebiz), and *dhene* as "lips". Now the expression *vi ṣyasva* occurs only in one more verse in the RV which occurs twice (III.4.9 = VII.2.9), being a common portion of the Āprī hymns of Viśvāmitra and Vasiṣṭhar. The expression conveys the meaning of 'letting loose' or 'Releasing'. Now, it is difficult to understand the set of teeth or even the jaws being let loose for drinking! Normally even, they are not set together. If, on the other hand, we take the word *śipre* to indicate the lips, they may well be described as 'loosening' for drinking; for, they are normally set together. But, in that case, what about *dhene*? Again, even if we take the word *dhene* to indicate the *jihvopajihve* (with Sāyaṇa) which are said to be 'a means for drinking' (from √*dhe*, to drink; Sāyaṇa-*pāna-sādhana-bhūte*), can the tongue and the lower tongue, or even the jaws, be really taken in the sense of the *sādhana* for *drinking?* It is, thus, clear that the hitherto accepted (but not doubtlessly; for, there are other alternatives as 'nose' etc.!) rendering of *śipre* as jaws and lips is unhappy. This does not suit the other words *viz. dhene* and *hanū* used with it, nor does it satisfactorily explain the comparison with the rising *soma*-plant.

Let us have the next expression about *śipre:*

sruveva yasya hariṇī vipetatuḥ
śipre vājāya hariṇī davidhvataḥ (X. 96.9)

[whose golden *śipre* move for the 'drink of strength (*vājāya*), as hasten the golden ladles]. The 'drink of strength' is Soma.

The idea of the *śipre* that we get here is that of the containers like ladles. This expression ill suits the jaws which are fixed and, with a human (or a god conceived as a human being) it is clearly ludicrous. If the *śipre* are as long as the ladles, one wonders if Indra could ever be called *su-śipra*, which is his favourite epithet. The description compares the *śipre* with the ladles pouring the offerings into the sacrificial fire. The *śipre* do not appear to be a part of the mouth; on the contrary, the image that this reference produces before the eyes is, that they are containers for drinking *soma* (*dhene,* but not *jihvopajihve!*), and pour *soma* into the mouth of Indra, who is voraciously fond of the drink, as the ladles pour offerings into the fire. Geldner's rendering of the word, here, as nostrils falls out of the arena like others which connect *śipre* with this or that part of the mouth or face.

Putting together all the points that we have noted about *śipre* we arrive at the following:

(i) The word *śiprā* (or *śipre* in the dual) indicates a container for the purpose of drinking from (*dhene* fr. the root √*dhā* "to hold")]
(ii) The container is such, as it could kill, may be, by piercing (*hanū*). So, pointed at one end;
(iii) It could be taken up, and could be placed to resemble the shoot of the *soma*-plant, or like the ladles; and
(iv) It could be fixed and loosened (*vi-ṣyasva, vi-sṛjasva*).

From the points we have deduced, it appears that *śiprā* (or *śipre)* was a *horn-like erection on the helmet.* We have already seen that scholars have suggested 'helmet' as an alternative rendering of the word but, it does not suit well with the drinking. RV attests to the fact that the *siprā-s* were worn on the head.[3] The *śiprā-s* appear to be fixed on the head-wear to be taken down, being released, for the purpose of drinking. This goes well with the expression "*vi-*

ṣyasva śipre vi-sṛjasva dhene." When Indra is invoked to drink *soma*, with the expression "*papṛthya śipre,*" (III.32.1) it indicates the forward extension of the horn-like container to get it filled with the drink, and not "filling the jaws or lips with the liquid", which is itself obscure.

Before we come to the etymology of the word *śiprā,* and compare it with other words, we may note that drinking from the horn was a widely current practice; and horns were worn on the head-wear or the helmet. Both these practices were current with the belief that the horn symbolized virility. Among others, we may note that silver horns were worn by married men among the Druses; and in China horn-cups, called *hsi chuen* were symbolic of happiness.[4]

In the Vedic tradition important deities wear horns and the horned head-dress forms a part of the bride-groom's attire at the marriage,[5] even to-day in certain castes.

With this in mind, let us examine other instances of *śiprā*. When Indra is invoked as *Śiprin,* it does not add anything special to his personality if it simply means "having a chin" or a moustache, or a set of teeth, or a jaw, or even a helmet. Even when Vṛtra is said to be *viśi-śipra,* (V. 45.6) the probability is of the meaning being, "high among his hord"; and *vṛṣa-śipra,* probably, indicates *śiprā* being of the bull as against the gold-*śiprā* of the Vedic gods. It also has to be noted that all the Vedic gods are not endowed with the *śiprā*. It is prominent with Indra. The Maruts occur next. Once *ayaḥ-śipra* occurs for Mitrā-Varuṇā; twice it occurs with the Ṛbhus (*ayaḥ-śipra* and *su-śipra*); and it is associated with Agni in a few cases.

An interesting passage about Indra is, "*vanoti śiprābhyām śipriṇīvān*" (X 105.5 only here). Sāyaṇa renders it as to mean that Indra requests by his jaws (*hanūbhyām*)! Geldner follows him, only changing it to, "mit geoffneten Lippen" (with open lips). The point is quite blunt even if the rendering is intended to convey frankness on the part of Indra. Sāyaṇa, already, feels it to be unhappy; and suggests an alternative (according to the variant to the commentary), without commenting on the word *śiprābhyām*. Does he mean to indicate that Indra vanquishes the enemies by his jaws? Though this picturesque idea brings to our mind the exploit of the Biblical Samson, who vanquished the enemies with the jaw-bone of an ass, the rendering has rarely any propriety here. Griffith is, however, impressed by the ingenuity of the commentator, and adds flight to it by stating that "with jaws" means "with a roar or the thunder."[6] Ludwig renders the passage as "er kamft (fur seine) mit seinen beiden Keifern," thus sticking to the jaw-fighting. The exact idea, however, appears to be that Indra asks for *soma* in his two long horn-cups. The word *śipriṇī-vān* has to be noted, though Sāyaṇa simply renders it as *śipra-van*. Ludwig, Geldner and Griffith do not come out of the lip-jaw-image; and Geldner thinks of the "*nustern*" (nostrils) here. The word *śipriṇī-vān* indicates mastery over the *śipriṇī*. Now the word *śipriṇī* occurs once more in RV where we read "*asmākam śipriṇīnām*" (I.30.11) and the *śipriṇī-s,* probably, indicate the cows as Sāyaṇa suggests. The meaning will be 'those having *śiprā*,' (but not 'having jaws'!). The word has association, in all probability, with the horns which is a speciality of the cows and cattle. The epithet *śipriṇī-vān* is unique with Indra, and may be compared with his another unique epithet, *go-pati*. Indra is *śiprin* and is the lord of the *śipriṇī-s*. If the *śiprā* is made of gold or any other metal, and is yet horn-like, we may not be far from the truth, if we see in *śiprin* or *su-śipra* a custom of wearing the golden or metal replicas of horns on the helmet. But a question may be asked—What is the propriety of the word *śipra* when already there is the word *śṛṅga*? If both the words indicate the same thing, what is the difference—if any? Before we answer this question we shall compare a word from the Semitic language. It is *shofar,* which was indicative of a musical instrument kept in synagogues. It was actually a ram's horn flattened by heat. Dr. Cyrus Adler, who wrote a note on the word,[7] says that the etymology of the word is not clear; but he compares the word to the Assyrian word *shafer*, meaning 'bright' or 'clear'. He further points out two words in the cuneiform list of animals, which are interesting and appear to be names of animals. One is *atudu,* and the other is *śapparu* or *śappartu.* The quotation, as given by Dr. Adler, is as follows:-

> *"turaha ina qaqqadisu u quarnisu ic,c,abit*
> *atuda sappar sadi sappartasunu ic,c,bi"*

(The mountain-goat, by its head and its horn, it seizes). The word *atudu* may be compared with the Tamil word *āṭṭu* (pronounced sometimes as *āḍu*), both meaning the ram or the he-goat. Though the word *Śappar* or *śappartu* has no exact parallel, including the meaning of horn, in the Sanskrit language, we may compare the word *śapha,* which indicates the hoof, especially the divided hoof of the cow. On the same analogy the word *śapha* denoted the two-pronged wooden implement used for taking away metal-pots from fire.[8] The position appears to be this, (i) **ṣapra>śapparu / śappartu>* shofar, indicating the horn; and (ii) **ṣapra>śaphra> *śapha* > Huf (German)/hoof (English). The probability as *śipra >*śapra,* cannot be denied.

It appears that in one direction the meaning of the horn waṣ retained.In *śipra,* as in *śapha,* the original idea seems to be of piercing. Though the Sanskrit language does not show *√śip,* the Avesta has '*śapha √śif,* meaning to pierce, which indicates *√śip* in the Vedic, giving *śiprā.* That *śiprā* was connected with the head is clear from the following passage from Mait. Sam. which refers to the sixfold consecration of the Soma-pandal at the sacrifice (the *havirdhāna),* in which the word *śipre* occurs.[9] In this rite poles are fixed and a roof is constructed over it. Frontal parts in it are addressed as "*Viṣṇoḥ pṛṣṭham asi, viṣṇo rarāṭam asi, viṣṇoḥ śipre sthaḥ*", thus connecting *śipre* with *rarāṭa* (*=lalāṭa,* which is head). This, connected with the idea of piercing, will indicate that the *śipre* were nothing else than the horns; and later, removable attachments for the two-horned helmet, having the shape of horns.

We may note another word from the Avesta *viz. śufra,* or *śuwra* the eliding of *f* being a later stage. This word has been rendered as "plough" by Sheftelowitz[10] and Hopkins.[11] This word has been formed, according to Hopkins, from √śif (to pierce). Now the ploughshare has a peculiar relationship with the earth in the belief of the people. It is the veritable ORGAN by which the earth is furrowed to sow the seed. In other words, it is the male organ for the lady Earth.[12] The word *lāṅgala,* which indicates both the ploughshare and the male-organ, may be compared. It is the very *śepa,* which itself is derived from √*śip*. It is in this peculiar sex-relationship that the word *śiprā* differs from the *śṛṅga,* though the latter was also the primitive tool for the tillage of the land prior to the use of the bull and the plough. Thus, the *śiprā* was primarily the 'digger'. This digger-tool itself was, in the origin, a horn of a ram or a goat, or even of a bull, indicating the virile power of the animal to fructify the earth. In the later period, it was worn on the head-dress, as a mark of virile distinction, in gold or copper as the word *ayas-śipra* indicates. The practice was just the same as that of wearing horns, with the addition that the *śiprā* was of a pastoral origin, indicating domestication of the animals as also the cultivation of the land. Another similar word is *kapṛt,* applied to the male-organ and the ploughshare.[13]

From what we have stated above it appears that the Avestan *śapha* √*śif* >*śufra* > *śuwra* were derived from √*śip* *śiprā,* and that the Semitic word *shofar* came from *śufra.* It appears that the Assyrian word *śapparu* or *śappartu* retained the *p,* changing the orignal *i* to *a*, as the Avestan changed it to *u* in *śufra,* the original meaning of piercing being lost in the Assyrian and the Semitic. It has to be noted that the word has a pastoral association in all the cases. In the Semitic *shofar* and the Germanic *hoof/Huf,* it is more probable that the direction of formation was: √*śip* > *śif* > *śufra* > hoof/Huf, with the connotation-change from "the pointed piercing horn" to the pointed "piercing hoof".

In the case of *śipiviṣṭa* also the original concept seems to be of the piercing horn, mixed with that of the pointed and virile male-organ. The word is acclaimed to be having a double-sense. The word occurs only thrice in the Ṛgveda.[14] It is supposed to mean the *ray* as also the male-organ.[15] Following one of the traditional meanings of the word, Johannson[16] and Charpentier[17] have rightly taken it to mean the male-organ. Even the tradition connects it with *śepa* (*membrum virile*). The connotation will, then be "one who entered the penis." It is also to be noted that the Vedic tradition connects the word prominently with the cattle. It is said that cattle are *śipi* and *śipi-viṣṭa* is "one who has entered the cattle as their lord."[18] *Śipi-viṣṭa* is also said to be the body of Prajāpati, which is established in the cattle (Mait. Sam. I. 11.9 *eṣa vai prajāpateḥ paśu-ṣṭhāḥ tanūr yat śipi-viṣṭam)*. This clearly establishes the association, in the Vedic tradition, between the cattle and *śipi-viṣṭa*; and this is corroborated by the later tradition, which makes Viṣṇu-Kṛṣṇa the lord of the cows. But, this does not yet clearly bring out the implication of *śipi*, which the tradition connects with *śepa*. Here we may, probably, get help from the context. The Taitt. Sam. starts one of its chapters with an episode about the cows where further it refers to the cattle being *śipi,* as we have noted above. The cows were without horns. They sat at sacrifice with the desire to get horns. Ten months they *sat* thus. And the horns cropped up.[19] Here, probably, we have the suggestion that it is the *śipi* (=horn?) that is the cause, why the Taitt. *Sam*. calls, later in the same context, the cattle *śipi*. The word *śipi* (fr. √*śip*) indicates the "piercing one" or the "shooting one;" and, hence it was taken to denote the *ray* in the sober sense, the *guhya* sense being "the one in the piercer" or "the one in the digger", indicating the penis and also the horn-share of the earth, of which Viṣṇu became the lord. In this unique aspect *śipi-viṣṭa* Viṣṇu exactly tallies with Indra, who is alone the *śiprin;* and it cannot be a mere accident that there is another epithet which *no other god,* in RV., except Indra and Viṣṇu share. It is *sthavira*. The unique sexual implication of this epithet about Indra is clear in the Saṁhitā-s where the *sthavira* Indra is said to be held by the expansive Pṛthvī Indrāṇī on her vulva.[20] It is to be noted that in the hymn from RV (VII.100) Viṣṇu's exploit in spreading the earth, to make her fertile for man, is alluded to just before that which refers to him as *śipi-viṣ*ṭa.[21]

NOTES

1. La Monde Oriental, XXX, p. 78 ff.
2. *Der Rigveda*, II, p.36.
3. Cf. V. 54. 11, where the Maruts are said to have them.
4. Gertrude Jobes, *Dictionary of Mythology, Folk-lore, and Symbols,* New York, 1962; see also James Hastings, *Encycl. Religion and Ethics,* Vol. VI, p. 792. It is clear that the practice of wearing horns or something resembling horns continued. At the Bhairavakonda temple near Udayagiri, the door-keepers show horned head-wear, O.C. Ganguli and A. Goswami, *Art of the Pallavas,* Rupa & Co. 1957, p. 13. A figurine at the excavated Ter shows her braid in horn-shape (I am obliged to [late] Dr. S.B. Deo, former Director, Deccan College, Pune for this information and for the figurine which he showed to me).
5. It is called *ba-shing (dvi-śṛṅga)*. We may compare the head-dress (pagḍī) of Sivaji's Maratha soldiers which showed horn-like slight elevations at both ends. Either of the ends was used to tuck a pearl-wreath.
6. *Hymns of the Rigveda,* relevant verse.
7. *JAOS,* XIV, *Proceedings,* p. clxxi ff.
8. Ai Br. I. 22.14; Śat Br. XIV 2.1. 16; See *Vedic Index.*
9. Mait. Sam. III. 8.7 *viṣṇoḥ śipre sthaḥ*; also, *ibid.,* I.2.9. the same.
10. *Zeitschrift fur Indologie und Iranistic,* II, 1923, p. 278.
11. *JAOS,* 1907, p.86, n.
12. Dange, *Vedic Concept of 'Field' and the Divine Fructification,* pp.83 ff.
13. *Ibid.*
14. VII. 99.7 = VII 100.7 and VII 100.5; 6.
15. Nirukta, V.8; also Sāyaṇa on RV noted above.
16. *Solfatgen Indien,* p.12 ff.
17. *Vienna* Or. J., XXX, p.427.
18. Taitt. Sam. VII. 5.5 *paśavaḥ śipiḥ ... śipi sabdaḥ paśu-vācī. teṣu svāmitvena praviṣṭaḥ.*
19. Taitt. Sam. VII.5.1.1

20. Mait. Sam. III 8.4; IV. 12.1; Taitt Br. II. 4.2, 7-8.
21. Also see Fig. IV.

* This chapter has been developed from part of a lecture delivered (among five total lectures) by the author in the University of Poona, under The Bhāu Vishnu Ashtekar Vedic Lecture Series, April 1968 (published, *Pastoral Symbolism from the Ṛgveda*, University of Poona, 1970).

Chapter 19

ADMA-SAD

The word *adma-sad,* in its different declensions, occurs six times in the Ṛgveda. No satisfactory explanation has been provided for this important word, the ordinary meaning given to it being 'guests at feast' or 'priests sitting at a feast or offering.[1]

Geldner suggests that the word means 'a fly' that sits on meals, following Durgā who explains it thus.[2] He changes this rendering in some contexts. Oldenberg rightly observes that this meaning is unacceptable.[3] The rendering 'fly' goes against such usages as *admasadām nṛṇām* (VII. 83.7) which indicate the *admasad*-s to be men. It would be advantageous to examine all the occurrences of this word to get at its real implication.

One thing that is remarkable with this word is that it is associated with the idea of waking or keeping awake, as also with chanting. Thus, we have Uṣas praised as *admasan na sasato bodhayantī* (like the *admasad*, awakening the sleepers) (RV I.124.4). Here, though Uṣas is being praised, it does not clearly show that *admasad* denotes a woman as Yāska and Sāyaṇa think. The greater probability is that it refers to a male with whom Uṣas is being compared with regard to the act of awakening. We have, elsewhere, *admasad* denoting a *vipra* (*admasad vipro na jāgṛviḥ* VIII 44.29). We have noted above *admasadām* as an epithet of *nṛṇām*. Again, it is used in reference to the mountains (VI. 30.3) in the masculine. Agni is said to be *admasadvā* (VI. 4.4).

It will be clear from the above, that the image in

admasad is that of a male. With this is associated the concept of awakening, most probably by means of the chanting of the *mantra*-s. The word *vipra* in *vipro na jāgṛviḥ* indicates the same thing. Where the word *admasad* is used along with *nṛṇām,* it is directly associated with praise (cf., *nṛṇām admasadām upastutiḥ*), and when Agni is said to be *admasadvā* he is also *vadmā,* suggesting praise. In the word *admasad,* the portion *adma* indicates 'food' *(ad + ma)* and this has been accepted by all. *Admasad* will, therefore, indicate a singer sitting at meals, or a chanting priest sitting at the offerings. It appears, that it was the duty of this priest to keep awake during the night or wake up early in the morning and awaken others. One priest awakening others is referred to also elsewhere in RV (e.g., X. 101.1). Of all the occurrences of the word *admasad,* the most original and suggestive seems to be *admasad vipraḥ jāgṛviḥ* which may be compared with *jāgṛvadbhir haviṣmadbhiḥ* (III 29.2). The word *jāgṛvadbhiḥ* occurs at two more places (VII 5.1 and X .91.1) and at the latter place the expression is *jāgṛvadbhir jaramāṇaḥ,* connecting it with the *mantra*-praise *(viz., jaramāṇaḥ)* in respect of Agni. There is another word with the same import, *viz. jāgṛvāmsaḥ,* which occurs thrice in RV (I.22.21; III.10.9 and VI.1.9; cf., also VIII 5.3, *jāgṛvāṁsam*). The words *jāgṛvat* and *jāgṛvi* seem to be derived from *jāgṛ,* from '√*gṛ* meaning 'to praise', and 'to keep awake, to praise' being the primary meaning. The concept is present also in the word *jāgaraṇa* which indicates not only the act of keeping awake (during the night) but also that of singing, and praising the deity. This is fully corroborated by the later word *mantra-jāgara.*

With the concept of *upastuti, bodhana* and *jāgṛvitva* associated with the word *admasad,* there should be no doubt about its indicating a priest who presided over the offerings and whose duty it was to rouse others, himself being awake before all; or, in other words, he is a high priest. Exactly here lies the importance of the fact that the Vasiṣṭhas pride themselves as *admasad*-s on whose account, the gods came to the help of Sudās (cf. VII 83.7, *satyā nṛṇām admasadām upastutir devā eṣām abhavan deva-hūtiṣu*). It is, again due to the fact of the status of the *admasad*-s that Agni is compared to a *vipra* who is an *admasad* (VIII. 44.29), and Uṣas directly to *admasad* (I.124.4). The word *admasadya* (VIII. 43.19) indicating the office or act of the *admasad,* is associated with Agni, who is referred to as *admasadvā* (VI 4.4).

The concept of *admasad* as the high priest officiating at the offerings (sacrificial food) and rousing Agni and the other priests by his *mantra*-s, has a close parallel in the *Vendidad* (*Sacred Books of the East*), where (Vol. I, p.56), Shraosh Varez is the god that awakens people for the prayer. The word *Śraosha* (cf. √*śru*) indicates 'hearing, 'awakening' and also 'punishing' (those who do not 'listen' to his orders). This god is compared with a cock awakening people in the morning. He is also supposed to pronounce the *shrashat* (cf. Vedic *Śrauṣaṭ*) which is the formula for the offering.

NOTES

1. Macdonell and Keith, *Vedic Index,* Indian Rep., Delhi, 1958.
2. *Der Rigveda* I, 1951, p.172 on I.124.4.
3. *Vedaforschung,* Stuttgart-Berlin, 1905, p. 90.

Chapter 20

ŚIŚNA-DEVA AND THE CULT OF THE NUDE

The word *śiśnadeva* has been put to various tests, and scholars have given various interpretations for it. Garbe renders it as *pucchadeva* ("Tail-gods"), the meaning being unclear; other scholars render it as the phallus, identified as *liṅga* in the later literature; Karmakar, A.P. renders it as "gods possessed with *śiśna*" (?); Shankarananda sees "weavers" in the word; and, to cut the list of scholars short, Sukumar Sen connects it with stump-worship, with Mūradeva=root worship.[1] The rendering "weavers" is based on the interpretation of Yāska (*āsnātāni sūtrāṇi*, "starched threads", Nir IV. 6), while the rendering "phallus" takes the word *śiśna* in the popularly known sense. It has been pointed out by the present author elsewhere,[2] that the word *śiśna-deva* does not indicate "phallus-worshippers", and that the word *śiśna* does not conclusively, in all cases, indicate the penis or the phallus. It has also been stated by him that there is no evidence of the killing of the *śiśnadeva*-s by Indra (a point not noticed by other scholars); on the contrary, Indra is said to have excelled them by his *varpas* (which does not necessarily mean bodily strength) at one place (RV X.99.3), the only other being where they are desired to be kept away from the sacrifice (RV VII. 21.5). The meaning *pucchadeva* implies the rendering *puccha* for *śiśna*; and, it tallies with another comparison, if we so make, *puccha*=*śepa*=(1) tail; (cf. *Śepaṭi* in Marathi; or *śepuṭ*, in the same language; and (2) male organ. Yāska himself is not quite sure about his meaning *āsnātāni sūtrāṇi*; for he rejoins, "*svāṅgābhidhānam vā syāt*, it may indicate the part of the body" (Nir. IV.6). When he comes to *śiśna-devāḥ*, he forwards no alternative interpretation, and takes *śiśna* as the male organ (*ib.*, 20 *śiśnam śnathateḥ*; and Durga thereon). In *śiśna-deva* there could, thus, be no doubt of any alternate rendering as *āsnātāni sūtrāṇi*; for that could hardly explain any person holding such "threads". It is to be noted that the word *deva* does not always indicate a physical object,[3] as is clear from such words as *anṛta-deva* (RV VII.104.14). Again, the word *deva* does not mean "god" always; it has the sense of "sporting", or "playing" (fr. √*div*). Thus, *anṛta-deva* would mean a person sporting with falsehood; and, by implication, it would mean a person who is given to false-speaking. This is exactly an abuse hit against Vasiṣṭha. Likewise, *śiśna-deva* would indicate a person who "sports the organ", though he may not actually "play" with it. The word *śiśna-deva*, very probably, is an abuse flung at the people who went about showing their organ. In other words, they were nude. But, they appear to be formidable; for, the hatred of the Vedic sacrificers for them, though they are referred to only twice, is evident. This conjecture gets fleshed up by references to the nude, though equally of less occurrence. They are of great significance, as they are indicative of a probable cult of the nude. We take them for study.

(i) RV VIII.2.12: *ūdhar na nagnā jarante*

["As do the nude praise the *ūdhas*", the *ūdhas* being the rain-cloud, the "udder" that releases the rain=milk.[4]]

(ii) RV X.61.9: *makṣū na vahniḥ prajāyā upabdir*
agnim na nagna upa sīdad ūdhaḥ!

[Here we have a pun on the word *udhaḥ*: (a) As the bull (*vahni*) approaches (sits upon) the *ūdhas* of his progeny; (b) so does the nude sit by the side of the fire (watching or attending on) the "udder".[5]]

In both the instances, the word *ūdhas* indicates the rain-cloud; and in the second image, in addition to the "udder", we have the fire near which the nude sits. The sitting of the nude by the side of the fire does not appear to be to ward off cold, as is understood by Geldner.[6] The mention of the nude in connection with the rain-cloud (*ūdhas*, used as metaphor) does have a deeper meaning. Apart from the fact that nudity is closely associated with the rituals for the gain of rain,[7] the nude is indicated to be hated by the Vedic sacrificer, in another verse; and though it is solitary, it is clear:

(iii) RV IV. 25.7: *na revatā paṇinā sakhyam indro*
(a)-sunvatā suta-pāḥ saṅgṛṇīte
(a-) sya vedaḥ khidati hanti nagnam
vi suṣvaye paktaye kevalo' (a-) bhūt

[Not with the wealthy Paṇi, who does not press (Soma for Indra), does the *Soma*-drinker Indra appreciate friendship; he destroys his (Paṇi's) wealth; kills the nude; for the well presser (of *soma*) and for the one who well fashions (cooks) the offering, alone, Indra becomes (friend).]

The verse marks the difference between a non-sacrificing wealthy person (here Paṇi) and the Vedic sacrificer. The point is, why should a *nagna* be mentioned here? There is only one more place where the word *nagna* occurs (RV VIII.89.2, where Soma is said to cover a nude), but that is not of any significance. The Panis, except for Bṛbu, have been exposed to vehement hatred by the Vedic seers.[8] It is against this background that the mention of the *nagna* with them here has to be examined. The killing of the *nagna* shows great hatred for him; and the mention of the *nagna* together with the Paṇi should indicate that these two were in close association. Though the help from other sources is meagre, the points put together would suggest:

(i) The *nagna* was a hated person for the Vedic sacrificer;
(ii) The reason, probably, was that he could bring rain by controlling the *ūdhas* (cloud), may be by a ritual in which the fire played a part; in other words, the *nagna* was a rival ritualist, and was patronised by

> the wealthy Paṇi, whom the Vedic seer-priests hated because he would not invite them to officiate at any rituals, nor would he accept the Vedic ritual. The only exception was Bṛbu, who is praised by the Vedic sacrificer in lofty terms.

To sum up: The Vedic sacrificers knew a cult of the nudes, which they hated. The hatred was more an economic issue, rather than a strictly religious one. This is clear from the glimpses of reconciliation of the Vedic priest-seers and sacrificers with people of other norms of life and rituals, such as Yatis and Munis, who, though of the same fold, followed different ways of life and did not accept the Vedic priestly rituals.[9] The nudes, being hated out of jealousy, were taunted as *śiśnā-deva*. But, these people never left the field. Though the name *śiśna-deva* lost currency in the later period, which only indicates that the nudes gained more acceptance in the then society, the practice of nudity continued as one of the distinguishing characteristics of the ascetic, who became and stayed on not only as a respected member of the ancient Indian (and even modern) society, but also came to be sought after.[10]

NOTES

1. See *Vedic Index of Names and Subjects,* under the term; also Macdonell, *Vedic Mythology* at the reference to this word; R.C. Jain, *The Most Ancient Jain Society,* Gangapur, 1964, pp.20 ff; Garbe, quoted by Hopkins, *The Religions of India,* London, 1896, p.150, n.; Karmarkar, *The Religions of India—The Vrātyas or The Dravidian System,* Lonavala, 1950, p.82; Shankarananda Swamy, *Sum. Papers AIOC,* 1957, Delhi; Sukumar Sen, *Renou Com. Vol.,* 1968, pp.680f.
2. *Cultural Sources from the Veda,* Bharatiya Vidya Bhavan, Bombay, 1977, pp. 30 f.
3. H.D. Velankar *Ṛgveda, Maṇḍala VII,* Bombay, p.60, n.5.
4. Oldenberg, *Noten,* on VIII. 2.12; also Griffith, Tr. of the passage, where he refers to Ludwig; cf. RV II. 34.10; III.1.9; 55.13; cf. *Noten* 11, p.76, "*Wie Nackte bei bewolktem Himmel*

(Regenwetter) wachen sie"; Griffith, though his negative sense is not acceptable, "The naked praise not when it rains"; it should, rightly be, "As *(na)* the naked praise so as to cause rain".

5. See Dange, *Vedic Concept of 'Field' and the Divine Fructification,* Bombay Uni., 1971, pp.131 ff.
6. *Der Rigveda,* on VIII 2.12 (which is implied in his rendering of X. 61.9), *"Wie Nackte in der kalte bleiben sie wach",* which is not warranted, nor corroborated, by the text.
7. See Dange, *Sexual Symbolism from the Vedic Ritual,* ch. on "Cosmosexualism"; also, *Vedic Concept...*, pp. 108 ff.
8. For the hatred of the Panis RV VI.53. 5-8; there are many other instances; see Macdonell, *Vedic Mythology* under Paṇi. For Bṛbu RV VI. 45.31-33.
9. *Cultural Sources from the Veda,* pp.85 f.
10. Not only the Jain saints of the Digambara sect adopted nudity as a way, but also the non-Jain Durvāsas is said to be roaming naked, Mb. Vana 260.11-*durvāso nṛpa digvāsāḥ tathā;* there are various references of Śiva roaming naked; actually, he is said to have attracted the wives of the sages, who hence, cut off his penis; various Puranic texts narrate this account, and one of the epithets of Śiva is Ūrdhvameṇḍhra, Mb. XIII, 17.46; for the account see Skanda-P., V.3. 38. 15-17; VI.228.10 ff; Kūrma-P. II.37.100-101; Brahmāṇḍa-P., I.2.26.15 ff.; also Dange, *Encyclopaedia of Puranic Beliefs and Practices*, under Śiva.

Chapter 21

AJĀMITĀ AND SPEECH-COUPLING

The words *jāmi* and *a-jāmi* occur at various places in RV in various combinations; and scholars have generally rendered them as indicating opposites in meaning, "related and foreign", "sister and non-sister" or "cognate and non-cognate" and the like. In RV the word *jāmi*-indicates "sister" at various places,[1] and at certain places *jāmi* and *a-jāmi* might indicate "friends and the enemies".[2] Yāska has understood the word *jāmi* as meaning, "something in excess (*atireka*)" in the first instance; also "foolish or boyish in appearance" and also "of the same species" as against *ajāmi* which means "of a different species" (Nir. IV. 20). At another place Yāska explains the word *jāmi* as "that which is expressed in the same way in one verse (Nir. X 16 *samānāyām ṛci samānābhivyāhāram bhavati taj jāmi bhavatyekam*); the example of this type given by Yāska is *madhu-mantam madhuścutam*" (RV IV. 57.2), where the word *madhu-mantam* occurs in the first quarter of the verse, while *madhus'cutam* in the third quarter; but both in the same verse. The meaning of both these words is alike; for, the second presupposes the first, and both have *madhu* in them. The example of the second type has been given in *hiraṇya-rūpaḥ sa hiraṇya-sandṛk* (RV II.35.10) where both the words occur in the first quarter; and this is explained by Yāska as "that which is expressed in the same way in a quarter" (*ibid., yad evā samāne pade samānābhivyāhāram bhavati taj jāmi bhavatītyaparam).* In these two types of *jāmi* the only difference is that the similar expression occurs in a verse or in the same quarter.

Yāska explains the word *a-jāmi* as indicating that pair of words which show even a little difference (*ibid. yathā-kathā ca viśeṣo-(a) jāmi bhavatītyaparam*). The example of this last type given by Yāska is *maṇḍūka ivodakān maṇḍūka udakād iva* (RV. X. 166.5), where the placement of the word *iva* is indicated to make a slight difference; and this is sufficient, according to Yāska, to have a case of *a-jāmi*. Now, the difference suggested by Yāska is not quite clear; for, if even a slight (*yathā-kathā*) difference makes the case for *a-jāmi,* we have such difference in the two earlier examples (given by Yāska as of *jāmi*). Reverting to the first set of meanings given by Yāska, we have him giving the example from the Yama-Yamī hymn ("where the *jāmi*-s might enact the *a-jāmi*"). Mehendale,[3] who has examined the meaning of these words, does not take into consideration the second set of examples given by Yāska; and, restricting himself to the Yama-Yamī hymn, follows Yāska and gives the final meaning of *ajāmi* as "Foolish twins or twins belonging to a different class (i.e. not human)". However, the expression is *jāmayaḥ kṛṇavann a-jāmi,* where it is the word *jāmi* that is in the plural. Again, the surmise of the "foolish twin" does not suit the sacred riddle of the hymn. This means, we have to probe the point further. The fact is that the expression in the Yama-Yamī hymn cannot be understood without taking into consideration the ritual-tradition, where the words *jāmi-ajāmi* occur often. The words are closely connected with the concept of duality (or coupling or pairing, i.e. *mithuna*). Gonda,[4] in his study of the dual deities has made a general survey of the concept of *mithuna* in the ritual set-up; and has rightly pointed out the case for *a-jāmitā* or *a-jāmitva,* which the ritual-texts stress for a specific purpose. This purpose is understood by Gonda as "disparity" and he renders the words *jāmi* and *a-jāmi* as "uniformity and un-uniformity". Thus, when two sacrificial cakes are offered in order, there is a silent offering between these two, with the purpose of *a-jāmitā* (Taitt. Sam. II.6.6.4; *ajāmitvāya*);[5] and the purpose, according to Gonda, is "to break the uniformity". The point is, why should this uniformity be broken? And it is here that Gonda does not seem to make a clear difference between the concept of *mithuna* and *jāmi*. The point is, that the silent offering changes the status of the subsequent sacrificial cake. The first cake is offered with a *yaju*s and the second one is preceded by silence. Here the coupling is of the vocal offering and the silent one; hence, they are different (*ajāmi*), though essentially the same (cakes). This slight difference (*yathā-kathā*) gives the two a different status, though they belong to the same class (i.e. of the cake). The concept in *a-jāmitā* is, hence, of a category and not of a class. And there is no question of un-uniformity or disparity.

The crux of the concept in *a-jāmitva* is not so much the disparity or the difference in class, as the speciality; and this speciality, in a wider sense, has to be understood in the context of ritual. In the references to *jāmi-ajāmi* from RV this point is not well marked; but the juxtaposition of these words in the hymn of Yama-Yamī is clearly on a different footing. This reference has become, or indicates, the basis of the concept of *jāmi-ajāmi* in the whole ritual set-up as we find it in the later ritual-texts; and the zeal of the Vedic ritualists to see that a pair does not remain *jāmi,* but that it has to be the *a-jāmi* one, has to be taken into account. This pair, then, has to be understood in the wider set-up of the *mithuna*. The special sense of the *mithuna* that this pair gets is absent in the other references to this pair of words in RV except for the Yama-Yamī hymn. The special difference between the *jāmi* and the *a-jāmi mithuna* is clearly expressed by the Jai. Br. in the following words: "What is *jāmi* is not (really) the *mithuna;* it is not procreative .... Indeed, what is the *ajāmi* is (in reality) the *mithuna;* that is procreative" (Jai. Br. I. 300). This is a clear advance from the general sense of the word *mithuna* that obtains elsewhere *viz.*, *mithunam prajananam* or *dvandvam mithunam prajananam* or even *daivyam mithunam prajananam*. In all these expressions the concept of *ajāmi*tā is implied, which is made clear by the Jai. Br. The *jāmi mithuna* is a simple pair, non-productive, as it is non-copulative, may be, because it comprises two males or two females,[6] or a pair of forbidden degrees. Yama and Yamī are *jāmi* in this latter sense; as they are brother and sister; and this latter sense is secondary. When the ritualists stressed the need for the *a-jāmi* pair, they had in mind the formation of a real copulative 'couple'; for the *jāmi* would be a homosexual pair, a non-productive one, which will be useless in view of the aim of the sacrifice, which was productivity.

The *a-jāmitva* is brought about by even a slight difference, as we have noted above. In the example we have taken at the beginning the *a-jāmitva* is accomplished in the offerings of the cake with and without the *yajus,* and that makes the difference in the sex, irrespective of the gender of the main word (*yajus* in the present context). It should be noted that the paraphrase of *a-jāmitā* as *atireka* is by the later interpreters[7] taking clue from Yāska; the ritual-texts use simply the word *a-jāmitā.* As the silent (*upaṁśu*) offering is the cause of creating *a-jāmitva,* there are also other ways of creating the same. One such method is 'non-utterance' of the same name. Thus in the context of the offerings to the various seasons, in the first round they are offered to by their names; and in the second round, they are offered to only "in the form of clarified butter" (Śat. Br I.3.2. 7-8). Now the non-utterance of the names for the second time would, naturally, be understood as doing away with unnecessary repetition (*atireka*); but there is hardly any evidence to show that the ritualists disliked or avoided repetition and cared for brevity; as a matter of fact, elaboration is the characteristic of ritual. Thus, the meaning of *a-jāmitā* cannot be "non-repetition". Like the silence, in the example above, the case is for the employment of a new method for creating *ajāmitā.* This is done by the direction, *ājyasyaiva rūpeṇa gṛhṇāti.* Thus, one form of the seasons is indicated by actually naming them, while the other by the clarified butter offered without the utterance of the name. The ultimate result is the same as silence; and the *ajāmi* pair is: Expression and Non-expression. It is specifically said that here clarified butter stands as the form of the season (*ājyasya rūpeṇa*); thus, in another aspect one form is the name of the season, while the other is that of the clarified butter. That the concept in *a-jāmitā* is not merely of avoiding repetition (*atireka*) is clear from another example. In the context of the invocation of Iḍā (personification of the offering) it is said that the various expressions, numbering four, are the four feet of the Cow (Iḍā). They are (*iḍā*) *upahūtā, upahūtā iḍā; upo asmān iḍāhvayatām; iḍā upahūtā* (Śat. Br. I. 8.1.24). It will be seen that the words are all repeated. What matters is the way; and this is to form the *a-jāmi* couple by changing the way of expression. The direction that has to be noted is: "variously, indeed, are they to be invoked; it will make *jāmi* if only it is said, '*iḍā upahūtā iḍā upahūtā*' or only '*upahūtā iḍā-upahūtā iḍā*' " (*ibid.,* 25).

The concept of speciality in the word *a-jāmi* has already been recorded by Yāska in the second set of his examples, when he describes it as *viśeṣa:* this is also borne out by his rendering of *a-jāmi* as *a-samānajātīya* in the earlier set of explanations of *jāmi.* It is to be noted that the explanation "foolish" for *jāmi* by him is influenced by the Yama-Yamī verse, where Yamī appears to *him* as '*bāliśa*'. His examples for *a-jāmi* are from the sphere of speech, or word; and there can hardly be any doubt about his being influenced in this by the ritual-tradition, which used pairs of dissimilar words having the same (or similar) meaning with the idea of forming copulative duals. There are any number of examples of this tendency. We may take a few examples. Thus, in the context of taking the various cups of *soma* (*graha*-s) it is said, that if the same name is uttered, it becomes *jāmi;* hence, slight difference (*viśeṣa)* is to be made: *upayāma-gṛhiṭo' si, āgrayaṇo'si, svāgrayaṇaḥ.* The addition of *su* to *āgrayaṇa* helps create an *a-jāmi* pair (Śat. Br. IV. 2.2.9). The case of *vetu* and *vyantu* is another example of this sort (Śat. Br. I. 5.3.15 *vyantu iti vai yoṣā, vetu iti vṛṣā vyantu* is a female; *vetu* is a male).

What has been said above will make clear that the concept of *jāmi-ajāmi* in the ritual context is an extension of the concept of the procreative *mithuna*. The same concept is extended to the sphere of speech and the formation of lauds (*sāman*-s), where the *ajāmi- tva* is indicated in the terms *nyūna* (also called *ūna* at certain places) and *atirikta*. Though it is not expressed in so many words, two *nyūna* lauds would be *jāmi;* and so would be the case with two *atirikta* lauds. The concept is as striking as it is interesting. The *nyūna,* ("minus") laud is said to be the female or woman, while the *atirikta* ("plus")[8] is the male or man. It is the *atirikta* that places the 'seed' in the *nyūna,* which then produces (cf. Ai Br. VI.9=28.1 *nyūnād vai prajāḥ prajāyante;* Śat. Br. I.3.17.18 *ūnād iva hi prajāḥ prajāyante;* this expression obtains at various places). Such pairs of *nyūna* and the *atirikta* were accomplished, or used at ritual, for procreation and weal (cf. Taitt. Sam. V.1.8.4 *ūnātiriktā mithunā prajātyai*). Various types of such pairs are noted. In the normal method the syllables in a quarter of the Virāj metre, ten in number, are taken as the unit; in certain cases the multiple of ten is the norm on the same basis; as the Virāj is of ten syllables (cf. Śat. Br. II.5.1.20 *daśākṣarā vai virāṭ*), a unit of nine verses in any metre is taken to form the female laud; and that of eleven forms the male laud. Thus, 200 or 240 total verses, or the exact multiple of ten is the norm; any combination having a verse less than this number is the female laud-unit (*stoma*), and that having more is male. Thus, in the triad technically known as the Trikadruka, there are three *stoma*-s: Jyotiṣṭoma, Goṣṭoma and the Āyuṣṭoma. Out of these, the Āyuṣṭoma is said to be the female; the Goṣṭoma is the male and the Jyotiṣṭoma is the offspring of these two. The Goṣṭoma consists of 241 *stotriya* verses (15 in the Bahiṣpavamāna laud + 36 in the four Ājyaśastras + 85 in the Mādhyandina Soma-pressing + 105 in the third pressing =241). As it is in excess by one, it is the male. The Āyuṣṭoma has respectively 9 + 60 + 85 + 105 = 259; this number is one less than the normal multiple of 10 (260);

this is the female laud (Pañc. Br. IV.8; XVI.I-3; also Kāṭhaka Sam. XXXIII.2; Jai. Br.II. 166; II.439; XXVII. 16; Taitt. Sam. VII.4.11.1-2; *ekayā gaur atiriktā, ekayā āyur ūnā*). Another example is the verse in the Gāyatrī metre; which has one syllables short (*ūṇakṣarā*). Here though there is no *atirikta* to represent the male, the normal quarter of 8 syllables serves for the same (cf. RV IX. 11.1; IX.64.28 etc.). Many more types may be cited.[9] Suffices to say that all these formations are, in essence, aspects of the central concept of the *mithuna* of the *a-jāmi* type which is the procreative spell of the Vedic ritualists.

NOTES

1. RV I. 23. 16; III. 31.2 etc.
2. I. 113.3; 124.6 etc.
3. *Summaries of Papers* AIOC, Jadavpur 1969, V-22, p.19.
4. *The Dual Deities in the Religion of the Veda,* Amsterdam, London, 1974
5. *Ibid.,* p.64
6. Cf. Jai. Br. I. 300 *yathā pumāṁsau vā saha śayātām striyau vā kim pumāṁsau saha śayānau prajanayetām; kim striyau.*
7. Cf. Sāyaṇa on Śat. Br. I. 5.3.8. *ajāmitvāya iti anatirekāya jāmi atirekanāma iti Yāskaḥ.*
8. Keith renders the word *nyūna* as "small", Rigveda *Br.* (Tr), p.206; Gonda renders the words as "deficient and redundant", *op.cit.,* p. 64. Both are not apt; for, they do not bring home the bodily structure of the male and the female, which the Vedic ritual tradition specifically intends.
9. See Dange, *Sexual Symboblism from the Vedic Ritual,* Delhi, 1979, pp.97-114.

Chapter 22

GARTA AND GARTA-ĀRUK

The word *garta,* which occurs in the Ṛgveda eight times, has been generally rendered as "chariot" by scholars, the chariot being actual or symbolic.[1] The tradition, as represented by Yāska and Sāyaṇa, also renders it as such generally, except at the place which refers to a brotherless girl ascending the *garta* (I.12.7), where it is rendered as "the place where the judges sit".[2] In addition, Yāska renders it as the S*abhā sthāṇu* ("an elevated platform in the assembly") and also as *śmaśāna-sañcayaḥ,* "elevated erection of stones on a dead body" (*ib.*). He also renders it as "chariot". These different meanings could not have been entirely different from one another in the origin; and it is necessary to investigate the original shade of the word. Giving these meanings, and referring to other authorities, B.H. Kapadia[3] has come to the conclusion that originally the word meant a chariot or an elevated seat in a chariot; then an elevated seat in the gambling hall, on which a person is required to sit in order to tell the truth; subsequently it meant a house and later the cemetery; and, according to him, it is "only in I. 124.7 that *garta*, because of *gartāruk,* can mean a board or a dais on which dice were thrown".[4] This is a rejoinder to the meaning of the word *garta-āruk* (*ā-ruh*) given by Yāska and explained by Durga, the commentator. Rightly does Kapadia question the propriety of the suggestion of Yāska, as understood by Durga, that here we have reference to a custom current in south India, according to which a sonless widow sits on the gambling dais to prove her chastity and gets the share of her husband's wealth from the relations of her husband; otherwise, the share might have gone to them.[5] His reason for not accepting the explanation is that RV could not probably refer to a custom in the southern part of India, for the Vedic Aryans had not penetrated to that part as yet. This is to be accepted. His suggestion that, here, the dawn may be compared to a "man ascending a chariot" is understandable, only insofar as it does not drag the word "brotherless". What seems true is, that here there are four different images, in which Dawn is set: (1) She is compared with a brotherless girl that reverts to the *gotra* of her father, as she is technically called *'putrikāsuta'*. This type of girl is supposed to be the 'son' of her father for all rituals meant for the manes, on such a condition to her marriage; or her son 'becomes' the son of her father.[6] The dawn disappears as soon as the sun (her man = husband) appears; hence, she is seen as going away to her father, the sky, and disappear. But this need not have any connection with the second image, which is (2) of the person who ascends the *garta* for the gain of the wealth. Yāska takes this image as that of the son-less widow; and he is believed to give the instance from the south, which poses difficulties as noted above. Here it may be pointed out that all the four images in this verse are of a woman; and it is doubtful if this second alone could be taken as that of "a man ascending a chariot". But, before we examine this image, let us refer to the other two images. (3) Dawn appears like a married woman, desirously expecting her husband after her period and donning charming garments; and (4) Like a smiling woman (a common woman) she exposes her form (*nirṇīte apsāḥ).* It is, thus, clear that in all these images the seer describes various types of women. As such, the one who ascends the *garta* need not be a man. These four images need not be mutually connected; and they are not, as the word indicative of comparison (*iva)* is used four times: *abhrātā-iva* (a), *gartārug-iva* (b), *jāyā-iva* (c), *hasrā-iva* (d). As such, the second type may be so described even if she is not brotherless. She may have a brother, or may not have; but, not having one might lead her to this state, for the gain of wealth. The text of RV does not mention if the second type of woman is without a brother, a son, or even if she is married! It is Yāska who brings in this point. It is probable that being *garta-āruk* indicates her profession; and, probably, we have to examine the word *dākṣiṇājī* used by Yāska for this type, in this light.

The word *dākṣiṇājī*, used by Yāska, is rendered by Durga as *dākṣiṇātyā strī.* It is clear, hence, that the idea of such a woman being from the "south" is not of Yāska, but of Durga; and it is not improbable that Durga misinterprets Yāska. There is no help for direct interpretation of this word used by Yāska; but it should be rather quite acceptable that he would not read in RV a custom from the south. What, then, is the explanation of the riddle that haunts this word? It is to be noted that even Durga, who sees a southern custom here, does not discard the suggestion of Yāska that the act refers to gambling. Yāska says that such a woman ascends the *garta,* because *garta* is a place of speaking the truth (*satya-saṅgaro bhavati*), and that here there is a throw of dice. The words of Yāska are *tām tatra-akṣair ā ghnanti, sā riktham labhate,* which are understood as "striking" with dice (Kapadia; Rajawade and others). Durga himself does not refer to striking with dice; for, these words (*tām...ā ghnanti*) do not occur in the copy of the script used by Durga. It is probable that they were not originally in the version of Yāska and were inserted by some one later. But, the fact seems to be that the woman had to prove her share by submitting to gambling in Yāska's period. Now, what about the word *dākṣiṇājī?* If we read the sentence as Yāska gives, *"gartārohiṇīva dhanalābhāya dākṣiṇājī",* it appears that the word *dākṣiṇājī,* in essence, explains *dhanalābhāya* ("for the gain of wealth"), and does not say anything more; and the "southern woman" might not have touched the imagination of Yāska. The context shows that the meaning of this word has to be fixed, according to Yāska, in the context of gambling, together with that of *dakṣiṇā / dākṣiṇa.* In this connection, it is to be remembered that the word *dakṣiṇā* is itself closely connected with the cow; and it is said that when no other sacrificial gift (*dakṣiṇā*) is mentioned, a cow is always meant.[7] In that case, *dakṣiṇā-jī* would mean "one who wins the *dakṣiṇā* =cow". We may compare here a ritual where the cow of the sacrificer is won by the cast of dice.[8] It is true that here we do not have the exact word *dākṣiṇājī*; but the point of gambling with dice and winning is clear. It might be that the word '*dākṣiṇājī* (*dakṣinām jayati; strī*)' is used, colloquially for winning the share of the husband by such an ordeal-like ritual (*divya*=divine help). Beyond this the point is dark. Dice-play has been a part of rituals and dice has been worshipped as having divine power.[9] Striking the woman in question with dice is to be seen only as an alternate method wherein the idea should have been to see the truth of the woman's claim by letting the dice actually touch her body and indicate justice as they fall. The proposition, hence, is that the word *dākṣiṇājī* is to be understood as a proverbial expression to indicate "the gainer of gifts" (*dakṣiṇām jayati iti dakṣiṇājiḥ,*[10] *dakṣiṇājir eva dākṣiṇājī; strī dākṣiṇājī*), which has the same sense as in *sanaye dhanānām* in the text of RV noted above. D*akṣiṇā* would, thus, indicate, 'money given through courtesy'. Yāska, thus, only explains the expression with the word *dākṣiṇājī*, which could not be taken to mean a southern woman. It should be noted in this connection that Sāyaṇa, himself a southern (Vijayanagara, Humpi), does not render the word as indicating a southern woman, though he quotes the explanation of Yāska. Durga's explanation of Yāska is, hence, questionable.

There is another point. Yāska renders the word *garta* here as *sabhā-sthāṇu,* which would simply mean 'a raised seat in the assembly hall'. As noted above, the version of Durga does not have the words "*tām tatra akṣair-āghnanti.*" The whole reading, then, would be "*gartārohiṇīva dhanalābhāya dākṣiṇājī; gartaḥ sabhāsthāṇur gṛṇāteḥ, satya-saṅgaro bhavati, tām tatra yā-aputrā yā-apatikā sā-ārohati; sā riktham labhate*". Whether all this is intended by the simple expression from RV, *garta-āruk,* is doubtful; for, *garta* is rendered by Yāska himself as indicating even other things. Out of the places that refer to *garta,* eight in all, three are from the same hymn (V. 62), while each of the rest is from various single hymns. The description of the *garta* at these would give an idea of its size and form. At four places it is associated with Mitra and Varuṇa, and they are called kings. They ascend the *garta* that is golden in hue and has the main pole made of *ayas* (hard metal);[11] from here these two gods supervise Diti and Aditi, which indicate the whole seen expanse of sky and the earth (V. 62.8). This *garta* is structured in an expansive and a holy place and has honey in it (*ib.,* 7). The *garta* is spacious (V. 88.5). Rudra sits on the *garta* (II.13.11). At one place the *garta* is associated with an archer, in standing posture, as Indra is compared with him while standing on his two horses (*tiṣṭhad-harī;* VI. 20.9).

The references noted above do not so much fit in the image of a chariot, as of a spacious dais or platform; and even if we take *garta* to refer to a chariot here, the image has to correspond to the *garta,* that is said to be 'ascended' by the *garta-āruk,* who is the woman. There it is clear that the *garta* is a high place, where the judges (or the gamblers) sit.[12] This seems to be a probable concept behind the word *garta.* The explanation of Yāska that it was a place from which only truth could be spoken *(satya-saṅgaro bhavati)* adds credibility to this concept. The *astā* (archer) could shoot his arrow from this place; and the image of the *astā* seems to be that of an archer in a shooting competition, rather than in a battle; here, probably, we have the glimpse of even the shooting competition at the marriage by choice. The *garta* being *satya-saṅgara* gives also the idea of a dais of proclamation. Honey and other gifts being associated with the *garta* would go well with the high dais whereupon the king sits, rather than with a chariot or a throne.[13] This would show that at the Ṛgvedic period the word *garta* had the connotation of a raised platform primarily, whatever may have been the later connotation. The word *garta-*

āruh(k) would indicate ascending the *garta*. Whether *garta* had a necessary association with gambling is doubtful; for, as Kapadia has pointed out, the famous gambling hymn[14] does not mention it at all; and never in RV is there any association of *garta* with gambling. As such, the image of the son-less woman going to the gambling house, or sitting on a seat surrounded by gamblers is not convincing. *Garta-āruk,* hence, would indicate a common woman who ascends a public dais for gaining gifts or money, may be by auction or by an art such as dancing. The dawn, who is compared to the *garta-āruk* here, is said to be a dancer at another place.[15] How *garta* came to indicate a pit, or a hollow ground, later, may be an interesting point for investigation. Probably, the reason lies in the practice of constructing the performing platform in the middle, while the seats are arranged around it gradually getting raised, as is the case with the amphitheatre.[16] This would make the *garta* a hollow ground; and also a pit, which is its connotation later.

NOTES

1. See Sāyaṇa at the places mentioned, except at I.124.7; *The Vedic Index of Names and Subjects,* under "Garta", says that it indicates the "seat in the chariot".
2. Sāyaṇa also Yāska, Nir. III.5.
3. "The word Garta in Ṛgveda", *J. Ganganath Jha Research Institute,* Vol. XXV, 1969, pp. 216-18; *Umesh Mishra Com. Vol.* 1970, pp. 221-26.
4. *Ibid.,* p. 226.
5. *Ibid.,* p. 225.
6. Yājñavalkya Sm. II. 128 and *Mitākṣarā* Com. which quotes Vasiṣṭha; also Kane P.V., *Hist. of Dharmaśāstra,* Vol. II-i, Poona, 1974 (I ed., 1941), pp. 435-36; also Nirukta III.4.
7. *Vedic Index* under *"Dakṣiṇā".*
8. *gām asya tad ahaḥ sabhāyam dīvyeyuḥ,* Mait. Sam. I.6.11.
9. Cf. RV X 27.17; AV XIV.1.36; Baudh. Śr. S. XVI.1.17.
10. For the form of, *ji,* ending in *ji* see W.D. Whitney, *The Roots, Verb-forms and Primary Derivatives of the Sanskrit Language,* Leipzig, 1885, p.53, under *ji,* 'to conquer'. We

may also derive as *dakṣiṇāyāḥ āgatam dākṣiṇam* (any gift); *tad jayati iti.*

11. *ayas* is not iron; see *Vedic Index,* under "*ayas*".
12. Cf. Sāyaṇa, *rājapuruṣair nyāya-nirṇetṛbhiśca-adhiṣṭhitam sthānam.*
13. Kapadia connects *garta* with *gaddī, gādī* etc.
14. RV. X.34.
15. *Ibid.*, I.92.4 *adhi peśāṁsi vapate nṛtūr iva.*
16. Some dancing-grounds are of this nature; see for example the one at Madurai in south India, in the palace of the Nayakars. However, there is no clear evidence from ancient India.

Chapter 23

DĪRGHATAMAS : HIS VISION OF JĪVA AND ĀTMAN

We have examined the various images presented by Dīrghatamas (ch. 2). Now we take a note of his contribution as a philosopher. Writers on Indian philosophy take to the Upaniṣads as the fountain-head, thinking that what stands beyond that period, in the ritual of the Brāhmaṇa-texts, is nothing else than mere Karma-Kāṇḍa. Naturally, they dwell only on names as Yājñavalkya, Pravāḥaṇa Jaivali, Āruni Uddālaka, Raikva, Aśvapati Kaikaya and the like. The philosophers of the Upaniṣadic period tried to solve the riddle of the ultimate Reality mainly through three approaches: (1) the consmological, (2) the physical, and (3) the psychological. The last was the best of approaches, as it was also the final and more subtle. The cosmological approach is one in which various cosmic forces such as water, fire, air, etc., are said individually to be the ultimate source of the universe. The physical one is where the forces of the human body such as breath, speech, etc., are concerned; and the psychological one is that wherein the experience of deep sleep is examined. The last has been very finely described by Ajātaśatru. The speculations went yet ahead; and it was propounded that the experienceless sleep is the best example of the stage of ultimate Reality, where there is no consciousness of the worldly experience whatsoever, the only consciousness being that of the self.

The Greek philosopher Thales, propounding Water as the ultimate principle, compares with the theory of ancient Egyptian thinkers that Nun (primeval waters) is the ultimate Reality, and also with the Indian thought that it is in water that all the gods were.[1] Raikva said that it is Air that is the ultimate Reality; and correspondingly the Greek philosopher Anaximenes propounded that the primeval substance is the Vapour. The theory that Fire is the ultimate Reality, which fact is propounded in the concept of the five fires (*pañcāgni*) in the Chāndogya Upaniṣad and the Bṛhadāraṇyaka Upaniṣad, corresponds to the thought of the Greek philosopher Heraclitus who taught that Fire was the source of all things. The Ākāśa (Ether) doctrine taught by Pravāḥaṇa Jaivali is reflected in the teaching of Philolaus, according to whom Space (Ether) is the ultimate Reality. These are only a few examples to show the influence of Upaniṣadic thought upon the Greek writers. However, the point to be noted in the philosophy of the Upaniṣads is the contribution of the Upaniṣadic thinkers to the theory of Ātmanism. It is generally believed that the difference of the body from the soul is the thought contributed by the Upaniṣadic thinkers. It is believed that this thought was not known before; and, naturally, the Upaniṣadic thinkers are given the credit for it. It has to be remembered, however, that beyond the period of the Upaniṣads, the Brahmanic ritualists had their own method of ritual-philosophy, which is clear in all their rituals; and the most striking example of this is the ritual of Agnicayana, which was the symbolic piling of the cosmos with the sun-fire, symbolized as a golden figure of man in a layer of the altar, as the central principle. In the hymns of RV various 'seers' have recorded glimpses of real philosophy; but their names are not known to the modern students of philosophy, who start from the Upaniṣads only. These seers relate their experiences as 'visions', and it is necessary to examine these 'visions' to get a first-hand idea of their *'darśana'* which is the real term for philosophy in the Hindu tradition. In a number of cases, true to the spirit of the Hindu tradition, the names of the ancient Vedic seers have not come down to us, though their thought has become famous. Thus the hymn known as the 'Nāsadīya' (X. 129) is referred to as the most ancient example of the Hindu (Aryan) approach to the speculations regarding the creation of this universe; and yet the name of the seer is unknown to us, the tradition saying that it is Prajāpati himself! Another important hymn is the one known as the 'Puruṣasūkta' (X.90), the seer of which is said to be Nārāyaṇa, of whom nothing more is known. There are many other seers whose names have been mentioned, and are plausible; but their thought has not been taken serious note of by modern scholarship on Hindu philosophy. The first Vedic seer who says, though casually, that there was the principle called *asat* in the beginning and that from it came *sat,* is named Bṛhaspati due to the fact that Brahmaṇaspati is mentioned in the hymn at one stage (X.72.2). This beginning of the philosophic discussion is mostly forgotten, though the Upaniṣadic discussions regarding there being *sat* or *asat* are well remembered. Likewise, the vision of the seer Vasukra regarding the working of the cosmos has not reached modern students (including such masters on this subject as Dr. Radhakrishnan and Hiriyanna), as they were not particular in probing the Ṛgvedic seers' 'visions'. The visions of the Ṛgvedic seers were mixed; with the cosmic workings they combined ritual details; for they believed that the latter are intimately connected with the former. But, because of this, they are thought to be more magical than philosophical. And this is the main reason why they are treated as less important by scholars. But that is a mistake; and in committing this mistake scholars shut their eyes to the very source of philosophical thought, not knowing that they are blind to the very '*darśana*' itself! In certain cases, the thought of the Ṛgvedic seers has been taken up by the Upaniṣads; and, through them, it was studied by the later scholars of '*darśana*'; but the pity is that it was believed to be from the Upaniṣads themselves! Having done so, new and fantastic (or rather philosophic!) interpretations were attached to it, not bothering to see the original context from which it was taken. The case of the seer Dīrghatamas is only one of many such. We have referred to him earlier (ch. 2); now a new aspect.

The personal history of Dīrghatamas is shrouded in mystery. The Mahābhārata and the Purāṇas mention him, the former only casually[2] and the latter weaving queer-looking accounts around him. The Vedic tradition, however, recognizes him as a great seer, who enjoyed a hundred years of life.[3] His greatest contribution to Indian thought is his concept of *Jīva* and its being separate from the mortal body. It is this thought that stands at the basis of the later Upaniṣadic philosophy of Ātmanism. RV knew the word 'Ātman'; but it was, for almost all the Vedic seers, only the principle of Air.[4] It is Dīrghatamas who differentiates Ātman, as the soul, as being separate from the body; not only this, he differentiates it from 'Prāṇa' (the principle of life-breath) and also from the subtle element called *'asu'*. This will be clear from a verse from one of his hymns, called the *'Asya-vāmīya'* which gets so named from its first verse which starts as *'Asya vāmasya palitasya hotuḥ'* (I. 164.1).

> Who saw the very first-born, when the boneless one bore the one having bones? Whence came the blood, the life-breath and the soul of Earth (*asuḥ, asṛk, ātmā)?* Who,indeed, went to the wise to ask? (I.164.4).

The difference between the *asu* and Ātman (the soul) is clear in the passage noted above, where the word *asu* indicates the subtle element of 'Prāṇa'; and Ātman is beyond it. At yet another place this difference is marked, though the word 'Ātman' is not used there. In the place of the word 'Ātman', we have the word *'jīva'*. The seer of that hymn is again Dīrghatamas; and the expression using the word *asu* is set in the imagery of the ritual-fire. The fire is said to be fondled by the flames; and the latter are said to be his 'sisters'. It is said to be taking off their old age, and giving them new life of brilliance. It is also said to be imparting them the *asu* and the *Jīva* (I.140.8). Though the word *Jīva* occurs at various places in RV, the distinction of the concept of *Jīva* from that of *asu* is marked prominently by Dīrghatamas. There is only one more place in

RV where *asu* and *Jīva* occur together, and there the sun is said to be both the *asu* and *Jīva* of the dawn (I. 113.16); but there the distinction is not made clear by the seer Kutsa of the family of Aṅgiras. As said above, the word *jīva* occurs at various places in RV; but, the seers do not show clear acquaintance with the exact meaning of the word, using it only in the general sense of 'a living creature'. But that the 'living' principle (principle of life) is to be termed *Jīva* is an innovation of Dīrghatamas, allowing some benefit of doubt to Kutsa of the family of Aṅgiras. Nowhere do we find in RV a clear distinction between the various elements of the human body (as blood, breath, bones) and the soul, as in the hymn ascribed to Dīrghatamas noted above. And comparing the two passages of Dīrghatamas himself,[5] we see that in one he uses the word Ātman and in the other *Jīva*, which leaves no doubt about the fact that it is he who first interprets (or, at least, is the first to know) the changed conception behind the word Ātman, and stresses that it is synonymous with *Jīva*. It is here that we have the first-ever concept of the Jīvātman. Hence, it has to be accepted that Dīrghatamas was the first seer-philosopher to contrast the terms 'Prāṇa' and 'Ātman', the former being '*asu*' and the latter '*Jiva*'. Actually, the controversy regarding the mutual superiority between 'Prāṇa', (the vital breath on the microcosmic level, and Air on the macrocosmic level) and Ākāśa continued even in the Upaniṣadic period. Raikva propounded, as was noted earlier by us, that Air was the chief element and the ultimate Reality; and Pravāhaṇa Jaivali chose a yet subtler element called Ākāśa (Ether) as the ultimate Reality. Dīrghatamas contributed to the pre-Upaniṣadic world of thinkers the concept of Jīvātman; but his contribution was forgotten in the later din of Upaniṣadic controversy. The reason, probably, was that the Ṛgvedic 'seer' was also a ritualist in addition to his being a mystic thinker! But his thought deserves further probe.

Not only did Dīrghatamas propound that the Jīvātman (soul) was different from, and subtler than, the element of Breath (Prāṇa), but also that it could be separated from the living organism which we call body, and which dies when bereft of the soul. The imagery of Dīrghatamas centres on the sun and the earth, as does that of Kutsa on the sacrificial fire; but, it is to be noted with pertinent care that Dīrghatamas bases his imagery of the cosmic relationship on that of the human body (or, for that matter, a living body) inasmuch as he refers to the blood, the bones, etc. He is quite clear in his concept of the soul wandering away from the body, when he says, "The *Jīva* of the dead (*mṛtasya*) wanders," (I.164.30) which enshrines the belief that the body dies, yet the soul remains and wanders to seek a fresh body. The other side of the belief, that the soul and the body stay together, is also clearly stated by him in the words, "The *Jīva* stays in the same abode that perishes"-*amartyo martyena sayoniḥ*. Thus, he shows a clear grasp of the concept of the soul that stays in the body, and yet gets away from it. This is the very basis of the principle of the transmigration of the soul. Though Dīrghatamas describes the upper cosmos and the daily rising and setting of the sun, his basic concept regarding the soul staying with the body and getting away from it can hardly be doubted. The belief recorded by this seer here is reflected finely in the later Upaniṣadic thought which says, "What is not endowed with *Jīva* dies; *Jīva* (soul) does not die."[6] Dīrghatamas says further that the soul enlivens the body, which, hence, gets born in various forms.[7]

Another contribution of Dīrghatamas is that it is he who first 'saw' the vision of the Two Birds that rest on the same tree, one of whom eats the sweet fruit of the tree (*pippalam*), while the other only looks on without eating. The verse is famous and has formed around it heaps of interpretation, if one may say so. The Muṇḍaka Upaniṣad and the Śvetāśvatara Upaniṣad,[8] each of which adds a verse to it, have incorporated the image to impart their philosophical teaching. As both have this and the next verse common, they certainly have borrowed both from the earlier tradition. As we have seen, the first verse (which shows the vision of the Two Birds) is from Dīrghatamas (I.164.20); the next is from the later Vedic tradition, but follows the image of the first, when it speaks of the Puruṣa sitting on the same tree. It is this second verse that speaks of two Puruṣas on the same tree, one of them being the Paramātman and the other the Jīvātman. But the basis of the thought is the vision of Dīrghatamas. As noted earlier, the seer Dīrghatamas applies the microcosmic (that is, of the individual body) observation regarding the soul and the body to the cosmos, where the sun is said to be the soul by him. On this analogy, he describes the sun as the 'animating, actively moving soul' that stands in the midst of the cosmic waters—*anat śaye turagātu Jīvam* (*ib.*, 30). Incidentally, the waters are often conceived as the females, or the foetus, in which the principle of fire stays to fructify them for fresh creation. Here the seer employs the same image, and states that the sun is the generating element, in addition to its being the very soul. He does not stop at the idea that the sun is the ultimate truth, that is, the soul; he says that the outer form (the orb) of the sun is to be distinguished from the inner principle of steady light and fire, which is the real essence of the divinity that is visible in the sky. The orb is the 'cover' (*vavri*), thus suggesting that even in the sun there is the outer 'body' and the inner soul. He never uses the word 'Puruṣa' in this imagery; but there is no doubt that the concept of "the Man-in-the-Waters" was already getting to the forefront in the Ṛgvedic age, which conveyed at a later stage, the concept of 'Puruṣa Narayana' (Man traversing in the cosmic Waters), which originally indicated the sun and, later, Viṣṇu on the serpent in the Waters. When this concept of "Man-in-the-Waters" got mixed with that of the bird in the cosmic or solar water, the two birds were seen anthropomorphically as the Jīvātman and the Paramātman. But in the pure image of the seer Dīrghatamas, the birds were never the Jīvātman and Paramātman, though he propagated the *Jīva* as a distinct element beyond the body, the 'cover' (*vavri*). The two birds, in the first aspect of his image, were the sun in the heavenly region, and the sacrificial fire on the terrestrial plane. This is clear if we note the verse that is earlier to the one that has the two birds. There he speaks of the Father and the Son (I.164.18), the former being the sacrificial fire that is believed to sustain the sun, the Son. This is how he connects the Sacrificial fire with the sun here and elsewhere in the hymn.[9] But taking his sap from the sacrificial set-up he goes a step ahead in the present image. He takes his stand on the already set belief that the sun is the other end of the cosmic tree, the branches being his rays. We have the image of the cosmic pillar (*stūpa)* of Varuṇa, whose root is up there, while the shoots come down, where it is further said that the shoots enter our hearts (I.124.7). This is the most original concept of the cosmic tree, borrowed later by the Kaṭha-Upaniṣad and the Bhagavad-Gītā.[10] After setting forth the vision of the two birds, Dīrghatamas takes it further; he says that the solar orb is the haunt of the birds (rays) that eat the honey (I.164.22), where he conceives the sun as the tree. At another stage in the same hymn he says that the sun is the bird that holds water to release for the creatures (*ib.*, 52). In the image of the tree, he says that the sun is full of nourishing fruit that stands at the top of it (*ib.*, 22); the ray-birds eat this sweet fruit. The next step is that these rays come down (or better, fly down) to the terrestrial plane and enter the individual souls, which then partake of the nourishing life-essence of the sun-fruit. So, the individual soul is the bird that eats of the fruit; but the other bird that does not eat is the one in the sun, the soul of the universe. The sun-bird is different from the ray-birds for Dīrghatamas. The individual soul gets its sap through the ray-birds; but the sun-bird simply holds the sap (fruit), as the tree simply holds the fruit, not eating it. The sun is, then, the abode of the supreme Bird (Paramātman) in the most original concept of the seer from whom the Upaniṣads have borrowed the imagery. That the 'Paramātman' is in the sun, is clear enough from the Muṇḍaka Upaniṣad also, which speaks of this Puruṣa as: 'Golden-hued' (III.3.3). This also speaks of the *saguṇa* Reality, prior to its being contemplated as the subtle Brahman (*ib.*, 4 ff).

The Śvetāśvatara Upaniṣad, which takes the verse of the Two Birds from Dīrghatamas, takes another verse from his hymn: 'In the highest heaven stands the *akṣara* of the shining *mantra* (*ṛc*); therein stay all the gods; (beyond that is the High One); one who does not know Him, what shall he do with the mere verse?[11] It will thus be seen that Dīrghatamas first gives the meaning of the *mantra* as the abode of the high God. But the concept of Akṣara for the seer is not limited to the mystic *syllable of the mantra.* On the analogy of the sun-tree, whose shoots come down to the individual souls, the Akṣara also is prone to ooze. The word Akṣara means 'non-oozing'; but Dīrghatamas clearly says that the Akṣara oozes.[12] Thus, the highest principle is steady; yet it oozes for nourishing the creatures on the earth. Dīrghatamas makes the image very simple and clear further on, when he says that the *Akṣara* that oozes is seen in the form of rain, which is the visible phase of the highest shining life-giving element of sustenance. For him, the sun is the visible Akṣara as it holds the waters that it releases in the form of rain. But, as the solar orb is only the 'cover' (*vavri*), the real Akṣara stands beyond it. It is both the source of light and of water. This is on the basis of the Vedic concept of the rain-waters being always sunny or full of light (*svar-vatī*). When the Śvetāśvatara Upaniṣad (IV.4) takes the idea, it still holds on to this original concept of light-water fusion; but the unborn (*aja*) god for it is not in the sun; it is the mid-region fire of the cloud, which it describes as, "the blue-black Bird of yellowish-green hue, of red eyes, that stays in the womb of the lightning." From this the next step is that of the various flames of the sacrificial fire having varied colours (*ib.*, 5); and the next is the image of the Two Birds; next comes the image of the Puruṣa on the tree, we have noted earlier; and the final one is the Highest principle beyond the *mantra* of the Akṣara. The whole scheme follows the imagery of Dīrghatamas, who fuses sacrificial concepts with his cosmic vision of the sun and the sun-waters (rain), and yet, in the context of the ritual, asserts the concept of the highest Soul of the cosmos.

What has been said above will prove that the seer Dīrghatamas has clearly influenced the philosophic thought of the Upaniṣads; and it is to be noted that the Upaniṣads also do not set away the images from the sacrificial ritual atmosphere, which speaks for the dominant ancient influence. It has to be admitted that the Upaniṣadic thinkers cannot do away with the 'vision' of the Ṛgvedic seers, which may be termed proto-philosophy. The points to be noted from the vision of Dīrghatamas are as follows:

1. *The Cosmic Tree* (Earlier Vedic Concept): The solar orb is the upper end; it holds the nourishing essence (the honey), which is twofold: (i) Light, and (ii) Water (seemingly); it holds also the essence of Life. The lower end (or the shoots) touches the individual souls.[13]
2. *The Two Birds*: (A) The original image known to Dīrghatamas—(i) the Bird in the solar orb, and (ii) the Bird in the sacrificial fire. (B) Innovation of Dīrghatamas—(i) the Bird in the solar orb= Cosmic Soul, and (ii) the Bird in the individual heart (=individual soul)-developed as the Puruṣas later.
3. *The Akṣara*: (A) Light-Fluid principle, Life-essence. (B) The subtle principle beyond words.
4. *The Concept of the 'Double'*: The concept of the *Jīva-Ātman*; *Jīva* (soul) and the body—the former immortal, self-moving, resorting to various bodies; the latter prone to vanish, subject to death; also indicated by the word *vavri* (Cover).

The belief in the double soul obtains at various places. Thus, among the Tasmanians obtains a belief that every individual has a shadow-soul, which is reincarnated. A similar belief obtains among the Haidas of British Columbia, according to which the shadow-soul returns after some definite time to enter the body of a pregnant woman; and the movement in the womb marks its advent. The belief in the *churinga* may be compared. It is with this soul that the idea of reincarnation is associated. The other soul is the Dream-soul, which leaves the body and wanders in sleep and gives various experiences. If the person is suddenly startled in sleep, the Dream-soul takes fright and the person sickens and also dies. In death the Dream-soul drops down to the underworld.[14]

In the case of the double soul the microcosmic position will be of two souls in the same body, one getting into the cycle of birth and rebirth, and the other resorting to a common habitat. Dīrghatamas shows knowledge of this belief when he speaks of the "honey-eating birds" that stay together on the divine tree (RV 1.164.22), the thought getting a clear tinge of the concept of the cosmic *pitṛ* (*ibid., yah pitaram na veda*). The concept is clearly ur-Vedic, though non-Vedic it cannot be said with certainty! We may note the ancient Egyptian belief, according to which everything has a double, including the body and the intellectual faculty. *Ka* is the spirit; it is also the double of the body. *Khu* is the soul and is also the double of the intellect. Thus, *Ka* and *Khu* represent the principles that are beyond the visible body; and both are subtle. This dual of the spirit and the soul (*Ka+Khu*), or we may say the double-soul, is represented as a bird with a human head, howering over the mummy seeking to re-enter it. Everything that exists has a *Ka*, including the trees and the water.[15] Though the *Ka* of a particular thing must be taken to be restricted to itself, it is seen that it could change its station as is seen in the story of Anpu and Bata, the two brothers. The wife of the elder brother, Anpu, being repulsed by the younger one, Bata, in her desire for the latter, poisons the mind of Anpu against Bata. Due to fear of being killed by the elder brother the innocent Bata transfers his soul in the blossom of the acasia plant. If the plant is cut, the soul would come out and be placed in a jar of water, whereupon Bata would come back to life. The soul of Bata transmigrates this-wise into the bull, thence into the tree, a chip from which impregnates his wife.[16]

The main motif of the transmigration of the soul in this story is the same as the thought in the verse from RV where the soul of the dead is said to go to the wind, his eye to the sun and he to the earth, the water or the plants (X. 16.3). The difference to be marked is that in the Ṛgvedic verse the cause for the various abodes is the *dharman* of the dead, while in the Bata-story there is no such cause, that is inherent in the action or the personality of the person. The only force for the change may, at the best, be called Desire; but it is not stated. This will mean that transmigration of the soul need not depend upon the action of a person.

NOTES

1. See RV X.72.6 The original reads. *yad devā adaḥ salile su sam-rabdhā atiṣṭhata.*
2. See Mb. Sabhā, 7. 11; and *Anuśāsana*, 165, 42.
3. See RV I. 158. 1, 6; 147.3; 152.6; IV.4. 13, etc.
4. See RV I.34. 7; VII, 87.2, etc.
5. See RV I. 160.4 and I. 140.8.
6. Chāndogya Upaniṣad, VI. 11.3.
7. See RV I. 164.32; the accent of *bahuprajāḥ* does not allow the meaning to be 'one who has many children' as suggested by scholars; Sāyaṇa, the commentator of RV is right in rendering the expression as 'one who takes many births'; *bahu-prajāḥ* has *udātta* on the second member; cf. *bahupāyya* at V. 66.6.
8. See Muṇḍaka Up., III.1.1; and Śvetāśvatara Up., IV.6.
9. See RV I.164.1, for the concept of the three brothers, the sun, the lightning-fire and the sacrificial fire; also see I. 164.17, 22 and 43.
10. See Kaṭha Up., II. iii. 1; and Bhagavad-Gītā, XV.
11. Śvetāśvatara Up., IV.8; and RV I, 164.39.
12. *tataḥ kṣarati-akṣaram* RV I.164. 42.
13. This concept develops later into the Vālakhilya sages, the thumbkins on the banyan tree; see Mb. Ādi 31.

14. G.P. Murdock, *Our Primitive Contemporaries,* 18th ed., New York, 1958, pp.311-37; 252.
15. Donald Mackenzie, *Egyptian Myth and Legend,* London (No year), p.87 ff; Rundle Clark, R.T., *Myth and Symbol in Ancient Egypt*, London, 1959, p.120.
16. Donald Mackenzie, *op.cit.*, p.49 ff.

Chapter 24

METEMPSYCHOSIS AND THE ṚGVEDA

In the *Hist. of Dharmāśāstra* (Vol. V-ii, pp. 1530-1612) Kane has dealt with the topic of "Karma and Punarjanma," and has tried to trace the development of this doctrine in the Sanskrit literature. He has rightly said that the belief in the migration of the soul is found in many tribes and, that hence, it is not quite true to say that it was borrowed by the Hindus from any other tribe (*ibid.*, p.1531). His observation that the theory of expiation (*prāyaścitta*) caused the edge of the theory of transmigration to be blunted (p. 1591) has to be accepted; for, the most important point about the theory of transmigration is supposed to be the concept of sin and virtue on the one hand, and the belief in retribution on the other; and *prāyaścitta* seeks to destroy sin in the current life itself, leaving nothing to be punished as a cause of the next birth. However, while commenting on the evolution of the theory of transmigration Kane says, "It must be conceded that a clear statement about the doctrine of *karma and punarjanma* is absent from the whole of the Ṛgveda." (*ibid.,* p. 1536). This is the position held by scholars generally. Thus Oldenberg says, "The thoughts that new wanderings, new repetitions of death and birth await the soul after death, are wholly foreign to the ancient times in which the hymns of the Ṛgveda are sung".[1]

It is, however, necessary to focus fresh attention on certain passages of the Ṛgveda. This is necessary, as Kane has entered into a controversy. Actually he tried to examine the position of Ranade in relation to certain passages from the Ṛgveda. He positively says that Ranade is "wrong" (p.1541). He has also taken into account the opinion of Karandikar regarding a Ṛgvedic passage, and has said that the meaning given by Karandikar is "incorrect" (p.1542). Ranade and Karandikar see traces of *punarjanma* in these passages, while Kane does not. Faced with this controversy, there is need of a fresh review of these passages, along with the whole question of the doctrine being reflected in RV. For this, certain other passages, missed by scholars, are to be studied very closely. At the outset, it is necessary to note that metempsychosis does not necessarily have any relationship with the idea of *karma,* originally, though in the later stages, they are closely associated. Also the doctrine of metempsychosis, irrespective of *karma,* obtains in other tribes. We restrict ourselves to these two points in our discussion further.

It is not necessary to refer to all the passages mentioned by Ranade and refuted by Kane, but the most important ones are, where the thought is very subtle and apt to be closely viewed. Ranade ushers into service certain of the verses of the *Asya vāmīya* hymn (I.164). He takes the following verse: (We have already studied it earlier, at ch. 23. But, we recapitulate).

> Who saw the very first-born, when the boneless one bore the one having bones? Whence was the blood, the life-breath and the soul of Earth? Who, indeed, went to the wise one to ask this?

There have been various interpretations of this verse; but the purport is not very difficult. It deals with the first ever creation of the earth; Ranade's efforts to see in this verse any idea of *punarjanma*[2] may not be acceptable; for, the verse does not speak of a normal birth, or a rebirth. But, at the same time, this verse underlines a very significant truth. It differentiates the *ātman*, not only from the rest of the material body but also, from the subtle *asu*, which is the principle of *prāṇa* on the microcosmic level and of wind on the macrocosmic one. The hymn has been composed (or, rather, seen) by Dīrghatamas; and it is only here in the whole of RV that the concept of *ātman* is separate from that of the wind or *prāṇa*. While in the rest of RV the word *ātman* remained undefined and not separated from the meaning of "wind" (RV I.34.7; VII. 87.2 etc.), here, in the vision of Dīrghatamas, it got the meaning of "soul", which came to be permanently associated with it in the later *Ātma*nism of the Upaniṣads. As such, though not noticed hitherto, Dīrghatamas must be taken to be the first seer, or *dārśanika,* to have 'seen' the *ātman* in the proper perspective and to have led the theory of *Ātma*nism as we have observed earlier. There is another passage in RV where *asu* is differentiated from the soul, which is called *Jīva* (RV. I. 140.8); and the seer, again, is Dīrghatamas. In the latter context the word *ātman* does not occur; but there is no doubt that Dīrghatamas uses the word *jīva* in place of *ātman,* as contrasted with the subtle *prāṇa* (*asu*) principle.[3] *Jīva*, itself non-perishable, is found in the same abode as that of the mortal one (v.30[d] *amartyo martyenā sayoniḥ).* Here we have the clear reference to the *Jīva* that gets free from the *martya,* and yet gets associated with the latter. Though the description is of the daily setting and rising sun, the idea of the *Jīva* and the non-*Jīva*, and their mutual relationship, without doubt, has been suggested from the beliefs current in those times. The expression finds the excellent and the fittest support from the statement of the Chāndogya Up. (VI. 11.3), that what is not endowed with the *Jīva* lives not; *Jīva* does not die (*jīvāpetam vāva kiledam mriyate na jīvo mriyate*). Ranade takes support of this verse to suggest rebirth, while Kane simply mentions it without comment. Though Kane notes that the verse "draws a sharp distinction between the self that is immortal and the body which is mortal" (p.1538), thus understanding it microcosmically, he does not dwell on the part *"jīvo mṛtasya carati svadhābhiḥ",* nor does he connect it with the latter part of the same hemistich. One feels that without connecting these two parts, the thought of Dīrghatamas cannot be understood. The point is clear. The soul remains in the body; goes out leaving the latter dead; and becomes also "*sayonī*" (living in the same unit) with the body, at a later stage. There is no mention that the body is the same. The soul is free to choose. That the belief in rebirth or transmigration had already shown its prevalence in the later Ṛgvedic period is clear from another expression of Dīrghatamas, "*bahu-prajā nirṛtim āviveśa*" (*ibid.,* v.32), where the word *bahu-prajāḥ* need not mean "having many issues", but, "having manifold births" with Sāyaṇa (*bahujanma-bhāk*). There seems to be no reason to push aside Sāyaṇa, and to say, that this verse does not show the belief in rebirth, especially when the word "*bahu-prajāḥ*" is used with the expression, "engulfed in the womb of the mother" (*ibid., māturyonā parivītaḥ*). A very important word, not noticed by either Ranade or Kane, but which deserves notice is *aprajāḥ* (in the plural), which means, 'having no further births' and used in the case of the enemies (RV I.21.5[d] *aprajāḥ santv 'atriṇaḥ,* and Sāyaṇa, pointing out the accent, "*anutpannāḥ*"). The point of the belief in rebirth gets support from such expressions as, Śuṣṇa was born again and again" (X. 61.13 *puruprajātasya)*: and Aryamā is "born many times" (VII 35.2). The latter expression indicates that the belief of rebirth was suggested from the solar movement; but, that it was current is beyond doubt. The purpose of the Ṛgvedic hymns was not to propound any particualr philosophy as such, and hence it is difficult to find a clear cut and argumentative style of expression. But from the passages noted above, there remains no doubt about the glimpses of the belief in the transmigration of the soul.

We have noted the relationship between the soul and the mortal body. The same is true when the word *tanū* is used in such a context. Thus, the deity Apām-napāt is said to have two forms; and when he comes on the terrestrial plane he pervades a different body (RV II.35.13 *anyasyeveha tanvā-viveśa)*. It cannot be argued that it is true only with the deity; for the very idea of getting enveloped in another body cannot come without a belief to that effect. This expression from the older RV cannot be bypassed in such an important discussion. A very interesting passage in this regard is where the *piṭr-s* are said to deposit their *tantu* called also *prajā,* among the people of the world below, along with their power, or that of the sun (RV X.56.6 *svām prajām pitaraḥ ā-avareṣv ādadhus tantum ātatam*); herein the use of the word *tantu* is significant, and it indicates 'progeny' in RV and later (cf. RV. II 28.5 *mā tantuśchedi;* X.53.6 *tantum tanvan,* which has the corresponding Brāhmaṇa passage as *prajā vai tantuh,* Ai Br. III. 38; and on the passage in question, *ayam hyātata-tantur yat prajāḥ*). What is believed is that the manes put their particles in the foetus to be born in the world below. It should be noted, that the *Pitṛ-s* have a collective appellation, indicative of the group of souls, from among whom some are to be placed in the world below. The belief in the group-souls (or, we may say the soul-group) is the most important concept, It is this belief that gave rise, at a further stage, to the concept of the transmigration of the individual soul. The belief of the soul-group has another aspect. It is that the receptacle of these souls is the orb of the sun. RV notes that the souls stay in the solar orb, whence they come to the earth (I.109. 7). The Chānd. Up. (V. 10.1) further extends this very belief and says that the *pitṛ-s* mix with the sun-rays and thence they enter the day. The concept develops further in the tree of the souls, as is seen in the account of the Vālakhilyas (Mb. Ādi 30-31) with which we are not here concerned.[4] The belief in the soul-group is closely associated with that of the *sukṛtām loka* (the world of the virtuous), where the soul of the dead is desired to go (RV X. 16.4). And here we come to the controversy again. The verse previous to this is, "O soul of the dead! May your eye go to the sun; your *ātman* (here life-breath) may go to the wind; ascend to heaven or go to the earth due to your *dharman;* go to the waters if there be your establishment (*hitam*); or stay in the plants" (v.3). Accroding to Ranade this is a clear enough case for the migration of the soul; it is not so according to Kane. It is necessary to place, side by side, the verse that refers to the *sukṛtām loka.* "(O Agni) Heat well the portion that is *aja* (in the body) by your heat; may your heat and may your flame heat it; which be your auspicious flames (*tanvaḥ*), O Agni! with them take him to the world of the virtuous". Ranade sees transmigration in these two verses, indicating that the first deals with the migration of the soul to various places due to his "qualities" (*dharmaṇā),* while in the next Agni is invoked to carry him straight to the world of the virtuous (we may add, irrespective of the *dharman*). To quote Kane, "There is no reason to suppose that in RV X.16.3 anything more is meant than what is prayed for in verse 4" (p. 1539). I accept Ranade; for, the meaning of the two verses is mutually different; their concept and the very purpose are varied. It is to insist that the soul of the dead might go to any place depending on the "*dharma*" (v.3), but that Agni should take him straight to the *sukṛtām loka* (v.4). One fails to understand how Kane does not see this difference. The word *dharma* is the cause of the difference in the future abodes, and has the sense of *karman* though it is not clearly used. Even according to Kane, *dharma* means "religious rite or sacrifice" (*ibid.*). But can the religious rite be different from *karma,* in view of the tradition of ritual itself being known as *karmakāṇḍa?* There is, hence, every reason to accept, with Ranade, that *dharma* (which is the *karma* itself) guides the soul to the abodes mentioned in v.3. It should be noted that Kane himself says, "In several other passages of the Ṛgveda 'Karma' means 'religious work' (p.1533)," which meaning he gives to *dharma,* as seen just now.

We now go to the next verse in the same hymn; and it is addressed to Agni. As the verse is important it will be better to quote it prior to discussion.

> *ava sṛja punar agne pitṛbhyo yasta āhutaś carati svadhābhiḥ*
> *āyur vasāna upa vetu śeṣaḥ sam gacchatām tanvā jātavedaḥ* (RV. X.16.5)

The verse has the following points: (i) Agni is invoked to release the dead (i.e. his soul) again (the words *punar ava sṛja* are to be noted); (ii) The soul of the dead is said to move on, or subsist on the *svadhā,* i.e. the offerings of the people on the earth that themselves turn into sustenance; (iii) He (the soul) is said to don new life (*āyur vasānaḥ*); (iv) He is desired to come to the *śeṣaḥ*; and (v) is to get associated with the body (*tanvā*).

The verse, which Karandikar[5] cites as an example to support rebirth, is denied by Kane as a support for that belief. Karandikar understands here the return to the relatives on the earth, while Kane (p. 1542) says, "There are no words for 'back to relatives". It is necessary to point out that the verse has the word *śeṣaḥ,* which, in RV means 'progeny' (cf. RV VII. 4.7 *na śeṣo agne anyajātam asti;* also *ibid.,* VII. 1.12 *svajanmanā śeṣasā*); hence, what Karandikar has said gets supported. The plan of the belief recorded in the said verse is, then, that the soul first goes to the *sukṛtām loka* or to the region of the *Pitṛs.* Thence it is to come back to the earthly region. It is not improbable that the word *pitṛbhyaḥ* is not the dative, but the ablative, and the meaning is not "for the p*itṛs* "but "from the p*itṛṣ*", especially in view of *punar* (again). It is difficult to understand how, once resorting to the *sukṛtām loka*, the soul is to go to the *Pitṛs.* Obviously they are two different strata. The idea is that, if the soul does not go to the *sukṛtām loka* which is heaven (as Kane rightly says), it is to go to that of the *Pitṛs.* From this latter, there is the way back to the earth, in the vicinity of the *śeṣas,* or as the *śeṣas.* This coming back is not for the annual offerings, for he is asked to come bodily (*tanvā*). In the other alternative, it goes to the various places mentioned in the earlier verse, such as the water and the plants. In the same breath it is good to examine another verse, from another *pitṛ*-hymn; for it has the same belief: "Associate with the p*itṛs*, with Yama, by means of the *iṣṭāpūrta;* leaving the censurable (aspect of your behaviour), come again to the abode (*punar astam ehi*) being lustrous, unite with the body (*sam* *gacchasva tanvā suvarcāḥ*)" (RV. X.14.8).

The points to be noted are: i) The soul is asked to associate with the *pitṛ*-s; ii) By *iṣṭāpūrta* (which is the same as the sacrificial rites, or the *dharma* of the passage noted earlier), performed while living, he is to leave the censurable portion of his behaviour or *karma* (*avadyam*); iii) He is asked to return to the *asta,* with a new body.

The most important words are *astam ehi*. The meaning of *ehi* has been taken by Sāyaṇa and, following him by Karandikar, as "returning" or coming back; but Kane renders it as "go"; and having taken this meaning, he sees here the going of the soul to the *pitṛ*-s. But the meaning cannot be "go"; for the word *ehi* has *ā* + *ihi*, which rightly means "coming", and, with *astam* "coming home". This home is on the terrestrial plane; and it is the same as the abode of the *śeṣas,* the son, as noted earlier. Geldner rightly renders as such; but his suggestion that here the soul is asked to return for the annual feast is not happy;[6] for, in that case it is difficult to understand the words *tanvā saṁ gacchasva*. The only meaning, then, is that they show the belief in the soul's return to the earth in the form of the son with a fresh body. It is difficult to understand how, from the second half of this verse Kane takes the meaning, that the departed is "to leave behind his sons" etc.

It is granted that in RV there is mention of only *sukṛtām loka*; and that the opposite, *duṣkṛtām loka* (indicative of the fate of the sinners) is rare. However, the belief of the evil-doers going to a bad state is corroborated. They are said to resort to the regions of total darkness (RV VII 104.3), indicating that they may never be reborn. The position, then, is this; RV does record the belief of rebirth in the case of the persons who abided by the way of good rites; but for the evil-doers, it was believed, there was no rebirth. For the virtuous there was either the enjoyment of heavenly pleasure, or rebirth in the homely atmosphere on the earth. For the evil-doers the only place was the doom, with all its darkness. The answer to this peculiar belief is, probably, to be sought in the concept of Ṛta, which gave expression only to the good aspect in life, wiping off the evil aspect (RV X. 124.5 *ṛtena rājann anṛtam viviñcan).* The effects of *anṛta,* or what may be called sin, were to be seen in the present life itself in the form of the various diseases. That Ṛta wiped off the effect of *anṛta* gave rise to the practice of *prāyaścitta,* which is to be taken as a belief older than the retribution theory of evil leading to a bad birth.

We have referred above to the indication of soul-groups in the belief of the Vedic people. The class of the *pitṛ*-s bears testimony to it, as we have pointed out; also that the souls of the *pitṛ*-s are said to be the cause of the birth on the earth. The concept of the group of souls here compares with that of the group of ancestral stones, representative of the souls of the dead, called *churinga.* It was believed that conception in the woman was due to the migration of one of the *churingas* and settling in her womb. At the first sign of movement in the womb she goes to the place where these *churingas* are deposited; she selects one of these at her own will; and it is believed that, that particular soul residing in that *churinga* has entered her body.[7] The Vedic concept of the group of *pitṛ*-s has a peculiarly solar trait; and it is not quite easy to ascertain if, prior to the solar aspect, there was another one like the stone-heap as is the case with the *churingas.* In any case, it is clear that RV attests belief in rebirth.

NOTES

1. *Buddha* (Eng. Tr.), 1882, p.43.
2. *A Constructive Survey of Upanishadic Philosophy,* Poona, 1926, pp.145.ff.
3. See ch. 23, *supra.*
4. According to J. Charpentier, the Vālakhilyas are "seelen-wesen" (soul-essences), *Die Supernasage,* Uppasala, 1920, p.333; according to Barnett, these thumbkins have grown in popular fancy out of the "*puruṣas*" residing in the hearts

of men, "Study in Indo-European Psychology", *JRAS,* 1929, p.743 note; see also Dange, *Legends in the Mahābhārata,* Delhi, 1969, p. 131; *Myths from the Mahābhārata*, Vol. I, pp.103ff.

5. *Gītātattvamañjarī* (Marathi), Poona, 1974, pp.175-76.
6. *Der Rigveda*, HOS, London, 1951, Vol. III, p.144.
7. G.P. Murdock, *Our Primitive Contemporaries,* p.32 ff.

Chapter 25

THE RIDDLE OF THE BLACK ANTELOPE

The black antelope has been a very auspicious beast in the Vedic ritual-tradition. The *smṛti*-s record the belief that the black antelope is closely associated with the country called Āryāvarta.[1] The Vedic ritual of sacrificial consecration attests to the sacredness of the beast, as its skins are used to signify the fresh birth of the person to be consecrated. According to Śat. Br. for the said consecration two black antelope-skins are spread to the south of the *Āhavanīya* fireplace, with their necks pointing to the east. If two skins are not available, even one suffices. The hairy part of the skins is to be kept outside in such a way that there should be mutual contact of the flesh sides of the two when the skins are placed upon each other (Kātyāyana Śr. S. 7.83: *māṁsa-sammite syutānte tardmasu;* and Āpastamba Śr. S. X. 8. 12: *antarmāṁsābhyām bahirlomabhyām*). When fitted one-upon-the-other they, together, would form a sort of a bag. If there be only one skin, the tail-portion or the neck portion of the same is folded to form a bag. According to the Śat. Br. (III. 2.1.1 ff), the two skins symbolize the heaven (upper) and the earth (lower skin). The person to be consecrated is to be placed in between the two, stating that he is to be consecrated in between the heaven and the earth (*tayor enam adhi dīkṣayati*). A step further, and it is said that the two (or the skin and the twisted end, if there be only one skin) form a couple, *viz.*, Heaven (Father) and Earth (Mother), so that the *dīkṣita* becomes the foetus (*ib.*, 2 *tad imau lokau mithunīkṛtya*). It is also said that the black hairs on the skin are the form of the heaven, while the white ones symbolize the earth; or, it may even be the other way. The tawny or yellowish hairs represent the mid-region (*antarikṣasya rūpam*). The person to be consecrated is required to sit in the space of the 'bag' formed by stitching the two skins, or by the one skin being folded. He stays there as a foetus to be born afresh, with a new ritual-body for the duration of the sacrifice. The same is the process when the shoots of *soma* are to be consecrated for use in the ritual-pressing at the sacrifice; and the same is the case when the grains are to be pounded for preparing a sacrificial cake (*puroḍāśa*) from them (Ai. Br. I.27=5.1 also Śat. Br. III. 9.4.1. ff).

After such consecration, the *dīkṣita* is covered with a cloth, which is said to be the inner cover of the 'foetus' (=sacrificer, newly consecrated), and upon this cloth the skin of the black antelope is placed; this is the outer cover of the foetus. The cloth is made of the fibres of the reeds (*śaṇa;* cf. Śat. Br. III.2.1.11 *sā vai śāṇī bhavati*); and both are said to be the inner and outer covers of Prajāpati, when he was born. At the end of the covering, the horn of the black antelope is tucked up (*ib.,* 18), with the opening up. This horn is the womb from which Indra is said to have been born, and now it is the womb of the sacrificer himself (*ib.,* 28-31). The symbolism of Vedic sacrifice is, obviously, a development later than the use of the black antelope-skin.

The bag formed from the skin(s) and the horn is the womb of the sacrificer for his ritual-birth. In other words, the black antelope is the birth-giver for the sacrificer, or is his womb. As the sacrificer is said to be born, in this way, from the black antelope-skin, which stands for the beast itself, he is also said to be born from the sacrifice (Mait. Sam. III 6.7 *sa vai yajñena jāyate;* cf. also Śat. Br. III. 2.1.11). At places it is said that the sacrifice ran away from the gods taking the form of the black antelope,[2] which makes it clear that the skin of the beast came to stand for the sacrifice, as also for Prajāpati. Now, a question presents itself before us. In the sacrificial rituals, as they are recorded in the texts, there is hardly any mention of the sacrificial immolation of the black antelope.[3] All beasts that are to be sacrificed are domesticated, such as the goat, the bull and even the horse at the Horse-sacrifice. Out of the strictly *Śrauta* sacrificial atmosphere, the skins to be used are those of a bull or a goat. Thus, for example, the bride and the bridegroom have to sit on the skin of a bull.[4] There is no doubt about the fact that the black antelope-skin to be used at the ritual was of the beast ritually killed, especially when the beast had such a haloed background as is noted above. Though there is mention of the skin of the tiger or that of the boar at such rituals as the *Rājasūya,*[5] the importance of the skin of the black antelope is unique as the beast is identified with the sacrifice or Prajāpati. The birth of the sacrificer from this skin, or a 'bag' formed from it, indicates the birth from the beast itself. This would mean that the beast was sacrificially killed in far ancient times, and the skin worn on special ritual-occasions. In other words, the black antelope was a *totem.*

This was, obviously, far prior to the fuller development of the Vedic ritual-tradition that we have it from the Ṛgveda, or later from the Brāhmaṇa texts. Hence it is that, though the black antelope might have been thus sacrificially killed, no mention of this process occurs in any of the extant Vedic ritual-text. The stage of the Vedic society when the said beast must have ritually been killed was the pre-pastoral stage. It may be noted that the black antelope is a beast which is more wild than domesticated; and though it is seen to be domesticated from references in literature, it is mainly associated with the hermitages of ascetics—the forest-dwellers.[6] With the growth of the sacrificial religion, domesticated beasts came to be sacrificed; and this was the agricultural stage of the Vedic society, which is the semi-static stage. The magical importance of the antelope, black or the tawny (as an alternative) in fertility or the gain of rain is clear from the tale of the sage Ṛṣyaśṛṅga, who is said to have in his head the horn of an antelope and who was specially brought by the king Romapāda to cause it to rain, by offering his daughter to the sage.[7] The skin, specially that of an antelope, marks an important stage in ritual-history; and the point can be seen from the beast's skin being used in rituals in also other regions and peoples.

Thus, among the ancient Cretan principalities when beasts of *totem* were sacrificially killed the priest-kings wore their skins; for, they believed that they were incarnations of the beast.[8] This is exactly as is the case of the person to be consecrated for the Vedic sacrifice wherein the concept of the birth was enacted at the special ritual as noted above. The Egyptian Pharaoh became identified with Osiris, who died and was to be resurrected; this was done by donning the skin of the gazelle (a soft-eyed antelope). This was done every year at the time of important rituals. Osiris was believed to be the antelope in one of his aspects. The skin was used also at the funeral of the Pharaoh.[9] In ancient Maithraic rituals, the priest who acted as the initiator of the novices wrapped himself in the hide of the fawn,[10] which is a deer with brownish colour, corresponding to the *ṛṣya* or *rohita* type of deer on the Indian stage, whose form the god Prajāpati is said to have taken in one account, as we shall see soon. There are many instances of cases where the *totem*-beast is the domesticated one, with which we are not concerned here. Fixing our attention on the antelope, it becomes pretty clear that there had been some type of a mystic consideration about this beast, probably due to its undomesticated wild nature coupled with the serene appearance of its eyes. Its status in the Vedic ritual-tradition, now, can be fairly ascertained as the first semi-domesticated and edible sacrificial beast. The use of the skin, and its identification with the sacrifice and the god Prajāpati, even after its complete substitution and extinction by a clearly domesticated beast, only stress its continued importance.

We have noted above that there is hardly any trace of the custom of ritually sacrificing the antelope, as far as the Vedic tradition is concerned. However, there is a faint indication of the antelope (though not the black variety) being ritually sacrificed. This is in the context of the rite associated with the *prāśitra*. The *prāśitra* is a portion of the *puroḍāśa* (sacrificial cake) to be partaken of by the Brahman priest at the sacrifice. And, by means of a laudatory account (*arthavāda*) it is associated with Prajāpati. It is said that when Prajāpati ran in lust after his own daughter, in the form of an antelope, the god Rudra got angry and shot an arrow at him. The arrow hit Prajāpati, who fell to the ground. As the arrow got stuck deep into his body it had to be taken away. When it was taken away, some portion of the flesh of Prajāpati (the antelope) came out; and it was sought to be offered to the gods, lest it should go waste.[11] Though the actual *prāśitra* used in the sacrifice is not the flesh of the beast, the very fact that, in the myth, it is associated with the antelope (=Prajāpati) indicates the beast being hunted and offered at the ancient ritual. Here the antelope is tawny, as Prajāpati is said to have taken the form of a *ṛṣya*, which marks a change in the custom, from the black to the tawny antelope. This indication of the sacrificial killing and offering of the black antelope (though tawny in this case) is substantially supported from the Rāmāyaṇa. Thus, in the context of the consecration of the newly built dwelling (*parṇaśālā*, "a dwelling made from leaves"), Rāma says to Lakṣmaṇa that he should hunt a black antelope so that it could be offered to the dwelling, in the ritual of *vāstuśamana* (pacification of the dwelling); and this is said to be accomplished according to the traditional rites (Rām. Ayodhyā, 56.22 ff; esp.23b *kartavyaḥ śāstra-dṛṣṭo hi vidhiḥ*). Accordingly, Lakṣmaṇa hunted a black antelope, and threw it into the fire. When it was completely roasted, and the blood was dried up, Rāma took bath and offered its portions to the gods and the manes. He then established the various fireplaces and the altars (*ib.*, 26-32).[12]

The reference is unique in the sense that the method of sacrificing the flesh of the beast is rather crude; and it is not according to the norm prescribed by the Vedic ritual-texts. The normal method, according to the Vedic tradition, is to immolate the beast and "silence" it by smothering, so that the life-principle should not go away. Even a sound from the beast, or breath, is inauspicious and warrants expiation. After the beast is thus immolated, it is skinned and flesh from its parts is offered to the gods. But, RV faintly indicates the practice of holding the beast over the fire and letting the fat drip on the fire (III.21. 2-5); and at the Mait. Sam. (II 5.10; cf. also Taitt. Sam. III. 3.9.1) a verse indicates that a bull is roasted. But, at the latter place it may be a lump of flesh; nothing definite is known. Now, the reference from the Rāmāyaṇa cannot be set aside; and yet, in the absence of any clear corroboration from the Vedic texts, the riddle of the sacrifice of the antelope persists. The only conclusion from the passage from the Rāmāyaṇa and the use of the black antelope skin in the Vedic rituals, would be that the rite mentioned at the Rāmāyaṇa is the most ancient form of antelope-sacrifice, giving place to the method of immolation by smothering, and skinning. It is in the new method of immolation that the importance of the antelope-skin got settled. The Rāmāyaṇa would indicate the continuation of the old method, though generally discarded, and that the antelope figured at the construction and consecration of the dwelling, while the Vedic consecration for sacrifice is closely associated only with the antelope-skin, as noted before. This would mean that the most original rite was the killing of the antelope (the symbol of the sacrifice) at the very beginning of the sacrifice, and at the consecration itself. At a later stage, the killing was discarded and only the skins remained in use. In the earlier stage, then, the would-be *dīkṣita* was to be placed under the skin of the freshly killed antelope, as is indicated by the one skin. And from the antelope (-skin) he was believed to be born. This was the new birth, at the ritual-level. There is already a parallel to this ritual in the Vedic tradition. Thus, in the case of a person who kept the three fires for the whole life, a cow is freshly immolated, skinned, and the entrails are placed on his body at his death, when it is placed on the funeral pyre. The body is then covered with the hide of the cow.[13] An example from the non-Vedic (or non-Indian) source is as follows. Among the Omalsa from Peru a dead person is wrapped in the hide of a freshly killed buffalo;[14] and among the Akikiyu of Africa the sacred goat is killed at the initiation; and the initiate is adorned with the strips of its skin.[15] Among the Akamba, the initiate is covered with the skin of the freshly killed goat.[16] The custom of the ancient Vedic people does not seem to be different, and the belief is also the same: Birth from the sacred beast. Herein lies also the solution of the riddle, as to why the sacrificial killing and offering of the flesh of the antelope are not mentioned in the Vedic texts. The fact is, that it had long ceased to form part of the main sacrifice to the gods; and its memory was kept alive only in the ritual of the *prāśitra* and the myth of the Father (Prajāpati) running after his own daughter. But it actully formed part of the rite of initiation only, when an antelope was killed and the initiate or the would-be *dīkṣita* had to don the skin to indicate new birth from the holy beast. But, as time went along, this ritual was discarded; and its place was taken by the symbolic birth wherein the person simply sat on the skin, or was covered with it (or two skins) which formed the womb. Out of the strict Vedic ritual, however, the ritual-killing continued to be practised, as is indicated by the Rāmāyaṇa till it was completely lost. At the *upanayana*, even to-day, the initiate has to wear the sacrificial thread, to which a piece of a deer-skin is tied.

NOTES

1. Yājñavalkya Smṛti 1.2. *yasmin deśe mṛgaḥ kṛṣṇaḥ tasmin dharmān nibodhata;* also Vasiṣṭha-Dharma-sūtra I.8.9; 12-13.
2. Śat. Br. I. 1.4.1. *yajño ha devebhyo'pacakrāma, sa kṛṣṇo bhūtvā cacāra; tasya devā anuvidya tvacam evāvacchāya*

ajarhuḥ; for Prajāpati=sacrifice, *ib.,* I.1.1.13.

3. See above note 2, where only the mention of the skin obtains. At another place it is clear that the sacrificial beasts were: man, whose sap entered the horse after the former's sacrificial killing; then comes the bull, then the goat, and the last the corn, Śat. Br. 1.2.3.6.; thus after man come directly the domesticated beasts. It is also said that when the sap went from the beasts that were killed, they became, respectively, a half-man *(kiṁpuruṣa), gaura, gavaya and śarabha;* all these are wild beasts; as they are without the sap, they are not recommended for being offered. The fact seems to be that they were once offered, but were discarded later in favour of the domesticated beasts (*ib.,* 9). Even here no antelope is mentioned.
4. Āśv.Gṛ.S. I.8.9. *vivāhāgnim upasaṁdhāya paścād ānaḍuham carmāstīrya...*
5. Śat. Br. IX. 3.4.8 ff; Kāt. Śr.S. 15.4.21 ff. etc.
6. Cf. Śākuntalam, Act. I, *āśrama-mṛgo'yam etc.*
7. Mb. Vana 113; Bhāgavata P. IX. 23.8 ff.
8. Donald Mackenzie, *Myths of Pre-Columbian America,* London, p.189.
9. James Hastings, *Encyclopaedia of Religion and Ethics,* Vol. IX, p.77a: also Vol. VII, p.318a.
10. *Ibid.*, Vol.II, p.374a.
11. Śat. Br. I.7.4.1 ff.
12. Cf. 26. *sa lakṣmaṇaḥ kṛṣṇa-mṛgam hatvā medhyam pratāpavān* | *atha cikṣepa saumitriḥ samiddhe jātavedasi.*
13. R.N. Dandekar and C.G. Kashikar, *Śrautakośa*, ii, Poona, 1958. p. 1071.
14. J.G. Frazer, *Folk-lore of the Old Testament,* Vol. I, London, 1918, p.31.
15. *Ibid.,* Vol. II, p.7.
16. *Ibid.*

Chapter 26

KUNTĀPA AND SYMBOLISM IN RITUAL-BIRTH

In the context of the Viśvajit sacrifice, in both the types, *viz.*, the Atirātra and the Agniṣṭoma, there is a mention of the hymns termed Śilpa. The tradition uses the term Kalpa for a sacrifice in general, and the Śilpa-s are a unique method for producing wonderful results. The term Śilpa occurs in the context of the rites of the Sixth day of the Pṛṣṭhya sacrifice;[1] and it is said that the combination of verses at a hymn, or certain methods of reciting the verses in a hymn (with a *nyūṅkha* etc.) are at the basis of the concept of Śilpa. These, then, are called Devā-śilpa, as we have the *śilpa* among the humans to be seen in producing an elephant, a mirror, ornaments of gold or even a chariot drawn by a female mule (*aśvatarī-rathaḥ*).[2] The purpose of these *Śilpas* is said to be to accomplish the sacrifice and to bring about the new birth of the sacrificer (*kalpata eva yajñaḥ kalpate yajamānasya prajātiḥ,* at Ai. Br. VI. 31. = 30.5). The *Śilpas* included in this special technique (*kalpa*) are based on the following hymns from RV: Nābhānediṣṭha (X. 61), Vālakhilya (VIII. 49-59), Vṛṣākapi (X.86) and Evayāmāruta (V. 87). These hymns are deftly combined with others, each combination being allotted to a separate priest among the Hotṛ, the Maitrāvaruṇa, the Brāhmaṇācchaṁsin and the Acchāvāka. The hymns combined with the four main noted above are Nārāśaṁsa, Sukīrti and the Kuntāpa.[3] Actually another set of the Nārāśaṁsa is included in the Kuntāpa, while the Sukīrti is from RV (X.131). Every hymn has a purpose and symbolic value. The Nābhānediṣṭha is without a clear deity; hence, it is said, it is to be recited first; because, the whole *Śilpa* is for the new birth of the sacrificer; and the Nābhānediṣṭha hymn stands for the semen; and, being without a clear deity it should be recited inaudibly, as semen is sprinkled in the vagina without its being seen openly (Ai.Br., *loc.cit.* 27 *aniruktam śaṁsaty 'aniruktam vai reto guhā yonyām sicyate*). This particular hymn is selected for this purpose, as it has the expression "With the earth does he unite sprinkling the semen" (X. 61. 7). The Hotṛ priest recites the hymn; and after this he recites what are called Nārāśaṁsyaḥ verses from the Kuntāpa group. This is so, because the Nārāśaṁsīs indicate 'progeny' (*narāḥ*) with the speech (*śaṁsaḥ*).

After this has been done by the Hotṛ priest, it is believed that the sacrificer is himself sprinkled in the form of the semen (*retobhūtam siktvā*). Thereafter the sacrificer (in the form of the semen) is given over to the Maitrāvaruṇa priest to work another symbolic wonder (*śilpam*). The Maitrāvaruṇa, now, recites the Vālakhilya hymns. The reason is that the sacrificer is on the way to be a full foetus. Along with being endowed with the faculty of "being born" with the Nārāśaṁsa hymn, which is *prajāḥ,* he is now got endowed with the vital breaths; that is why the Vālakhilya hymns are to be recited (*ib.,* 28). Here, again, out of the first eight Vālakhilya hymns only the first six are to be recited. The reason is (obviously) that this is the *Śilpa* of the Sixth day of the Pṛṣṭhya Ṣaḍaha sacrifice, and it is known in the tradition that the "sixth" is a symbol of new birth or new life.[4] These six hymns are to be recited as separated from each other; because the vital breaths (*prāṇāḥ*) are separated-the Prāṇa, the Vyāna, and the Apāna. The first two are to be recited according to the hemistiches (*pac-śaḥ=pad-śaḥ)*, the next two in halves and the next two in a whole verse. Thus, the sacrificer is endowed with the vital breaths, and also with speech, with eyes and mind and with the ears and the soul. (Other details are left out.) After this is done, the last two are to be recited with mutual inversion: the eighth first and the seventh thereafter (*ib.*, 28). Thereafter the sacrificer is (conceptually) handed over to the Brāhmaṇācchaṁsin priest, who recites the Sukīrti (X. 131) hymn, which is supposed to be the divine womb. By reciting this hymn, the said priest places the sacrificer in the divine womb for being born on the divine plane of the sacrifice. He, then, recites the Vṛṣākapi-hymn, which is symbolically the soul and provides also the food, as one gives milk to the new-born child. After this new birth, the sacrificer is handed over to the Acchāvāka priest, who provides him with stable ground to stand; and this is done by means of the recitation of the Evayāmāruta hymn (mentioned above).

While the process of the new birth of the sacrificer goes on, the Kuntāpa hymns are ushered in after the recitation of the Sukīrti and the Vṛṣākapi hymns by the Brāhmaṇācchaṁsin. The Vṛṣākapi hymn is symbolic also of the five vital breaths, as it has the Paṅkti metre in its structure (*ib.*, *sa pāṅkto bhavati pāṅkto 'yam puruṣaḥ pañcadhā vihitaḥ*, the five being hair, bones, marrow, flesh and skin). The Kuntāpas are to be recited by the Brāhmaṇācchaṁsin himself. This means that the Kuntāpas are to be recited at the end of the birth process of the sacrificer, but prior to his *pratiṣṭhā* (establishment) by the Evayāmāruta hymn by the Acchāvāka. The sixth day is thus closely associated with the Kuntāpas; and without these hymns the foetus cannot be complete. It may be noted that the normal foetus gets fully grown by the sixth month, for which the sixth day is symbolically used. As noted above, this birth at the sacrifice is brought about with the recitation of the hymns. But, according to the belief recorded by the Ai. Br., the essence of the normal metres went away on the sixth day. Prajāpati got afraid feeling that the essence (*rasaḥ*) would never turn back; but he managed to get it turn back. He, however, could not use the same original metres, but the Kuntāpas. The essence of the Gāyatrī he got with the help of the hymns called Nārāśaṁsyaḥ, the first of the Kuntāpa hymns. That of the

Triṣṭubh by the Raibhīs (i.e. the hymns that have the word *rebha* in it), that of the Jagatī in the hymns called Pārikṣityaḥ (having the word *parikṣit*), that of the Anuṣṭubh in the Kāravyaḥ (where the word *kāru* is present); and after gathering the essence this way, he placed it again on the original hymns (VI.32=30.6). About the method of recitation in the case of these Kuntāpa hymns, the norm is the Vṛṣākapi hymn, but with the difference that in the Vṛṣākapi Nyūṅkha[5] is employed, while in these its place is taken by the mode called Nardana (or, Ninarda). This Ninarda is said to be equal to the Nyūṅkha for these hymns (*ib.,* 32). Other Kuntāpa hymns to be similarly recited are Diśāṅ-kḷptayaḥ, Janakalpāḥ, and Indragāthāḥ. These are the main Kuntāpa hymns, the verses numbering thirty.[6] Others that are loosely included in the same category are Aitaśa-pralāpāḥ, Pravahlikāḥ, Ājijñāsenyāḥ, Pratirādhyaḥ, Ativādaḥ, Devanīthāḥ, Bhutecchadaḥ and Āhanasyāḥ. All except the last are enjoined to be recited with breaks, with the Ninarda, but not the Nyūṅkha. The last have the Nyūṅkha, again. If we examine the statement of the Ai. Br. about the metres and the essence of the original metres and the Kuntāpa hymns it appears that the Kuntāpa hymns are believed to be on par with the original ones. But the fact is that there are variations, metrically. Let us take the example of the Nārāśaṁsyaḥ which are said to have the essence of the Gāyatrī. These are only three verses. The analysis of the hemistiches in each of them is as follows. (For the verses, see Ṛgveda-saṁhitā, Khila V. 8.)

> Verse 1. 8 + 8 + 8, which is Gāyatrī all right. But the verse does not end here. It goes further and has 12 more letters, so total letters 36, while the Gāyatrī has 24.
>
> Verse 2. 8 + 7; the latter portion is confused, with 20 letters, so total letters 35.
>
> Verse 3. 8 + 8; and further 14, these 14 could be 15, with a split at *śatāni arvatām*; so in all 30 or 31.

Barring the last of the three Nārāśaṁsyaḥ, which is their total number, the first two could be arranged as having a uniform pattern with 12 + 8 in the later part, thus:

(1) 8+ 8 + 8; 12 + 8; also (2) 8 + 7; 12 + 8. Even then the last is a difficulty, which may be solved by reading the latter half as 7 (= 8 with *śatāni-arvatām* in the place of *śatānyarvatām*) leaving the last portion with only 7. So, (3) 8 + 8; 8 (with split) + 7.

What has been stated above would show how the legend at the Ai. Br. has to be taken with a discount, unless we believe that the Nārāśaṁsyaḥ, from the Kuntāpa, were slightly changed later. But there is nothing to admit the latter supposition, as at all occurrences they are uniform, with a slight change of word or so. The Ai. Br. states that the Raibhī-s were fashioned from the Triṣṭubh; but, this is not correct; for, the Raibhī verses are perfectly in the Anuṣṭubh, which is the metre mentioned for the Kāravyaḥ by the Ai. Br. Actually, the Kāravyaḥ are in the Anuṣṭubh metre, except for the last verse which has an added *pāda* of 8, making it split like the Gāyatrī. This puts the statement of the Ai. Br. to confusion. The only conclusion is that the statement is not exact; nor, probably, was it to be taken as mentioning the exact position of the syllables in the verses. The same inexactitude is seen in the case of the Pārikṣityaḥ, which do not answer the statement of the Ai. Br. that they were fashioned from the Jagatī. The Ai. Br. which mentions the legend of the original hymns losing their essence, which is then gathered in the Kuntāpa hymns, does not explain the name Kuntāpa. The Gopatha Br., however, explains it. According to it *kuyam* (not *ku)* is "the despised"; as they burn what is despised, they are called Kuntāpa (*kuyam + tapa;√tap,* "to burn"; cf. Uttara, VI. 12 *kuyam ha vai nāma kutsitam bhavati, tad yat tapati tasmāt* Kuntāpaḥ). The verb *tapati* (in singular) would indicate that by reciting the hymns, the despised thing gets itself burnt up. The sacrificer, in whose favour these hymns are recited, is termed *kuyaḥ;* and when the hymns are recited he gets settled in heaven (after death) and gets all prosperity in food and cattle in this world (*ib.*). The Gopatha Br. also mentions the account of the essence of the metres flowing away and being collected in the Kuntāpa hymns. It, like the Ai. Br., states that by reciting the Kuntāpa-s the metres (original ones) get the essence (Ai. Br. VI. 32=30.6; Gop. Br. *loc.cit.* 11). The Gopatha Br. closely follows the treatment of the hymns as seen from the Ai. Br., and even the explanation of the various names of the hymns included in the Kuntāpa is about the same. It seems, however, that the names of these hymns are due to the key-words therein; and the explanation of these names is a later phase. For example, the name Raibhī is due to the word *rebha* that occurs at the verse in that hymn (*vacyasva rebha vacyasva*). This name is already settled and is taken as such by the Ai. Br. or the Gop. Br.; and, then, it is explained thus: "*rebhanta vai devāś carṣayaś ca svargam lokam āyan* etc.)".[7] This would indicate that:

(i) These hymns had already been taken as sanctified by the priests, though they were not actually part of the accepted normal hymns;

(ii) They had no definite measured metre; but, they were akin to the accepted metrical measurement; hence, they were described in comparison with the normal metres; mostly they had about eight syllables in a *pāda,* which appears to be a normal, popular way suitable for singing;

(iii) They were given the status of the four important hymns, and were mixed with them, as the *śilpa,* as they were already settled in belief as wonder-producing. Here, probably, we have the difference between the *Brahman* and the '*Śilpa*', the former being thought 'divine', the latter human and artificial.

An important point to be noted in this connection is that the Kuntāpa and the following hymns (included under the Kuntāpaḥ) are preserved in the Ṛgvedic tradition, as is seen from the fact that they occur in the Ai Br, Śāṇk. Br., and also in the Āśv., Śr. S. The Yajurveda tradition (see Vāj. Sam., XXIII. 28, 29) has only two verses from the last of these hymns, known as Āhanasyāḥ (RV Khila V. 22.1 and 4). However, the Atharvaveda and its Gopatha Br., have all the hymns mentioned above; and we have seen it above. These two verses are enjoined by the Vāj. Sam. (*loc. cit.*) to be recited at the Horse-sacrifice, along with others of similar nature (i.e. having sexual tone), which are common in the Yajurveda tradition.[8] An interesting remark may be noted in this connection. The Gop. Br. (of the Atharvaveda) says that the Kāravyaḥ are, in reality *gāthā*-s,; and it includes the Pārikṣityaḥ also under the same term.[9] Actually, we have the verses called Indra-gāthā among the main Kuntāpa-group which is said to contain only thirty verses in all. Taking into account these points, and also the looseness of structure, as noted above, it could be said that all these verses were only popular verses, *gāthā*-s or Nārāśaṁsīs[10] or, in other words, verses meant for, or of, the common people, as against those of the priestly class. In essence, they were folk-songs! Being so, they were devoid of any strict and measured metre. Getting once embedded in the Ṛgveda ritual-tradition, they continued to have the halo, and were indispensable, though not included in the Saṁhitā proper. Like the verses in the Yajurveda tradition, used at the Horse-sacrifice, these ones known as Kuntāpa, have to be taken as a grafting from the secular common folk-tradition (*śilpa*) on to the priestly ritual-tradition (*brahma*). This is supported by the hymns (from among the Kuntāpa) that are termed Aitaśa-pralāpa, which is verily the "mad man's prattle". The Ai. Br. has an interesting account of the origin of this "Pralāpa", in which it states that Aitaśa told his sons that he knew the special group of *mantra*-s called "life of Fire", and that they should not disturb him when he prattled. The verses are so confused, apparently, that they make no sense (Ai. Br. VI.33=30.7). The Gop. Br. also records the same account.

The Pravahlikāḥ and the Āhanasyāḥ are decidedly sexual in tone.

The Kuntāpa-s show a variety of ideas mingled together; and they are not always coherent. A few examples would be welcome in this context. Thus Nārāśaṁsyaḥ make sense; and they are in praise of one Kaurama (Kaurava at RV-Khila and certain other texts) and Iṣa. The Raibhī-s praise the *rebha* (the singer) and his clan; but, the expression "your tongue moves on like a razor" (*niṣ ṭe jihvā carcarīti kṣuro na*) is rather un-suiting a sober assembly.[11] The Pārikṣityaḥ are in praise of king Parikṣit and refer to the king at every verse (in all four). The Kāravyaḥ praise the Kāru (artisan), and refer to the favour of Indra for him. The whole picture is complete. Actually these can be taken together with other hymns in this collection that praise Indra; and this is done by the Śāṅk. Śr. S. (XII. 15-16). The verses called Diśām-kḷptayaḥ speak of various persons that are installed by gods at the different quarters. The good man who offers to the gods, presses Soma at the sacrifice, and is worthy of an assembly, is placed to the East; one who censures his friend and commits fault against his near relations (*jāmayaḥ*), also one being the eldest but inconsiderate (*apracetāḥ)*, is placed to the South; one who is the son of a gentleman and is bold, for him the priest, Gandharva, utters fruitful desire (*kāmyam vacaḥ*), and he is in the North; the Paṇi who is non-generous (*abhujiṣyaḥ*), and the rich who is a miser and not favouring the noble, are relegated to the West. Here, the belief regarding the various quarters is to be noted. Good is associated with the East and the North, while bad with the West or the South. This holds good even in later times, as it did in the earlier.[12] Here the simple sober (so we may say!) hymns end. The next, called Janakalpāḥ, is a mixture of the sober and the sexy. It has the refrain: *tvo tā kalpeṣu saṁ-mitā,* indicating that the persons and things mentioned herein are to be included in the *kalpa* (rituals). They are: The son of a *brāhmaṇa* who is himself not practising (or knowing) *brahman,* having his eyes without collyrium, having not taken bath, not having gold or a jewel; in contrast to this, the son of a *brāhmaṇa* who is himself a *brahman,* washed and bathed, having gold and jewels etc. These contrasting pairs are mentioned even further. A pond without (and with) water-supply, a rich donor (and a rich miser), a beautiful maiden not admitting (and admitting) sex (*ayabhyā* and *suyabhyā*); a rejected wife (queen, Parivṛktā), a soldier (*yudhiṅgamaḥ*), a not active (and active) horse. Here there is clear indication of the three queens that took part in the horse-ritual at the Horse-sacrifice, along with the horse (*anāśur aśvaḥ* and, in contrast, *svāśur aśvaḥ*). It may be noted, however, that at the ritual in the Horse-sacrifice, mentioned in the Yajurveda Saṁhitās, these verses do not occur. But, as the mention of the Horse (along with the names of the queens) occurs here, there is ground to believe that these verses are from the earlier phase of the Horse-sacrifice, or, at least, a ritual connected with the queens and the horse. If so, we could safely believe that the ritual was lost. The ritual was, obviously, that from the Ṛgvedic tradition, as the Kuntāpa hymns are all seen in the Ṛgvedic Brāhmaṇas, and in the Śrautasūtras of the same branch. There seems to be no doubt that this Ṛgvedic ritual tradition with the *mantra*-s was superseded by the Yajurveda ritual tradition, which also used other verses at the Horse-sacrifice that were of similar nature. The Pravahlikāḥ are fully sexual in tone, in expression being riddle-like. Thus, for example: "Extended are the two rays (*kiraṇau*); them does the male press. Not so it is, O maiden, as you think!" ("Not so... think" is the refrain for all the six verses in this hymn). Further, "The two 'Ṛays' of your mother go asunder, without a male; Not so...". The images that follow are of a woman falling on her back; a man covering her and.... It ends with the expression, 'the 'slippery' one has been concealed into the 'slippery' one (that of the male into that of the woman); the slippery one has slipped into the hairy pond![13] Every time the maiden is told that the verses do not mean as she would think, i.e., they are not to be taken with the literal sense; they are to be understood with their inner meaning! The dialogue had already gained a ritual context; and, as noted above, it might have been also like the one at the Horse-sacrifice or the Mahāvrata, but it was already a lost tradition—the Ṛgvedic one. The Śāṅk. Śr. S. (XII.22), which records these verses, adds one more, which is the most eloquent and well grounded in the ritual-sex symbolism: "What is Minus and what is Plus, that all does he conceal". "Minus" refers to the organ of the woman, "plus" to that of the man."[14] The last of the hymns is called Āhanasyāḥ; and, in the ritual tradition, these verses are associated with the concept of releasing the semen (Ai. Br. VI.36=30.10), as noted above. Before that group of verses, the group called Aitaśa-parlāpāḥ is enjoined. Some specimens of these are as follows: "These mares gallop against Prātisatvan; one of them is the fallow one (*hariklikā*)...". It is not necessary to translate the whole passage; it is too difficult, as it uses obscure words, suiting the "prattle". But some of the images are: The *hariklikā* desires a son of noble character and endowed with gold; a man with his face turned says that he is at a place where there are the three Śiṁśapa trees, round which sit three scorpions (*pṛdākavaḥ*). They blow the horn etc.". The language is elliptical, and appears to be made so on purpose.

The conclusion that may be drawn from the record of the Kuntāpa hymns is that they once formed part of a regular ritual for fertility. The mention of Ruśamas and Kaurama on the one hand, and of Parikṣit on the other, would indicate that these were popular in their period, and the persons are mentioned as donors. They must have been a necessary ritual-accompaniment for a pretty long period and formed the older tradition of such popular songs for fertility. Their recital was believed to destroy evil (*ku or kuya*) and ensure prosperity. The element of sex was a necessary charm, as is seen in other Vedic texts and rituals.[15] Why this older Ṛgvedic tradition was set aside, giving place to the similar practice in the Yajurveda tradition is not quite clear. This is a matter of further investigation. The probable reason is the hymns appearing prominently in AV. and the latter was their source! But, there can be no doubt that the Kuntāpa hymns are an important link between the Yajurveda tradition and that of the Ṛgveda. Also these and such other hymns with loose metrical set-up are to be taken as the remnants of the Folk-traditions of the Vedic period which the ancient Purohitas could not set aside, and had to adjust in their ritual set-up for popularity and the spread of their cult.[16] (See Post-script).

NOTES

1. See Sāyaṇa on Ai. Br. VI. 27 (=30.1).
2. *Ibid;* Gopatha Br. Uttara VI.12. For a detailed treatment, see Dange, Sindhu S., *Aspects of Speech in Vedic Ritual.*
3. For the *Kuntāpa* hymns see *Ṛgveda Saṁhitā*, Vaidika Samśodhana Maṇḍala, Poona, Vol. IV, Khila V. 8-22. The name *Kuntāpa* is explained further in our discussion.
4. Cf. Śat. Br. IV. 5.9.4. *atha ṣa'ṣṭhe 'hani śukrāgrān gṛhṇāti.* The Ai. Br. says in the present context that the sixth day is heaven, *loc.cit.*, 36, *svargo vai lokaḥ ṣaṣṭham ahaḥ.*
5. The *nyūṅkha* is accomplished by the utterance of short 0 sounds, thirteen times, followed by the same long; see Sāyaṇa on Ai. Br. VI. 30=30.4 According to the Āśv. Śr.S. the *nyūṅkha* is to be imposed on the second vowel of each of the two halves of the verse VIII. 3. Also VII. II.1-3; see also Kashikar, C.G., *A Survey of the Śrauta Sutras,* Bombay University, Bombay, (Journal), Sept. 1966, p.85.
6. Sāyaṇa on Ai. Br., *loc.cit.*,6.
7. For others, cf. *śaṁsanto vai devāḥ svargam lokam āyan* (Nārāśaṁsyaḥ); *kalyāṇam karma akurvans tat kāravyaḥ*; etc.
8. Cf. Vāj. Sam. XX. 18 ff; Mait. *Sam.* III. 12.20 ff; Taitt. Sam. VII 4.19 ff; Śat. Br. XIII. 2.8.3 ff.
9. Gop. Br. Uttara VI. 12. *atho khalv āhuḥ gāthā evaitāḥ kāravya rājñaḥ parikṣita iti.*
10. Cf. AV XV. 6.11-12 which mentions these as different from the Vedic verses (*ṛc*-s), as following the Mahāvrātya, indicating a mixture of these two types in popular rituals and festivals. The Ai. Br. mentions various *gāthā*-s as mixed

with the Vedic ritual; VII. 8=32.7 where we have the mention also of a verse called *yajña-gāthā*. The famous Śunaḥśepa legend is full of such *gāthā*-s. The legend forms part of the Rājasūya sacrifice. Śat. Br. also has many *gāthā*-s at various rituals.

11. The latter part of the expression occurs at RV. VIII. 4.16a: *bhūrijor iva kṣuram,* but the expression *niṣ ṭe jihvā carcarīti* is unique. See *Vedic Index of Names and Subjects,* under *bhūrij.*
12. Cf. RV. X. 101.2; *prāñcam yajñam; prāgvaṁśa* etc.
13. The tr. is from Caland' Śāṅk. Śr. S., Nagpur, 1953, XII, 22.1-6. For *kiraṇau* he has "reins"; and in the bracket, "slang for *romaṇvantau bhedau or ūne* at the Pañc. Br. *romaṇvantau bhedau is* RV. IX. 112.4c; these and *ūna (ūne)* stand for the female organ.
14. Śāṅk. Śr.S. XII. 22.7; even AV which records these hymns does not have the verse. For the symbolism of the Minus and Plus (*ūna-atirikta*), see *Sexual Symbolism from the Vedic Ritual,* pp.105 ff.
15. *Ibid.*
16. It may be noted that the 'Bhūtecchads' verses are called lauds (*sāmāni*); and they were sung at the Mahāvrata, which was a mixture of a Vedic sacrifice and popular festivities for fertility; c.f. Taitt. Sam. VII.5.9.4 *yad bhūtecchadām sāmāni bhavanti-ubhayasya-avaruddhyai*; they are associated with ritual sex, which is mentioned immediately afterwards (*antarvedi mithunam sam bhavataḥ*) which refers to that act by a prostitute and a *māgadha* male.

Post-Script

KUNTĀPA-S AND HUMAN BODY

The word *Kuntāpa* occurs also in the Śat. Br., though the context is not of the verses from the *Kuntāpa*-sūkta. Keith does not show knowledge of this word, nor does he connect the *Kuntāpa sūkta* of the Ait. Br. or the Kau. Br. with this word (*Rigveda Brahmanas*, pp. 58; 526; also 283). Eggeling, in his note to the relevant passage from the Śat. Br. (XII.2.4.12) admits that the meaning of the word *kuntāpa* is doubtful; but, even he does not connect the word with the *Kuntāpa* hymn. It is to be particularly noted in this context, that there is close and subtle affinity between the word *kuntāpa* from the Śat. Br. and the placement and purpose of the *Kuntāpa* hymns. As has been noted in the chapter, the context is the making of the sacrificial body of the sacrificer; and, at the *pratiṣthā* stage of the newly formed 'body' the *Kuntāpa* verses are ushered in. This means that these verses have relation to the body. Now, the Śat. Br. at one place (XII.2.4.1ff) identifies various lauds with the parts of the body of Puruṣa. This is in line with the usual belief of the *Chandomaya puruṣa* (as there is also the concept of the *nakṣatramaya puruṣa* and so on). Among other things, the *ekaviṁśa stoma* (twenty-onefold laud) is said to be the belly; and, in this belly there are said to be twenty *kuntāpa*-s the belly itself being the twenty-first (*viṁśatir vā antar udare kuntāpāni; udaram ekaviṁśam*). Commenting on the word *kuntāpa* at this place, Eggeling refers to the St. Petersberg Dictionary, which says that *kuntāpa* is some gland. Eggeling's own suggestion is that *kuntāpa*-s may refer to transverse processes (forming spikes) on both the sides of the ten lower spinal vertebrae of the last true rib, i.e. of the five lower dorsal and the five lumbar vertebrae (SBE, Vol.44, p.164, n. 1). This is acceptable. Just in the earlier passage there is reference to the chest (*ib.*, 11 *uraḥ saptadaśaḥ*) and later to the two sides of the chest (13 *pārśve triṇava*). As the *kuntāpa*-s of the Puruṣa are formed with twenty-one lauds, the two sides (*pārśve*) are formed with twenty-seven. This falsifies the etymological explanation of the Gopatha Br. (noted in the chapter). There is another reference to the *kuntāpa*-s in the Śat. Br. (XIII.4.4.8), in the context of the production of the trees suitable for making the sacrificial stakes from. All trees, recommended for preparing the stakes (*yūpa*) from, are said to have been created from the various substances from the body of Prajāpati. This is, of course, to mythically elevate the status of the trees. Among these trees the Bilva tree (Aegle Marmelos) is said to have been produced from the *Kuntāpa* and the marrow that flowed together and burst through the ear of Prajāpati (*atha yat kuntāpam āsit yo majjā*). Here the word *kuntāpa* is in the Singular. The final comment of Eggeling, after the one noted above, is, "It would certainly seem to be something connected with the spinal cord". The mention of *Kuntāpa* in the Plural at one place and in the Singular at another need not be taken as contradictory to each other. Actually, according to the Āyurveda (Hindu medical system), right from the skull to the lower belly the *Kuntāpa*-s are stationed on both sides of the spine and have a parasympathetic status. In modern terminology they are called 'ganglions'. They are powerful and intimate to the brain even what is not, accidentally, conveyed to it by other parts of the living body. Thus, the myth of the *kuntāpa* falling out from the ear is understandable this way. According to the Āyurveda the *kuntāpa*-s are globular in shape. This is why, the Bilva-fruit is seen in the myth as the *kuntāpa* and is said to be sweet and eatable (*ib.*, 8). In the first imagery about the *kuntāpa*-s being ten, their position being *antarudare*, the sense is that the ten *kuntāpa*-s from top to the *udara* on both sides of the spine come to twenty; and, with the *udara*, they make twenty-one. (I am obliged for this information to my friend Dr. Indubhushan Bade. Dr. Bade is a senior practioner in Āyurveda with strong base in Allopathy. He is stationed in Bombay = Mumbai, Western India.)

The position of the *Kuntāpa*-s in the body and of the hymns, that were used in the formation of the body of the sacrificer, is similar. These hymns sustained the metres, and also the body of the sacrificer.

Chapter 27

FEATURES OF TANTRISM AND THE VEDA

Like most of the later Hindu sciences (*śāstra*-s) and religious sects, Tantrism, especially the Śaiva Tantrism is said to express its relationship with the Veda. There have been efforts on the part of some scholars to connect Tantrism with the Veda, the latter being said to be its source. But, no final opinion has yet been set. As Kane has said, most of the texts on Tantrism are from a very late period. Yet the beginning of Tantrism has been accepted to go back at least to the seventh century A.D. Works of John Woodroffe (Arthur Avalon), Haraprasad Shastri and Dr. B. Bhattacharya are very well known in this connection.[1] But the relationship of the Veda with Tantrism has not been made clear by scholars; and general statements on this subject would lead us nowhere. Thus when the *Kulārṇavatantra,* for example, states that there is no lore beyond the Veda (*na hi vedādhikā vidyā*) and that the Kaulaśāstra is *vedātmaka*,[2] it only vibrates with the traditional view and no one expects the text to explain the statement. But when Woodroffe says that the Tantric concepts and rituals are the counterparts of the Veda,[3] one expects details of correlationship between the two. He gives the details which do not go to convince a careful reader. He says, that the offering of flesh in fire and the use of wine and Soma in rituals are the source of Tantric practices. In these offerings he sees the seed of the Tantric *ma-kāras, māṁsa and madya.* He also sees in the *puroḍāśa* (sacrificial cake offered at the sacrifice) the *mudrā* of the Tantric practice.[4] This is not to say, that the Veda cannot be taken to be the source of the Tantric practices; or that Tantric practices have absolutely no connection with the Vedic ritual-concepts. What is wanted is a closer look at the Vedic sources. We have to keep in mind, for example, that Soma and *surā* (Wine) were used in different contexts in the Vedic rituals, and that there was maintained a clear difference between Soma and *surā*. Moreover, these drinks cannot be said to be special to the Tantric practices; for, flesh of the sacrificially holy beast and the holy drink have a wider range of religious use, even in non-Indian and non-Vedic contexts.[5] Fish is known to have been used in the Vedic ritual-context; but, it is in the context of *śṛāddha;*[6] and this special context cannot be too strongly exploited to attest the Tantric practice. The point to note is, that in the Vedic sacrificial context, as such, fish has hardly any relevance. It is impossible to find a single example in the Vedic sacrificial context to attest the use of fish as an offering. The meaning of term *mudrā* is not fixed in the Tantric context. Apart from certain mixtures accomplished from flour,[7] the term *mudrā* is applied to whatever gives pleasure (*mud*)[8] and four types of *mudrā*-s are mentioned, namely: Karma-mudrā, Dharma-mudrā, Mahā-mudrā, and Samaya-mudrā. Two more types are: Jñāna-mudrā and Phala-mudrā.[9] Mudrā is also the woman who participates in the ritual-act of sex; and she is termed Mahā-mudrā.[10] Mahā-mudrā is also said to be the most important among the *mudrā*-s; and it comprises sexual union with women drawn from various strata of the society.[11] Mudrā, or Mahā-mudrā, thus, has a close connection with the act of sex, which is said to be the fifth and the most important of the *ma-kāras.*[12] The excellent "joy-giver" (mudrā = *mudam rāti iti*), thus, is the sexual partner in the Tantric ritual. And the crux of the Tantric practice, whether Śākta or Buddhistic, is, hence, Sex. The other *makāra*-s are only stages to this final ritual.[13]

Kane, who has dwelt elaborately on this subject in his *History of Dharmaśāstra,* traces the antiquity of the Tantric practices; and, refuting the opinion that it was a gift of the Tibetan religion, maintains that Tantrism has its roots in the Indian context. This is acceptable. But, he also gives stress on the three earlier *makāra*-s leaving the Mahāmudrā and *maithuna,* in writing about the connection of Tantrism and the Veda. He discards the sexual union that marks the Mahāvrata as indicative of the Tantric germ (and rightly so, if taken flatly), pointing out that in the former the performer himself does not take part in the said ritual, unlike the Tantric practice.[14] It might, however, be said that an exact act may not always be noted in the earliest practices. Again, it has to be stressed that to say that the act in the Mahāvrata is symbolic, as against the Tantric, is rather too spacious an argument! Sex in the precincts of religious rites can be nothing but symbolic, whether from the Vedic context or from the Tantric. This is clear from the fact that even in the Buddistic Tantric context, where sex achieved extravagant levels, symbolism underlines the ritual. Thus, the *Prajñopāya-viniścaya-siddhi* states that Prajñā is the woman and Upāya is the man, who approaches (*upa-āya*) the former for sex. The symbolism in the word *evam* is explained as follows: the letter *e* is the Mother; *va* is the Father; and *ṁ* (nasal after *va*) is the *bindu* indicating the release of the fluid.[15] A further step in the Tantric symbolism is that the *sādhaka* is not to release his semen (*bindu*), indicating full control in the ritual-act.[16] The same thought obtains in the symbolism of the word *evam* at the Devendraparipṛcchā-tantra,[17] which states that the union of *e* and *va* is completed, symbolically, in the sound of *ṁ*. This is the cause of the whole range of letters (*varṇa-mālā*). The whole creation in the universe and the multitudes of letters are, thus, symbolically, the product of the 'sexual' union of the symbolized parents. The act of sex in the Tantric practices, howsoever it might have degenerated later on, is, hence, nothing but the symbolic union of the two supreme forces in nature... the Mother and the Father... that are the great parents. The Mahāmudrā has to be seen from this angle.

To go to the root of this concept of the union of the two Great forces is, hence, to go to the source of the main concept of Tantrism.

From the angle that has been hinted at above, it is not sufficient to see only the prevalence of a mother-goddess, but to see whether the great Mother is associated with the concept of sexual union. Kane's effort to take a note of the wide range of female deities like Śacī, Indrāṇī, Varuṇāṇī, Vāk (Speech), or even the concept of the Gnāḥ (a collective name for the wives of the gods)[18] falls too short of the mark. This is only an enumeration of the female deities, which are not related to the process of procreation, as such. They are suggested from the male gods, and are only reflected deities, as against the prime Mother-goddesses. Kane, rightly refuting the views that see the source of the Tantric practices in China or Tibet, goes as far as Bhadrakālī, a form of Durgā, in Śāṇk Gṛ.S. crossing and mentioning Caṇḍikā referred to by Bāṇa.[19] It is acceptable, with Kane, that Tantric glimpses are to be noted in the Mahābhārata. But, it is also necessary to note references from the Rāmāyaṇa in this context, before we go still back. Wine and flesh are generally mentioned as offerings to female deities in the Rāmāyaṇa. Thus, when Rāma sets to the forest with his brother and Sītā, and they come to the place where they have to cross the Gaṅgā, Sītā prays to the river and says that she would offer to the Brāhmaṇas a thousand cows, to her (i.e. the Gaṅgā) she would offer 'a thousand jars of wine and boiled rice mixed with flesh' and the same she would offer to the deities on her bank (Rām., Ayodhyā 80-90). She invokes the Yamunā in the same words (*ib.,* 56.20-21). It is to be marked, however, that when she comes to the Vaṭa tree, named Śyāma, she simply circumambulates it invoking it for the safe return of her husband and the regain of his royal glory (*ib.,* 56. 19-25). The offering of wine and flesh to the rivers is due to their being considered as Mothers. That wine and flesh are the offering for the Mothers is clear also from elsewhere (cf. Viṣṇu P., V. 7.6; we leave away the Purāṇas; for, we have to go back). There is reason to believe that wine (*surā*) formed a speciality for the female powers in ritual. Thus, at the ritual for the manes, known as the Anvaṣṭakya, the male ancestors were offered balls of boiled rice (*odana*), while the females were offered *surā* and *odana,* as is clear from the Gṛhya texts.[20] This would mean that the female deities, or female ancestors believed as deities, are associated with *surā* even at the Sūtra period (from 600 B.C. to 200 B.C.). But, we have a clear association of the Vedic Mother-goddess with not only *surā* but also with sex. This Mother-goddess, missed by scholars until now, is known to the Veda as Mahānagnī (RV Khila V. 22.5-9) a name that very much resembles the later Mahāmudrā. According to the Śukranītisāra (IV. 3.39) Tantra is the *upa-veda* of the Atharvaveda (*atharvaṇāñ copavedas tantra-rūpaḥ sa eva hi*). It is difficult to say on what basis this is said; and Kane does not agree with this statement, nor does he mention Mahānagnī. But, it is to be noted that, as the variant Mahānagnī, she is clearly mentioned in the Atharvaveda; and that too in the context of marriage, as a prototype of the bride. It is desired that the bride be sprinkled by the gods Aśvins with the same fluid which they sprinkled on the genitals of Mahānagnī (AV, *mahānagnī* XIV. 1.36). And here there is mention also of the *surā,* said to be sprinkled over by the Aśvins. Though here there is no offering of *surā* to Mahānagnī, their mutual association is clear. It may be marked that in the "sprinkling of the genitals" of Mahānagnī, there is a couched indication to sexual union. Moreover, there is mention of the male partner of Mahānagnī; and he is called Mahānagna (RV. Khila *loc. cit.,* 9). The Vedic ritual-texts abound in sexual rituals, and sex has been a formidable aspect therein.[21] The presence of Mahānagnī is seen, symbolically, in many rituals. The context of marriage is already mentioned above, where Mahānagnī is mentioned. Mahānagnī is also the name of the cow, in exchange of which Soma is to be purchased, according to Ai. Br. (I.27=5.1)[22] which shows the Ṛgvedic tradition. Thus, Mahānagnī is well preserved in the

Atharvaveda and the Ṛgveda traditions, along with the holy drink. At the purchase of Soma, the cow called Mahānagnī is the sexual counterpart of Soma, the bull. It is in this concept, which is backed by rituals, of a Mother-goddess and her mate, and in the concept of ritual-sex that the seeds of the later Tantric concept appear to be hidden. In the context of the purchase of Soma, an interesting expression obtains in Ai. Br. (*op.cit.*). Soma is with the Gandharvas, and it is to be purchased by sending a woman to them. Vāk (Speech) tells the gods that she would become Mahānagnī, whom they could send to the Gandharvas. This would mean, that, though in the Vedic rite a cow figured, actually, in the original rite a woman might have figured. And she was Mahānagnī. It should be remembered that the word Mahānagnī indicates also a "prostitute", which means that a prostitute, originally, figured in the ritual of the purchase of Soma (?). The Mahāvrata is marked by the sexual intercourse of a prostitute (*puṁścalū*) and a Māgadha.[23] As we noted above, a difference is sought to be made in this act and the later Tantric act of sex, stating that in the latter sexual intercourse is on the part of the *sādhaka* (performer) himself. We have indicated that the early phase may not exactly tally with the later one. But, there is another point to be noted. The Māgadha-prostitute sex-act seems to be a substitution for the one by the performers themselves. Thus, Taitt. Sam. refers to the performers, and suggests that the substitute (in the form of the Māgadha-prostitute) is to preserve the vịrility of the performers; because, the performers themselves, for a year, do not indulge in sex-act (VII. 5.9.4).[24] The Tantric practices prescribe the prostitute in certain cases; and, according to the type called Devacakra prostitutes are of five types.[25] Another point to be noted is that, even in the Horse-sacrifice, the performing king and his wives figured. Thus, when the sacrifice started, in one rite the performer had to lie for the whole night between the thighs of one of his wives without moving.[26] At the end of the period of the roaming of the horse, the horse had symbolic sex with the eldest wife, Mahiṣī and others. The first rite is only the symbolic counterpart of the latter. The concept of *maithuna* at the holy stage is the same in the Vedic rites and the Tantric, the difference being only in degrees and phases. It is here that the earliest phase of Tantrism is discernible.

We have noted above the symbolism in the mystic word *evam*. The Vedic ritual-tradition had already a fully developed letter-symbolism based on sexual imagery. Thus, the latter Om, or Hum and even Hiñ, is said to be the male, while the verse is said to be the female.[27] There are cases where the verse-female is arranged in such a way in utterance that its two feet are separated and the prose utterance called *nivid* is inserted into them to form a virtual coitus.[28] A variety of such speech-couples are formed with a view to aid prosperity and fertility.

The Vedic sacrifice shows a variety of sex-symbols, where the wife of the sacrificer gets to have symbolic union with a variety of objects, including the priest; and the sacrificial beast is her divine male partner, the most striking example being that of the horse in the Horse-sacrifice.[29] It will be, hence, seen that the most important *ma-kāra* (the fifth one: *maithuna*) is firmly embedded in the Vedic ritual tradition. Though *surā* does not directly get associated with sex in the Vedic ritual-tradition, it has its own unique importance in the Vedic tradition, and has a unique association with Mahānagnī, as noted above. As an example of sex-coupling, on a bit lower level, obtains the couple of the Māgadha and the prostitute which is said to be constantly associated with the Mahāvrātya in the Atharvaveda.[30] This couple has to be understood as only another phase of the Māgadha-prostitute couple that works at the Mahāvrata. The Mahāvrātya has to be taken as an earlier aspect of Śiva Mahādeva, and of none else, which is clear from his unique attire and the *rajata niṣka* (AV XV. 1.5, 14 and other places in the same hymn) round his neck. As such, here we have, in the Māgadha-prostitute couple, the first ever glimpse of the later Śākta couple. There is no doubt that the concept of the couple in close embrace, one getting mixed into the body of the other, is the crux of Śaiva Tantrism. The same gets extended in the letter-symbolism in the form of the Buddhist Prajñopāya and the Śaiva Evaṁ. Another aspect of the same is the Buddhist concept: *Oṁ Maṇi Padme Hum.* The Kāmakalāvilāsa presents the concept of Speech (female) and Meaning (Male) in constant union like Śiva and Śakti. The same thought was already presented by Kālīdasa in the starting verse of the Rahuvaṁśa,[31] which would indicate the prevalence of Śaiva Tantric concepts at the time of Kālidāsa, which period may be the first century B.C. or the fourth century A.D. This is the generally accepted Ardha-nārī concept. But, it should be noted that this concept goes yet back; and it is first prominently seen in the couple of Indra-Indrāṇī, where the same divinity is said to have two forms: the Male and the Female. Thus, it is said that in the right eye of the sacrificer stays Indra, the male; and in his left eye stays Indra as a female, Indrāṇī. These two enter the realm of the heart and have union there. This is what is said by the Śat Br.[32] and there we have the concept of the *kāntā-saṁmiśra-deha* deity, Śiva, praised as such by Kālidāsa later.[33] The main Tantric concept, thus, is far ancient than is supposed to be; and it is rooted in the Vedic concept of *mithunīkaraṇa* ("coupling"). The Mahānagna-Mahānagnī couple fell back, along with the polished Indra-Indrāṇī couple, giving place to the Śiva-Śakti couple somewhere in the beginning of the Christian era. The same period is marked by terracotta figures showing couples in amorous poses,[34] which cannot so much be adornments for walls as votive offerings. These do not seem to be of the Vedic origin; but they correspond to the sexual symbolic practices of the Vedic ritual tradition, and appear to be forerunners of the later erotic sculptures.[35] *Maithuna, surā, 'māṁsa* and *mudrā* (in the sense of the Mahāmudrā-prostitute; the ritual woman) appear to be, thus, common to both the Vedic and the non-Vedic traditions, though the Vedic tradition has a clear and neat record of these practices in the various texts. Whether

Tantrism that shows itself prominently after the seventh century A.D. is a clear development from the pure Vedic tradition, or whether it is a mixture is a difficult question. But, one thing is pretty certain: Tantrism is an ancient Indian creed, in essence. It is not improbable that in the hey-day of Vedic practices and sacrifices, with a predominant sexual note, a mixed mystic cult got created and fostered wherein the ancient Mahānagnī changed into Śakti and the Mahānagna turned into Śiva with his nudity, with new dimensions, adding the fish to the already existing *makāra*-s (*māṁsa, madya (surā), mudrā* and *maithuna*). And, as this one mode of worship got believed to solve all worldly and heavenly problems, it came to be called TANTRA.[36]

NOTES

1. For a brief account of these opinions, see P.V. Kane, *History of Dharmaśāstra,* Vol. V-ii, Poona, 1977, pp.1039ff.
2. Kulārṇavatantra II.141; II. 113.
3. *Śakti and Śākta,* Luzac and Co., London, 1918, p. 132.
4. *Ibid.,* p.27. His statement that in the "Vaidika usage meat, fish and Mudrā (the latter in the form of a *puroḍāśa*) were consumed" has to be taken cautiously.
5. For ex. the Buriat of Siberia eat flesh and drink the special wine, prepared from sour butter-milk and called '*tarasum*', after offering it into the fire; the Aztecs used the wine called *pulque* from the Mayauel tree and so on. See Donald Mackenzie, *Indian Myth and Legend,* London, p.90; also *Myths of Pre-Columbian America,* London, p.177.
6. Āpastamba-Dharma-Sūtra II.7.17.2 mentions the *śatabali* fish in this context.
7. For the various meanings of this term, see Kane, *op.cit.,* p.1123.
8. *Ibid.,* note 1836.
9. Guenther, H.V., *Yuganaddha,* Varanasi, 1952, p. 87, where he refers to Indrabhūti and Advayarāja.
10. *Ibid.,* p.45; also Prajñopāyaviniścayasiddhiḥ, vv.38-40.
11. Guhyasamājatantra, Gaekwad Or. Ser., Vol. III, Baroda, p. 42; also text published by the Mithila Instt, Darbhanga, 1965, X. 20,21.

12. Mahānirvāṇatantra 1.57ff.
13. *Op. cit., loc.cit.*
14. *Op.cit.,* p.1080
15. Guenther, *op.cit.,* p. 93, where he quotes from the Devendraparipṛcchātantra; *ekāras tu bhaven mātā vakaras tu pitā smṛtaḥ bindus tatra bhaved yogaḥ sa yogaḥ paramākṣaraḥ; ekārastu bhavet prajñā vakāraḥ suratādhipaḥ. bindus' cānāhatam tattvam tajjātāny akṣarāṇi ca* and from Prajñopāyaviniścayasiddhiḥ at p.154.
16. Kalivilāsatantra X. 21 *na bindoḥ patanam kāryam kṛte ca brahmahā bhavet.* This is in connection with sex with a woman, who is not one's own wife.
17. See note 15 above. The same symbolism of letters occurs at the Mahānirvāṇatantra.
18. *Op.cit.,* p. 1043f; actually Kane would have done well in referring to the concept of Indra-Indrāṇī, Indrāṇī described as lying flat, with her genitals thirty *yojana*-s spacious, and holding Indra steadily in her *upastha,* Kāṭhaka Saṁhitā VIII.17.62, Maitrāyaṇī Sam. III.8.4 (Indrāṇī) *trimśad asyā jaghanam yojanāni, upastha indram sthaviram bibharti.*
19. *Op.cit.,* p.1042.
20. *Āśv.* Gṛ.S. II.5.8. Pāraskara Gṛ. S. III.3.11; Kāṭhaka Gṛ. S. 85.7.8; see Mrs. S.S. Dange, *Hindu Domestic Rituals,* ch. "Wine and Female Ancestors", Delhi, 1985.
21. See Dange, *Sexual Symbolism from the Vedic Ritual,* Ajanta Books International, Delhi, 1979.
22. I.27=5.1, where the cow is said to be the imitation of Mahānagnī:
tayā mahānagnayā bhūtayā somam rājānam akrīṇan tāmanukṛtim áskannām vatsatarīm ājanti; also earlier, 25. A. A. Macdonell and A.B. Keith, *Vedic Index of Names and Subjects,* London, 1912, under "Mahānagnī ", say that she is a prostitute. Obviously, she is not a common prostitute; in ritual she is the divine woman counterpart of the ritual-male. On this point reference may be made to Dange, *Vedic myths in Social Perspective* (ch. II, "Myths in Vedic Ritual-Setting"), Panjab University, Chandigarh, Published at Hoshiarpur, 1982.
23. Jaim. Br. II.206 *māgadhañca pumscalūñ ca dakṣine vedyante mithunīkārayanti.*
The sexual conversation of the Ārya and the Śūdrā, along with the sexual intercourse of the animals (*bhūtānāñca*

maithunam) seems to be an adaptation of the original sexual union between humans; cf. Ai. Ār. V.1.5. Was this a substitute for the giving of the prostitute (Mahānagnī = ritual woman) to the Gandharvas, referred to at the Ai. Br.?

24. Taitt. Sam VII. 5.9.4, *antarvedi mithunam saṁbhavataḥ,* which refers to the Māgadha and the prostitute; but further, *tenaiva mithunan na yanti;* see also J. Gonda, "Ascetics and Courtesans", *Adyar Library Bulletin,* Jubilee Vol. XXV, 1-4, 1964, p.92; cf. Kāṭhaka Sam. XXXIV.5
25. Arthur Avalon, Mahānirvāṇatantra, p. x; Rājaveśyā, Nāgarī, Guptaveśyā, Devaveśyā", and Brahmaveśyā.
26. Śat. Br. XIII. 4.1-8; Eggeling, SBE V, p.349. We may compare the instruction of one of the Tantric texts, Mahānirvāṇa-tantra (VIII.40), which states that when one's own wife is available, the *sādhaka* should not touch another woman. The Kālīvilāsatantra (X.20-21) ordains that when he has sex with another woman, he should take care not to eject the semen. The motif of controlled and symbolic sex is the same in the Tantric text mentioned above and in the rite at the Horse-sacrifice. The Vedic sex was for fertility and prosperity, while at the "Tantra" level it is taken to mystic heights!
27. Cf. Ai. Br., II.38-*prāṇo vai retaḥ vāg yoniḥ;* also Śat. Br. I.4.1.2; Pañcaviṁśa Br. VI. 8.5.; for other example, see Dange, *Sexual Symbolism ...,* p.100ff.
28. *Ibid.,* also Ai. Br. II. 35 = 10.3; and Sāyaṇa thereon.
29. See *Sexual Symbolism,* chapter on "The "Wife" and her Divine Mates".
30. Rudra has the *yajata niṣka,* which is unique with him; it is not associated with any other deity. On the identity of the Mahāvrātya and Rudra-Śiva, see Dange, *Cultural Sources from the Veda,* Bharatiya Vidya Bhavan, Bombay, 1977, pp.31, 33.
31. Raghuvaṁśa. I.1. *vagarthāviva saṁpṛktau pārvatī-parameśvarau* and Kāmavilāsa, 12 *vāgarthau nityayuktau parasparam śiva-śaktimayāvetau.*
32. Śat. Br. X 5.2.8-11; also Bṛhadāraṇyaka Up. IV. 2.3.
33. Mālavikāgnimitram, Act I, v.1. It would be better to refer to the opinion, and explanation, of Guenther, *op.cit.,* p.154, about Prajñā and Upāya. He says, "When pictured in anthropomorphic shape they embrace each other touching

all points of contact. This shows that the one cannot be without the other, and that they are basically one". We add that the first concept of the "Two-in-One" is recorded by the Veda in Indra-Indrāṇī, as noted above.

34. Devangana Desai, *Erotic Sculptures of India,* Tata McGraw Hill, Delhi, 1975, pp.1,11,12.
35. *Sexual Symbolism...* pp.213-34.
36. This is the Mīmāṁsaka idea of *tantra;* cf. Śabara's comment on Jaiminīya Sūtra XI 4.1. *yat sakṛt kṛtam bahūnām upakaroti tat tantram ity ucyate yathā bahūnām brāhmaṇānām madhye kṛtaḥ pradīpaḥ.*

Asko Parpola ("Metamorphoses of Mahiṣa Asura and Prajāpati" in *Ritual, State and History in South Asia-* Essays in honour of J.C. Heesterman, E.J. Brill, Leiden, New York Koln, p.280) suggests that the Śākta Tantric *cakrapūjā* with its nude virgin is a counterpart of the virgin *(Kumārī)* who is mentioned in the context of the Horse-sacrifice (Śat.Br. XIII. 5.2.4). He refers to more details from the Vādhūlasūtra (III.93) to support his suggestion.

Chapter 28

MOTHER-GODDESS ON THE VEDIC SCENE

There is a basic difference in a sacrifice offered to a Mother-goddess and to a Vedic deity, as far as the animal-sacrifice is concerned. Unlike that for the Mother-goddess, the one for a Vedic deity excludes blood which is offered to evil spirits, except for Rudra; and to Rudra also it is offered outside the locality.[1] Moreover, details from the Vedic ritual texts show that the sacrificial beast was smothered and was not allowed to make any noise, so that it could be 'whole'. The victims to the Mother-goddess have been, on the other hand, regularly beheaded.[2] The only exception in the Veda is that of Śunaḥśepa; for, in his case, there is a clear reference of his being about to be slaughtered like any other beast.[3] This, then, has to be taken as the very early practice among the Vedic people, if at all it was prevalent. But even in this case, there is no killing ultimately. Another point of difference to be noted is, that some of the Vedic gods are offered female beasts,[4] while such is hardly the case with the Mother-goddess. The reason is that, for the Mother-goddess manly fluid in any form is necessary for continued procreative powers. This is true in both of her aspects—(i) Productive Earth; and (ii) Generating Female. However, there are certain indications in the Vedic belief, which have conceptual similarity to the cult of the Mother-goddess.

According to a general belief, the victim to the Mother-goddess, especially in her aspect of the procreative earth, is her "son-husband", to be ever new and young.[5] The concept appears in RV, though in the later stratum of the Veda it has almost faded out. This is the concept of "*vṛṣa-śiśu*" (the 'seeder' who is also the child). This epithet appears for the god Apām-napāt, the Indo-Iranian god of waters,[6] who is at once the "Child of the waters" and also their "seeder" husband (RV II. 35; esp. vv.4 and 13). This god comes to be identified in the Vedic context with the fire-god; but, he is originally the spirit of the river-waters, as is clear from the context. At the place mentioned above, we have many water-mothers for this One Seeder; but, they came to be symbolised also as the river Sarasvatī (RV VII. 95; X. 30). However, the Sarasvatī is not offered any sacrifice specially and independently, to figure prominently as a Mother-goddess. But, in the list of victims one for the Sarasvatī figures, and also for Sarasvant, who is her male counterpart.[7]

Sarasvant has to be taken as a later reflected deity from the Sarasvatī, due to the influence and prominence of the male deities. A close view reveals that Sarasvant is only a phase of Apām-napāt. The point to be noted is that, unlike a victim of the Mother-goddess, who is the "son-husband", Apām-napāt (or, Sarasvant) is not himself offered, in any symbolic form to the Sarasvatī. Now, let us see the position at the Soma-sacrifice.

At the Soma-sacrifice the waters, technically called Ekadhanā and Vasatīvarī, used for the swelling of the pressed out shoots of Soma, are conceptually from the Sarasvatī. Soma (in the form of these shoots) is said to unite with them and gets swelled up again; thus, he is their child and also the uniting "seeder" (RV X. 30.5 *yābhiḥ somo modate harṣate ca kalyāṇībhir yuvatibhir na maryaḥ*). As against Apām-napāt, the "seeder" Soma is ritually "killed", as the offering par excellence.[8] However, there is a difference. As against the victim to the Mother-goddess, Soma is not offered as sacrificial victim to the Mother(s) (here, waters) or the Sarasvatī. But, the image of the "seeder" as victim is complete, especially when Soma is called "King". Let us probe the point further, and examine the status of the (deity) Sarasvatī. It is to be noted, in this context, that it is the Sarasvatī alone, of all the rivers, that is addressed as *ambi;* and, though the term *ambī* is applied to the rivers generally in their aspect as the Mothers (and not so much for their making sound, from √*amb,* like *nadī* from √*nad),* it is only the Sarasvatī that is called *nadī-tamā* and *ambī-tamā* in her address (RV II. 41.16). This would indicate that this river was considered to be the supreme mother, as also the most important river. Though the Ṛgveda mentions other things as *mātṛ* (Mother), the epithet *mātṛ-tamā* (only thrice) occurs only for rivers. This would suggest that for the Ṛgvedic people, the river was a potential Mother-goddess, and the Sarasvatī was the supreme Mother. This is, probably, why an animal was sacrificed to her, and also to her male counterpart, Sarasvant, while Aditi, the mother of the gods, was offered a *caru* of boiled rice.[9] It is to be further noted, that, unlike Aditi, Sarasvatī gets to be a regular fertility goddess in the post-Vedic pantheon, getting identified with Gaurī, her aspect of the goddess of fertility.[10] Another indication of Sarasvatī's claim for being the Mother-goddess in the making during the Ṛgvedic period itself is, that, in the Āprī hymns of the Ṛgveda, Sarasvatī is the most concrete goddess (developed from the visible river), the other two—Bharatī and Iḍā—being hazy.

Along with the river-mother the earth-mother persisted in the Vedic society in the form of Indrāṇī. Though she was unclear in the Brahmanic Śrauta ritual as a Mother-goddess, she had her sway in the domestic *(gṛhya)* ritual. As early as RV she appears as the Mother *(ambā),* with traits that are usual with the Mother-goddess. She has a young sex-partner, the virile monkey *(vṛṣākapi),* who is also her "son". He addresses her and describes her in sexual terms; he is described in the coitus position, and is ultimately sacrificially killed, so that Indra may get his glory (RV X. 86).[11] Reading closely, and scratching the outer crust of the myth, which is in fact based on a ritual, it becomes pretty clear that the *vṛṣā* (Virile) *kapi* (Monkey), is the post-type of an earlier male victim, and was sacrificed to Indrāṇī in her aspect of the earth-mother, who is referred to as becoming pregnant (*ib.*, V. 23). That Indrāṇī is the earth-mother is clear from her description in other Vedic texts, where she is said to have hips thirty *yojana*-s spacious.[12] In domestic rituals she gets to be worshipped for happy married life, as is the case with Gaurī.[13]

It is to be noted, that, unlike other goddesses such as Varuṇāṇī, Brahmāṇī etc. that are reflected females, on the basis of their male originals, Indrāṇī has an independent status. She does not depend on Indra for her status. Another goddess of a similar status is Vārāhī who appears in the post-Vedic period. She is a perfect Mother-goddess, sometimes shown with a symbolic fish in her hand.[14] The Mother-goddesses Indrāṇī and Sarasvatī could not have their special and independent cult in the Vedic pantheon due to the dominant male-centred religion; and, in the post-vedic period they got assimilated with the popular Mother-goddesses through the bridge of Durgā-Kātyāyanī. Such goddesses of the Vedic pantheon may be termed "Shadow Mothers" rather than being completely ignored as non-Mother-goddesses. One of the most siginificant of such "Shadow Mothers" is the *vedi* (altar). The Ṛgveda already speaks of her as "the beautiful woman having four tufts" (X.114.3); and, later, she is seen in the form of Vāgīśvarī being altar-based.[15] Though the *vedi* is not sacrificed to, she is constantly identified with the earth; and its preparation (*saṁbhāra)* is set with almost all types, and symbols, of the earth, including the earth from the ant-hill (*valmīka-vapā)*, which appears as an important symbol of the Mother-goddess in later times (cf. Reṇukā).[16] Already in the Vedic ritual the *vedi* is conceived as a woman embracing the Āhavanīya fire-place.[17] Another important Mother is the *ukhā* described as the mother of the fire-god; and she is portrayed as having teats, which is a clear fertility symbol common with the later Mother-goddesses.[18] The *ukhā* is the prototype of the later goddess found at excavation-sites, and known as the "head-less goddess".

There can be hardly any doubt that these later Mother-goddesses, are and have to be taken as, the visuals of their Vedic proto-types such as Indrāṇī and Sarasvatī who had to remain dormant in the hey-day of the male deities. With the mixture of cults, and with the contact with bolder popular Mother-goddesses, they asserted their status, influencing the latter and getting influenced by them.

Recalling the sacrifice offered to the Mothers, a thing to be noted is the importance of wine, curds or butter-milk. All these indicate fermentation. Now, in the Vedic context in the ritual of the manes (*pitṛ-śrāddha*) women ancestors are offered wine;[19] and though in the Sautrāmaṇī the manes, as a group, are offered wine without any distinction of sex, there is room to believe that this is so due to the presence of the female ancestors.

Among the deities along with the Aśvins and Indra, only Sarasvatī is offered wine.[20] In such offerings the idea seems to be of fermentation as a symbol of new creation. This explains why the Tantric cult gives so much importance to the menstruating Mother-goddess and wine. The Atharvaveda (IV. I. 36) already mentions wine and woman's fertility together. As such wine would symbolically indicate fermentation and pregnancy leading to reproduction. The earliest reference to fermentation in the womb, indicating pregnancy, occurs in the context of Indrāṇī and Vṛṣākapi in the Ṛgveda (X. 86. 23 *yasyā udaram āmayat*). The womb (*udaram*) in this context is, obviously, of Indrāṇī, called here Parśu Mānavī,[21] the veritable Mother-earth, whose another form is the Mahānagnī.[22]

NOTES

1. As is the case in the Śūlagava, see Kane, *History of Dharmaśāstra,* Vol. II-ii, Poona, 1974, p.832.
2. Henry Whitehead, *The Village Gods of South India,* Delhi, 1976 (1921), at various places.
3. Ai. Br., VII.16=33.4, read *viśasitāram,* and *asim niḥśāna eyāya;* and further *amānuṣam iva mā viśasiṣyanti.*

4. Cf. the sacrifice of the *vaśā* cow; the speckled cow (or she-goat) for Agni and the Maruts etc., Mait. Sam. II. 5.7.
5. Donald Mackenzie, *Myths of Babylonia and Assyria,* London (1915), p.91; see also ch.V, *supra.*
6. This aspect of the fire-god in the Veda is a later one; see R.N. Dandekar, *Vaidika Agni Daivata-śāstra,* Pune, 1972, p.45ff.
7. *Āśv*.Śr.S. III 7-8.
8. Śat. Br. III. 9.4.2; Jai. Br. 1.82; Taitt. Br. 1.3.1 etc.
9. Ai. Br. II.1=6.1
10. Skanda P. VII I.185.2, where she is said to have a mare's face.
11. RV X.86; see Dange, *Vedic Concept of "Field" and the Divine Fructification,* Bombay Uni. Pbn. 1971; pp.49-67.
12. Mait. Sam. III.8.4; Kāṭhaka Sam.VIII. 17.62; Taitt. Sam. VII. 5.10.
13. Śāṅkh. Gṛ.S.I. 11; the ritual is called Indrāṇī-karma at marriage; cf. RV Khila III. 17.4; AV XIV. 1.52.
14. J.N. Banerjea, at *Mirashi Fel. Vol.,* Nagpur, 1965, p.350, pl.2
15. Liṅga P. II 25. 67-68; she is identified with Sarasvatī; Brahmavaivarta P., *Śṛṣṭikhaṇḍa,* 35, 19-23.
16. Mb. Vana 99.42; 116.4 etc. At Skanda P. II 1.9.60; she is described as *Valmīkākāra-saṁsthitā.*
17. Śat. Br. 1.2.5. 16.
18. *Ibid.,* VI. 5.2. 17-19.
19. Pāraskara Gṛ. S. III 3.10 f; see S.S. Dange, *Hindu Domestic Rituals,* Delhi, 1985, pp.53-58.
20. Śat. Br. V. 5.4 24ff; Taitt. Br. II. 6.2., remnants of wine are poured on the ant-hill earth (*valmīka-vapā*); also see Kane, *op.cit.*, p.1226. This indicates the direction of identification as Ant-hill=Sarasvatī=EarthMother-goddess, and explains the use of wine in the worship of the goddess.
21. She is called Parśu Mānavī; for Mānavī as earth (though also as sky), cf. RV IX 98.9.
22. See p.240, *supra.*

Chapter 29

THE GODDESS OF SPEECH PUṀŚCALĪ

Speech (Vāk) is regarded as a divinity in the Hindu tradition and has a unique importance in the Vedic ritual-tradition. She is also identified with Sarasvatī, the popular goddess of learning and literature. The Vedic tradition shows her various aspects.[1] In one of her aspects, she is conceived as a *puṁścalī* (Puṁ-calī, the word indicating a prostitute, or a courtesan). On the whole, this aspect of hers is rather subdued, but subtle. However, it is important, and the Kauṣītaki-Br. (Kau. Br.) directly refers to speech as a *puṁścalī* (XVII.1). This passage is said to be in the Anuṣṭubh metre at the said Br. and yet it was missed by scholars, as Keith has rightly pointed out in his translation of the said text.[2] It forms part of the tenth (and final) day rites of the Daśarātra (Ten-night) Soma-sacrifice. This day is called 'divine' and is believed to be sacred to the metre Anuṣṭubh (*tad deva-karma yad daśamam ahar anuṣṭub-eva*); and in the Anuṣṭubh all metres of Speech are resorted. Due to the speciality of the day and of the Anuṣṭubh at this rite, it is said that none should try to interfere and explain if there be any mistake. But, this is one view. According to Kauṣītaki, however, one may explain if one is sure of his knowledge; for, by the right meaning the sacrifice gets joy. The point in the discussion is regarding the release of Speech, after the rites are over, through the Anuṣṭubh. It is said, that up to this juncture speech was overburdened due to the use of her various aspects, viz. metres, lauds, *nivid-s*, *yajus*-es and so on. Due to this burden, it is suggested, she became hoarse and unpalatable[3] (in voice, and uncompromising in attitude!). Hence, she is to be released (for some rest) with the consideration, 'Let us not close-sit with her' (*na-id vācam ā-sīdāma*).[4] And here a verse in the Anuṣṭubh (with the fourth foot a bit extended) is ushered in. The text says," This is the Anuṣṭubh sung on the tenth day (*anuṣṭub-eṣā daśame ahan parigītā*)," with the comment, "One should not vacate the abode of the Anuṣṭubh. One should follow with the recitation of the Virāj; because Virāj and Anuṣṭubh are similar (*samānam*) metres. Not, indeed, by one syllable or by two a metre becomes another".[5] The passage is not separated from the rest and appears as if it were prose. However, the initial words, *tad enān* (=*tad enām*) have to be separated and the verse would have the form as presented below:

> *Vāhevābhimṛśe śūdrām, no enān pra-sasṛkṣāṇi*
> *na tvevānyatra yāmaka, puṁścalyā ayanam me asti*
> (Like a carrier (*vāhā iva*; she is)! I (merely) touch her, the *śūdrā*. I shall not, indeed, leave her. Elsewhere certainly I would not go. With the courtesan (*puṁścalyā*) is my going)".[6]

Seen closely the verse reflects a hesitation, deliberation and the final conviction, that in spite of Speech being a '*puṁścalī*' the poet will constantly follow her. She is termed *śūdrā*, as she carries the burden like a female Śūdrā (cf. *vāhā-iva*).[7] The burden is of the various metres and types of expressions. This explains why she gets her voice going hoarse (the *śūdrā* due to fatigue; Speech due to over exercise of her faculty). It may be noted that *vāhā* means also 'beast of burden'. And, Speech is such a one for the burden of *mantra*-s she bears in ritual, the pitch and tone constantly changing affecting her vocal cords. The divinity associated with Speech, together with her being termed Śūdrā *puṁścalī* reflects the status of the courtesan in the Vedic society. It was low yet auspicious, the latter because she was engaged for dancing, singing and ritual dialogue as a charm for productional prosperity. This is a marked trait in the ritual texts and is already suggested in the

Ṛgveda.[8] Speech has been a vehicle of all sorts of vocal ritual-expressions, including the erotic. Hence, it is not surprising that the Kau. Br. equates her with the *puṁścalī*. The equation between Speech and the courtesan holds good also in the word *vāhā*. Speech is *vahā* for her male clients. Speech is *puṁścalī* as she moves to the (mouths of) various priests and the sacrificer, who are invariably male, while the *puṁścalī* moves among men and changes them. When Speech is said to be *puṁścalī*, there is a subtle indication that, in the sacrificial rites family women were not to utter the *mantra*-s.[9] The Ṛgveda does not have the word *puṁścalī*. The contrast is interesting from the point of the status of women, in the Ṛgvedic and the post-Ṛgvedic period.

The case of Speech being equated with a courtesan is not a solitary one. Another Vedic example is of Mahānagnī, who is mentioned variously. She is not mentioned in the Ṛgveda (except for the Khila, V.22.5-9, which are covered by Atharvaveda X.136.5-14 where more references to her occur). The Atharvaveda mentions her in the context of the marriage also, where Aśvins are invoked to favour the bride in the same way as they 'sprinkled' the vagina of the Mahānagnī. The idea is that the bride should gain the ability to render marital pleasure and progeny to her husband after the marriage.[10] The Mahānagnī appears as a woman bartered for Soma in a myth in connection with purchase of Soma, wherein she is to be sent to the Gandharvas who had Soma. In fact she is Speech, who was to be sent as a woman, for the Gandharvas had a weakness for women. Speech says, "Send me as I assume the form of a woman (*mayaiva strī-bhūtayā*); and when thus you gain Soma, I shall come back to you" (Ait. Br. I.27=5.1). But, the myth goes on to say that the gods bartered Mahānagnī for Soma; and, to conform with the earlier suggestion of speech to the gods she should be a woman—and, a special woman. The myth ends here and the actual ritual has a young immaculate cow (*vatsatarī*), which is given to the soma-seller and taken back from him in exchange (of other things). This will show that there is variance between the myth and the ritual, with the probable indication that in an earlier stage of the rite a woman figured. She was called Mahānagnī, which term indicates that she was a prototype of the *puṁścalī*, in ritual-status, though there is hardly any help to precisely say that she was a courtesan or a prostitute. The term never again occurs in later literature, and even in the Vedic texts it is restricted only to the Atharvaveda (as we have seen), Ait.Br. and the Śāṅkhāyana Śr. S., which would indicate that the post-Ṛgvedic tradition borrowed it from the Atharvaveda (or, from the diluted Ṛgvedic tradition? of the Khila). In a variant of the myth of the Speech-woman being sent to the Gandharvas and that she was replaced by the immaculate cow (in the ritual), there is a further turn when it is said that the female cow assumed the form of a tawny female antelope (*rohidrūpām kṛtvā*) and bolted from the Gandharvas to reach the gods. The tawny female antelope here (Taitt. Sam. VI.1.6.4f.) is suggested from the original myth of Prajāpati and the daughter, where the latter is said to have run away from the former in the same form (of the tawny antelope) and in the context of the purchase of *soma* the colour (*rohit-rohitā*) matches that of the cow that is bartered for *soma* in the ritual.[12] There is further confusion between the myth and the ritual, as both occur at the Taitt. *Sam*. This text says that the gods send Speech changing her into a female, one-year-old (*ib., striyam ekāhayanīm kṛtvā*) with the thought that the Gandharvas are fond of women. This can hardly go well with the 'one-year-old', who is just a child, though referred to as woman (*strī*). Yet, the text says further that Soma was purchased with *her*; because, a 'one-year-old' human can speak. This is to explain the ritual-use of the cow[13] (heifer) at this stage. So, the expression 'one-year-old' indicates the actual faculty of speech (speaking) but not the age of the human *strī* from the myth (and the earlier ritual?), and age but not actual speech in the case of the cow at this stage of the ritual. The Ait. Br. (I.27=5.1) is very clear when it says, that the gods purchased *soma* with Speech who, on her own advice, became Mahānagnī and, further, that an immaculate cow (*vatsatarī*) is made to walk to the *soma*-seller as, her representative, or, better, her imitation (*tām anukṛtim askannām-vatsatarīm ājanti*). The Ait. Br. does not go to say that the Gandharvas are fond of women and all that, while the Taitt. Sam. says further that the gods sang because women are fond of songs, and that thereby Speech (who had taken the form of a woman) came back to them leaving the Gandharvas. This could be amazing in the case of a one year old woman (!=child), or a one-year-old cow, unless we understand that in both these cases of camouflage (at the ritual) there lurked the youthful reality of the Speech represented by a woman. The Śat. Br. (of the White Yajurveda) generally follows the Taitt. Sam. (Black Yajurveda); it does not mix the images and, like the Ait. Br., maintains that Vāk (Speech) was a woman (*yoṣā*) and that the gods enticed her from the Gandharvas by playing on lute, singing and dancing. "Because women are, even this day, given to worthless things" (cf. Śat. Br. III.2.4.2-6; *mogha-saṁhitāḥ*). And Speech returned. This is right; for, a young woman could be enticed by such things.

It will be, thus, clear, that Speech was equated with Mahānagnī in the earliest symbolization, at the purchase of *soma*; and the woman, or Mahānagnī (though of restricted mention, as noted above) was a young woman. This is to be taken as the first stage of the ritual. The woman could not have been a family-woman. At a later period when a *vatsatarī* or the one-year-old cow was substituted, the former ritual became a myth, with the result that the actual woman was mythicised. However, to keep the memory of the earlier ritual in the revised rite, when the cow was introduced, the earlier ritual-woman got assimilated in the tradition through memory and mention. The process is not new, and to use an expression from the Vedic ritual context, it was for continuity (*santatyai*).[14] In the study of myths, such a process is said to give rise to 'charters'.[15] We could say that the earlier ritual wherein a woman figured became a charter and was joined to the new practice of the employment of a cow. As in the case of the *puṁśćalī*, in the case of the Mahānagnī also Speech is released with a verse in the Anuṣṭubh metre after Soma has been actually, and finally, purchased. During the purchase (and during the arguments with the Soma-seller) Speech is supposed to be with the Gandharvas. There is a slight difference. In the Mahānagnī account and ritual a verse from the Ṛgveda (X.176.3) is prescribed (Ait. Br. *loc.cit.*), while at the release of Speech at the Ten-day sacrifice the Kau. Br. prescribes a secular verse (as noted above) with the remark that Anuṣṭubh and the Virāj are similar metres. Actually this verse shows the structure of the Anuṣṭubh in three feet, while the fourth foot has more than eight syllables, which could be even ten with slight modifications:

puṁśćaliyā ayanam me asti.[16]

At an earlier place, in the context of the carrying of the fire and Soma (Kau.Br.IX.1) it is stated, that the gods were about to consecrate for sacrifice and resorted to Speech. The expression is to be noted, as it indicates the status of Speech. As the gods resort to her she is to be supposed as being intimate to them, and is divine. They make her sit close to them (*vācam upa-āsādayanta*) and say to her, "You go about much and variedly" (*bahu tvam uccāvacam nigacchasi*), which would also mean "You are of much and varied 'experience' (cf. *nigacchasi*);[17] but,we are truthful and have restraint (*satyamayā u damamayāḥ*)." The contrast is obvious. It is between free behaviour and control. This would show that Speech was close to the gods and, hence, divine; but, she was also unrestricted in approach to others. This was the belief about Speech among the Vedic Aryans, which is noted even later as we shall presently see. The expression *vācam upa-ā-sādayanta* (indicating close intimacy) compares well with *vācam ā-sīdāma* noted earlier above. These expressions go well with the *puṁśćalī* or the Mahānagnī aspect of Speech. This also hints at the twofold aspect and importance of the prostitute for the Vedic people. We might compare Urvaśī and Uṣas in the Ṛgveda, though the terms *puṁścalī* and Mahānagnī are not used for them. But, for that matter, these terms never occur in the Ṛgveda, as we have noted.

It will be proper to examine the Sarasvatī aspect of Speech, which is popular in the post-Vedic literature. The identification of Sarasvatī with Speech had already started in the later Vedic period. It is evident not only from the expression "Speech, indeed, is Sarasvatī" (*vag vai sarasvatī*) occurring at many places (cf. Ait. Br. VI.7=27.4; Kau. Br. V.7.; XII.8; XIV.4; Śat Br. III.9.1.7 and other places and texts), but also from the fact that Speech is prescribed to be released, after a span of silence, with an offering to Sarasvatī desiring to be favoured by Speech (cf. Taitt. Sam. III. 1.10.1 for example).[18] In the Purāṇas Speech appears as Sarasvatī; but, in her aspect of the goddess Vāgīśvarī an interesting detail obtains. She is said to have been censured by Brahmā as *puṁścalī*, when she asked him for sexual favour. She is also called Bhāratī, the presiding deity of all lores, holding the lute in one hand and a book in another. Saying to her that he has now become old, Brahmā asks, "What desire do I have for the prostitutes?" (*kā ratiḥ puṁścalīṣu me,* cf. Brahmavaivarta P. Śrīkṛṣṇa-janma-khaṇḍa 35. 12. 22). She is said to be blooming with youth and being in constant youth (Liṅga P.p.25, 68). Though Speech is not called *puṁścalī* in the Ṛgveda, this trait of hers is indicated when she is said to expose her body before any learned person as does a wife before her husband (X.71.4). The contrast is clear. The wife does so only before her husband. Speech does so before any man, who acquires her; because she is an unrestricted 'mover' (*calī*) among men (*puṁ*): she is *puṁścalī*.

NOTES

1. (Mrs.) Sindhu S. Dange, has dealt with this topic in her book, *Aspects of Speech in Vedic Ritual*.
2. *Rigveda Brahmanas* (HOS, Vol. 25, London, 1920), Delhi,

1981 (1971), p.508, n. 5. He feels that the verse is a relic of old Indian Nīti literature and that the verse is in "very free Anuṣṭubh form". The *Vedic Concordance* does not record it.

3. Keith feels that the (variant) reading *krūravāheva* (which he translates as "bearer of a dread thing") is correct "though the comm. has *krūraraveva*". But he does not explain how Speech is "bearer of a dread thing". The reading *krūraraveva* is from the Ānandāśrama ed., though Keith does not seem to have noticed it.
4. The reading is *nedvācamāsīdama*. Keith, "Let us not consort with speech".
5. Keith translates,"... are the same metre". The reading is *samānam vā-etacchando yad virāḍ vā-anuṣṭup ca*. Similarity would allow a difference of one or two syllables. Sameness would not.
6. Keith translates the first foot as, "Her I touch not as being a śūdrā; also Aufrecht (ZDMG xxxvi, 75, 76)," neither touch nor deal with any (noisy; his German, 'larmenden'), Śūdrā-wife". The reading at the Anand. Ed. is *tadenānvāheva*, which I follow as real, and not *tadenān-na vāheva*, which these scholars appear to read (or have before them from another source).
7. *Vāhā-iva* goes well with *pra-tad-ohuṣī krūra-ravā-iva bhavati* just before; the variant *krūra-vāhā-iva* after *ohuṣī* and before *vāheva* (*vāhā-iva*) in the verse (but taken as a prose passage by Linder and Aufrecht) is tautologous-*vāhā*, *ohuṣī*, *vāhā* all signifying the same thing.
8. Cf. Atharvaveda XV.2.5ff; Vāj. Sam.30.22; Taitt. Br.III. 4.1; Jai. Br.II. 405; RV, dancing VIII. 20.22; 68.7; X.72.6; I.92.4 etc.
9. Though in certain cases the wife of the sacrificer is made to repeat what is recited by the priest, it does not amount to independent allowance; cf. at the Varuṇapraghāsāḥ, for ex., *vācayati*.
10. See Dange, *Vedic Concept of 'Field' and the Divine Fructification*, Bombay, 1971, pp.68-82. The word *Mahānagnī* has variants: *mahānagnī* (Ait. Br. I.27=5.1) and *mahānaghnī* (AV XX.136.5 etc.); but they are taken as the same; also AV XIV.1.36.
11. RV I.71.5;X 61.5-7; esp. later versions Ai.Br.III.33; *rohitam bhūtām* and Taitt. Sam. at the context here.

12. Taitt. Sam. VI.1.6.7 *aruṇayā piṅgākṣyā.*
13. A.B. Keith, Taittirīya Sam. HOS, Indian reprint, Delhi, 1967, p.433, translates, "a woman one-year-old". This is rather curious, esp. without any comment.
14. For this trait see, "The Principle of Continuity in the Vedic Ritual", ch. 30, *infra*.
15. A term proposed by Bronislaw Malinowski, *Myth in Primitive Psychology*, reprint, in *Magic, Science and Religion*, Garden City, New York, 1959 (1948), p.32, n.; also G.S. Kirk, *The Nature of Greek Myths*, Penguin, Harmondsworth, 1976 (1974),p.59; also Dange, *Purākathāñcā Artha, —— Vāda āṇi Vivecana* (Marathi), Continental Prakashan, Pune, 1994, p.45f; also, Dange, *Towards Understanding Hindu Myths,* Aryan Books International, New Delhi, 1996, ch.3.
16. Such a split is common; cf. RV I.33.15 *tugryāsu* (=*tugriyāsu*); I.162.9 *te api.*
17. For the meaning of *nigacchāt* with a sexual slant we may compare RV X.10.11 and 12 where a double-implication is suggested: Yamī to Yama (11d) *yan nirṛtir nigacchāt* (Sāyaṇa, *niyamena gacchāt*; and Yama to Yamī (12d): *pāpam āhur yaḥ svasāram nigacchāt* (Sāyaṇa, *niyamena upagacchati sambhuṅkte ityarthaḥ*). With this may be compared *nigama* indicating source of (and) knowledge. Cf. *Nir. athāpi nigamo bhavati*, or *ityapi nigamo bhavati* (II.4); also *nighaṇṭavaḥ kasmāt? nigamā ime bhavanti chandobhyaḥ samāhṛtya samāhṛtya samāmnātāḥ.*
18. Taitt. Sam. III.1.10.1 *juṣṭo vācā bhūyasām juṣṭo vācaspataye devī vāk svāhā sarasvatyai*; the same at Mait. Sam.I.3.1; Gopatha Br. II.1.17.

Chapter 30

THE PRINCIPLE OF CONTINUITY IN VEDIC RITUAL

Though Vedic sacrifices are divided into various types, such as Agnihotṛa, Darśapūrṇa-māsa (i.e. the New-moon and the Full-moon rites), Cāturmāsyas (i.e. the 'four-monthly' rites) etc., this division is only for convenience rather than completion of every division. It will be noticed, that the idea is that of a continuous chain (*santati*); and though there is a difference between the *iṣṭi* and the *Yāga*, the latter indicating the Soma-sacrifice, the ritual-philosophers appear to stress that the main *iṣṭi* (i.e. the *prakṛti*), the Darśapūrṇa-māsa, and its *vikṛti*-s, the Cāturmāsya rites, are on par with the Soma-sacrifice. It will be interesting to take some examples to see how this principle of continuity worked.

In the context of the establishment of the sacrificial fires, boiled rice for four priests (*cātuṣprāśya*) is cooked in the afternoon on the day previous to that of the actual establishment. The fire for this is produced by attrition, or a portion of fire from the household fire (*gṛhya* or *aupāsana*) of the sacrificer is taken out, to the west of the place meant for the Gārhapatya. This fire is called *brahmaudanika*. After the rice for the *brāhmaṇa*-s is cooked, and after it is served to them, a portion of the fire is kept to be used as the Dakṣiṇa fire (also called Anvāhāryapacana). According to another practice, the fire is extinguished. But, in that case, the apparatus for kindling the fire (the two *araṇī*-s and the churning rod) are heated on the *brahmaudanika* fire,[1] with two verses indicating that the *brahmaudanika* fire has now entered the *araṇī*-s. Then the fire is extinguished. A new fire is produced from those *araṇī*-s, the next morning. The belief is that the fire, that had entered the *araṇī*-s, would come out again at attrition. This procedure is said to be for the continuity of the fire (cf. Taitt.Br.I.1.9.10 *sāgneḥ santatiḥ*). In the first practice, where the fire was not extinguished but was kept to be made into Anvāhāryapacana, the idea of the same old *gṛhya* fire being present, and now extended to this new status, is clear. In the second practice, the idea of *santati* is seen in the heat being transferred to the fire-kindling apparatus. Where the fire remains the same, as in Agnihotra, the concept of *santati* is seen in the clear blaze of the fire. Thus, in the context of the daily Agnihotra rite, the fire has to be cleaned by ashes being brushed, and faggots are offered into it so that it could flare up prior to the daily offering is poured into it. It is ordained, that the offering must be continuous; hence, daily; for that, indeed, is the *santati* of the Agnihotra (cf. Kau. *Br.* VII.3 *eṣā'gnihotrasya santatiḥ*). Actually, the daily Agnihotra offerings are cast into the fire daily in the morning and in the evening; and they are closely associated with the rise and setting of the sun.[2] Those offerings are for the continuation of the lights-the sun and the fire. Hence, they are so closely associated with sun-rise and sunset.

In the actual rite of *agnyādhāna* (establishment of the three fires), the same fire, which was taken up in the *araṇī*-s is produced freshly by attrition; and it is to be extended and deposited in all the three fire-places *viz.* the Gārhapatya, Dakṣiṇa and Āhavanīya. This is done by carrying a portion of the fire to the two other places after it is established in the Gārhapatya fire-place.[3] The principle of continuity (*santati*) is also seen when, at the two middle phases (*parvan*) of the Cāturmāsya rites (namely Varuṇapraghāsa and Sākamedha only, not in the first, i.e. Vaiśvadeva and the later added Śunāsīrīya) fire from the Āhavanīya (or Gārhapatya according to a variant practice) is carried to the new altars-called *uttaravedi* (as it is raised and also as it is to the north of the other new altar) and the *dakṣiṇavedi* (which is to its south and is hence so called). Both these altars are structured to the east of the original Āhavanīya. The belief is that the fire in the new altars is the same as the original one in the Āhavanīya[4] or the Gārhapatya, which, in its turn, is the same old one, the *gṛhya* or the *aupāsana* fire of the sacrificer kept ablaze in his house constantly and continuously. An interesting example of this principle of *santati* is seen in the *sānnāyya*. There has been variation in opinion as to who should offer the *sānnāyya*-only a sacrificer who has previously performed a Soma-sacrifice, or any body who is regularly performing the New-moon and Full-moon sacrifices. That point is not important here. What is important is the belief, that the *sānnāyya* offering is a bridge between the Darśapūrṇamāsa and the Soma-sacrifice. The *sānnāyya* is a mixture of curds prepared from milk of the cows milked on the previous day, afternoon, and fresh heated milk on the day of the actual New-moon sacrifice. As these two, i.e. the curd and milk, are brought together (*sam* + *naya* fr. √*nī*, to carry), the offering-mixture is called *sānnāyya* (as it is prepared by *sam-naya* = *sānnāyya*). Now the milk of the previous day is curdled (with a drop of curds) with a *mantra* which says that the curdling agent is Soma. The *sānnāyya* actually is the offering at the Darśapūrṇamāsa; but the *mantra* (*somena ā tanacmi*)[5] indicates that the *sānnāyya* connects this *iṣṭi* (i.e. Darśapūrṇamāsa) with the Soma-sacrifice. There is noted an effort to further identify the two (the *iṣṭi* and the *yāga*). It is said, that the offering of the first day in each case (New-moon and Full-moon days) is like constructing the *mahāvedi* (that is a special and great altar at the Soma-sacrifice); the warding off of the calves from the cows, to milk them, is equal to building the *sadas* (the fire-chamber at the *mahāvedi*, in its western portion where the *dhiṣṇya* fire-places are structured) and with the structuring of the *havirdhāna-maṇḍapa* (in the mid-portion of the *mahāvedi* at the Soma-sacrifice, where two small carts and the utensils for the juice of Soma are kept; Taitt. Sam. III.2.5.5ff) etc. Likewise the final offering at the Darśapūrṇamāsa, called *sviṣṭakṛt* (which is offered to Agni *sviṣṭakṛt* = *su-iṣṭakṛt,* i.e. one who fulfils the desire) is likened to the third and the last offering of Soma on the day of pressing the shoots of Soma (cf. Śat. Br. I.7.2.16 *tṛtīyasavanam vai sviṣṭakṛt*).

Now, we take an example from the Soma-sacrifice itself. This is of the rites called *prāyaṇīya* and *udayanīya*. The *prāyaṇīya* is the opening rite (*iṣṭi*) of the Soma-sacrifice, after the day of the consecration (*dīkṣā*) of the sacrificer. At the conclusion of the whole sacrifice there is the *udayanīya* rite. These two rites are separated by various intermediary rites and about five days. However, to mark their mutual continuation (*santati*) the remainder (*niṣkāsa*) in the utensil in which the offering at the *prāyaṇīya* was prepared is mixed with the offerings for the *udayanīya*, thus connecting both, and, sort of, enclosing all intermediary rites in between these two-the 'opening' and the 'concluding' rites. (Ait. Br. I.11=2.5).[6]

These are some examples to show how *santati* was sought to be formulated. The same principle is seen where care is taken to keep the unity and continuity of the sacrifice and the persons participating in it. We take the example of the carrying of the *prāśitra* at the Darśapūrṇamāsa sacrifice. In concept, *prāśitra* was the portion of the flesh of Prajāpati whom Rudra shot with an arrow (as the former ran after his own daughter, according to a well known myth).[7] In ritual, it was a barley-sized portion of the *puroḍāśa* (like *iḍā*); and it was to be eaten by the Brahmā priest. Now, the position of the Brahmā priest is to the south of the Āhavanīaya fire, while the Adhvaryu priest sits to the north-west of the Āhavanīya, both being inside the precincts of the altar. The Adhvaryu has to carry the *prāśitra* to the Brahmā. According to one practice, probably older, the Adhvaryu got up, went to the east to the northern corner of the Āhavanīya, crossed along the east of the Āhavanīya to the south, turned to the west and reached the Brahmā priest. The Śat. Br. (I.7.4.12ff) does not approve of this method. The reason is, obviously because the Adhvaryu has to go beyond the Āhavanīya which is the eastern boundary of the altar. Hence, he, actually, gets disconnected from the altar and the sacrifice. Here, the Śat.Br. does not mention this as the reason, though it is expected if we consider another example given below. The reason given, here, is that on this (eastern) side the cattle of the sacrificer are made to stand, facing west (i.e. facing the Āhavanīya); also, that the *prāśitra* belongs to Rudra; so, if the Adhvaryu were to go along the eastern side of the Āhavanīya, Rudra would harm the cattle! But, now, let us examine another rite. This is the Patnī-saṁyāja, forming part of the Darśapūrṇamāsa itself. In it the Adhvaryu has to carry the offering to the Gārhapatya altar, where the wife of the sacrificer is seated, to the south-west of the Gārhapatya. Two other priests (Āgnīdhra and Hotṛ) follow him going a bit separately. Now, according to one (older) practice the Adhvaryu (as in the older practice at the *prāśitra* mentioned above) has to go along the eastern side of the Āhavanīya, to the south, turn to the west, and reach the Gārhapatya (Śat.Br.I. 9.2.2). The Śat.Br. disapproves of it, giving the reason that, thereby he would be cut off from the sacrifice, as he would go out of the eastern precincts of the altar. The opinion of the Śat.Br. is, that he should pass along the inner (western) side of the Āhavanīya, come to the Gārhapatya altar, pass along its eastern side, to the south, turn to the west, where the wife of the sacrificer is seated, and reach the Gārhapatya. This way he is not separated from the sacrifice as he moves within the altar. This text, which has always stood for reformist and intellectually proper methods, also does not approve of the Adhvaryu going in between the Gārhapatya fire-altar and the wife; as that would, according to it, cut away the wife from the contact of that fire, which would be tantamount to excluding her from the sacrifice. As here, according to Śat.Br., continuity is in keeping contact with the fires—and within the limits of the altar—so should be the case at the *prāśitra* rite noted above. We could explain by saying that, if the priest goes along the east of the Āhavanīya, he would break the continuity between the cattle and the fire; cattle belong to Rudra; as such Rudra would harm him.

An interesting feature of this principle of continuity is the principle of inclusion. As is well known, the altar was believed to be the earth itself (Taitt. Sam.II.6.4.1; Śat.Br.I.2.5.7 etc.). So, what is outside the altar is what is beyond the earth. In other words, it is the other world—mid-region and heaven-conceptually. To include both these appears to be the idea in certain structures. The location of the sacrificial pole and the Havirdhāna pandal (the first at the Paśubandha, i.e. animal-sacrifice, and both at the Soma-sacrifice) may be examined from this angle. About the sacrificial pole (*yūpa*), it is said that it should be fixed half inside the altar (i.e. in the centre on the eastern boundary of the *mahāvedi* in the Soma-sacrifice), or of the altar at the *paśubandha*, to the east of the Āhavanīya. It is glossed, that if it is fixed inside the altar, the sacrificer would control (*only*) the heavenly world; if out, he would control (*only*) this world.[8] So, one should fix it at the juncture (i.e. half inside, half outside). So that he could control both these worlds (Taitt. Sam.VI.6.4.1.). The sacrificial pole, thus, connects (through the eastern boundary line) the two worlds (for the *havirdhāna-maṇḍapa,* Śat.Br.III.6.1.26). A variant of the practice of *santati* could be seen, in the context of the Cāturmāsya rites, where the new altars (one to the north of the other) are joined to the old usual altar (at the Darśapūrṇamāsa) by a line, which is drawn from the old Āhavanīya to the northern hind corner (called *Śroṇi* = buttock) of the new southern altar or the new northern altar (Kat. Śr. S. V.4.9-10); the two new altars are also mutually connected (Āpastamba Śrauta-sūtra).[9] This practice is marked prominently in the later (Śrauta) literature; but the concept of continuity is clear.[10]

NOTES

1. P.V. Kane, *History of Dharmāśāstra*, Vol.II, 2nd Ed., Poona, 1974, p.992; also see Taittirīya Brāhmaṇa, I.2.1ff.
2. For the divergent views regarding when to offer-whether when the sun is yet to rise or set or when it has risen or set—see Kauṣitaki-Br. II.9; Aitareya Br. V. 29=25.4. Accordingly, the persons were termed *uditahomin* and *an-uditahomin*.
3. Variations are seen in the actual mode of carrying the fire. See Taitt. Br. I.1.4.3; see the modes mentioned by Iḍā; *ibid.*, I.1.4.3-7; cf. also Mait. Sam.I.6.14.
4. In this context see Śat. Br. XII.9.3.1-16 (the whole *adhyāya*), where, through a discussion between Bālhīka, the son of Pratipīya, and Sthapati, the son of Cakra, ultimately it is proved that, at the Sautrāmaṇī rite, the fire on the new southern altar is Āhavanīya, in addition to its being the Dakṣiṇa, as it was carried from the Āhavanīya. This was, obviously, through the principle of *santati*.
5. For *sānnāyya*, see Taittirīya Sam.II.5.5.1ff; Śat.Br. I.6.4.10. and Taitt.Sam.I.1.3.1 *somena tvā-ātanacmi-indrāya dadhi*; cf. Taitt.Br.III.2.3.10; Vāj. Sam. I.4, and Mahīdhara, *somena somavallī-rasena*; i.e. curd is equal to *soma* here.
6. Ai.Br. I. 11=2.5 *prāyaṇīyasya niṣkāsam ni dadhyād, tām udayanīyena-abhinirvaped, yajñasya santatyai, yajñasyā-vyavacchedāya.*
7. For the myth and discussion regarding it, see Dange, *Sexual Symbolism from the Vedic Ritual*, Delhi, 1979, pp.141-60; see also Ṛgveda I.71.5; X.61.5-7; Ait. Br.III.33=13.9; Śat. Br.I.7.4.1ff.
8. Here the altar is taken as the heavenly world, the outside being the earth. However, the general belief in the *vedi* being the earth is quite prominent and often expressed; cf. Śat.Br.I.2.5.7; III.7.2.1; Taitt. Sam.II.6.4.1;-3 etc.
9. P.V. Kane, *op.cit.*, p.1097.
10. Cf. the dragging of the pot of boiled milk from the fire, where it was placed for being boiled, in such a way that the ashes would mark a line, at the Agnihotra, Taitt.Br.II.1.3.5 *vartma karoti yajñasya santatyai*; also, the jar of the *prokṣaṇī* water is placed on the lines drawn by the *sphya* (wooden sword), *yajñasya santatyai*, Taitt.Br.III.2.9.4.

Chapter 31

HOTṚVŪRYA

The word *hotṛvūrya* occurs only twice in the Ṛgveda (RV) *viz.* at I.31.3 and at VI.70.4; and at both the places, there is the theme of the kindling and flaring of the sacrificial fire. Thus, it is said,

> Agni, show yourself to Mātariśvan (and) Vivasvant first of all with (your) desire for an auspicious exploit. The twain-Heaven and Earth (females)-have shaken (with joy) at the *hotṛvūrya*; you have offered to the great gods, O Vasu! (I.31.3):
>
> (*tvām agne prathamo mātariśvane*
> *āvir bhava sukratūyā vivasvate*
> *arejetām rodasī hotṛvūrye*
> *a'saghnorbhāram ayajo maho vaso*)

This would show that the activities at the *hotṛvūrya* concern the kindling, or flaring up of the fire. The time is indicated to be the morning, as there is mention of Vivasvant (Āditya); and the flaring up here is likened to the first ever expression of the fire, as is clear from the mention of Mātariśvan, who is famous as the bringer of the fire from heaven.[1] At his flare-up the divine females (Heaven-Earth) shake with joy. The next activity is the carrying of the offering to the gods, which is also the worship of the gods, and the carrying of the 'load' (*bhāram*) of offerings:

> Heaven and Earth are covered with *ghṛta*; they are rich in *ghṛta*; increasing with *ghṛta*. Wide, spread up

(as they are), they are (as if) the two priests at the *hotṛvūrya*. Them do the singers (*viprāḥ*) praise for well being at the sacrifice (VI.70.4.):

(ghṛtena dyāvāpṛthivī abhīvṛte
ghṛtaśriyā ghṛtapṛcā ghṛtāvṛdhā
ūrvī pṛthvī hotṛvūrye purohite
te id viprā īḷate sumnam iṣṭaye)

Some additional points that we get here are: Though this is a praise of Heaven and Earth, they are likened to two priests which mark the *hotṛvūrya*. The symbolic word *ghṛta* stands for the nourishing fluid (may be, dewdrops) that forms in between these two, suggesting the early morning time.

Taken together, these two references indicate that *hotṛvūrya* is the occasion of the first flaring up of the fire at the daybreak, may be, as soon as the ashes are brushed off from the fire, and it is prepared for the first offering (of clarified butter) of the day. But, what exactly was *hotṛvūrya*? There is no help from the Ṛgveda; and the word does not occur later as would throw light on its exact nature. Sāyaṇa (at the first place, I.31.3) states that *hotṛvūrya* is "sacrifice" (*hotrā vriyate iti hotṛvūryo yajñaḥ*). This actually confuses his earlier explanation, in the same context just above in his comments on the same verse, that *hotṛvūrya* is the "act of selecting the Hotṛ priest" (hotṛ*varaṇayukte karmaṇi*). Thus, once he says, that hot*ṛvūrya* is a *karma* (being an *aṅga*, part) of a sacrifice; and, in the same breath, that it is whole "sacrifice". This would show that the commentator (Sāyaṇa, or a *brāhmaṇa* in his school) does not exactly know what hot*ṛvūrya* is, though he is beating about the safe bush of the sacrifice! At the other place (RV VI.70.4) he renders the word simply as "*yajñe*".

Geldner renders the word as "Hotṛ-selection" (Hotṛ-wahl); and in the note, he explains that Heaven and Earth shake with joy at the prospect of getting their share of the offering through the Hotṛ-selection of Agni. He, thus, suggests, that *hotṛvūrya* is the selection of Agni as the Hotṛ (see his note on I.31.3, *Der Rigveda*, Harward Uni. Press, 1978 [1951] vol.I, p.34). At the other place (VI.70.4) he renders the word as "Hotṛwahl" (selection of the Hotṛ), without giving any further explanation.

That Agni is seen, and is praised, as the Hotṛ is clear at various places at RV.[2] However, *hotṛvūrya* has to be taken as a regular rite in a sacrificial set-up (and not as sacrifice, as such). The picture that we get from the two passages from RV, noted above, is that Agni is himself the Hotṛ here, as elsewhere, as he invokes (*hve*) the gods, and also helps offer to (*hu*) them. As he has this double function, his selection as Hotṛ is the first step. This is clear also from later ritual texts, where the human Hotṛ had his unique importance. Though RV does not have any further suggestion, or indication, to the method of selecting the Hotṛ, there is no doubt that it knew a regular rite to that effect. This is clear if we compare the later ritual, where the concept is present, though the word *hotṛvūrya* is absent. The selection is termed, there, '*pravara*' (also hotṛ-*pravara*, *hotṛ-pravaraṇa*), starting with the selection of Agni, and coming to the selection of the human priest of that name. Such expressions as *agnir devānām hotā tam agre pravṛṇīte* etc. (cf. Taitt. Sam. II.5.9.5; Śat. Br.I.5.1.5), and further, *atha ārṣeyam pravṛṇīte*, and *mānuṣam hotāram pravṛṇīte* (Śat. Br. *loc.cit.* 9;13) make the point clear. It is to be noted, that the word *vūrya*, like *varaṇa (pravara)* is from the root √*vṛ*, "to select" (see Sāyaṇa on RV I.31.3).[3]

An interesting detail is to be noted in this context. In the ritual at the selection of the Hotṛ priest, as it is seen in the later Saṁhitās, and Brāhmaṇas, three priests figure, in addition to the Hotṛ who is to be selected: The Adhvaryu, Āgnīdhra and the Brahmā. Prior to the selection of the Hotṛ, there is already the selection of the Brahmā. The Adhvaryu is the priest for the sacrificer. With his help the sacrificer selects the Brahmā priest; and then the Hotṛ. There is another priest, the Āgnīdhra, in the later rite of *pravara* (selection, and also reciting the names of the *ṛṣi*-s in the line of the Hotṛ, to indicate his capability). After the Brahmā priest consents, he advises the Āgnīdhra to go ahead with the selection. Thus, it is clear, that it is the Adhvaryu who selects the Hotṛ. Hence, Sāyaṇa's comment, *hotrā vriyate iti hotṛvūryo yajñaḥ*, is beside the actual practical. While in the later practice, there are three priests, leaving the Hotṛ to be selected yet, in the passage from RV (VI.70.4) we have mention of two priests *(purohite)*, who are said to be seen in the form of Heaven and Earth. Now, RV clearly mentions the priests Brahmā and the Adhvaryu, while for the Āgnīdhra the reference is not quite clear (II.36.4), where Agni is invoked to drink *soma* from the *āgnīdhra* (*āgnīdhrāt*), which Sāyaṇa renders as *"āgnīdhra-yāgāt"* (which has the variant as *āgnīdhra-yāgāt*). Geldner renders the word *āgnīdhrāt* as "from the beaker of the Āgnīdhra". The hymn (II.36) starts with the invocation of Agni to drink from the Hotra *(hotrāt)*, then *Potra (potrāt)* and at these places also Sāyaṇa renders the words as "from the *yāga* of ...". There should be no difficulty in believing that RV knew the Āgnīdhra priest (there is no other mention of him in RV). But, who actually figured at the *hotṛvūrya* is a dark point, though there should be no doubt regarding the presence of the Adhvaryu and the Brahmā; and, probably, the dual (in *purohite)* indicates them, the feminine gender (*purohite* in place of *purohitau*) notwithstanding; it is due to Heaven and Earth seen as females.[4] The expression is just a simile.

From what has been said above, it would be clear that *Hotṛvūrya* was the prototype of the later Hotṛ-*pravara*, where Agni is to be selected and offered to in his aspect of the divine Hotṛ, prior to the selection of human Hotṛ. In the later ritual the rite formed part of the Darśapūrṇamāsa sacrifice, while at the Ṛgveda there is no indication of any particular rite. However, the *hotṛvūrya* must have been a usual rite at the selection of the Hotṛ[5] for all family sacrifices, or the Hotṛ for the family as such.

NOTES

1. Cf. RV III.5.10 and 2.13; Mātariśvan is also said to be the messenger of Vivasvant, VI.8.4 etc.
2. RV I.1.1 *purohitam...hotāram*; I.13.4 *hotā manurhitaḥ* etc.
3. √*vr.* + *kyap* (Pāṇ.III.1.109); then, *ud oṣṭhyapūrvasya*; the accent is by *kṛd-uttara-prakṛtisvaratvam*.cf *vurīta* at RV V.50.1. *marto vurīta sakhyam* (= Vāj. Sam. XI.67); also VI.14.1.
4. We have noted, how Heaven and Earth are associated with the *Hotṛvūrya* at RV. This detail obtains also at the *hotṛ-pravara* as it occurs in later texts. Thus, Agni, being selected as the Hotṛ, is invoked to realize the *hotram* and also *dūtyam*; that the Heaven and Earth should protect him in this task; that he also should protect Heaven and Earth (Vāj.Sam.II.9 *agne ver hotram ver dūtyam, avatam tyā dyāvāpṛthivī ava tvām dyāvāpṛthivī)*. The mention of Heaven and Earth as females, in this context, goes well with Agni being called *dvimātā hotā* (RV III.55.7).
5. It may be, incidentally, noted that the office of the Hotṛ was very important and called for special care, as he had to know the suitable *mantra*-s and proper offerings. He was to guide other priests. A lively discussion appears, in this regard, at Ait. Br. (I.3).

Chapter 32

ANTARVEDI-BAHIRVEDI

The expression *ardham antarvedi ardham bahirvedi* occurs in the context of the fixing of the sacrificial pole and also in that of the Āgnīdhra shed in the Vedic ritual texts as noted earlier. We shall refer to this point further in more detail; but, it is to be noted, that, though the expression as such is seen in the context of the sacrificial pole and the said shed, the concept is not restricted to them. The altar, for the Vedic ritualists, was the most sacred place on the earth; and it was also, symbolically, seen as the whole earth.[1] It was termed "region of the virtuous" *(sukṛtasya loka)* and "womb of the Universal Order" *(ṛtasya yoni)*.[2] The usual altar at the Darśapūrṇamāsa *vihāra* (called also *Prācīnavaṁśa*) and the Mahāvedi at the Soma-sacrifice (or the other at the Paśubandha) were bounded by limits; and the main fires were within these limits. Yet, outside the limit there were two important spots, which were conceptually connected with the altar. One of these spots was the *utkara*[3] (the place where used up things in the sacrifice were to be dumped), which was seen in both the types of sacrifices *viz.* the *iṣṭi* (of Darśapūrṇamāsa) and the Soma-sacrifice (the main, and the norm, being the Agniṣṭoma). The other one, the *cātvāla* was to be structured only at the Soma-sacrifice and at the Paśubandha, which were both animal sacrifices and termed *yāga*. The *utkara* was to be made slightly outside the northern boundary of the usual altar and also of the Mahāvedi, at about two steps from it. The earth dug-up and dust from the place where the altar was situated, were deposited on the spot for the *utkara*; hence, it was supposed to be the altar, conceptually. Hence, though outside the northern boundary of the altar, it was believed to be 'within' it. The same was the case with the *cātvāla*. It was structured to the east of the *utkara*, a bit away, the distance being enough for a person to pass in between it and the *utkara*. Through this place in between the *utkara* and the *cātvāla* in the animal sacrifices (i.e. Soma and the Paśubandha), the sacrificer or the priests would pass. This passage was termed *'tīrtha'*. The same was the case at the *iṣṭi* types of sacrifices, noted above; but here the passage was in between the *utkara* and the jar of waters called Praṇītā, which was deposited to the north of the Āhavanīya fire (as the *cātvāla* was absent).

As the *utkara* was closely associated with the altar *(vedi)*, being formed from the dug-up earth from the altar and also as the dust swept from the altar was deposited in it, the *cātvāla* was also, verily, the satellite of the altar; for, the earth dug from the pit, to be called *cātvāla*, was deposited on the *uttara-vedi* ('raised up altar') on the main altar; thus, the *cātvāla* provided the earth for raising the *uttravedi* in the animal sacrifice, or the Mahāvedi in the Soma-sacrifice. Hence, though outside the precincts of the altar, the *cātvāla* was, conceptually, within it. This is also clear from the fact that the *tīrtha*-passage was in between the *utkara* and the *cātvāla* in these sacrifices. The *cātvāla* had another importance at the Soma-sacrifice. The waters called Vasatīvarī, collected on the previous day in the afternoon, and those collected on the morning of the day of pressing, and called Ekadhanā, were to be mixed; and this was done at the *cātvāla*-actually by holding the cups above the *cātvāla* (Śat. Br.III. 9.3.29). It was also believed that the *cātvāla* was the place whence the gods return to heaven after attending the sacrifice (*ib.,* 30). It was, hence, considered as the divine station for the path to heaven (*svargyam panthānam*) on the plane of the sacrifice. Likewise, the *utkara* was seen as the exterior boundary of the altar, beyond the northern boundary; and it marked the farthest limit of the altar, out of it. The pounding of the grain to prepare the offerings (such as *puroḍāśa*) from it, was done near the *utkara,* to its west. This means, it was done out of the altar, yet it was conceptually done within the broader limit of the altar. That, like the *cātvāla,* the *utkara* indicated the extended limit of the altar is clear when Agni is said to block the Asuras as they were fleeing to the north. He said that he would go to the north of the altar, beyond the usual boundary for it. The indication is that he would check them at the *utkara.*[4] Thus both the *cātvāla* and the *utkara* were, conceptually, *antarvedi* though actually and visibly they were *bahirvedi.*

The position of the *cātvāla* and the *utkara* being both *antarvedi* and *bahirvedi* (if we may say so, following the expressions in other contexts) is not an isolated one. This is in line with the belief expressly stated in the case of the sacrificial pole and the Āgnīdhra fire-shed. The Saṁhitā and the Brāhmaṇa texts are not uniform in stating the position of these two, the expression being: *ardham antarvedi minoti ardham bahirvedi,* or the like. In some texts this direction occurs only in the case of the sacrificial pole (cf. Taitt. Sam.VI.7.4.4. for the sacrificial pole), while in others it occurs in the case of the Āgnīdhra shed (Śat. Br. III. 6.1.26), while in yet others it occurs for both (Mait. Sam. III. 8.9 for the Āgnīdhra; and III. 9.4 for the pole). For the Mārjālīya fire-shed which is on the southern boundary, there is no such mention in the texts noted above; and it could be hardly found in other older texts also. It is structured on the southern boundary; and, according to the tradition, it has to be, like the Āgnīdhra shed, half inside the altar and half outside. The Śat. Br. (*loc.cit.*) does not strictly prescribe the norm of half-inside-half-outside suggesting that the Āgnīdhra may be more than half outside and less inside– or it may be wholly inside the altar.[5] It is implied that the same may be for Mārjālīya shed. The Mait. Sam. (*loc.cit.*) explains that the shed should be half inside and half outside, as it symbolizes the mid-region; and the mid-region *(antarikṣa)* is half with heaven and half of it is with the earth.[6] Going by this explanation we may understand that the Āgnīdhra shed (and also the Mārjālīya) is the connecting spot for heaven and earth. Apart from variation in the identification of the altar some times with heaven, or some time with the earth, the fact remains that the boundaries of the altar were believed to demarkate the ritual-world from the common world. The belief is expressed by the Taitt. Sam. (VI.6.4.1) in the context of the 'unit of eleven poles' in the animal sacrifice (cf. *yupaikādaśinī).* It says, that, if the poles are fixed inside the altar, the sacrificer conquers (only) the heavenly world. If they are fixed outside of the altar, he would conquer (only) the region of the humans. Hence, it says, they should be fixed at the joint of the precincts of the altar *(vedyantasya sandhau).* The 'joint' is, obviously, the boundary—in the case of the sacrificial pole it is the eastern boundary of the altar. The Mait. Sam. (III.9.4) does not speak in terms of the two worlds etc., when it prescribes that the sacrificial pole be fixed half inside the altar and half outside. It explains, that if it is fixed wholly inside it may burn the sacrificer; and if it is fixed wholly out of the altar, it would be unprotected (insecure, *an-avaruddhaḥ).* Both these alternatives are not convincing, if we mark the general trend of beliefs, which is that the position at the boundary is for the control of both the worlds, or spheres. The insistence of the pole or the shed being half inside and half outside is maintained throughout (barring the variation of the shed being wholly inside the altar, at the Śat.Br.). The reason for this becomes clear in the belief in the double aspect of the pole and the sheds. They are both outside and inside; for they are believed to join both these spheres at the sacrifice. In other words, they are, conceptually, similar to the *utkara* and the *cātvāla,* which are both inside and outside. In the wider sphere, the sacrifice itself is to be taken as both heavenly and earthly—or, in other words, the heavenly on the earth. Other aspects of the same belief are the *dehali* (threshold) in the later period, and the concept of the *dvibarhas*[7] in the Ṛgveda (I.71.6:IV.5.3 and other places), indicating control of both spheres. In the same category we may place the cow called *ubhayatomukhī*, of later period.[8] See Fig.III at the end.

NOTES

1. Śat. Br.I.2.5.7 *Yāvatī vedis tāvatī pṛthivī;* also III. 7.2.1.; Taitt. Sam. II.6.4.3 *etāvatī vai pṛthivī yāvatī vediḥ* etc.
2. Ṛgveda III.29.8 *sukṛtasya yonau*; 62.18;X.85.24 *ṛtasya yonau sukṛtasya loke.*
3. It was also called *go-sthāna;* and the Āgnīdhra priest sat near it.
4. Cf. J. Eggeling, Tr. of Śat. Br., SBE, vol.12, p.25 and p.54, n.2.
5. This laxity might have marked even the fixation of the *yūpa*; see Mait. *Sam.* referred to further. 'half' did not exactly mean half; cf. Jaimini III. 7.13-14.
6. Mait. Sam. III.8.9 *ardham āgnīdhrasya-antarvedi minoti-ardham bahirvedi, ardham hyantarikṣasyā-sminlloke-ardham amuṣmin*; and at III. 9.1 *gārhapatyenāmum (imam ?) lokam āgnīdhreṇa-antarikṣam-āhavanīyena-amum lokam.*
7. See, "Dvibarhas", ch.17 supra;
8. Cf. Yājñavalkya Smṛti I. 206-7, which is cited in Garuḍa Purāṇa I. 98.9 and Skanda P. V.3.51.56. The cow is termed *ubhayatomukhī* when in the act of delivery, her calf's face is seen out. So, she faces one quarter while the calf faces the opposite. In this position she was believed to be most auspicious.

Chapter 33

HAVIRDHĀNA-MAṆḌAPA AND THE TEMPLE

In the Mahāvedi at the Agniṣṭoma sacrifice, among other structures, the Havirdhāna shed is an important structure. It holds the two small carts that hold the shoots of Soma, and are hence themselves called *havirdhāna-śakaṭe* (dual). These carts with shafts pointing to the east, are placed on two sides of the middle line (called *pṛṣṭhyā*) that divides the Mahāvedi east-west. The cart to the south is larger than the one to the north. The Havirdhāna-*maṇḍapa* is situated to the south of the Āgnīdhra fireplace and to the west of the Āhavanīya. It is higher in the east than the west, answering the concept that also underlies the Prācīna-vaṁśa which is the chamber for the fires at the Darśapūrṇamāsa sacrifice, in line with the set symbolism of facing the east (cf. Ṛgveda X. 101.2 *prāñcam yajñam nayata sakhāyaḥ*). It has two doors one to the east and the other to the west. This is the general plan of the *maṇḍapa*. The *maṇḍapa* is structured, generally, on six posts to the east and six to the west, having a bamboo connecting them on the east and the west and running south-north. From the front (eastern) part of the *maṇḍapa* a garland (or rope) of twisted grass is made to dangle.[1] This garland is called *rarāṭī* — or *rarāṭyā* (top, *lalāṭa*) of the *maṇḍapa*. It is also addressed as *viṣṇor rarāṭam asi,* or, *rarāṭyā* which makes it virtually the "brow" of the sacrifice.

It is interesting to note that, in spite of the general structure of the maṇḍapa (Havirdhāna-*maṇḍapa*), and its situation, in the Sūtra period, there are variations in the details associated with it in the earlier period. It is said that the carts in the *maṇḍapa* should be so placed that they are at three strides (*prakramā*) from the western side of the *uttaravedi*. However, this was not to be followed strictly. Thus, the Śat. Br. (III.5.3.19), which mentions the view about the three strides says that they may be placed wherever one may like *(nātra mātrāsti)*, but not very far. Though the carts are said to have Viṣṇu as their deity, through his identification with sacrifice, there is indication that they symbolised Heaven and Earth. This is clear if we compare the *mantra*-s used at the Ait Br. and the Yajurveda Brāhmaṇas. The Ait.Br. starts a discussion in the context of the carrying of the carts to their place in the shed,[2] posing a question: Why is the unit of three verses *(tṛc)* to Dyāvāpṛthivī to be recited when the Adhvaryu gives the order, "Recite after the *Havirdhāna* carts being carried"? The explanation is that the earth and heaven were the *havirdhāna* of the gods. They continue to be the *havirdhāna* even to-day, as whatever material for offering (*havis*) there be, stands in between them ! When the carts are placed in their proper place, the cover to complete the Havirdhāna shed is laid. This cover is called *chadis*.

There seems to be some variation (and confusion) regarding the *chadis*.[3] The Śat. Br. (III. 5.3.9) simply says, that when the carts are carried and placed at the proper place, a *chadis* is arranged over them (*tayoḥ sam avavṛttayoś chadir adhi nidadhāti)*; and, that, if there be no *chadis* available, a *bhitti* of the size of the *chadis* is to be tied *(chadiḥ-saṁmitām vā bhittim pratyānahyanti)*. After this is done, the *rarāṭyā* garland of sacred grass is to be tied in the front (to the *chadis* or the *bhitti*). Then, again, at the back, on two poles there is the *chadis* or *bhitti*, as mentioned above. Thus there would be two *chadis-es*, one in front and the other at the back. Though it is not quite clear, it appears that the *chadis* was a half-rounded (curved) cover, as is generally seen on a cart; and the *bhitti* was a plain and flat cover. At any rate a difference is clearly sought to be made between the *chadis* and the *bhitti*.

Another detail that obtains at the Śat. Br. regarding the *chadis*, in the same context but a little further, is that there is one more *chadis*, which is in between these two that are at the two sides (front and back). Whether this third one was laid before the two mentioned above, or after them, is not clear. But, there is no doubt that it was higher than the two, as it is said to be the upper skull-bone of Viṣṇu,[4] and that it is much above (Śat.Br. *loc.cit.*23 *atha madhyamam chadir upaspṛṣya vācayati ...idam haivāsyaitac chīrṣakapālam yad idam upariṣṭād, adhīva hyetat),* while the other two are lower than this one. The verse that accompanies the touching of this one is that one for Viṣṇu which refers to the three strides, thus supporting the three *chadis*-es (the verse is RV I.154.2). It has to be noted, that for this *madhyama chadis* there is no alternative as is seen in the case of the two other *chadis*-es (the *bhitti*). This would mean, that the middle *chadis* had to be a half rounded one, and seen above the other two, giving dome-like appearance resembling also the head! This would show that the *chadis* or the *bhitti* (the former being prepared from reed-grass, and the latter from split-cane, as Eggeling suggests), along with the middle *chadis*, are to be part of the Havirdhāna shed. There is no clear indication whether the carts themselves were covered. It is also to be noted that the structure on six bamboos, as mentioned (obviously on the basis of information from the Śrauta-sūtras) also is not corroborated from the Śat. Br. From this text, the only surmise that can be had is that the straight six poles might be on the south and the north side. Well, the point is dark. Though there is no clear mention of the carts being themselves covered (with the *chadis*), the expression *tayoḥ samavavṛttayoḥ* is puzzling. It may mean, "after the two (carts) are turned round" (and are placed in their places), the *chadis* is placed as to cover the front portion of the Havirdhāna shed; and, it may also mean, that a *chadis* is placed over the carts themselves. In the first case, the expression *tayoḥ samavavṛttayoḥ* has to be understood as involving the locative absolute. But, the fact that to the front *chadis* the *rarāṭyā* (the frontal garland, mentioned above) is tied, would indicate that the frontal *chadis* is separate from the carts. Now, with the fact that there are in all three *chadis*-es, as noted above, the middle one appears to be over and above the carts, the carts themselves not having any *chadis* each. This middle *chadis* is a common cover for the carts, and is high above. This seems to be the position at the Śat.Br.

Now, let us examine the position at the Ait.Br.(I.29= 5.3). Here, in the context of the carts being led to the Mahāvedi at their place in the Havirdhāna shed, from the *sadas* (hall) which is structured in the western portion of the Mahāvedi, a question is raised and also answered. It is about the propriety of the three verses to Heaven and Earth, as we have already referred to above. As the carts (representing Heaven and Earth) are placed side by side, they are conceived as forming a couple, in the image of the sacrificer and his wife. The image of a couple in relation to the carts appears to be appropriate, if we remember that the cart on the south (right side) was to be larger (indicating the man) than the one to the north (woman), with the often spoken of position of the woman to the north[5] (=left). If we accept the explanation of Sāyaṇa it is clear that the two carts were each covered with a separate *chadis (dve chadiṣī dvayor havirdhānayor avasthāpya)* and, over and above these two, a third *chadis* was arranged (Ai. Br. *loc.cit. dvayor hyetat tyṛtīyam chadir adhi nidhīyate).*[6] A comparison between the passage from the Śat.Br. (with Sāyaña's comment) would show, that, in the original ritual the two carts were each covered with a *chadis;* and, when they were placed side by side (in the Havirdhāna shed?) a third one was arranged over them. This third one developed later (as is seen from the Śat.Br.) into the high middle, when two *chadis*-es were thus laid. The construction of the Havirdhāna shed started, with the *rarāṭyā* being arranged on the poles (cf. Sāyaṇa *sa rarāṭyām īkṣamāṇo'nu brūyāt, havirdhāna-maṇḍapasya cikīrṣitasya,* which would show that the shed is now to be structured). However, there is no indication of a regular *maṇḍapa* at the Ait.Br. which mentions only the *rarāṭyā,* the covering for the carts being only in the form of a *yajus* formula (*yajuṣā vā ete saṁpariśrayete yad havirdhāne)*, looking at the *rarāṭyā*. The *maṇḍapa* and the restriction not to eat or drink in it, appears to be a later development. As noted earlier from the Śat.Br. it appears that the carts were not covered separately with a *chadis* each, the "middle" *chadis* high up serving that purpose. The Śat.Br. does not have any alternative to the middle *chadis,* probably retaining the old custom, though it has alternatives to the front and the back *chadis*-es (in the *bhitti*) which had to be spacious being parts of the whole *maṇḍapa,* which is specifically mentioned (III 5.3.7 *ubhayatodvāram havirdhānam bhavati).*

It may be noted in this context, that the Taitt. Sam, indicates the "third" *chadis* to stand for the third *havirdhāna-śakaṭa,* though in actual practice, as attested from the Brāhmaṇa texts (and later the Śrautasūtra-s) only two carts are used. The Taitt. Sam. (VI.2.9.4), states: "Daṇḍa, the son of *Upara,*[7] broke the axle of the third *havirdhāna* (cart) with the Vaṣaṭ sound (uttered at the actual offering of the oblation). As to the third *chadis*, that is laid above the two *havirdhāna* carts, it is for supplying the third *havirdhāna* (cart); the Havirdhāna (shed) is indeed the head of the Sacrifice". The Maitrāyaṇī-Sam. (III.8.7) also refers to Daṇḍa, the son of Upara, in the context of the *havirdhāna;* but, there it seems to refer to the Havirdhāna shed, and not the "third cart", as we have it in the Taitt. Sam. For comparison it would be better to place side by side the expressions from the two texts:

> Taitt. *Sam*.: *daṇḍo vā auparas tṛtīyasya havirdhānasya vasaṭkāreṇākṣam acchinat; yat tṛtīyam chadir havirdhānayor udāhriyate tṛtīyasya havirdhānasyāvaruddhyai śiro vā eted yajñasya yad havirdhānam.*
>
> Mait.*Sam*.: This text refers to the Havirdhāna shed as the ritual-abode of the gods, who are to be offered

to on the next day, and indicates that the *havirdhāna* shed itself was destroyed by the Vaṣaṭkāra by Daṇḍa the son of Upara:

ya eva devā yajñiyās tān havirdhānā āsādayati, tān śvo bhūte 'bhi yajate; daṇḍo vā etad auparo vaṣaṭkāreṇa nirahan, yacchadir abhi ni dadhāti apihityā achidratvāya.

The difference in the two versions is clear; and it is important. In the version of the Mait. Sam., we have explanation for the cover (*chadis*) of the shed and it is indicated that the shed had an upper cover, originally. This is a situation slightly similar to the one indicated by the Ait.Br. The Taitt. Sam., on the other hand, speaks of the third *havirdhāna*, which is a cart whose axle is said to have been broken, and at once refers to the Havirdhāna shed. The problem is, what was the original practice?

On comparing the accounts from the two Saṁhitā texts, in respect of Daṇḍa and his utterance of Vaṣaṭ, it is difficult to assume that, originally, three *havirdhāna* carts actually figured in the ritual, unless it be taken as a speciality of the ancient Taittirīyas! Apart from the difference, both the Saṁhitās use the account to explain the *chadis* of the H*avirdhāna* shed, which must have been an innovation, the earlier structure being only a simple topless semi-enclosure. In all probability it was Daṇḍa himself who innovated the common *chadis* over the two carts, with the explanation, that otherwise the carts (and the gods, to refer to the Mait.Sam.) would be exposed! In later times, the explanation gave rise to the myth that the Havirdhāna was actually destroyed by the Vaṣaṭ of Daṇḍa. The Taitt. Sam., simply echoes the account to explain the curved cover (*chadis*) which looked like the cover of the common and popular cart, in addition to the *chadis*-es of the two carts, and fancied it to be a cart without an axle. It appears that, in the ancient ritual as it was originally followed, there was only one method as regards the *chadis*—either on the two carts or on the enclosure for them, which formed a unit of three. Sāyaṇa on the Ait. Br., would make us believe that, in addition to the *chadis* over and above them, the two carts themselves had a *chadis* each. But the Kauṣītaki-Br. (IX.3) indicates that the carts were uncovered, and that the *chadis* above both of them was the "third" being common for both (*dve havirdhāne bhavataḥ chadis tṛtīyam abhi nidadhati*), and that whatever is triple is auspicious (cf. *yat kiñ ca trividham).* Now, the position from the Ait.Br, as it is, without the gloss of Sāyaṇa, is not different: "On these two the third, the cover, is arranged" (*dvayor hyetat tṛtīyam chadir adhi nidhīyate).* This does not say that the two carts were endowed with the *chadis.* Sayaṇa's comment, that the two carts had *chadis* may be from the tradition which he followed. At the best, it comes nearer to the explanation at the Taittirīya Saṁhitā.

From what has been said above, it appears that the earliest structure (or an enclosure) was a simple one, without the cover at the top, above the two carts. A later one had a *chadis* (curved cover), which in all probability, was an innovation by Daṇḍa. Its eastern limit was the *rarāṭyā* on the poles, which, to give the idea of the forehead (*rarāṭa*) of Viṣṇu just below the head, was connected with the *chadis.* The Śat.Br. shows a later stage, when an additional *chadis* (or *bhitti*) was added each to the east and west of this central original *chadis*, which had no substitute in the form of the *bhitti*-like cover; for it was the head of Viṣṇu[8] and had to be visibly rounded in shape. As regards the carts themselves, they might be originally uncovered, except in the case of the Taittirīyas, who had a cover for each cart, and envisaged the top cover as being reminiscent of a "third" cart. The identification of the sacrifice with Viṣṇu has to be taken as a marked phase in the development of Vedic ritual tradition. Now, with the *rarāṭyā*, just before the 'head' of Viṣṇu in the form of the Havirdhāna shed, the structure has to be taken as the germ of the later temple structure in India, with the *toraṇa.*

A point regarding the deity of the Havirdhāna is worth

noting. While the Yajurveda texts (Saṁhitā and Brāhmaṇa) say that the deity of the Havirdhāna is Viṣṇu, and prescribe verses from the RV and the *yajus* formulas for Viṣṇu,[9] the Ait. Br. nowhere mentions Viṣṇu on this occasion. The same is the case with the Kau. Br. The Ṛgveda Brāhmaṇa texts prescribe a verse in praise of Savitṛ (RV V.81.2 *viśvā rūpāṇi prati muñcate kaviḥ)*-the Kau.Br., while the "third" *chadis* is being placed, and the Ait. Br. while looking at the *rarāṭyā*[10] with "Thou art the forehead of Viṣṇu" and not merely with a look at it. However, the touch is not mentioned in the Saṁhitā texts (Mait. and Taitt.). Apart from the difference in the details—the touch and look—as regards the *rarāṭyā* it may not be wrong to presume that Savitṛ, as the deity of the Havirdhāna, gave place to Viṣṇu.

We have indicated above the probability of the Vedic Havirdhāna *maṇḍapa* being the source of the later temple-structure of the Hindus. A further observation on this point would be in the fitness of things. As noted above, the Mait. Sam. says: "Those that are, indeed, sacrifice-worthy them does he seat in the Havirdhāna. On the next day, he offers to them through worship" (see quotation cited earlier). The practice of maintaining a *devālaya* or a *devakula* (shrine, or a temple) goes back to at least the fifth century B.C.[11] Yet the plan of the exact structure of a temple is not known at this period. According to one opinion, the structure of a Hindu temple is suggested from the *stūpa* which is structured on the relics of the Buddha.[12] In the period after the death of the Christ, through the expanse of the Puranic period, the *Prāsāda* (*devālaya*) of the god gets elaborate mention of its being the body of the god himself with the various parts of the structure, such as the *jaṅghā* (the part of the leg from the ankle to the knee), *aṅghri* (foot), *kaṭi* (waist), *nāsā* (nose; also called *śuka-nāsā* its shape being like the beak of a parrot), *kaṇṭha* (throat, neck) and others.[13] At this period another popular belief was that the god (*hari*) stands in the form of the *prāsāda* (cf. Agni P.61.26, *eka evā hariḥ sākṣāt prāsādatvena saṁ-sthitaḥ*). We have seen earlier, that the sacrificial pole (*yūpa*) was fixed in the centre of the eastern boundary line of the Mahavedi.[14] The Mahāvedi was sufficiently spacious, as it held in its centre the Havirdhāna-*maṇḍapa*; two sheds, one each to its northern and the southern boundary-lines, and also an assembly-hall (*sadas*) with six round fire-altars; in line with these six altars there was also a leafy branch of the Uduṁbara-tree (called *auduṁbarī*). Apart from the fact that the in-set Havirdhāna-*maṇḍapa* was believed to be Viṣṇu (and we have indicated that, in origin, it was dedicated to the sun-god Savitṛ, who came to be later identified with Viṣṇu), the bigger structure of the Mahāvedi is described as follows: "Sacrifice is the Man (the *Puruṣa*); the Āhavanīya fire in the *uttara* (raised) *vedi* (altar) is its mouth (because, the offerings are cast into it); the sacrificial pole *(yūpa)* is its head; the Āgnīdhrīya and the Mārjālīya sheds (which are on the northern and the southern boundary, respectively, are his arms; the *sadas* (with the six fire-places) is his stomach; and the (former) Āhavanīya and the Gārhapatya fire-altars (at the west of the Mahāvedi, in the shed called *Prācīnavaṁśa*, which is the common scheme for the usual three fireplaces) are his legs" (Śat. Br. III.5.3.1-7).

The concept and image of the Mahāvedi here is that of the *Puruṣa* (God) lying horizontal on the ground. At the Havirdhāna-*maṇḍapa* it is of the standing Viṣṇu, with his head *(rarāṭa)* erect, with the garland for it *(rarāṭī / rarāṭyā)* tucked at the proper place. Taken together, we have the image of the Puruṣa lying and also standing erect. If we take the first image, the *yūpa* is seen as the head, which, in later times, gives place to the *dhvaja*[15] at the front of the temple, while the *sadas* with the fires acts as the later *garbha-gṛha*. In the *sadas* various priests sat. Behind the line of these six small fire-altars the branch of the Uduṁbara tree (*auduṁbarī*) was fixed. As the Vedic people were not idol-worshippers (at that period) the *sadas* did not have any idols; but, the fires could be taken as the gods. However, the gods that are said to arrive at the Havirdhāna-*maṇḍapa*[15] are not the fire-gods. They are the popular Vedic gods, though not mentioned by names. They have to be understood as a group of gods, or Viśve deva-s. It may be of interest to note, in this connection, that the threshold of a house or a temple is called *uṁbaraṭhā* (in Maharashtra, Western India), which would indicate the practice of it being made from the wood of the Umbara tree (Marathi; Sanskrit Uduṁbara), or where a branch of the *uduṁbara (Ficus Glomerata)* tree was to be fixed at the start of the construction of the house. As the Mahāvedi was not a permanent structure, the branch at the Vedic sacrifice stayed till the conclusion of the sacrifice. But, there could hardly be any doubt that the plan for the Hindu temple of later times had its origin in the Mahāvedi, which had the *yūpa* (later *dhvaja*) in the east and Audumbarī at the west, the *sadas* and the fires in it giving place to the idol in the *sanctum sanctorum*. (See Fig.III and Fig.V at the end).

NOTES

1. Kane, P.V., *History of Dharmāśāstra*, Vol.II-ii, Poona, 1974, p.1123f. His information is based mainly on the Śrautasūtras.
2. Here the wife of the sacrificer anoints the axle of the cart with clarified butter; and the carts, one by one, are taken to the east from the Prācīnavaṁśa pandal (the usual shed at the Darśapūrṇamāsa sacrifices), which is to the west.
3. On this see Eggeling, J., *Śatapatha Brāhmaṇa* (Tr. in SBE, Vol. 26), pt.II, Delhi, 1978 (1885), p.128,n.1. He admits confusion.
4. The RV verse for this is I. 154, 2; Śat. Br.III. 5.3.23; Mait. Sam.III.8.7; Taitt. Sam. VI.2.9.3 where it is said to be the head of the sacrifice; see also 1.2.13.3 for the *mantra*-s.
5. Śat.Br. I.1.1.20 *uttarato hi strī pumāṁsam upa śete.* The expression is very common in the rituals; see Dange, *Sexual Symbolism from the Vedic Ritual*, Delhi, p. 52ff.
6. This is done the moment the carts are supported on the post.
7. Sāyaṇa misses the actual expression and writes

audumbaraḥ for Auparaḥ; see his com. on Ait. Br. I.29=5.3).

8. The structure seems to be the origin of the later Hindu temple structure. The point discussed below.
9. The formulas are: *viṣṇor dhruvo 'si; viṣṇo rarāṭam asi* etc.
10. It is to be noted that the first oblation prior to the bringing of the carts is to Savitṛ, by whom they are said to be impelled; see the texts and places mentioned above.
11. Kane, *op.cit.*, Vol.I-ii (2nd Ed.), Poona, 1974, p.710.
12. Deshpande, M.N., "Some Thoughts on Indian Symbolism", *Symbolism in Temple Art and Architecture* (Proceedings of the Seminar), Ananthacharya Indological Research Instt., Bombay, 1982, p.4. This opinion is untenable in view of the discussion that follows.
13. Dange, *Encyclopaedia of Puranic Beliefs and Practices*, Vol.I, New Delhi, 1986, p.314f.
14. See ch.32, *supra*.
15. The arrival of the gods at the sacrifice is a very common motif in RV; the exact *mantra* recited at the completion of the over-cover (the third *chadis*) is RV II.41.21, which has *devāḥ sīdantu yajñiyāḥ, iha-adya soma-pītaye.*

ILLUSTRATIONS

प्राचीन-वंश

fig.I

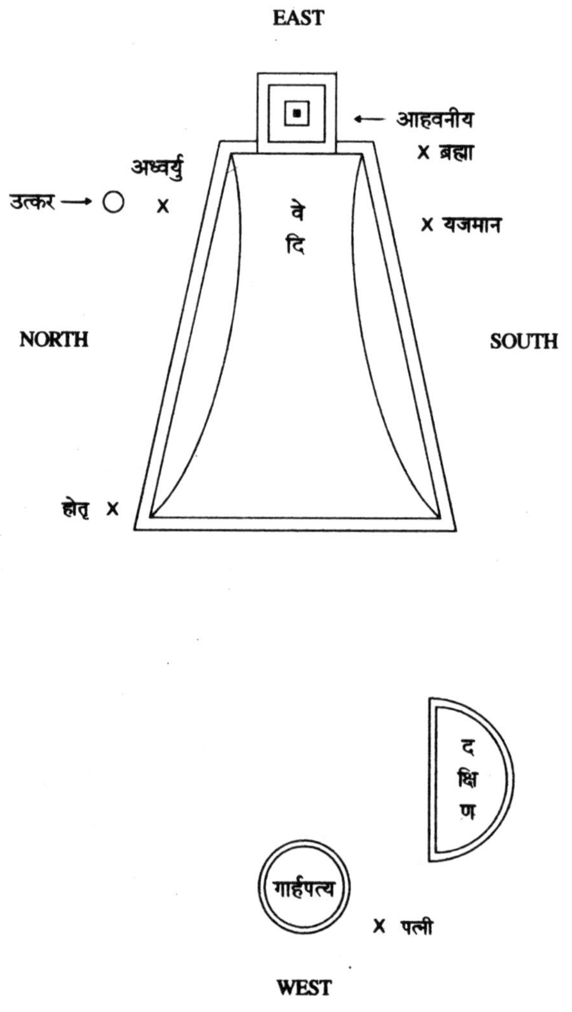

The usual altar at Darśapūrṇamāsa; also called PRĀCĪNAVAMŚA

प्राचीन-वंश

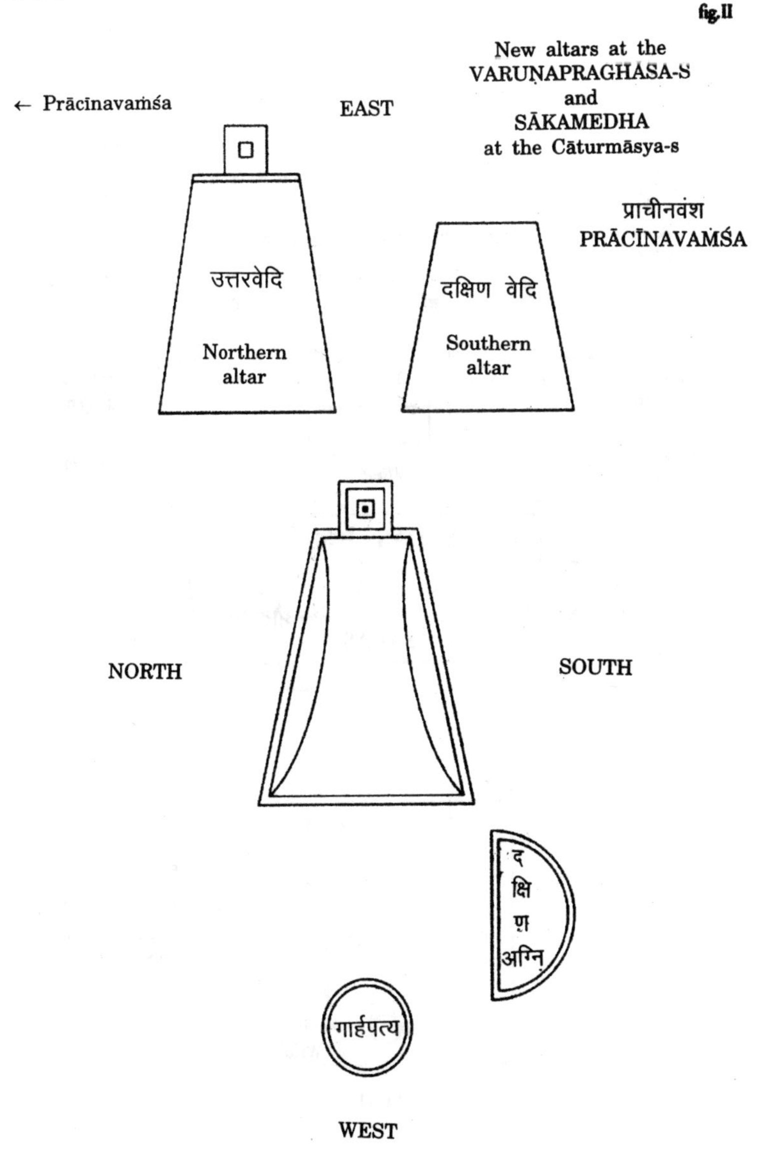

Altar – plan at the two middle phases at the Cāturmāsya-s

← Prācīnavaṁśa Prācīnavaṁśa →

fig.III

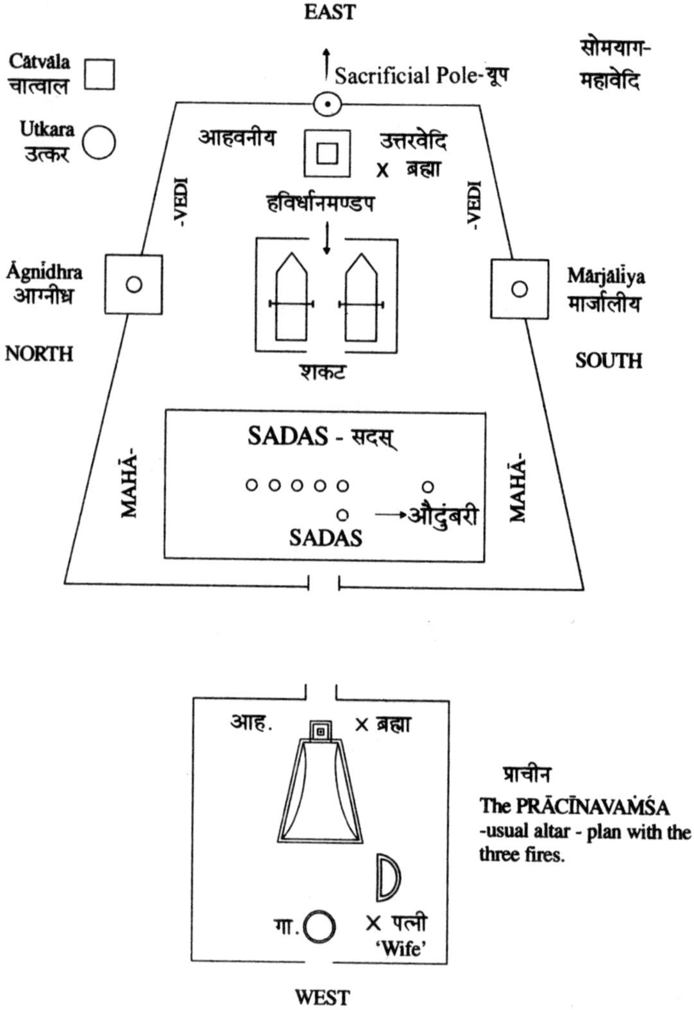

The New altar at the Agniṣṭoma (Soma) sacrifice, with the usual altars in the Prācīnavaṁśa

fig.IV

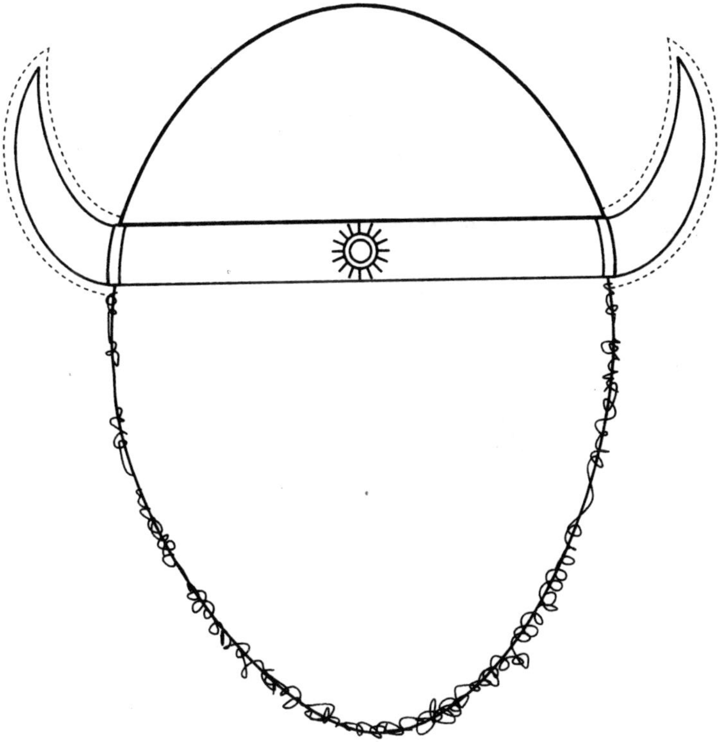

Dotted lines indicate Śipra on either side,
on the horned helmet probably to be fastened
with a string each;but could be unfastened
for drinking from.

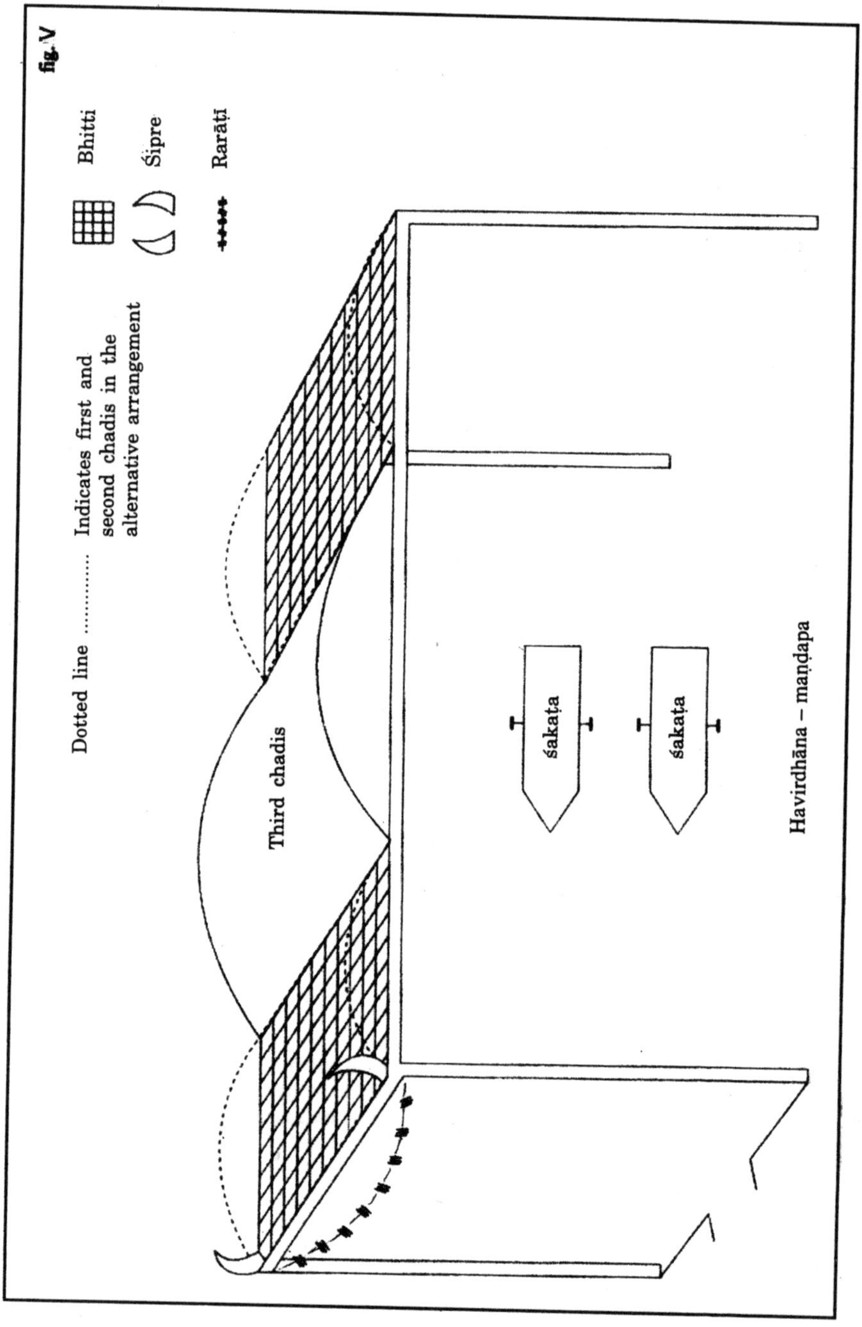
fig. V
Dotted line .... Indicates first and second chadis in the alternative arrangement
Bhitti
Śipre
Rarāṭī
Third chadis
śakaṭa
śakaṭa
Havirdhāna – maṇḍapa

BIBLIOGRAPHY

Important Sanskrit Texts (with abbreviations), arranged typewise.

Saṁhitā-s

Atharvaveda (AV)
Kāṭhaka-Saṁhitā (Kāṭh. Sam.)
Maitrāyaṇī-Saṁhitā (Mait. Sam.)
Ṛgveda (RV)
Taittirīya Saṁhitā (Taitt. Saṁ.)
Vājasaneyi-Saṁhitā (Vāj. Sam.)

Brāhmaṇa-s (Br.)

Aitareya-Brāhmaṇa (Ai.Br.; Ait.Br.)
Brāhmaṇa (Br.)
Gopatha-Brāhmaṇa (Gop. Br.)
Jaiminīya-Brāhmaṇa (Jai.Br.)
Kauṣītaki-Br. (Kau. Br.)
Pañcaviṁśa-Brāhmaṇa (Pañc.Br.)
Śatapatha-Brāhmaṇa (Śat. Br.)
Taittirīya Br. (Taitt. Br.)

Upaniṣad-s (Up.)

Chāndogya-Upaniṣad (Chānd. Up.)
Śvetāśvatara-Upaniṣad (Śvet. Up.)
Muṇḍaka-Upaniṣad

Āpastamba-Dharmasūtra (Āp. Dh. S.)
Āśvalāyana-Śrauta-sūtra (Āśv. Śr. S.)
Āśvalāyana-Gṛhya-sūtra (Āśv. Gṛ. S.)
Baudhāyana-Śrauta-sūtra (Baudh. Śr. S.)

Kāṭhaka-Gṛhya-sūtra (Kāṭh. Gṛ. S.)
Kātyāyana-Śrauta-sūtra (Kāt. Śr. S.)
Pāraskara-Gṛhya-sūtra (Pār. Gṛ.S.)
Vasiṣṭha-Dharma-sūtra (Vasiṣṭha Dh. S.)

Manusmṛti (Manu Sm.)
Yājñavalkya-smṛti (Yājñ. Sm.)

Rāmāyaṇa (Rām.)
Mahābhārata (Mb.)
Bhagavadgītā
Purāṇa (P.)
Agni-Purāṇa
Bhāgavata-Purāṇa (Bhāg. P.)
Brahmāṇḍa-Purāṇa (Brahmāṇḍa P.)
Mārkaṇḍeya-Purāṇa (Mārk. P.)
Vāmana-Purāṇa (Vām. P.)

Bṛhatsaṁhitā

Devendraparipṛcchā-tantra
Guhyasamāja-tantra
Kālīvilāsa-taṇtra
Kulārṇava-tantra
Mahānirvāṇa-taṇtra
Prajñopāyaviniścaya-siddhi

Others:

Agrawala V.S., *The Thousand-Syllabled Speech*, Varanasi, 1963
Banerjea J.N., *Development of Hindu Iconography*, Calcutta, 1956
Berden Frances F., *The Aztecs*, Chalsea House Publishers, New York, Philadelphia, 1989
Bergaigne A., *La Religion Vedique.*, Vols. I-III, 1878-1883
Blair C.A., *Heat in the Ṛgveda and the Atharvaveda*, New Haven, 1961
Buitenen Von, *Pravargya,* Deccan College, Poona, 1968
Caland W., *Pañcaviṁśa Brāhmaṇa,* Calcutta, 1931
Charpentier J., *Die Suparṇasage,* Uppsala, 1920
Clark Rundle T., *Myth and Symbol in Ancient Egypt.,* London, 1959
Crooke W., *Popular* Religion & *Folklore of Northern India.* Vols. I-II, Westminster Centre, 1896

Dandekar R.N., *Vaidika Agni, Daivataśāstra* (Marathi), Poona, 1972
——, *Vedic Mythological Tracts*, Delhi, 1979
——, *Śrauta-kośa* (Eng. Tr. of Skt. by Kashikar C.G.), Poona, 1958
Dange Sadashiv A., *Legends in the Mahābhārata*, Delhi, 1969
——, *Pastoral Symbolism from the Ṛgveda,* Poona, 1970
——, *Vedic Concept of 'Field' and the Divine Fructification,* Bombay, 1971
——, *Cultural Sources from the Veda*, Bombay, 1973
——, *Sexual Symbolism from the Vedic Ritual*, Delhi, 1979
——, *Encyclopaedia of Puranic Beliefs and Practices* Vols.I-V, Navrang, New Delhi, 1986-1990
——, *Towards Understanding Hindu Myths*, Aryan Books International, New Delhi, 1996
——, *Myths from the Mahābhārata*, Vol. I, Aryan Books International, New Delhi, 1997
Dange, Mrs. S.S., *Aspects of Speech in Vedic Ritual*, Aryan Books International, New Delhi, 1996
Darmesteter J., (Tr. of) *The Zend Avesta* in SBE Vols. IV., XXIII, XXXI, Delhi, 1965 (Rep.)
Deo S.B., *History of Jain Monachism*, Poona, 1956
Desai Devangana, *Erotic Sculptures of India*, Delhi, 1975
Eggeling J., (Tr.). *The Śatapatha Brāhmaṇa*, SBE, Vols. XII, XXVI, XLI, XLIII, XLIV, Delhi, 1965 (Rep.)
Frazer J.G., *Magic Art.*, London, 1932.
——, *Folk-lore of the Old-Testament*, Vols. I-III, London, 1918.
Ganguli O.C. & Goswami A., *Art of the Pallavas*, Delhi, 1957
Geldner K.F., *Der Rig-veda,* Vols. I-III (HOS 33-35), Cambridge, London, 1978 (1951)
Gomme G.L., *Folk-lore as an Historical Science*, London, 1908
Gonda J., *Aspects of Early Viṣṇuism*, Utrecht, 1954
——, *Dual Deities in the Religion of the Veda*, Amsterdam-London, 1974
Griffith R.T.H., *Hymns of the Rigveda*, Vols. I-II, Benares, 1963 (Rep.)
Guenther, H.V., *Yuganaddha*, Varanasi, 1992.
Hastings J., *Encyclopaedia of Religion and Ethics (Encl. Rel. and E.*) Vols. 1-12;13 Index
Hillebrandt A., *Vedische Mythologie*, Vols. I-III, Breslau, 1891-1902
Hopkins E.W., *The Religions of India*, Delhi, 1970 (1896)
Jobes Gertrude, *Dictionary of Mythology, Folk-lore and Symbols*, New York, 1962

Kane P.V., *History of Dharmāśāstra*, Vols. I-V, Poona, 1974 (Rep.)
Karandikar J.S., *Gītā-tattva-mañjarī*, Poona, 1947
Karamarkar A.P., *The Vrātyas or the Dravidian System*, Lonavla, 1950
Keith A.B., *Rigveda Brahmanas (Rigveda Br. Tr.)*, HOS, Cambridge, London, 1920
——, The *Religion and Philosophy of the Veda and Upanishads*, HOS Vols. 31-32, Cambridge, London, 1925
Kersenboomstory Saskia, *Nityasumaṅgalī-Devadāsī Tradition in South India*, Motilal Banarsidass, Delhi, 1981
Kirk, G.S., *The Nature of Greek Myths*, Penguin, Harmonsworth, 1976 (1974).
Lang A., *Myth, Ritual and Religion*, London, 1913
Macdonell A.A., *Vedic Mythology*, Ramkumar Rai (Hindi), Varanasi, 1961 (Strassburg, 1897)
Macdonell A.A. and Keith A.B., *Vedic Index of Names and Subjects*, London, 1912
Mackenzie D., *Myths of China and Japan*, London
——, *Myths of Babylonia and Assyria*, London
——, *Myths of Crete and pre-Hellenic Europe,* London,
——, *Myths of Pre-Columbian America,* London, (1913-1915)
Malinowski Bronislaw, *Myth in Primitive Psychology*, London, 1926
Max Müller, *Chips from a German Workshop*, Vols. I-IV, London, 1896-1907
Murdock G.P., *Our Primitive Contemporaries*, New York, 1958 (18th Ed.)
O'Flaherty W.D., *Sextual Metaphors and Animal Symbols in Indian Mythology*, Delhi, Motilal Banarsidass, 1981
Olcott W.T., *Sun-lore of All Ages*, London, New York, 1914
Oldenberg H., *Buddha, His Life and His Doctrine* (Eng. Tr.), Belfast, 1885
——, *Rigveda Textcritische und Exegetische Noten (Noten),* Vols. I-II, Berlin, 1909, 1912
——, *Vedaforschung,* Stuttgart, Berlin, 1905
——, *Die Religion des Veda*, Berlin, 1894
Pischel R. & Geldner K.F., *Vedische Studien*, Vols. I-III, Stuttgart, 1889-1901
Raja Kunhan, *Asya vāmīya Hymn* (The Riddle of the Universe), Madras, 1956
Ram Gopal, *India of Vedic Kalpasūtras*, Delhi, 1959
——, *Ṛgveda Vyākhyā Vivecana* (Hindi), Delhi, 1979

Ranade R.D., *A Constructive Survey of Upanishadic Philosophy*, Poona, 1926 (later ed. Bombay, 1968, 1986)
Sengupta Nilakshi, *Evolution of Hindu Marriage*, Bombay, 1965
Shastri A.M., *India as seen in the Bṛhatsaṁhitā of Varāhamihira*, Delhi, 1969
——, *Varāhamihira and His Times*, Jodhpur, 1991
Schroeder L.V., *Mysterium und Mimus in Rigveda*, Leipzig, 1908
Tilak B.G., *Orion*, Poona, 1955 (1916)
Velankar H.D., *Ṛgveda Maṇḍala VII*, Bombay, 1963
——, *Ṛgveda Maṇḍala* II, Bombay, 1966
——, *Ṛgveda Maṇḍala* III, 1968
——, *Ṛksūkta-śatī*, Bharatiya Vidya Bhavan, Bombay, 1972
Vogel J.Ph., *The Indian Serpent Lore*, London, 1926
Waterman T.T., and Croeber W., *Source-book in Anthropology*, New York, 1931
Whitehead H., *Village Gods of South India*, Delhi, 1970 (1921)

Articles: (Selected list)

Barnett L.D., "Study in Indo-European Psychology", JRAS, 1929
Bloomfield M., "The Legend of Soma and the Eagle", JAOS, Vol. 15
Bodewitz H., "What did Indra do with the Yatis", *Amṛtadhārā* (R.N.Dandekar Fel. Vol.),1984
Brown N., "Agni, Sun, Sacrifice and Vāc", JAOS, Vol.88
Buitenen Von, "Akṣara", JAOS, Vol.79
Chaube G., "Behir Songs of Rain", *Bhāratīya Vidyā*, Vol. VI, Jan.-Feb.
Dange S.A. "About the words Garut and Garutman in the *Ṛgveda*" *IHQ*, Vol. 39, No. 1 & 2
——, "Root-germinants in the Sanskrit Language", *Indian Antiquary* (New Series), Vol. V-i, Jan. 1971
Dange S.S., "Autovertism from the *Ṛgveda*", VIJ., Vol. XIV-i
Grey G., "The Creation according to the Maori", in A.L. Kroeber & T.T. Waterman, *Source-book in Anthropology*, New York
Gonda J., "Ābharaṇa", *New Indian Antiquary*, Vol. II. 1939
——, "Ascetics and Courtesans", *Adyar Library Bulletin*, (Jub. Vol.) XXV, 1-4, 1964
Guillemin J., "Heraclitus and Iran", *History of Religions*, Chicago Uni., Vol. III-1, 1968
Kapadia B., "The word Garta in the *Ṛgveda*", J.Ganganath Jha Res. Instt., Vol. XXV, 1969

Kashikar C.G., "Apropos *Pravargya*", Bulletin CASS, Poona Uni., March 1973

Mitra S., "Frog in North Indian Rain-controlling Rites", *Folk-lore and Traditions in India*, Vol. IV

Parpola Asko, "The Metamorphoses of Mahiṣa Asura and Prajāpati", *Ritual, State and History in South Asia* (Essays in honour of J.C. Heesterman), Ed. by. A. W. Van Den Hoek and others, E.J. Brill, Leiden, New York, Koln, 1992.

Seidenberg A., "The Separation of the Sky and the Earth", *Folk-lore*, Vol. 70, 1959

Schrader O., "Aryan Religion", *Encl. Rel. and Ethics*, Vol. II.

Velankar H. D, "Viśvāmitra and Vasiṣṭha in the Ṛgveda", *Mirashi Fel.* Vol., Nagpur, 1965

IHQ	=	*Indian Historical Quarterly*
JRAS	=	*Journal of the Royal Asiatic Society*
JAOS	=	*Journal of the American Oriental Society*
VIJ	=	*Vishveshvarananda Indological Journal*
CASS	=	*Centre of Advanced Study in Sanskrit*

INDEX

Sāyaṇa and Yāska have been referred to at a number of places. Hence their names, at all places, do not appear in the Index. Numbers in the brackets indicate notes on that particular page.

NOTES

NOTES

NOTES

NOTES

NOTES